Corona and Work around the Globe

Work in Global and Historical Perspective

Edited by
Andreas Eckert, Sidney Chalhoub, Mahua Sarkar,
Dmitri van den Bersselaar, Christian G. De Vito

Work in Global and Historical Perspective is an interdisciplinary series that welcomes scholarship on work/labor that engages a historical perspective in and from any part of the world. The series advocates a definition of work/labor that is broad, and especially encourages contributions that explore interconnections across political and geographic frontiers, time frames, disciplinary boundaries, as well as conceptual divisions among various forms of commodified work, and between work and 'non-work.'

Volume 11

Corona and Work around the Globe

—

Edited by
Andreas Eckert and Felicitas Hentschke

DE GRUYTER
OLDENBOURG

ISBN 978-3-11-071689-4
e-ISBN (PDF) 978-3-11-071824-9
e-ISBN (EPUB) 978-3-11-071828-7
ISSN 2509-8861

Library of Congress Control Number: 2020950021

Bibliografische Information der Deutschen Nationalbibliothek
TDie Deutsche Nationalbibliothek verzeichnet diese Publikation in der Deutschen Nationalbibliografie; detaillierte bibliografische Daten sind im Internet über http://dnb.dnb.de abrufbar.

This book is dedicated to young people across the world, who will have to make the most of what we leave behind.

Miguel Corrêa Fontes (4) "Coronavirus", Rio de Janeiro, April, 28, 2020.

Table of Contents

Despair and Indifference at the Margins

Being 'Relevant to the System' is Female

Shutter Release I. Current Issues in the World, Told Visually

When Private and Public Spaces Become Blurred

Acknowledgements

Corona and Work around the Globe came into being at the international research center Work and Human Lifecycle in Global History (re:work) at Humboldt-Universität zu Berlin.

re:work is one of ten Käte Hamburger Centers currently funded by the German Federal Ministry of Education and Research (BMBF). We would like to thank the BMBF for its extended support for re:work and for making projects like this book possible.

We would also like to thank the Berlin Center for Global Engagement (BCGE), an initiative of the Berlin University Alliance, which funded a substantial part of the production costs. Our cooperation partners Tobias Berger and Miles Larmer provided important support for the book project. We are also grateful to Jeremy Adelman, without whom this idea would never have borne fruit.

A special mention must go to Sebastian Marggraff, who managed to keep constant track of the huge amount of information and texts that were being exchanged among the great number of people involved. And of course we would also like to thank the whole re:work team, which has participated in this project time and time again. We were particularly pleased that our excellent copyeditor, Helen Veitch, could work with us again.

We are proud to be able to include visual contributions in this book, in the form of an outstanding image series by Ellen Rothenberg and Maurice Weiss.

We would also like to thank Rabea Rittgerodt for her constant encouragement, and De Gruyter Oldenbourg and the editors of the *Work in Global and Historical Perspective* series at De Gruyter for their support. Mahua Sarkar kindly wrote a prologue for this volume on behalf of the editors.

Finally, we would like to thank our contributors, all of whom are former fellows or close cooperation partners. It was a special experience to embark on such a book project in the middle of the coronavirus period, without being able to come together spatially and within a time frame of just a few months. We are very happy that it worked.

This book is dedicated to young people across the world and to all those throughout the world who were robbed of their basic rights and existence in connection with the coronavirus crisis, and those who oppose the injustice that happens to them – sometimes risking their lives in the process.

Andreas Eckert and Felicitas Hentschke

Mahua Sarkar
Prologue

The Incident

It was around 10:15 am on April 1, 2020. As on every Monday and Wednesday morning since the beginning of the spring semester, the lecture hour for Sociology 100 (Introduction to Sociology) at a public university in New York state was in full swing. Except, the campus had been in lockdown mode since the third week of March, and all classes had moved online as part of a statewide effort to stem the rising tide of COVID-19 infections. For many of the students with homes in New York City (especially those from the relatively underprivileged boroughs of the Bronx, Queens, and Staten Island) and Long Island, this had meant returning to a far more dangerous context than the sleepy university town where the infection rates were – and would remain – comparatively insignificant. Just that morning, the number of people infected with COVID-19 had surged past 47,000 in New York City alone; while statewide figures had surpassed 83,000, with nearly 2,000 reported deaths. By the end of the semester, several students in the class would be afflicted by the virus, and a few would lose people close to them in a battle with the beast.

That morning, however, the peak of the pandemic's first wave was still a few weeks away, and despite the increasing gloom in the air, the students – nearly two hundred in all – appeared lively and engaged. The topic was flexible labor and global migration, and the documentary (*The Supermarket Slave Trail, The Guardian*) they had watched in preparation for the class on the exploitation of 'slave' (or functionally enslaved) labor in the global shrimping industry seemed to have touched a nerve. Students – many women, non-white, and/or international students among them – seemed particularly interested in learning about the global value chains that linked the lives of severely coerced workers in other parts of the world with their own lives as consumers in the United States.

It was at this point that two young men suddenly appeared on the screen, intervening in the conversation in a manner that seemed both insistent and oddly disjointed. At first, they were polite enough, but as the minutes passed, their tone turned increasingly sarcastic and disrespectful. Soon, it was obvious that they were intent on disrupting rather than constructively engaging with the perfectly intelligent discussion that was underway. As the confusion and tension mounted, the vigilant and tech-savvy graduate teaching assistants realized that the class was being 'Zoombombed' – a term used to refer to unwanted infiltrations of virtual meetings – and they moved swiftly to expel the two intruders.

Despite being rattled, the class began to regroup and focus collectively on salvaging the discussion. However, a few minutes later it was disrupted once again – this time by a posse of six or seven young men sporting masks and other disguises conjuring up images of the Islamic State. To the utter shock and bewilderment of everyone present, they shouted obscenities and *Allah hu Akbar* in the same breath, made barking noises, smeared racist and pornographic content across the screen and, most egregiously, invited female students and the professor alike to partake in sexual acts. The teaching assistants once again swung into action, but this time it proved well-nigh impossible to expel the intruders, because they had hijacked the names of students – specifically non-white students – who were in the class. A few minutes into this mayhem, the professor was left with no choice but to abandon the class for the day. Indeed, eventually all synchronous Zoom meetings for the course were cancelled for the rest of the semester in the absence of guaranteed, credible protection against further attacks from the university administration, already struggling with the sudden fallout from the pandemic lockdown.

In the aftermath of this deeply disturbing incident – described by students and teaching assistants alike as "traumatic" – reports surfaced about the Zoom-bombing of two other classes on campus that week: Social-Cultural Anthropology and African-American Literature. The three affected courses share important commonalities: as broad introductory courses that critically examine social structures such as race, class, gender, sexuality, culture, and religion in a global/ national context, they draw students from diverse backgrounds. The specific targeting of these courses suggests that this was no mindless prank by students breaking into a class for a bit of juvenile fun. Rather, as a number of the students and teaching assistants later observed, this was an "organized, preplanned, and coordinated action." The fact that the intruders singled out women and/or non-white students for racist and misogynist gibes further points toward a supremacist politics of intimidation motivating these specific disruptions. Indeed, reports emerging from universities across the United States around this time would seem to support these suspicions. Apparently, the two young men who appeared first as hecklers in the incident described above were known entities with possible links to white supremacist groups on the FBI's radar.

Implications

Nine months into the COVID-19 pandemic, it is clear that the impact of the crisis on human life and livelihoods is – and will likely continue to be – colossal. And while the virus – dubbed the "great equalizer" – does not seem to discriminate in its choice of victims, the severity of its afflictions is in fact far from equal, with particularly devastating consequences for underprivileged communities across the world. The pandemic has also ushered in profound and likely irreversible transformations in the world of work. Even as essential workers, represented overwhelming by black, latinx, and poor (im)migrant labor, are compelled to toil in dangerous conditions on farms, in food processing factories, hospitals, and in transportation, others are forced into workspaces that range from the near dystopic for those who live alone, to a daily struggle for quiet for those who live with families, sometimes in small spaces.

A university campus, with the many different forms of work that it supports, can be seen as a microcosm of sorts for the world of work at large. The particular story of disruption in one class at a public university in an ethno-racially super-diverse state such as New York indexes many of these troubling questions that the COVID-19 crisis throws up. Let me highlight a few.

There is no doubt that the pandemic has delivered a massive fillip to ideas of distance learning and virtual conferencing that have been on the horizon for some time now. Much of the discussion about the transition to a virtual world of conferencing, teaching, and learning, spearheaded by tech companies that stand to make windfall profits from it, tends to be celebratory. However, virtual learning and working online offer no ready panacea. The experiences of students mentioned above spotlight some enduring structural problems – beyond the disproportionately pernicious effects of Zoom-bombing on some (women/students of color) as related above. For instance, not all students have the kind of space at home that supports uninterrupted class attendance. Many lack access to stable internet connections, while some are obliged to share a single computer with multiple working members of the household. But perhaps more than anything else, the pandemic-induced social distancing invites us to recognize anew the significance of campus life as a crucial social site for the complex, sometimes fraught, and lifelong process of learning.

Some faculty members – those who have secure positions that have not been eliminated due to the pandemic – have undoubtedly come to appreciate the flexibility of teaching online asynchronously while living elsewhere. For many others, however, the loss of frequent human contact with colleagues and students, the (not always necessary but pleasurable) forays into the library, the possibility of learning from casual exchanges in the corridors, or after the occasional film or concert or other academic/artistic events – things that make university campuses so different from other sites of employment – have been disorienting, to say the least. Perhaps more than anything else, what has really transformed the experience of teaching as a profession is the loss of the ever-so-delicate affective dimensions of pedagogy in physical classrooms. The imperceptible nods, the light (or confusion) in the eyes of students as they comprehend something (or not), the satisfaction (or frustration) of succeeding (or failing) to get a point across, and the inevitable milling around after lectures when the more shy or differentially able students haltingly articulate their questions – all such cues that add depth, meaning, and texture to communication, so central to intellectual labor in all its iterations, are flattened, *virtually*.

Beyond the immediate experience of teaching on campus, there are other structural ramifications on the horizon for the world of academic work. The standardized 40/40/20 (research/teaching/service) model that has defined employment contracts of tenured faculty in many institutions across the world has been under pressure for some time. Now, as the pandemic threatens to shrink overall funding for both research and casual teaching jobs – disproportionately affecting early-career academics who depend on them – the familiar models of employment relations in academia may well be a casualty in the near future.

The immediate and daunting task facing instructors across the world, however, is of reinventing pedagogical tools to make them consistent with the demands of virtual classrooms. So, for now, we grapple with online platforms and PowerPoint presentations, on shared screens dotted with one-inch-square student/speaker slots, carrying faces and names that can be hijacked by ever novel forms of cyber aggression.

Andreas Eckert and Felicitas Hentschke
Introduction: Corona and Work around the Globe

Corona and Work around the Globe is about the simultaneity of events that have affected people and their daily lives, their work routine, and their understanding of what it means to be a citizen in different parts of the world during this global pandemic. In many cases, experiences of lockdown, standstill, empty streets, closed shops, and no-go public areas are similar.

These similarities between government measures to contain the crisis – social distancing, disinfection and, in many places, mask requirements – are impressive, but sometimes worrying. There are also vast differences. Where do welfare concepts work, where do they not? Where are parliamentary rights suspended and where are they not? Where are human rights trampled on and where are they not? How much has work changed under coronavirus conditions? And what does that mean for a possible 'Post Corona' scenario? We tried to find out.

The Lockdown

On March 11, 2020, the federal state of Berlin directed coronavirus measures at the institutions of higher education in Berlin. As of the end of the working day on March 20, 2020, operations at all Berlin scientific institutions and thus also at the Humboldt-Universität were limited to emergency levels, and they closed their doors. re:work closed its doors, too. Our center remained empty until June 2020. Since then, the strict measures have been gradually relaxed, but even today the university has not returned to normal operations. Currently, due to rapidly rising infection rates, the university is even re-introducing a number of restrictions.

Overnight, all communication switched to online or via telephone. During this ghostly time, we received a lot of messages from our alumni group of fellows. All thoughts revolved around this new, decisive, and hitherto unknown experience, from which everyone was now equally affected: COVID-19. In the aim of sharing this with everyone we know, scattered around the globe, the idea for the book at hand arose. We invited colleagues living and working in various parts of the world to bring this idea to life with us. The Berlin Center for Global Engagement (BCGE), an initiative of the Berlin University Alliance, provided financial support.

Corona and Work around the Globe

There is little doubt that the coronavirus pandemic has fundamentally disrupted the world of work, causing massive human suffering and laying bare the extreme vulnerability of many millions of workers and self-employed individuals. According to estimates by the International Labour Organization (ILO), the large-scale workplace closures in response to COVID-19 have led to a worldwide reduction in hours worked of 10.7 percent in the second quarter of this year, which translates into a loss of more than three hundred million jobs. In the world of work, coronavirus has been particularly damaging for the most disadvantaged and vulnerable, thus dramatically exposing the devastating consequences of the massive inequalities underpinning societies across the globe. Worldwide, over six out of ten working people make their living in the informal economy. Referring again to ILO data, out of more than two billion workers, 1.6 billion face an imminent threat to their livelihoods as average income in the informal economy shrunk by approximately sixty percent in the first month of the pandemic alone. This breathtaking decline has intensified global poverty. Moreover, the pandemic has impacted women and men in the world of work in specific ways. For instance, women are over-represented in the more affected sectors such as services or in occupations dealing with the pandemic on the frontline, for example health care and care work. Finally, young people all over the world, many of them already squeezed in labor markets before the pandemic broke out, have seen their prospects deteriorate sharply. Those leaving or soon to leave education now face a bleak future in labor markets reeling under the impact of COVID-19. Some commentators are already describing them as the "lockdown generation."

Views from Different Corners of the World

Against this backdrop, this volume aims to provide a global perspective on the transformations in the world of work brought about by the coronavirus pandemic.[1] It enables us to reflect on the effects of coronavirus by bringing together case studies from various corners of the globe. These case studies explore the ways in which coronavirus has shaped labor relations and work practices in different parts of the world, locating these insights within a broader historical perspective and conversation. We aim to break down the general statistics and trends into glimpses of concrete experiences of workers during the pandemic, of workplaces transformed or destroyed, of workers protesting against political measures, of professions particularly exposed to coronavirus, and also of the changing nature of some professions.

The coronavirus crisis has also strengthened populist and anti-democratic forces in the United States, Western and Eastern Europe, Brazil, and India. This has led, among other things, to a blatant denial of scientific expertise and fierce attacks on international organizations such as the World Health Organization. These tendencies have coincided with a transformation of universities and scholarly work in many parts of the world, with scholars facing increasing constraints on their academic freedom, as some participants in our project, for example those based in Brazil, India, or even Japan, are currently experiencing for themselves.

This book is based on a truly global academic cooperation. We asked each of the authors to write an essay on how coronavirus has changed work and labor in particular neighborhoods, cities, regions, or even states. This main theme was refined by questions such as to what extent disruptions and intensifications had instituted changes for the better or worse, or if changing features of labor had also changed (or were related to changes in) the cityscape, welfare politics, an awareness of the strength or failure of government, the democratic order. We did not specify the format. The authors were free to write in any way they chose. Accordingly, the spectrum ranges from reports and heavily source-based analyzes to more literary forms. In this kaleidoscope, some authors used photographs, drawings, or interviews, some used statistics and graphics, others did without all of that. In terms of the main content, some essays focus on people and their professions and activities. Others are interested in labor law and labor rights, or draw historical comparisons. The protagonists of the essays range from informal workers and industrial workers, to artists, employees

---

1 There are currently a number of efforts to analyze the effects of Cornona on work. See e.g. Aaron Benanav, "Service Work in the Pandemic Economy," In *International Labor and Working-Class History* 2020 (online, October 12, 2020).

in public offices and universities, and unemployed people. All essays are based on the personal experiences of the authors and their concerns in these difficult times. What was most important for us was the regional spectrum, that our authors focused on the region they are living in, where they witnessed the coronavirus pandemic.

Amid the diversity, two main themes emerge: Inequality and contestations of democratic principles and parlamentarism. The authors approach these overarching focal points using different examples. Accordingly, we have bundled the essays into six subject areas.

They are preceded by a prologue. MAHUA SARKAR, one of the editors of this book series, writes about the university as a work site in times of Corona – which is appropriate, since, after all, all authors come from the university environment.

The essays in the first section, *Despair and Indifference at the Margins,* describe the force with which the poorest, the people at the margins of various societies, have been hit by coronavirus and the measures to contain the pandemic. SUPURNA BANERJEE conducted numerous interviews with migrant and local workers in the informal sector of Kolkata. She spoke to people who have acquired skills in niche areas of the informal sector so as to earn a modest but reliable income. With the lockdown, many activities were lost and those affected had to be inventive in order to find a job – often in areas in which they had no skills at all – and earn at least enough to feed themselves and their families. For the protagonists of ALINA SANDRA CUCU's essay, the professional flexibility that the workers in Banerjee's essay find challenging seems to be a familiar normal. Cucu analyzes the lives of those in Romania who have always had to switch from job to job and take whatever they can get, regardless of their skills and talents. NICOLE MAYER-AHUJA moves this topic to Germany. Coronavirus and associated measures to stop it from spreading bring the issue of inequality onto the agenda. Mayer-Ahuja reconstructs the supposed solidarity that emerged in certain German cities across class, gender, and race boundaries in the first period after the lockdown, as well as the sharp decline in this trend and its subsequent reversal over the course of the pandemic – even though solidarity is one of the few ways we can tackle the new social challenges. CHITRA JOSHI compares the severity with which Indian labor migrants were and are affected by catastrophic pandemics and the measures taken against them today and in the past.

The section *Being 'Relevant to the System' Is Female* contains three essays that address so-called systemic relevance in very different ways. LARISSA ROSA CORRÊA and PAULO FONTES study the situation of domestic workers forced to risk their lives in the pandemic mainly for three reasons: they have to stay at home in their favelas in Rio de Janeiro shaped by high infection rates; they have to endure financial shortages rendering them unable to support their families; or they have to expose themselves to the virus on public transport or through their employers while being exploited for extra work that goes unpaid. BRIDGET KENNY examines the constraints on low-paid service workers under the various government security levels to contain the pandemic in Johannesburg, especially the female cleaning personnel who maintain streets and buildings in the center of the city. Her findings are strikingly similar to those of her Brazilian colleagues. The suffering related to COVID-19 is female in many places. BAHRU ZEWDE tells a refreshing counter-story about a female fashion designer in Addis Ababa, who makes a virtue out of necessity and takes to producing masks in a system-relevant manner.

All over the world, attempts are being made, again and again, to relate the number of deaths in the coronavirus crisis to the quality of the respective health care systems. The better a system works, the fewer deaths there are. In the section *The Health System in Which We Live,* four essays discuss the possibilities and limitations of welfare systems in the countries in which the authors live. MARCEL VAN DER LINDEN focuses on nurses, who often work under poor conditions and who are chronically underpaid. At the height of the pandemic, they were hailed as heroines. When they tried to use this praise to fight for better wages, the hype fell silent. DEBORAH JAMES, a member of London School of Economics Department of Anthropology's Covid and Care Research Group, presents a jointly-authored analysis of the changing care networks in the United Kingdom during the coronavirus crisis and the importance of the third sector in the face of state withdrawal and state-driven austerity. PREBEN KAARSHOLM writes about the sudden changes in the care system in Denmark that accompanied the coronavirus crisis, drawing comparisons with Norway and Sweden, which have followed different paths in many respects. He reflects on the potential return of Keynesianism and economic policies of debt financing, public investments, and multiplier effects after a long drought of neoliberalism. YOKO TANAKA writes about the comparatively harmless course of the coronavirus crisis in Japan, which may be due to fortunate circumstances but has been claimed by the Japanese government as a product of their success, while their measures have remained inadequate and dysfunctional.

The fourth section, *Thwarted Youth*, comprises three essays dealing with problems and opportunities, especially concerning young people and their career prospects – as well as those who provide their start in life, namely the teachers. MARY JO MAYNES and ANN WALTNER describe the situation faced by young people between the ages of sixteen and twenty-four in Minneapolis in the United States who are disconnected from work and school under the current pandemic conditions. The interruption of their plans for first jobs, internships, volunteer work, etc. has an effect far beyond simple life planning. Insecurity and depression contrast with new forms of empowerment, such as engagement in the Black Lives Matter protests as observable generational markers of the new COVID-19 generation. The essay by JAMES WILLIAMS considers the mandatory school closures in Great Britain during lockdown. How does this affect learning and teaching? Williams examines how the various actors – the children and their parents, the teachers and school administrators and the teachers' union – have reacted to this. BABACAR FALL reports from one of the world's poorest regions, the Sahel, covering countries such as Burkina Faso, Côte d'Ivoire, Mali, Mauritania, Niger, and Chad. He writes about the Sahel Women's Empowerment and Demographic Dividend (SWEDD), an initiative that was set up to give young girls from this region a professional perspective. A large-scale project has enabled girls to produce masks for the entire Sahel zone and make a useful contribution to prevention during the pandemic.

In the section *Fighting for Justice in the Pandemic*, LEON FINK compares low-wage immigrant poultry workers and the United States police, two groups whose very polarity at opposite ends of the spectrum of control and collective influence raises increasingly pressing challenges for community health, welfare, and democratic self-rule. CRISTIANA SCHETTINI shows how sex workers in Argentina fought long struggles for their work to be recognized and how state policy has taken back hard-won rights as a side effect of measures to limit the pandemic. Airlines around the world were among the first and particularly hardest hit by the spread of coronavirus. ON BARAK traces the connection between military and civil aviation and explains the resulting protections for Israeli pilots with a military background in the global aviation crisis compared with their colleagues around the world.

The last section, *When Private and Public Spaces Become Blurred*, brings together essays on changes in working conditions and working methods that have emerged in the wake of local pandemic lockdowns. In the history of work, the division between the private sphere and the workplace has been fiercely contested. Against this background and with a look at historical pandemic experiences, JÜRGEN KOCKA and SANDRINE KOTT look at the phenomenon of the 'home office.' DANIEL EISENBERG also addresses remote working, but approaches it in a methodologically different way. In a kind of self-observation, he describes the simultaneity of the experience of being at home, of being in intensive exchange with colleagues via the internet, the neighborhood's empty streets, and the news of the coronavirus crisis and the demonstrations against racism in many American cities.

Current Issues in the World, Told Visually

This book also includes visual contributions that do not require words. The documentary photographer and artist MAURICE WEISS accompanied a medical team in an emergency ward for coronavirus patients at the Ernst-von-Bergmann hospital in Potsdam for three weeks in March/April 2020. His photo series "Black Ward" depicts their pressures, stress, and helplessness in the face of coronavirus, about which little was still known at the time. ELLEN ROTHENBERG is a concept artist and feminist political activist. In her collage "'This is Ridiculous,' Voting as Labor During COVID-19: A Report from the United States," she considers inequality in the United States, which emerged more strongly than ever during the coronavirus crisis. She observed the primary elections in Wisconsin and Georgia, which took place on April 7 and June 9, 2020, and demonstrates the effort and cost of exercising the right to vote under coronavirus conditions. Interviews with Rothenberg and Weiss contextualize their work as artists as well as their art around the subject of work.

The chapters for this book were written over the European summer months of 2020. By the time it goes to print in December 2020, the world may once again look completely different. It is and can only be a snapshot of a completely unexpected, unusual time for everyone – from the Americas and Africa to Europe to Asia.

Despair and Indifference at the Margins

Supurna Banerjee
Skill, Informality, and Work in Pandemic Times: Insights from India

Rajindar came to Kolkata from a small village near Muzzafarpur in Bihar. Prior to COVID-19, he worked with his cousin as a presser in one of the city's neighborhoods. Having worked in the same area for a long time they enjoyed a steady income. During festival periods, the pace was quite frenzied and they would often call for extra help from their village, young lads who could come and earn some money and also explore the city at the same time. In March 2020, his cousin returned to the village. It was not long since his previous visit (they took turns so as not to lose business) to bring back his ten-year-old daughter. She had been supposed to stay for two weeks and would then return with one of the many people moving between the village and the city. The lockdown, however, changed all that. With the closure of the trains, movement was no longer possible. An even more severe blow, however, was the total loss of earnings. With offices shutting down and the fear of contagion, people stopped bringing clothes to be ironed. For someone who had over one hundred articles of clothing to iron on an average day, now he was faced with weeks of no work. His paltry savings dried up in no time. On the verge of starvation, and especially for the sake of his young daughter, Rajinder asked around for help with food. "All my life I have earned an honest living. To be reduced to begging like this is so humiliating. So I started then assisting people by doing their groceries and bringing their medicines, in return for which they gave me one hundred rupees."[1]

Tamanna lives in a village close to Kolkata with her daughter. She works part-time as a live-out domestic worker in three houses in Kolkata, commuting daily by train early in the morning and returning late afternoon. With the outbreak of COVID-19 and the consequent lockdown resulting in a suspension of trains, she has been unable to go to work. Only one of her employers has promised to pay her wages during the lockdown period, while the others argued that they couldn't pay her because they had to do all of the work themselves. But even with the relaxation of the lockdown, the train services remain suspended, thus preventing workers like Tamanna from getting to their workplaces. "I have lost all the jobs that I had, they have all employed domestic workers locally. Who will wait for five months? I don't blame them, but what is to become of us?" Left with no earnings, Tamanna doesn't know if she can even afford for her daughter to continue schooling. "There were days when we had nothing to eat and just kept our stomachs filled with water. Now I have started selling fruit in the locality. I buy them from the market and then go from street to street selling them. Sales are low and there are far too many vendors but at least we can eat a meal."[2]

These two extracts, from interviews I conducted during the lockdown, provide glimpses into the destitution facing informal workers in India during this period. These are, unfortunately, not exceptional moments of suffering that the pandemic and the consequent anti-poor response have unleashed on the working population of the country. After a brief contextualization of the working

---

1 Face-to-face interviews, Kolkata, March-June 2020. One hundred INR is currently 1.4 USD.
2 Telephone interview, June 10, 2020.

conditions of this vast majority of India's workforce, this essay looks at the experiences of insecurity, destitution, and the resulting need for fluidity for such workers who do not have any employment security or social safety net to fall back upon.

Introduction

The outbreak of COVID-19 necessitated stringent measures globally to arrest the rapid spread of the virus. Much like other countries, India, too, decided to opt for complete lockdown. The difference, however, was that this policy was mostly based on gimmicks rather than on well-thought out protective measures. With only four hours' warning and a lack of either measures to protect marginalized populations or safeguards to prevent domestic violence, what began as a public health crisis quickly escalated into a humanitarian one. As factories, shops, and other establishments closed their gates, street vending was wound down to a bare minimum, and household labor was prohibited, it became evident that the main brunt of the economic shutdown was to be borne by workers in the informal sector, which, estimated to comprise 450 million, is the majority of the country's working population.[3] The plight continued not only during the lockdown but also in the post-lockdown period.

There has been much written about the precarity of informal labor both generally[4] and specifically[5] during the pandemic. This essay builds on this body of work to think about what the lockdown – the economic shutdown – signifies for work itself, specifically in the informal sector for both migrant and local workers. The informal job market is characterized by tenuous employment contracts, a lack of acknowledgement of skill, depressed wages, and a general precarity.[6] While this generates conditions for the movement of workers from one sector to another, such fluidity is not entirely the norm. Apart from agricultural labor, which can involve a large number of workers during a particular season, the segmentation of non-farm labor is quite stable. Generally, workers tend to be engaged in similar work (with the higher skilled more likely to be tied to a particular occupation) as far as it is consistently available. The experience of work in a specific industry equips workers with a certain amount of experience, if not skill, allowing them to attain efficiency. But during periods of economic downturn – either in general or during specific crises such as the closure of firms – workers are compelled to look for other sources of livelihood, often in fields that are less remunerative, more competitive, and less economically productive. The COVID-19-induced lockdown and unprecedented economic shutdown meant a loss of jobs, drying up of earnings, and even conditions akin to destitution.[7] In the absence of government data, there are no exact

---

3 Yogima Seth Sharma, "National Database of Workers in Informal Sector in the Works," *Economic Times,* January 19, 2020, https://economictimes.indiatimes.com/news/economy/indicators/national-database-of-workers-in-informal-sector-in-the-works/articleshow/73394732.cms, accessed September 3, 2020.
4 E.g. Snehashish Bhattacharya and Surbhi Kesar, "Precarity and Development: Production and Labor Processes in the Informal Economy in India," *Review of Radical Political Economy* 52/3 (2020): 387-408.
5 Sunanda Sen, "Rethinking Migration and the Informal Indian Economy at the Time of a Pandemic," *The Wire,* June 1, 2020, https://thewire.in/economy/rethinking-migration-and-the-informal-indian-economy-in-the-time-of-a-pandemic, accessed August 9, 2020.
6 E.g. Tom Barnes, *Informal Labour in Urban Cities: Three Cities, Three Journeys* (London: Routledge, 2015).
7 Anil Dharkar, "COVID-19 has Made Migrant Workers' Plight, State Apathy Visible," *Indian Express,* May 25, 2020, https://indianexpress.com/article/opinion/columns/invisible-india-migrant-exodus-coronavirus-6425627/, accessed September 3, 2020.

numbers but news reports, activist accounts, and personal experience suggest that the loss of more remunerative, stable jobs has forced workers to become self-employed in low-productivity sectors on an almost unparalleled scale. It is not the intention of this essay to predict the magnitude of this crisis; but rather to illustrate how compulsory fluidity in the informal sector plunged workers into livelihoods they were ill-equipped to handle and also brought forward the risk of deskilling, thus causing further precariatization.

This essay is based on observations and informal conversations with workers in and around my neighborhood in Kolkata as well as phone conversations with returning migrant workers from other states. Kolkata, as a metropolitan area and the capital of West Bengal, provides employment for migrants from the districts of West Bengal as well as neighboring states of Bihar and Orissa. In recent years West Bengal has also seen high out-migration to states such as Delhi, Maharashtra, and Kerala, but this essay deals with the former. Fleeting conversations – sometime repeated, often isolated – during a single tract of time do not offer deep ethnographic insight. Rather, these glimpses into the working lives of informal workers trace the precarity of their location as laborers within the larger questions of skill and informal work in India.

Context

Informal workers constitute almost ninety-three percent – the vast majority – of India's working population.[8] A lack of social security benefits (although some firms offer social security entitlements on paper) and the absence of any job security characterizes informal employment in India.[9] Informal workers are contractual and casual workers both in the unorganized informal sector but also increasingly in the formal economy through its links to subcontracting and outsourcing of cheap contract labor. Chowdhury points out that between 1999-2000 and 2004-05 the entire increase in employment in the formal sector was represented by informal workers.[10] This shows a paradoxical process of a growing GDP with an almost complete absence of formal employment, a trend which continues. The National Sample Survey of 2004-05[11] (NSSO) demonstrates that the increase in employment was primarily due to an increase in self-employment. Srivastava argues that workers involved in various kinds of putting-out systems and subcontracting arrangements are characterized as self-employed based on their activity status.[12] However, they differ from independently self-employed workers. While they may use some of their own capital they are in reality disguised wage workers.[13] The precarity of self-employed workers is evident from the NSSO survey, which reveals that a large proportion of such workers do not consider their employment to

---

8 Department of Economic Affairs, Ministry of Finance, Government of India, "Economic Survey 2018-19 Vol-2".

9 Tom Barnes, *Informal Labour in Urban Cities*; Ravi Srivastava, "Structural Changes and Non-Standard Forms of Employment in India," *ILO Conditions of Work and Employment Series* 68 (2016), https://www.ilo.org/public/libdoc/ilo /2016/116B09_9_engl.pdf, accessed August 9, 2020.

10 Subhanil Chowdhury, "Employment and Growth under Capitalism: Some Critical Issues with Special Reference to India," *Institute of Development Studies Kolkata Occasional Paper* 27 (2011): 1-40.

11 NSS Report No. 515: *Employment and Unemployment Situation In India*, 2004-05, http://mospi.nic.in/sites/default/files/publication_reports/515part1_final.pdf, accessed on September 3, 2020.

12 Ravi Srivastava, "Structural Changes and Non-Standard Forms of Employment in India,": 16.

13 Ravi Srivastava, "Structural Changes and Non-Standard Forms of Employment in India": 13.

be remunerative.[14] The growing difficulty of finding a regular job and the rise in self-employment therefore suggests that much of this form of employment is in fact distress driven. Accompanying this crisis in regular employment has been the worsening of earnings. This sector of the labor force is offered scant protection under laws which were largely designed for the formal sector. The few laws which exist are limited either by their inapplicability (e.g. Contract Labor Regulation and Abolition Act) or by implemental lapses on the part of the employer and the state (e.g. Building and Other Construction Workers Act), all of which consolidates the power relations skewed against the informal sector.

The post-lockdown difficulties facing workers are therefore neither unexpected nor sudden, but rather emerge from the structural constraints characterizing these sectors. Further, the pandemic comes in the wake of the highest unemployment in four decades.[15] The economic distress caused by the lockdown was met with limited measures by the central and the various state governments (Kerala being an exception), which lacked a grounding in reality and political will to implement. On top of receiving paltry or no compensation for their loss of earnings, no provisions were made for migrant workers to return home. This led more than a million workers to set out from the cities to their villages by foot, hand-cart, or bicycle, facing police repression, detention, and even being sprayed with disinfectant on their way.

Informality, Work, and Fluidity

Rajindar and Tamanna's experiences, described at the beginning of this essay, point to the precarity and lack of security that workers in the informal sector face, whether employed or self-employed. Another aspect underlying the nature of their labor is the question of work itself and skill. Informal work is commonly associated with unskilled labor (although skilled informal workers receive higher wages as we will see below). While the Ministry of Labour and Employment's 2019 Code on Wages sets out detailed criteria for determining the minimum wage for different categories of workers, it does not specify the classification criteria. The Indian government uses the International Labour Organization's taxonomy in its general classification, which sees skill associated with formal education and technical qualifications and thus categorizes most blue-collar work as unskilled. Tandon notes that such a system of classification is based on a hierarchy that privileges college degrees and devalues experience gained through work.[16] The experience and knowledge of workers categorized as unskilled or elementary has therefore been economically unrewarded. That said, there is some level of on-the-job acknowledgment of skill, which allows workers to become efficient in their work, accomplish more in a shorter time, and often even rise in rank. None of this maps onto the state's skill register per se but does provide certain advantages to the working lives of those in the informal sector.

---

14 Subhanil Chowdhury, "Employment and Growth under Capitalism: Some Critical Issues with Special Reference to India" *Institute of Development Studies Kolkata Occasional Paper* 27 (2011): 1-40.

15 Anand Patel, "Cat Finally Out of the Bag: Unemployment at 45-Year High, Government Defends Data" *India Today,* May 31, 2019, https://www.indiatoday.in/business/story/india-unemployment-rate-6-1-per-cent-45-year-high-nsso-report-1539580-2019-05-31, accessed August 9, 2020.

16 Rajesh Tandon, "Who is Unskilled?" *Times of India*, July 10, 2020, https://timesofindia.indiatimes.com/blogs/voices/who-is-unskilled/, accessed August 9, 2020.

Raju used to work as a supplier to a mason in Kolkata. He had worked for many years in this role, and while his wages were low there was a consistent supply of work. Teams of construction workers are often recruited through the contractor's social or village networks. For unskilled workers like Raju, being attached to such a team provides steady access to work. He had been working in this sector for seven years, illustrating that even among unskilled workers at the lowest rung of employment there is a tendency to persist in that sector if work is regularly available. One of the reasons behind this persistence was the scope of opportunities to learn other better paid skills associated with construction work.

> On the (construction) site you observe all the work being done and you learn new things. I have learnt from Pal da (the painter) how to mix colors. The more you learn the more you can access these jobs in case someone is absent. It is all about being quick on your feet and always learning, if you keep your eyes closed and mechanically do your work then you will never get anywhere.[17]

This conversation with Raju in 2016 suggests that workers engaged in low-paid, unskilled work also aim to skill up through active learning and experience. This understanding, echoed by others during my 2016 fieldwork, challenges the official understanding of skill, which devalues the role of experience and initiative on the job. For precarious yet aspiring workers like Raju, the sudden loss of work due to COVID-19 spelled destitution. His wages amounted to just subsistence wages for his family and they had no savings. While the central and state government had announced policies to safeguard construction workers,[18] Raju and many other unregistered suppliers were not eligible for any relief. The government rations were inadequate and intermittent. After barely surviving for some weeks on assistance from charitable organizations, Raju had to find other means of sustaining himself. Even with the relaxation of the lockdown, construction work is hard to come by. Without recourse to any other options to secure a livelihood, Raju now sells vegetables. He buys them from the local vendor in the village at cost price and then sells them in the nearest town.

> There are many people who prefer to not go to the market because they are afraid of contracting Corona. I go through the neighborhoods selling my wares. On some days of the week sales are good but on other days I am hardly able to make a couple of sales. There are many others who have taken to selling vegetables so the competition is high.[19]

At a time when only essentials such as food are being purchased on a regular basis, many like Tamanna and Raju have resorted to selling such items. It is evident that for workers located in the unskilled segment of the informal job market this further lowers their bargaining power. Chowdhury holds that in a society offering no unemployment benefits, joblessness is unsustainable.[20] Instead, workers resort to low-paid, low-productivity work, which, according to Joan Robinson, constitutes disguised unemployment.[21] Without the provision of productive jobs, we see a crowding effect in low-productivity work such as food-vending. The increase in people looking for the

---

17 Face-to-face interview, Kolkata, October 9, 2016.
18 Somesh Jha, "COVID-19: Government Directs States to Transfer Cash to Construction Workers," *Business Standard*, March 24, 2020, https://www.business-standard.com/article/economy-policy/covid-19-govt-directs-states-to-transfer-cash-to-construction-workers-120032400746_1.html, accessed August 9, 2020.
19 Telephone interview, May 20, 2020.
20 Subhanil Chowdhury, "Employment and Growth under Capitalism: Some Critical Issues with Special Reference to India": 21.
21 Joan Robinson, "Disguised Unemployment," *The Economic Journal* 46 (1936): 226.

same opportunities in what is already low-productivity, low-paid work brings down earnings even further.[22] This kind of disguised unemployment then results in further deskilling.

Paid domestic workers – while consistently underpaid, over-exploited, and classified as unskilled – had, over time, been able to negotiate some task specialization in the discharge of their labor. Domestic workers were employed as cooks, for cleaning and maintenance work, and for care work, all of which had different scales of pay. The uncertainty, non-payment of wages, and the threat of losing their job during COVID-19, however, in many instances reversed this hard-fought task specialization. The rise in unemployment has pushed many women previously engaged in other jobs or with working husbands to look for jobs as paid domestic workers, bringing increased competition and the risk of depressing wages. Another effect of this increased competition and job insecurity has been the diffusion of the nascent job specialization.

Mamata, a part-time, live-out domestic worker used to sweep, wash dishes and sometimes chop vegetables at her employer's house, where another woman was employed for cooking. During the lockdown, the latter, who was a live-in worker, had to undertake the additional tasks of sweeping and washing as Mamata could not come to work. After the lockdown, Mamata's employer asked her not to return to work. They had increased their live-in worker's wages (albeit not commensurate with the increased workload) in return for her taking on these additional duties.[23] Similarly, Sarika, who was employed in childcare, has been asked to take on additional maintenance tasks such as washing dishes and laundering and folding clothes.

> They argue that they are doing me a favor by keeping me in employment as with all the family staying at home, there is no need for a childminder. My husband has lost his job in the factory and if my job goes too how will I feed my two daughters? So I had to agree. They have not even increased the wages for the extra work.[24]

Paid domestic work is not just underpaid; it is invisible, unlegislated, and rarely recognized as hard labor. In view of this already marginalized position, pushing workers to combine multiple tasks on slightly increased or the same wages erodes their claim for task specialization and skills quotient.

In this period of COVID-19, however, skill does not protect workers from sliding into low-paid, low-productivity precarious work. Suresh was a carpenter, an occupation categorized as skilled. Much like Raju he also had no work and was forced to resort to food-vending, in his case, fish. The work of selling fish, however, also involves preparing and portioning it according to each buyer's request. Suresh had no expertise in this area and this inexperience cost him customers. He now sells whole fish at a slightly cheaper price to achieve some sales but the return is expectedly paltry. Suresh's experience shows the limits of the idea of the transferability which characterizes informal work. The work of fish-scaling and cutting was a specialized task that required learning, as Suresh found out. This work, however, is not classified or remunerated as skilled.

Sarjul, a mason, was unable to work when construction sites closed down. While he reported receiving some governmental benefit earmarked for construction workers, this was minimal. In the absence of other avenues, he resorted to selling masks at traffic lights. Needless to say, the amount he earned through this was less than half of what he used to earn as a mason and barely enough to sustain his family.

---

22 Subhanil Chowdhury, "Employment and Growth under Capitalism: Some Critical Issues with Special Reference to India": 22.
23 Telephone interview, June 7, 2020.
24 Face-to-face interview, Kolkata, June 7, 2020.

As is evident from Rajindar's account, self-employed workers faced similar conditions of extreme difficulty. Anwar worked as a tailor in Durgapur. He had a small shop and received regular tailoring, repairing, and alteration orders from the neighborhood, through which he was able to live relatively comfortably. In the initial period of the lockdown he survived on his savings but soon they too ran dry. Being in his fifties, he also had medical expenses to cover for his ailing daughter. At first, he tried his hand at selling fruit but with the long trek through neighborhoods, police harassment, and very low sales it soon became evident that he would not be able to sustain himself in this way.

> All my life I had done tailoring work; I had not learnt anything else. During the lockdown, I went to different houses asking people if they had clothes to be mended but no one was forthcoming. I was also not making money selling fruit. Finally, to make ends meet my wife decided to ask around in the nearby neighborhood if someone needed a domestic worker. With police restrictions many of the regular workers were not able to come to work, so she managed to find work in some houses. If someone needs utensils washed or their rooms swept, she does it and they pay her for it.[25]

Anwar's skilled labor had rendered him unskilled in other areas of work. The extreme economic crisis of the lockdown period sent the household spiraling from skilled self-employed to daily wage labor on barely subsistence wages. These instances of penury make it evident that the informal sector across its spectrums functions without any state protection and is completely dependent on the vicissitudes of the market.

Conclusion

It has been reported that 100 million workers have lost their jobs in the COVID-19 pandemic.[26] The pandemic has exacerbated an already extant crisis of labor and illustrates the agency of workers who, left to their own devices, have managed, even if in minimal ways, to continue to earn a living wage. At the same time this agency cannot eclipse the structural inequalities within work itself and the tenuous relation between skill and security. The pandemic has pushed down the skills quotient of workers unprotected by social security or wage guarantees. Both unskilled and skilled workers are forced to sustain themselves through low-productivity, highly competitive low(er)-waged jobs which barely allow them to eke out a living in the present crisis period. Further, for segments like domestic workers, such reversals of task specialization could have long-term effects on their conditions of labor, pushing them to perform more work for less wages. Informal labor categorized as unskilled presumes a fluidity and transferability between various kinds of work. The experiences highlighted in this essay, however, shows that this is inaccurate. Every job entails certain knowledge and skills, and the fluidity pushing workers from one job to the other is, in fact, a condition of precarity.

25 Telephone interview, April 21, 2020.
26 Govindraj Ethiraj, "100-120 Million Jobs Lost Due to Covid-19 Lockdown", *India Spend*, April 20, 2020, https://www.indiaspend.com/100-120-million-jobs-lost-due-to-covid-19-lockdown/, accessed September 3, 2020.

Alina-Sandra Cucu

'It was Quiet': Pandemics as Normal Life in a Romanian Town

"These idiots have put all these restrictions in place, and now I cannot do anything."
"I don't know if I will still have a job when we get back to normal."
"Life will never get back to normal."
"I hope we'll all get back to normal soon."

Everybody I've been talking to in Craiova in the last five months just wanted their lives to "get back to normal."[27] During everyday conversations and hours of complaining on the phone, taxi drivers, street vendors, industrial workers, supermarket employees, shopkeepers, veterinary doctors, personal trainers, and managers have been denoting the pandemic as an existential break, a stop, a suspension of living. More dramatically, in relation to school closures, comments drew not only on a deferral of the present but also on a "destruction of children's futures."

What kind of biographical imaginary have people in Craiova been employing when thinking about themselves as "stopping" or "putting on hold" their lives during the pandemic? While answers to these questions can get very personal when it comes to people's relational universe, one thing was clear: what was actually being put on hold was work. The lockdown made visible a biographical imaginary that equates work – or rather labor – with life itself. Furthermore, it is a productive imaginary that assumes a continuity and stability of our working-lives that is long gone, but still functions as a retrograde historical illusion, and frames the ways in which we define certain moments as ruptures, or as eventful landmarks of a before and after.

The consequences of the lockdowns everywhere have played out differently for various social categories. The poor, the migrants, the commuters, the old, and the informal workers have disproportionately paid the price for a crisis policy that failed to take into account both the fact that, as social beings, individuals are not equivalent nodes in epidemiological networks, and that this structural non-equivalence would produce a wide range of behaviors, ideological commitments, and emotional responses. Whole societies in the global south and large categories of populations everywhere have simply collapsed as millions lost their jobs, went unpaid, or had to flee the area where they worked and return home. While the uneven geography of capital and labor constantly pushes individuals out of their immediate environment in search of remote survival opportunities, the pandemic has made it clear how, in the long-run, capitalism survives on people's capacity and willingness to fall back on their kinship support structures whenever the elusiveness of these opportunities is revealed.[28] Another failure is predictable: as authoritarian regimes seek to make

---

27 The essay draws on my very personal experience with how people in Craiova, a town in the south of Romania, have dealt with the spread of *SARS*-CoV-2, with the COVID-19 pandemic, and with the economic, social, and emotional consequences of the national lockdown. Until mid-August, I was living in Craiova, conducting ethnographic fieldwork for a project on the 'advance' of flexible capitalism in Eastern Europe, which focuses on the main private employer in the region: the automotive factory, now part of Ford Company.

28 See also James Ferguson, *Expectations of Modernity: Myths and Meanings of Urban Life on the Zambian Copperbelt* (Berkeley: University of California Press, 1999).

a state of exception into the norm,[29] there is little hope of new articulations of a radical political imaginary that would refuse the return to a 'normal' of existential fragility, social inequality, and injustice.

The ways in which polities everywhere have faced the menace of COVID-19 have resulted in the systematic "destruction of lives and livelihoods in the name of survival,"[30] and in an illusory scientification of the biological through little more than "evidentiary charisma."[31] The multidimensional threat we are facing cuts through flesh and bones, and "it is the poor, the marginalized, and the vulnerable who are most affected by drastic measures, exacerbating already existing inequalities."[32] However, even the most fierce critics of the ways in which the political dealt with the social, civic, and economic consequences of the health crisis we are traversing have little to say about those cases in which being destitute, peripheral, and precarious results in an existence that is so fragmented and unstable that there is basically no 'normal' to return to. For certain social categories, the crisis of a global pandemic is just part and parcel of an everyday vulnerability they have been carrying around for a long time. For many whose precariousness is an ordinary experience, the pandemic is lived not as an unprecedented sweeping of the everyday, but as 'just life.'

This essay delves into the ways in which Denisa, a twenty-three-year-old woman in Craiova, has lived through the Romanian national lockdown and its aftermath, and offers a glimpse into a (working-)life in which crisis is *always* the 'normal.' It places the current situation within her fragmented and fragile employment trajectory of constantly being in-between jobs, trying to acquire new skills without knowing what they would be good for, and moving across borders overnight. Denisa's very personal experience of the pandemic as a non-event questions the normal we are supposed to go back to: a normal that glorifies narratives of honest labor, while making stable and reliable work a thing of the past; a normal that does not allow the transformation of large categories into surplus populations to be recognized for what it is – a structural feature of late capitalism – but translates it into a repertoire of personal moral obligations and failures.

A Very Ordinary Work Trajectory

Denisa moved to Craiova when she was fifteen, after her parents got divorced. While her father remained in his hometown, her mother took the migration path and left for Italy, for what in the beginning was supposed to be a temporary series of work-gigs. Initially, Denisa lived with her sister and her grandparents, who died soon after. As a teenager, she was isolated and lonely, with no family close-by and with no structure of support. Her home situation spilled over into her high school hierarchy, where it was expressed in comments about her "weirdness" – as if leaving alone, not dressing fancily, and not being supervised in her studies were personal choices or tangible character features. But what Denisa experienced most as a teenager was a generalized invisibility,

29 Selam Gebrekidan, "For Autocrats, and Others, Coronavirus Is a Chance to Grab Even More Power," *The New York Times*, March 30, 2020, https://www.nytimes.com/2020/03/30/world/europe/coronavirus-governments-power.html, accessed August 16, 2020.

30 Carlo Caduff, "What Went Wrong: Corona and the World after the Full Stop," *Medical Anthropology Quarterly* 0 (2020): 2.

31 Ann H. Kelly, "Ebola Vaccines, Evidentiary Charisma and the Rise of Global Health Emergency Research," *Economy and Society* 47 (2018): 135–161.

32 Carlo Caduff, "What Went Wrong": 2.

which meant that she could barely recall this period of torment beyond the broad strokes and the pale shades of feeling "like a shadow," because "nothing really happened."

When she moved to Craiova, she had to leave behind the intensive English training she had opted for in her hometown and enroll in a high school with an economic services profile. According to her own evaluation and to the opinion of other people in town, her high school was low-ranked, "full of gypsies," a place where "nobody truly wanted to learn anything." While in school, she liked sports, English, and geography, and when she graduated, she had vague thoughts about enrolling in the physical education department at the local university. She abandoned the idea almost immediately because "it wasn't going to help with anything" anyway. So, she said to herself: "I should go to Italy to earn some money, 'cause well, this was how things were, everybody had to earn money."

Her 2016 Italian experience started with a new form of isolation, in her mother's home, where she could not find a way to get close to or avoid conflict with her mother's husband. Soon enough, she was going to replace her mother in two of her part-time jobs: dog-sitting and cleaning.

> I worked in mom's place, she was taking care of some dogs and she was cleaning after them... There was a Labrador, or I don't know, a Rottweiler, she reached to my breasts when she jumped on me. She was a girl, and she thought she was still a puppy, but she was very big. And she had one of those collars so she couldn't bark, so I didn't get scared. And there were four more little dogs. I worked in my mom's place and meanwhile, I tried to find something else. I also worked for some banks; I was doing the cleaning.

Her mother's salary was four hundred euros (around 470 US dollars) a month for her dog-sitting job, where she worked for two to four hours in the morning, and three to six hundred euros a month for the cleaning job, where she worked three or four hours in the evening. Denisa covered both jobs for two weeks, allowing her mother to take care of her family issues, rest a bit, and focus on her third part-time job: weekend elderly care, for which she earned fifty euros a night. Denisa could not find any other type of work, so she returned to Craiova after three months. She came home with all the money she had earned: approximately four hundred euros. She started to search for work immediately and landed a night job as a pretzel maker in a bakery.

> In my first job, I lasted for three days; no, three nights, because I was working at night. It was at a bakery. Their ad said they were hiring people with no experience. I said: 'ah, this is great.' I went there and they started to mock me, say I was good for nothing, say that I didn't know how to do anything. I told them I didn't have experience, I was just out of school, of course I didn't know what to do there. They said: 'yes, but you have to catch up; if you don't catch up, that's it...' My colleagues were really awful. After three days, I didn't go there anymore.

The job search resumed, and after a few weeks, Denisa got her "first real job," which came with retirement benefits and health insurance. She was to work as a bus ticket vendor for the first private public transport company in the city. She was hired on October 10, and for the first three weeks, she only had to work for the three or four hours a day that her colleagues could not cover during their normal shifts. The next month, Denisa transitioned to full-time, working from 5:30 am to 2:00 pm on the first shift; or from 2:00 pm to 11:00 pm on the second shift, when she also had to stay behind to clean up the buses, even though this task was not specified in her work contract. But when Denisa got her first salary, she was glowing, and said to herself: "God, I'm so rich!" "I went to buy some sweets and then I started to look for rent." The salary that made her feel so rich, so suddenly, was "thirteen million" [approximately 320 US dollars][33].

---

33 Denisa's salary would actually be 1,300 RON, but people in Craiova continue to use the 'old money,' with basically no reference to the latest monetary expressions of prices and wages.

Out of the thirteen "millions," Denisa ended up paying seven for a room in the house of an aunt, where she didn't have heating or a television, and her door had a window so the aunt could check up on her at all times and deny her any amount of privacy. In November, she was already filling bottles with hot water and placing them under her blanket for a bit of warmth. She slept wearing her cap and gloves, before running to work at the other end of the city at 4:30 in the morning, fearing the aggressive dog packs and the late-night drunkards.

Acute loneliness pushed her in the arms of a much older bus driver, who had a wife, two children, and a permanent mistress. Reflecting on this, she says: "I didn't know about sexual harassment back then, but the truth is the bus drivers tried their luck with all of us and they had a chance with me because I felt so alone. I just wanted someone to talk to me." Telling me this, her voice goes flat, as it does every time she speaks about human connections, almost as if, in spite of her openly declared need for others, 'people' are a category that is alien and functions according to an obscure logic that Denisa gave up grasping.

In the same voice, she tells me about her long-term ex-boyfriend, with whom she left for Lugoj, a small city in the west of Romania, where they were offered work and accommodation together with another couple, back in 2017. He was hired as a builder, she was hired as a cleaning lady, with ironing as her main task. They stayed for one month, until they got into a big fight and she stormed back to Craiova. A new attempt at working abroad soon followed. She left for Italy once again, where she searched for work in vain for a few weeks, before deciding to train as a manicurist, "just to have a skill." Now, she regrets the money she invested in those courses, instead of getting her driving license sooner, which might have given her a better chance for a job. After a while, she invited her boyfriend to live with her and her mother's family in Genoa, while she continued to search for a decent job. Although agreeing to find work as a construction worker while in Italy, her boyfriend started gambling, often spending his nights with the slot machines [*păcănele*]. The second attempt at a life in Italy fell apart pretty soon for both of them, so they came back to Romania. The relationship didn't last much longer after that.

In 2018, after a few months without an income, Denisa got a diploma as a Zumba instructor and found a job at a gym, where she was paid by the hour, with no contract. She worked there for a month before being laid off because the gym found it too expensive to offer her the part-time contract she was asking for. She also took up dog-sitting more seriously, placing an ad on the only online platform offering pet-related services in Craiova. For a while, she hosted dogs and cats at almost absurdly low prices, although she felt she made a lot of money out of this erratic activity.

At some point, she found a job at a veterinary surgery, where, although she had no training, she was asked from the start to perform risky procedures – including injections and blood shedding – on cats and dogs. When she questioned her capacity to do this and "tried to be useful in other ways," her bosses and colleagues started to shout at her and pressured her to "do the work" and relax, because "animals don't die so easily." She remained afraid of performing procedures she wasn't trained for, so she left after less than a week. At the end of 2018, she was again searching for a job, to the dismay of her new boyfriend, a kinesis therapist born into an intellectual family, who had been pretty happy to be able to say that his partner was a nurse at a vet's office. Not a pretzel maker; not a dog-sitter; not a ticket vendor.

After three more jobless months, Denisa became clinically depressed. For the first time in her life, her aimlessness felt unbearable. In February 2019, she joined a wooden frames workshop, but she did not last there either, because of her lack of physical and emotional strength. Depression made interpersonal communication difficult and laughter came hard to her in those days. After two weeks, her employer called her into his office and in a half-fatherly, half-contemptuous manner, he lectured her on the dangers of being a "lone wolf" and not knowing what she wanted to do with her life. When she stated, almost bursting into tears, that she wanted to become a psychologist, he drily replied: "You could never become a psychologist, you actually need one."

For almost a year, hopelessness flooded her life, and her depressive episode became so severe that she could not keep up the search for yet another job. But that was the first thing she did at the end of 2019, when her depression started to lift, and she found another job as a Zumba instructor at a gym, where she was paid less than twenty Romanian lei (five US dollars) for an hour and she had no legal contract. In February 2020, the owner of the gym offered her part-time work as a cleaning lady at an afterschool program she ran in a different part of the city. She was offered a monthly wage of five hundred lei (approximately 120 US dollars) for four hours a day, which she supplemented with the money she got for walking my dog when needed.

The last workplace brought with it the double shame of a low-pay/low-status job. To this, Denisa responds with compensatory but contradictory statements. First, she moves the emphasis from status to activity, or in more fundamental terms, from being to doing: "I don't consider myself a cleaning lady. I believe I do something good when going there to disinfect the place. Who wouldn't want to clean and make money at the same time? At home, I clean all the time, and nobody is paying me, like so many others." "Like most women here," I reacted, smiling. "Like all women," she said, starting to laugh. But later in the conversation, she talked about feeling degraded and humiliated, both financially and in relation to her boyfriend and his family.

> When I bought food, I bought it with my own money. When I got the money, I tried to save something, to buy something, to pay something, so they can't say I do nothing. Anyway, for him, what I do, that I go there [to the afterschool] and that I come here [to my place] to walk the dog is equal to zero. Because it is normal... If we go somewhere and somebody asks: 'What do you work as?' 'I'm a kinesis therapist' 'And you?' 'I'm a cleaning lady.' He is ashamed if I tell this to somebody. I'm not bragging about it either. I know people who work in sanitation get a shame bonus and I don't understand why, because it's not a shame to take out the trash. I don't know why it's shameful, but it is. And it makes me feel embarrassed to do this job, to do the cleaning. But it is not shameful... But I have always been ashamed to say where I work. And when I worked at the veterinary office, why should I have felt good for three seconds when telling someone that I work there but feel horrible every time I go there? It's better here: I go, I clean... at least I'm in peace.

Denisa is twenty-three. In five years, she has entered into twelve employment relations, has gained two qualifications, and has gone through three moves to different cities or countries. To all these, she concludes: "I haven't worked on a contract since 2015. I paid retirement benefits for two or three months, I think, and I don't have health insurance." With the last cleaning job, she has finally been promised a double part-time contract: half at the gym, half at the afterschool program, but although this sounded really good to Denisa, the pandemic paralyzed Craiova before the promise could materialize.

An Uneventful Pandemic... for Some

The nationwide state of emergency was instituted by presidential decree in March, and imposed a complete lockdown, including production stoppages and restrictions to all economic operators.[34] The

---

[34] Between March and August, several legislative measures have been adopted as a frame for the emergency measures required by the spread of SARS-CoV-2: Decree 195/2020, which instituted the state of emergency, MO, I/212/ March 16, 2020; Emergency Ordinance no. 30/2020, MO 231, March 21, 2020; Decree 240/2020, MO 311, April 14, 2020;

Romanian economy has faced the worst period since the last global financial crisis. 400,000 jobs have disappeared in only sixty-seven days: in April, between five and seven thousand work contracts were being terminated daily; in May, their number reached ten thousand.[35] Over 1.5 million people became the beneficiaries of technical unemployment support. Many others lost their jobs, and it is impossible to say at the moment how many will be able to re-enter the labor market and when.

The pandemic exacerbated three lines of fracture in Craiova's labor landscape. First, the one between the permanent and the temporary employees of the biggest companies in town – mainly Ford, its suppliers, and hypermarkets like Lidl. For instance, the six thousand workers at Ford, the strongest economic agent, and the largest private employer in the region, were kept in technical unemployment between March 19 and May 4, and had seventy-eight percent of their wages covered (by the company in the first two weeks; seventy-five percent from the state unemployment insurance budget and three percent from Ford afterward).[36] This represented a crisis departure from the Romanian Labour Code provisions that state that in the event of a temporary reduction in economic activity, the individual work agreements may be suspended but the employer must cover a monthly technical unemployment indemnity of at least seventy-five percent of their wages (without bonuses).

From June onwards, the state support went down to 41.5 percent of gross wages, but not more than 41.5 percent of the average gross income, even if the employee's salary is higher than that.[37] To stimulate the re-entry onto the labor market of the most vulnerable age groups – ages sixteen to twenty-nine, and the over-fifties – the state decided to cover fifty percent of their wages for one year, up to a limit of 2,500 Romanian lei (approximately six hundred US dollars).[38] Companies could benefit from both types of state help for three months and could not terminate the work contracts of their employees before the end of the year, with the exception of seasonal or temporary workers. And it was precisely the temporary workers who were left in the air in Craiova. For instance, after the lockdown was lifted and production restarted, Ford was unable or unwilling to extend many temporary working-contracts. As the sales crisis in the automotive industry

Emergency Ordinance no. 70/2020, MO 394, May 14, 2020; Decision no. 394/2020, MO 410, May 18, 2020; Law 59/2020, MO 416, May 19, 2020; Emergency Ordinance no. 92/2020, MO 459, May 29, 2020.

35 Ramona Cornea, "Cea mai dură perioadă pentru angajați din 2009 încoace: 400.000 de locuri de muncă au fost șterse din economie în numai 67 de zile," *Ziarul Financiar*, May 21, 2020, https://www.zf.ro/profesii/cea-mai-dura-perioada-pentru-angajati-din-2009-incoace-400-000-de-19163962, accessed August 8, 2020.

36 "Ministrul Finanțelor: Ford va susține șomajul tehnic primele două saptamani. Vedem cum putem să ajutăm după aceea," March 18, 2020, https://www.mediafax.ro/economic/ministrul-finantelor-ford-va-sustine-somajul-tehnic-primele-doua-saptamani-vedem-cum-putem-sa-ajutam-dupa-aceea-18996523, accessed September 2, 2020.

37 The European Union has recognized that its member states, especially the peripheral ones, would come under increasing pressure, and adopted as a policy guidance the International Labour Organization predictions that employment in these states would suffer worse than during the global financial crisis, which could lead to a loss of 7.8 percent of Europe's total working hours in the second quarter of 2020 (equivalent to 12 million full-time workers). In March 2020, the European Commission praised the effectiveness of short-time work (STW) schemes, and committed to financially bearing some of the burden for the public support offered to those firms who had to temporarily reduce the number of working-hours for their employees but still pay them. The debates and proposals led to the adoption of a financial instrument – Support to mitigate Unemployment Risks in an Emergency (SURE) – that allows member states to access up to 100 billion dollars in cheap loans, contracted by the European Unions on behalf of its members on the international financial markets, and guaranteed by the European Investment Bank temporary support to mitigate unemployment risks in an emergency. See Alessandro D'Alfonso, "Temporary Support to Mitigate Unemployment Risks in an Emergency (SURE)," *EPRS/European Parliamentary Research Service*, April 15, 2020, https://www.europarl.europa.eu/RegData/etudes/ATAG/2020/649375/EPRS_ATA(2020)649375_EN.pdf, accessed August 15, 2020.

38 Governmental Emergency Ordinance no. 92/2020, MO 459, May 29, 2020.

deepened, temporary workers had no protection in the face of the instability of the labor market provoked by the pandemic. Many of them were commuters from nearby towns or villages; others were middle-age women and men who had recently returned from abroad when hearing that Ford was going to increase its productive capacities in Craiova in the near future. In some cases, entire families who had been employed on temporary contracts had to leave the factory in May, with no prospects of finding other jobs during the pandemic.

The second line of fracture marked by the current crisis was the one between employees of large firms and those employed by shopkeepers, smaller factories, workshops, and carriers. Until recently, the biggest companies paid their workers only the national minimum as an entry wage[39] but their employees worked regular hours, had their contributions paid, and were compensated for overtime. Although Craiova definitely functioning as a reservoir of cheap labor in global supply chains, some of the biggest companies in the city had to increase their workers' wages because union representation was still strong enough to ensure some pressure on management. In contrast, as Denisa's story makes it clear, even before the COVID-19 situation exploded, the world of the smaller firms was dominated by irregular working times, multiple attempts to escape the requirements of legal contracts, unpaid extra hours, wages under the legal minimum, and the possibility of being laid off with no warning. This meant that even if the government also infused the small and medium enterprises with some blood, by increasing their credit cap, by offering to guarantee their investment and working capital, by refunding VAT up to a certain limit, and by subsidizing the interest on their loans and the payment of technical unemployment benefits for their employees, thousands of people in Craiova have lived the pandemic with the sword of unemployment hanging over their heads.[40]

During the lockdown, Denisa belonged to a category of workers who could not benefit from the financial help designed to mitigate unemployment risks, and had no health insurance. She was invisible in the public space, where social protection was concerned, just like the one million people who came back from Western Europe after losing their jobs in Italy, Spain, or the United Kingdom, with no unemployment benefit and, in many cases, with no national health insurance. Calls for a universal basic income and immediate health insurance for the entire population from a Romanian academic fell on deaf ears,[41] and more radical measures to support the population during the crisis – such as suspending rent or mortgage payments, debt cancelling, or the nationalization of certain key industries and parts of the health care system – remain unthinkable in mainstream politics.[42] Of course, the full lockdown policy of most European countries, which immediately left migrant workers without an income, had exceptions: governmental special permissions were granted for the opening of flight corridors that took the much-needed Romanian

---

39 The 2020 gross minimum wage in Romania is 2,230 RON (1,346 RON net), HG 935/2019 regarding the increase of the minimum wage from January 1, 2020, MO 1010/I, December 16, 2019.

40 Alina Grigoras, "Gov't Economic Measures on Coronavirus Crisis: Aid for SMEs, the State Will Cover the Employees' Technical Unemployment," *The Romania Journal*, March 19, 2020, https://www.romaniajournal.ro/business/govt-economic-measures-on-coronavirus-crisis-aid-for-smes-the-state-will-cover-the-employees-technical-unemployment/, accessed August 15, 2020.

41 "Planul anti-Coronavirus. Scrisoare deschisă," *CriticAtac*, March 31, 2020, http://www.criticatac.ro/planul-anti-coronavirus-scrisoare-deschisa, accessed March 31, 2020.

42 Georgi Marinov, "Coronavirus: Scientific Realities vs. Economic Fallacies," *LeftEast*, May 03, 2020, https://www.criticatac.ro/lefteast/coronavirus-scientific-realities-vs-economic-fallacies, accessed May 6, 2020.

seasonal workers to Germany.[43] After all, there are worse catastrophes than a global pandemic, such as a North Rhein-Westphalia without its sausages, or an undersupplied Berlin during the *Spargel* season ...

Further on, the lockdown deepened a third line of fracture: the one that separates state employees from all others. Denisa's boyfriend, Dan, his family, as well as all of his friends, work for the biggest employer in the country: the Romanian state. They are clerks, policemen, doctors, or army corps; they feel protected and stable, and benefit from the luxury of being able to make plans for the future. For them, Craiova is a world of conspicuous consumption, where showing one's money off is more important than actually having it. Denisa's boyfriend has his own flat and three cars, and dreams about buying some land to build a house. His brother – the only one in the family working in the private sector, as a low-level manager at Ford – owns six cars, most of them flashy but not functional. Sometimes, money is privately borrowed with absurdly high interest, cars and flats are bought and sold rapidly, and gambling is rampant. As Denisa says, in Craiova, whether one is rich or poor, "everybody spends their time at *păcănele.*"

For women in their group, having a good (state) job is desirable but finding a man with one is still the safest bet. As a consequence, while Denisa's low-status job, lack of family protection, and dire financial situation trigger contempt, her relationship with a man who has a flat and a good job is envied, an envy that is many times explicitly and aggressively expressed. This gives rise to immediate interactions that articulate a painful paradox: while Denisa's "unexplainable luck" with men is seen as remarkable, the human being behind this luck is ignored in all her closest relationships and her very usefulness in those relationships denied. This became more obvious with the COVID-19 crisis. During the pandemic, the income of state employees has been one hundred percent safe, which left a large category of the city's population not worrying about tomorrow and imagining their fate disconnected from the private sector's. However, in rare cases, their installments were delayed, which also happened to Dan, Denisa's current boyfriend. In a family conversation decrying the situation, Denisa jumped in to say: "I got paid, we will be OK for a while." Her boyfriend's mother pitifully commented: "Oh, but given how much you are making, this solves nothing." This made Denisa bitterly remark: "I feel like a third wheel. Maybe she didn't say it meanly, but that's how I felt."

Like her boyfriend's family, many in Craiova would consider Denisa's life as one of non-work. The idea of 'non-work' [*nemuncă*] has traversed the entire recent history of Eastern Europe, it has been pervasive in the formulation of redistributive policies and imaginaries of social justice, and it was instrumental in the articulation of populist discourses across the region. It stubbornly survived the austerity measures of late socialist regimes, the chaos and disintegration of the 1990s, and the neoliberalization of the region in the 2000s. And while as a discursive trope, *nemuncă* has played a central role in the reconfiguration of the relationship between the state, society, and economy in the last four decades, it has also come to life in people's ordinary interactions and routines, and in establishing personal hierarchies of worth. These hierarchies move in a fluid manner to address both the disgrace of the unemployed, and a more generalized incapacity to find good jobs or keep them. Living one's life as cheap labor is shameful even in a city where good and stable work is a

43 "Racism in the Flesh. German Meat Industry and East European Migrant Labor," June 28, 2020, *open letter written by FemBunt, a Bulgarian feminist collective based in Berlin, in response to the outrageous declarations of Mr. Laschet, the prime minister of North Rhein-Westphalia that stated that Bulgarian and Romanian workers are responsible for the Coronavirus outbreak at the meat processing plant Tönnies,* https://www.transnational-strike.info/2020/06/22/racism-in-the-flesh-german-meat-industry-and-eastern-european-migrant-labor/, *accessed August 10, 2020.*

rarity, and precariousness is structural and ubiquitous. As Denisa says, "I am still seen as if I didn't work. As if waking up early in the morning is nothing; as if washing toilets is nothing; as if my money doesn't count. Yes, it's five million, but it's mine."

Because of her structural position that offers her the "freedom" of not having much to lose, Denisa has not been able to emotionally participate in the panic and anxiety of the city. What the lockdown brought into her life was rather the luxury of not searching, of not anxiously waiting for replies to job applications, of not hitting dead end after dead end, in short, of simply not trying, while at the same time not having to feel like giving up or justifying herself to others. Empty streets matched her inner calm, although she knew well that the respite was both illusory and temporary. "I felt very well because I'm an introvert, and I liked it so much. There was quiet in the streets, quiet in the stores, no bustle. I liked it very much. And I had no problem with this, although I know people got very agitated: 'oh my, oh my' [aoleu, aoleu]."

When it came to the quarantine procedures, Denisa has been careful. She has done more than the governmental health and safety regulations have asked of the Romanian population: she has been washing her hands obsessively, has always worn a mask in the street, has tried to stay away from other people on the bus, and has refused physical contact at all times. She is used to doing things in an unusually responsible manner, and according to her own, not easily readable definition of "proper." When we first met, her concern for physical safety, routine effectiveness, and personal boundaries appeared rather excessive, and I experienced her presence as a surprising combination of old-school rigidity and adolescent newly-found assertiveness. The blend was sometimes uneasy, like I was unintendingly reaching some dark corners, which no previous knowledge of the person could render navigable. But the life-long assemblage of habits and reactions meant that preventing any glimpses into her existential fragility served her well during the pandemic, when rules that look unbearable to others seemed to make her rather happy.

At some level, her attitude has been a breath of fresh air amid the surreal positionings of both virus negationists and fear-paralyzed denizens. Despite trying to stay open and non-judgmental, adopting a proper 'ethnographic attitude' became a harder thing to do as the lockdown isolation started to wear me down. I came to meet both the endless conspiracy theories and the doomsday visions with increasing irritation. Lately, as medical anthropologists have shown, "[t]o be afraid has become an obligation, a responsibility, a duty. People are afraid not just because of what they experience but because they are told to be afraid and encouraged to inhabit the world with fear of 'foreign bodies' and 'invisible enemies'."[44] In Craiova, the opposite "duty" was to deny any danger of contamination. As a consequence, I appreciated Denisa's "no comment" and "matter of fact" compliance with mask wearing and social distancing "because this is what the law requires," although I preferred not to delve into the depths of her reasoning when she once commented that she does it "even if the virus doesn't exist."

During the lockdown, Denisa lost both her jobs. Just before I left Craiova, she was called back to her part-time cleaning job at the afterschool program but not for the one as a Zumba instructor at the gym. When I asked her how she felt when she thought she was going to lose both her jobs, she said: "it didn't bother me too much because I took the money for one month and a half during the lockdown. It wasn't much but I took it..." I tried to edge her toward self-introspection, maybe unconsciously searching for the traces of fear and confusion I found in my interviews with the temporary workers from Ford. "So, for you, losing your job and having to search for another is ...." Denisa replied quickly: "Just normal."

---

44 Carlo Caduff, "What Went Wrong": 12.

Nicole Mayer-Ahuja

'Solidarity' in Times of Corona? Of Migrant Ghettos, Low-Wage Heroines, and Empty Public Coffers[45]

When coronavirus (SARS COVID-19) hit Germany in spring 2020, a traditional rallying cry of the labor movement could be heard in politics and the media: 'Solidarity!' This was unexpected, given the fact that neoliberal economics had, for many decades, more or less subscribed to Margaret Thatcher's famous statement: "There is no such thing as society!" Suddenly, however, 'society' was supposed to display a new quality of cohesion (*gesellschaftlicher Zusammenhalt*), encompassing basically 'all of us' (*uns alle*). 'Solidarity' was evoked – between the young and the old, between capital and labor, between chief physician and hospital nurse, between the graphic designer working from home and her migrant cleaner. Most of all, solidarity was now showered over the newly appointed 'heroes' and, especially, 'heroines' of everyday life (*HeldInnen des Alltags*). The well-to-do assembled on their balconies at 6 pm, applauding the nurses in hospitals and retirement homes, sales assistants at supermarket cashiers, delivery drivers, cleaners, and others who did not have the option to stay at home, but more or less faced the risk of infecting themselves in their quest to 'keep things going' during the weeks of the coronavirus lockdown. Even the head of a powerful works council in one of the biggest industrial companies (Volkswagen) stated: "This crisis makes it very clear: If we do not produce cars for eight or twelve weeks, this has no effect on this country. Our product is obviously not systemically relevant."[46] Instead, the work of (mostly) women who contribute to the reproduction of labor and of social structures, on low pay, on precarious contracts, and typically 'invisible' to those who use their services, was now (finally!) acknowledged as crucial for the functioning of 'the system,' whatever that was supposed to be.

The Dark Side of Anti-virus Solidarity

The medium-sized university town of Göttingen, where I live and work, gained some notoriety in June 2020, not for solidarity, but for its "eighteen floors of stigma."[47] This headline in the weekly magazine *Die ZEIT* referred to a high-rise building with six to seven hundred inhabitants (Iduna Zentrum), just opposite the main university campus. When the first cases of COVID-19 were discovered in that building (eventually 147 persons turned out to be infected), the city government imposed an immediate quarantine. From one day to the next, the tenants of Iduna Zentrum (and a few weeks later, of a second high-riser, at Groner Landstraße 9) were confined to their homes, even before medical support and food supplies had been ensured. City representatives spread hearsay about 'extended families' who had apparently ignored all the rules of 'social distancing' in order to celebrate the end of Ramadan together, thus endangering the whole city. In no time, it

---

45 For a more extensive version of the argument (in German) see: Nicole Mayer-Ahuja and Richard Detje (2020), "'Solidarität' in Zeiten der Pandemie? Potentiale für eine neue Politik der Arbeit," In *WSI-Mitteilungen* 6/2020 [forthcoming].

46 Carsten Bätzold and Michael Lacher (2020), "Die Autoindustrie am Scheideweg," *denknetz.ch* (May 26, 2020), http://www.denknetz.ch/wp-content/uploads/2020/05/Baetzold_Autoindustrie_Scheideweg.pdf, accessed August 19, 2020 (Translation by Nicole Mayer-Ahuja).

47 Lucia Heisterkamp and Henning Sussebach, "18 Stockwerke Stigma," *Die ZEIT*, June 10, 2020: 3.

was common knowledge that the delinquents were not only Muslim, but also part of the Roma community, whose members (as the average liberal Göttingen citizen would not hesitate to state in private conversation) were known for their semi-legal activities and non-compliance with rules of good citizenship anyway. The Roma community protested publicly, leftist groups organized a rally in support of the inhabitants of Groner Landstraße 9, and there was a clash with the police, when several residents tried to break through the fences to leave the building – whether this was to join the demonstration or simply to go to the supermarket, since they had nothing to eat, is open to discussion.

This local conflict is interesting in its own right, but it also reveals social dynamics which are of relevance far beyond Göttingen, and also beyond Germany: the deepening of divisions among working people under conditions of a pandemic and lockdown. The very concept of solidarity implies notions of mutual obligation and assistance, among those who belong to the same group (however this group may define itself), but also of defense against those who do not. I will argue in the following paragraphs that coronavirus, and especially the measures applied to contain the spread of the disease and to come to terms with its social and economic consequences, has been utilized to increase the differences and competition among workers, thus diminishing their capacity to stand up to capital and to exert democratic influence on the emerging 'strong state.'

Old Lines of Division Revitalized: Ethnicity and Migration Status

First of all, the ruptures brought about by the coronavirus crisis shed some light on the lines of division that run along the axes of ethnicity and migration status. As soon as the virus arrived, most nation states closed their borders. In Germany, the migrant workers from Eastern and Southeastern Europe who typically come to the country in spring to harvest strawberries and asparagus were among the first to be denied entry. It was not long, however, before politicians realized that the valuable crops were rotting in the fields, and that the long-term unemployed and students who had been dispatched to the desperate farmers as a replacement in some regions lacked the experience and skills to ensure that these seasonal delicacies would actually end up on German tables. Hence, migrant workers were allowed back into the country as long as they respected the rules of 'social distancing.' In their case, this implied accepting being confined to the more or less improvised accommodation provided by their temporary rural employers.

For the German public, the problem was thus solved, even though the lack of access to medical care proved fatal in the case of at least one migrant worker from Romania. He died after contracting coronavirus in April 2020 without receiving any treatment.[48] When 150 seasonal workers went on strike in Bornheim, Hessia, to protest against the non-payment of wages and unacceptable working and living conditions, there was hardly any coverage in the national press.[49] Just a few weeks later, however, the German public could no longer ignore the fact that parts of the economy, and even 'systemically relevant' companies in food production, almost exclusively relied on migrant workers – but again, they were perceived, first and foremost, as a threat to public health. In June 2020, the first coronavirus infections were reported in slaughterhouses in the northwest of

48 Merlind Theile, "Tod eines Erntehelfers," *Die ZEIT*, April 23, 2020: 3.
49 "[Ausstehende Löhne und Missstände in Verpflegung und Unterbringung im Spargelbetrieb Ritter] Massenprotest von 150 Feldarbeitern in Bornheim," https://www.labournet.de/?p=172526, accessed August 12, 2020.

Germany. The region (covering parts of North Rhine-Westphalia and Lower Saxony) is known as the German 'Pig Belt' (*Schweinegürtel*), as it is here that the meat industry has expanded massively over the last years. This sector operates with extensive subcontracting arrangements: Employment agencies (initially from Poland, later from Romania and Bulgaria) recruit entire teams of workers, bring them to Germany, and provide them not only with a job, but also with a place to stay and with transport between 'home' and work. From time to time, journalists and social scientists have drawn public attention to the harsh working conditions on the assembly lines of these large-scale abattoirs, to the filthy and semi-dilapidated shared flats, and to wages that, on paper, meet the legal minimum wage (as established in 2015), but in fact are often much lower due to massive deductions (for accommodation, transport, work tools, and protective clothing and equipment).[50] In the wake of such scandals, several 'reforms' were launched, but most of them relied on the voluntary 'self-obligation' of the very companies that had just established Germany as a low-wage destination for slaughtering companies from Denmark (i.e. Danish Crown), for instance. Not surprisingly, conditions remained unaltered.[51] This would change only when 1,500 migrant workers at a meat factory in Rheda-Wiedenbrueck were found to be infected with coronavirus (their number would eventually exceed 2,100). Local authorities halted production immediately, the workers were confined to their shabby apartments, where far too many people per room made 'social distancing' impossible, and not all of them received their wages during quarantine.

Finally, the federal government announced that the infamous 'service contracts' (*Werkverträge*), on which the sector's subcontracting arrangements are based, would be abolished by the end of the year. At the same time, Clemens Tönnies, the owner of this slaughterhouse, which is one of the biggest meat factories in Germany, applied (unsuccessfully) for state compensation, pointing to the financial consequences of the interruption of production. The German public, however, was mainly concerned with two problems: the meat quality (which was more or less linked to animal rights) and the broader lockdown that was being inflicted upon the entire district of Gütersloh (where the Tönnies plant is located) due to the high infection rates. However, the chief minister of North Rhine-Westphalia, Armin Laschet, expressed his hope of being able to control the virus: "We do what we can, in order to prevent [the infection] from spreading to the population."[52] Just like in Göttingen, migrant workers were obviously not perceived to be part of 'the population' that could hope for solidarity in times of coronavirus.

Highlighting Class Differences

The upheavals caused by the pandemic accentuated not only ethnic, but also socioeconomic lines of division. When one of my colleagues, a young social scientist, reported her coronavirus infection to the Göttingen authorities, they did their best to reassure her (and us) that there was no need to shut down the research institute she had been attending in just before her infection was

---

50 Anne Kunze, "Fleischwirtschaft. Die Schlachtordnung," *Die ZEIT*, December 11, 2014: 21; Nicole Mayer-Ahuja, "Stellungnahme zur schriftlichen Anhörung der Mindestlohn-Kommission," May 1, 2020, http://www.sofi-goettingen. de/fileadmin/Nicole_Mayer-Ahuja/Stellungnahme_Mindestlohn_Mayer-Ahuja__.pdf, accessed August 10, 2020.
51 Peter Birke and Felix Bluhm, "Arbeitskräfte willkommen. Neue Migration zwischen Grenzregime und Erwerbsarbeit," *Sozialgeschichte Online* 25 (2019): 11–43.
52 *Armin Laschet zu Gütersloh: Lockdown nicht ausgeschlossen*, Redaktionsnetzwerk Deutschland, June 21, 2020, https://www.rnd.de/politik/laschet-lockdown-in-guetersloh-nicht-ausgeschlossen-54456b3a-5906-482d-8c80-8e22ae-57c1a7.html, accessed September 8, 2020 (Translation by Nicole Mayer-Ahuja).

discovered. When two (out of seven hundred) inhabitants of Groner Landstrasse 9 tested positive, instead, this was reason enough to lock the doors of the building without prior notice. This striking difference in the official approach to handling a disease that apparently affects 'all of us' is all the more relevant as it is working people from the lower echelons of society who are especially prone to being infected. As Matthias Richter, a sociologist of medicine, has rightly pointed out, jobs which are now ascribed 'systemic relevance' (in hospitals, supermarkets, or logistics) cannot be transferred to the 'home office' and hence imply higher risks of infection. Most of these women and men left school with basic or mid-level qualifications and are now working in the low-wage sector. On average, these workers die eight to ten years earlier than those earning at least 150 percent of the German average. Moreover, pre-existing illnesses are not distributed equally in socioeconomic terms. Those who belong to the lowest quintile of society are two to three times more likely to suffer from chronic diseases than the highest quintile. This applies to cancer, diabetes, coronary failures, but also to severe asthma, which represent virtually all of the diseases that make a person particularly susceptible to COVID-19.[53] All in all, the risk of being infected with and dying of coronavirus is especially high for those who cannot avoid direct contact with their clients or customers and are paid low wages – both of which applies to many of the inhabitants of the two high-risers in Göttingen.

In the German context, these striking interrelations are of particular interest, since the country's low-wage sector is a relatively new phenomenon. It has been systematically established over the last decades by successive federal governments, which have pursued policies of precarization since the 1980s in an attempt to combat unemployment. Through 'reforms' of labor law, social security, and labor market policies, they boosted the share of agency work, temporary contracts, and so-called 'marginal employment' (*geringfügige Beschäftigung*) or 'mini jobs,' which fall below the threshold of social insurance coverage. Around the turn of the millennium, however, the ruling coalition of social democrats and greens placed additional emphasis on the promotion of the low-wage sector, based upon the assumption that especially the United States of America enjoyed greater economic stability, and a more dynamic labor market, due to its high share of low-wage personal services. Hence, chancellor Gerhard Schröder boasted in a speech to the World Economic Forum in Davos on January 28, 2005, that Germany had "built up one of the best low-wage sectors in all of Europe."[54] Particularly between 1995 and 2008, the share of low-wage employment increased sharply. Since then, it has constantly comprised roughly one quarter of all wage-earners in Germany.[55] It is this group of working people who face an especially high risk of being infected with COVID-19 as well as of developing a particularly serious form of the disease. Thus, government policies of precarization, which have been pursued in the global north and south for several decades now,[56] have not only played an important role in deteriorating working and living conditions – they have also weakened physical resistance against the new and dangerous disease caused by the coronavirus.

53 Robert Pausch, "Risikogruppen: 'Gesundheit ist eine zutiefst ungleich verteilte Ressource'," *ZEIT online*, April 05, 2020, https://www.zeit.de/gesellschaft/2020-04/risikogruppen-coronavirus-einkommen-gesundheit-vorerkrankungen-gesellschaft, accessed August 12, 2020 (Translation by Nicole Mayer-Ahuja).
54 Gerhard Schröder, "Rede vor dem World Economic Forum in Davos," http://www.gewerkschaft-von-unten.de/Rede_Davos.pdf, accessed August 12, 2020 (Translation by Nicole Mayer-Ahuja).
55 Markus M. Grabka und Carsten Schröder, "Der Niedriglohnsektor in Deutschland ist größer als bislang angenommen," *DIW-Wochenbericht* 14 (2019): 252, https://www.diw.de/documents/publikationen/73/diw_01.c.618178.de/19-14-3.pdf, accessed August 12, 2020.
56 Nicole Mayer-Ahuja, "Die Globalität unsicherer Arbeit als konzeptionelle Provokation: Zum Zusammenhang zwischen Informalität im Globalen Süden und Prekarität im Globalen Norden," *Geschichte und Gesellschaft. Zeitschrift für Historische Sozialwissenschaft* 43 (2017): 264–296.

Short-time Work Money and Working from Home: Boosting Distinction

The most important measures implemented during the first months of the pandemic in Germany, such as *Kurzarbeitergeld* ('short-time work money') and 'working from home,' are generally (and rightly) praised for their success. At the same time, though, it can be argued that they have served as a marker of social distinction, deepening the lines of division between working people even further. Obviously, it makes a huge difference whether you are granted permission to work from home – or whether you are locked up against your own will and prevented from going to work, as experienced by the inhabitants of Göttingen's high-risers, or the migrant workers in meat production. But even apart from these drastic examples, the working and living conditions of working people seem to have drifted apart in the course of the coronavirus crisis.

First of all, many workers simply lost their jobs. This applied to agency workers, to those on temporary contracts, who were 'sent home' when business plummeted, and to 'mini jobbers,' who are, by definition, excluded from unemployment insurance and thus not entitled to *Kurzarbeitergeld*. Moreover, many of those in formal self-employment (who work alone and are often fully dependent on employer-like 'clients'), were out of business from one day to the next. For other groups, who stayed in employment, *Kurzarbeitergeld* provided temporary relief. According to this scheme, German unemployment insurance pays sixty to sixty-seven percent (depending on individual family status) of the full salary if working hours are reduced or terminated completely by the company in response to economic problems. Due to coronavirus, the percentage was temporarily increased in June 2020 to seventy/seventy-seven percent from month four of *Kurzarbeit*, and eighty/eighty-seven percent from month eight onward. In the same month, seven million (out of a working population of 44.6 million) received *Kurzarbeitergeld* in Germany. Even some workers in the low-wage sector are entitled to these payments, especially if they have permanent and stable full-time jobs. However, since the remuneration that they actually receive already falls short of a 'living wage,' two-thirds of that sum is certainly not enough to make a living. In big and well-organized industrial companies, instead, where wages are much higher, and powerful works councils represent the interests of the workforce, *Kurzarbeitergeld* is sometimes even topped up by company payments.

Finally, while many blue-collar workers, as well as employees in direct customer-facing roles whose jobs were not considered 'systemically relevant' (e.g. in restaurants, or non-food shops), were forced to accept hefty wage-cuts when their hours were reduced (since *Kurzarbeitergeld* covers only part of the deficit), white-collar employees with office jobs (sometimes in the same company) could move their work into the 'home' without suffering any reduction of hours or pay. Even among this privileged group, however, working from home was experienced in strikingly different ways. In a privately owned house or spacious apartment, a 'home office' can be pleasant enough, but this changes when the number of people per room or per square meter is higher – which takes us back to the high-rise buildings in Göttingen, where flats are small and often overcrowded. Moreover, the intensification of work, which is a typical consequence of working from home (due to the lack of interaction with colleagues, for instance) has proved especially challenging for parents, when kindergartens and schools were closed during the lockdown. Mothers seem to have taken over a decisively bigger share of additional reproductive tasks (such as home-schooling) than fathers. Accordingly, it is no surprise that it is mainly women with young children who have reduced their working hours, from an average of thirty-one hours before coronavirus to an average of twenty-six hours in June 2020.[57] Hence the pandemic crisis seems to have markedly different consequences for working people. Moreover, lockdown meant that some colleagues have not been able to meet for months, and works councils have lost touch with those they are supposed to represent. If Lessenich is right that solidarity is "performative" in the sense that it is constituted in the active process of its own making, it is rigorously put to the test under conditions of increasing socioeconomic differentiation and 'social distancing.'[58]

Short-lived, and Merely Symbolic, Solidarity with the 'Heroes of Everyday Life'

The ostentatious solidarity with the 'heroes and heroines of everyday life' has not survived the lockdown. When infection rates were at their peak in the last days of March and first days of April, many politicians had argued that nurses, shop assistants, and others in 'systemically relevant jobs' should receive much better pay and be granted much better working conditions in future, since it had become apparent that 'all of us' rely on their services in such fundamental ways. Some supermarkets, in fact, issued shopping vouchers for their employees, and the owner of a medium-sized bakery chain in Hannover, Gerhard Bosselmann, promised, tearfully, to provide hospital staff with free bread and rolls – a message, which received widespread publicity, first by Germany's leading tabloid newspaper *BILD* and later on YouTube.[59] Such initiatives were applauded by the federal government, deciding generously that vouchers as well as one-time bonus payments would not be taxed. A few weeks later, however, this enthusiasm had faded. Bosselmann threatened to sack employees who called in sick without producing a positive coronavirus test,[60] and the employers' association of retail companies (Handelsverband Deutschland) demanded that the pay rise due in May 2020 under the sector's collective agreement be postponed, at least to the end of the year, in order to avoid additional strain on shops that had already suffered so much from the economic crisis. What is more, the Handelsverband bluntly refused to even enter into a discussion about a generalization of the existing 'collective agreement' (*Allgemeinverbindlichkeitserklärung*), which could, in principle, be decreed by the labor minister to oblige every company, whether it is a member of an employers' association or not, to pay the wages agreed upon by the 'social partners.'[61] When the coronavirus shed light upon working conditions, especially in supermarkets, trade unions tried to push for the generalization of this collective agreement – after all, more and more retail companies had already turned their backs on the employers' association during the last years, and utilized increasingly complex subcontracting pyramids, stretching all the way down to those who fill shelves as individual, formally self-employed entrepreneurs, in order to undermine

---

57 "Coronakrise verschärft soziale Ungleichheit," *Böckler Impuls* 12 (2020): 2, https://www.boeckler.de/data/impuls_2020_12_S1-2.pdf, accessed August 12, 2020.

58 Stephan Lessenich, *Grenzen der Demokratie: Teilhabe als Verteilungsproblem* (Stuttgart: Reclam, 2019): 99.

59 *Verzweifelter Aufruf vom Chef der Bäckerei Bosselmann an seine Kunden*, YouTube Channel of BILD, March 20, 2020, https://www.youtube.com/watch?v=Sg7_ly6nM20, accessed July 27, 2020.

60 "Weinender Bäcker droht Mitarbeitern bei Krankschreibung mit Entlassung", *Die Welt*, March 21, 2020, https://www.welt.de/vermischtes/article206709257/Bosselmann-Weinender-Baecker-droht-kranken-Mitarbeitern-mit-Entlassung.html.

61 Michael Kläsgen, "Handelsverband will Lohnerhöhungen aufschieben," *Süddeutsche Zeitung*, April 01, 2020, https://sz.de/1.4863176, accessed August 12, 2020.

collective standards. However, the brusque refusal by the Handelsverband marked the end of a brief discussion, in which the federal government did not even actively participate.

As far as nurses in hospitals and retirement homes are concerned, the coronavirus crisis had even fewer positive consequences for wages and working conditions. The lack of qualified staff had been a topic of discussion for years, long before the onset of the pandemic. According to Ulrich Schneider, head of one of the most influential German welfare associations (Paritätischer Wohlfahrtsverband), 100,000 positions in professional care are currently vacant, and it has proved difficult to fill them, despite all government efforts to reform the system of qualification or to recruit trained staff from all over the world. This is not surprising, given the relatively low salaries, and especially the high level of rationalization that hospitals and other care institutions have been subject to during the last decades. In order to boost the return on investment (in private, privatized, and even public institutions), for instance, a system of flat-rate payments (Fallpauschalen) has been introduced, defining a specific sum for each and every treatment – irrespective of the actual needs of patients, but also of the professional standards of paramedical staff. Under conditions of a continuing shortage of labor and ever increasing profitability targets, the work pressure in many German hospitals and retirement homes has increased to such an extent that well-trained staff, despite their passion for their work, are quitting long before the age of retirement, because they cannot bear the physical and mental strain, nor accept responsibility for what many perceive to be a grossly negligent system of (increasingly un-) professional care. With the advent of coronavirus, some voices have stated the obvious: as long as pay and working conditions fail to improve massively, the German 'care crisis' (Pflegenotstand) will not be overcome. The president of the Federal Chamber of Physicians (Bundesärztekammer) even urged that we etch into the collective memory that hospitals are there to serve their patients, not to generate profits.[62] When the German government announced its economic stimulus package in the first days of June, amounting to 130 billion euros (150 billion US dollars), however, the term 'professional care' (Pflege) was not mentioned once. A journalist asked Chancellor Angela Merkel on television whether this meant that our heroes and heroines, much acclaimed during the coronavirus crisis, would ultimately be left empty-handed, that there would be no permanent improvement. She offered an interesting answer: the government's main aim was "to keep contributions stable and to prevent an extra imposition on citizens and also on companies."[63] According to Merkel, then, solidarity implies, in the first instance, preventing an increase in insurance contributions, which are paid in equal shares by employer and employee in the German system. In fact, the quest to reduce the cost of social insurance, and thus of labor (in order to keep Germany attractive as a location for corporate investment), had been a powerful argument in all (successful) attempts to cut back on social security provisions, ever since the 1980s. Obviously, even the traumatic experiences of coronavirus (including videos about coffins being transported through Bergamo by the Italian military) could not change the government's priorities. Professional care has to be cheap, according to this logic, and must not put too much strain on those (citizens and employers) whose contributions feed the system.

---

62 "Reinhardt: 'Schulen gut auf schrittweise Öffnung vorbereiten'," *Bundesärztekammer*, April 21, 2020, https://www.bundesaerztekammer.de/presse/pressemitteilungen/news-detail/reinhardt-schulen-gut-auf-schrittweise-oeffnung-vorbereiten, accessed August 12, 2020 (Translation by Nicole Mayer-Ahuja).

63 "'Farbe bekennen' mit Bundeskanzlerin Angela Merkel," (*Das Erste*, June 04, 2020), https://www.ardmediathek.de/daserste/video/farbe-bekennen/-farbe-bekennen--mit-bundeskanzlerin-angela-merkel/das-erste/Y3JpZDovL3d-kci5kZS9CZWl0cmFnLTAxN2M0Yjg2LTc1ZGEtNGFlZS1hZWVlLWUwYTZkZjUxODU1ZA, accessed August 12, 2020 (Translation by Nicole Mayer-Ahuja).

While COVID-19 is far from being defeated, discussions about a fundamental re-orientation with regard to public (health) services have already quieted down. This is despite the shocking realization that hospitals cannot make available the staff, facilities, or equipment required for an emergency situation like coronavirus if their most eminent aim is profit generation – thus free market ideologies prove fatal, in the literal sense of the term. At the same time, it is interesting to note from the perspective of global labor history that restrictions on 'freedom' were by no means treated as a 'no-go,' neither with regard to lockdown rules nor to the questioning of 'free wage labor.' The government of North Rhine-Westphalia, for instance, seriously considered issuing an emergency decree to force workers in 'systemically relevant' occupations into service (*Dienstverpflichtung*). Following protests, the plan was abandoned, but still, the fact that the discussion even took place highlights that the 'freedom of wage labor' remains disputed under conditions of capitalism, even in present-day Germany. In Göttingen, incidentally, considerable excitement was caused by the rumor that several inhabitants of Iduna Zentrum and Groner Landstrasse 9 were actually working in retirement homes. But this did not entitle them to a certain degree of solidarity from 'all of us' in a situation in which their own health was at stake – instead, 'the population' was just worried about them functioning as 'super spreaders.'

Towards a New Politics of Solidarity?

There is much more to say about 'solidarity' under the conditions of coronavirus, especially from a transnational perspective. Nobody knows how the pandemic crisis will develop, but the prospects for a politics that promotes solidarity among working people do not look too bright. In Germany, many companies have announced massive job cuts for the months to come, and there are reports about employers refusing to heed agreements, now that coronavirus has shifted the balance of power in their favor. During the weeks of lockdown, the German government had pushed through several reforms, which trade unions had long been fighting for in vain (like the temporary suspension of the 'brake on debts' or of sanctions for recipients of the infamous unemployment benefit, Hartz IV). Faced with the impending economic downturn and exploding public debt, however, the tide has turned, and the tendency to postpone or even cancel social reforms (like the introduction of a new scheme for minimum pensions or *Grundrente*) looks more likely to prevail.

Under capitalist conditions, solidarity is the exception, rather than the rule. After all, difference and competition between wage-earners are constantly spurred, as locations, companies, workforces, and individual workers are induced to pit their strength against each other. The history of labor movements abounds with examples of failed, but also of successful attempts to establish a different logic in society and economy, to the benefit of working people. During the first months of the coronavirus pandemic, the lines of division between the young and the old, between the skilled and the unskilled, between blue-collar and white-collar workers, between parents and single people, between men and women have considerably deepened. At the same time, however, the 'common sense' of the neoclassical economy has been challenged. The 'strong state' has resurfaced, which may well provoke debates about the democratic control of politics, but also of the economy. The importance of 'social property' (*propriété sociale*)[64] in the shape of public services has been widely acknowledged, and it has become obvious that 'the system' is not based on production and profit-seeking alone, but also on the reliable reproduction of labor power and social

---

64 Robert Castel, *Die Metamorphosen der sozialen Frage: Eine Chronik der Lohnarbeit* (Konstanz: UVK, 2000).

structures. The neoliberal claim that "there is no alternative" (TINA) has lost at least some of its former power of persuasion – but alternatives do not necessarily have to be more humane and democratic than the status quo. Solidarity among working people, as advocated by the labor movement, is certainly not a natural companion of the current pandemic crisis – but one of the few answers to this challenge that are compatible with human emancipation.

Chitra Joshi
Fear, Flight, and the Labor Question: Looking at Two Pandemics

For weeks after a national lockdown was declared in India, images of hundreds of thousands of workers walking on highways, railway tracks, any path that would lead them 'home' – away from the cities where they had lived and worked – flooded the print and visual media in India.[65] This was reverse migration on a scale witnessed never before. What makes this different from flows to rural areas in times of pandemics in the past?

The reverse flow of migrant workers in recent months was triggered by the declaration of a national lockdown on March 24, 2020 (with four hours' notice), an order that meant a sudden closure of factories, business, trade, and transport. The total lockdown continued until the end of May, and a phased and halting 'unlocking' began only in June 2020. In the first phase itself, "the entire economy, both agricultural and non-agricultural ground to a halt."[66] The first to be hit by the stoppage of work were the vast numbers of urban 'informal' workers who lived on daily cash earnings. They were left with no wages, no food and shelter. Hunger, a fear of starvation, drove millions onto the roads. According to unofficial estimates more than thirty million migrants, or around fifteen to twenty per cent of the urban workforce moved out of the urban areas after mid-March.[67] Despite gross under estimation, official figures, too, admit that over 10.6 million people migrated back to the villages.[68] These are astounding numbers.

The plague pandemic around the turn of the last century also saw a flight of workers, with large numbers returning from cities like Ahmedabad, Mumbai, Bangalore, Kanpur, and Surat to their villages.[69] In Mumbai, signs of the first epidemic wave appeared toward the end of 1896. By January 1897, around 400,000 people – almost half the city's population – had fled.[70] In Kanpur, 1900 ushered in reports of a labor shortage; large numbers had returned to their villages. In 1902, the Chamber of Commerce noted: "During October, November, and December the supply of labor was less than half, in some cases only a third, of the requirements. Workpeople seized with panic left the town."[71]

---

65 For a moving and compelling day by day visual documentation of migrants moving in the weeks after the lockdown see: *NDTV*, https://www.ndtv.com/video/list/shows/des-ki-baat, and the BBC coverage in *BBC*, https://www.bbc.com/news/world-asia-india-52086274, both accessed September 23, 2020.

66 Ravi Srivastava, *Understanding Circular Migration in India: Its Nature and Dimension, the Crisis under Lockdown and the Response of the State* (Delhi: Institute for Human Development, 2020): 1.

67 These are estimates drawn by Chinmay Tumbe, cited in Seema Chishti, "Explained: How Many Migrant Workers Displaced?," *The Indian Express*, June 08, 2020, https://indianexpress.com/article/explained/coronavirus-how-many-migrant-workers-displaced-a-range-of-estimates-6447840/, accessed June 09, 2020.

68 Avishek Dastidar, "1.06 Million Migrants Returned from Cities to Home States During Lockdown: Govt," *The Indian Express*, September 23, 2020, https://indianexpress.com/article/india/1-06-cr-migrants-returned-from-cities-to-home-states-during-lockdown-govt-6606918/#:~:text=Around%201.06%20crore%20migrants%20left,Singh%20told%20the%20Lok%20Sabha, accessed September 23, 2020.

69 On the global geography of the plague pandemic see Jacques M. May, "Map of the World Distribution of Plague," *Geographical Review* 42, no. 4 (October 1952): 628–630, https://doi.org/10.2307/211842, accessed September 23, 2020.

70 Aditya Sarkar, *Trouble at the Mill: Factory Law and the Emergence of the Labour Question in Late Nineteenth-Century Bombay* (New Delhi: Oxford University Press, 2018): 280.

71 *Report of the Upper India Chamber of Commerce* (Kanpur annual: 1902): piv.

Yet, there are important differences between the rural return in the years between 1896 and 1902 and the reverse migration in the summer of 2020. The exodus of workers from the cities during the plague pandemic was largely a result of the ruthlessness with which the plague regulations, formalized in the Epidemic Diseases Act of 1897, were implemented. There was widespread hostility to the rules enforcing the segregation and quarantine of affected people.[72]

Opposition to plague regulations in the late nineteenth century drew on solidarities that in many instances cut across class and community lines.[73] There was general hostility to rules that allowed health officials to enter homes and forcibly remove plague patients to segregation camps. The intrusion of the police, soldiers, and the cavalry into neighborhoods in Mumbai spread alarm and created panic. In Kanpur, there was an uproar over the forcible removal of a woman from a 'respectable' merchant family to a segregation camp. News of the kidnapping of a child and rumors that he was to be burnt alive at a plague camp culminated in a violent outburst.[74] A crowd of over fifteen hundred gathered to attack the plague camp. The police were the targets; several officers were killed and the huts of the plague camp were set on fire. Groups of men moved through the city, closing down shops. Workers stayed away from factories and large numbers left for their villages. Factory production in cities such as Kanpur came to a standstill. Industrial establishments, shops, and businesses in the city shut down because of a fear of violence. For several years afterward, there were reports of a crisis in the labor market and "a very acute state of affairs in mills and factories who find themselves without some of their most useful hands."[75]

The fears of the migrant workers fleeing the cities in recent months are different from those underlining the exodus during the plague pandemic. The immediate response of the state in late March 2020 was the announcement of a series of prohibitions on movement and activity, almost creating a sense that locking people in would protect everyone from the disease. The lockdown denied access to varieties of occupations like vending and portering – forms of low paid jobs that provided sustenance for those out of work from factories. There were others for whom moving between different low paid occupations was part of an everyday survival strategy. Common to the narratives of people leaving, walking away from places where they worked, was the motif of hunger. More than the disease, those taking the long road home were stalked by joblessness and starvation.

State initiatives to provide food in the form of dry rations or cooked food through soup kitchens covered a miniscule proportion of the unemployed. Besides, the pre-requisite of elaborate documentary proof of entitlement meant that official relief measures were a fiction for many. Those who belonged to 'minority' communities found it even more difficult. Women trying to reach the food vans were terrified of being driven away and beaten up by the police. They were told to complete their identification documents (aadhar), link these with their mobile numbers, and wait for a response on their phones. The wait for many was indefinite. The story of a female worker from

72 Rajnarayan Chandravarkar, "Plague Panic and Epidemic Politics in India, 1896–1914," in: Terence Ranger and Paul Slack, eds., *Epidemics and Ideas: Essays on the Historical Perception of Pestilence* (Cambridge: Cambridge University Press, 1992). See also Prashant Kidambi, "'An Infection of Locality': Plague Pythogenesis and the Poor in Bombay," *Urban History* 31 (2004): 249–267; Pratik Chakrabarti, "Covid-19 and the Spectres of Colonialism," *The India Forum*, July 14, 2020, https://www.theindiaforum.in/article/covid-19-and-spectres-colonialism, accessed September 02, 2020.
73 Chitra Joshi, *Lost Worlds: Indian Labour and its Forgotten Histories* (New Delhi: Permanent Black, 2003, London: Anthem, 2005).
74 Times of India, "The Cawnpore Riots: Orders of Government," *Times of India*, May 24, 1900, ProQuest Historical Newspapers: 5.
75 Times of India, "Cawnpore Notes: Plague and the Labour Market," *Times of India*, December 11, 1906, ProQuest Historical Newspapers: 7.

"The Long Trek Home": Jobless workers leave the city (end of March 2020) with their families and meager belongings, on a long journey back home.

Delhi trying to access government rations captures an experience shared by many. She was told: "Get your aadhar linked and you will get a message on your mobile. Without that message you cannot come this side. If you are a law-abiding citizen you will be spared or else we will beat you up."[76]

Queuing for food often began at the crack of dawn. Serpentine files of people waiting: a wait that could stretch into the searing heat of the afternoon. Queuing and waiting long hours was often impossible for women with young children and the burden of domestic work at home. Standing and waiting at a soup kitchen with a bowl was experienced as humiliating. For many who prided themselves in working with their hands – skilled laborers, masons, carpenters, weavers, and others from garment and textile factories – the act of turning back, walking thousands of miles to their rural homes, meant, also, a refusal to suffer the daily indignities and fears of intimidation by the police.

The anxieties that lay behind the flight of workers from cities during the plague pandemic of the past were different. It was not the specter of joblessness and hunger so much as the social opposition to plague measures: the intrusion of plague officials into the inner space of the home, the forcible removal of family members to segregation camps. In Kanpur, there was a huge outcry against regulations that authorized the removal and physical examination of suspected plague patients, including women. Actions like these were seen as a violation of norms of ritual pollution,

---

[76] Centre for Equity Studies, Delhi Research Group and Karwan e Mohabbat, *Labouring Lives: A Report on Hunger, Precarity and Despair amid Lockdown* (New Delhi: Centre for Equity Studies, 2020): 37.

of caste hierarchies, and codes of honor for women. Opposition to the plague regulations brought together a cross section of people cutting across class and community lines, who saw state action as a threat to their cultural sensibilities and affective worlds.

The Pandemic as a Moment of Rupture

The flight of workers from the cities during the plague years at the turn of the nineteenth century marked in many ways a moment of rupture. These years, as Aditya Sarkar powerfully argues, were marked by a "snapping of ties" that defined relations between workers and employers in the Mumbai mills. The forms of control that capital exercised over labor were unsettled and managements had to confront questions concerning labor in new ways. Even if it was momentary, the scales seemed to have shifted in favor of labor. Workers returning to the Mumbai mills in the months after the plague found work again and often on better terms than before. A classic image from Mumbai in 1897 is of recruiting agents standing at the mill gates, luring workers with ready cash payments: "Ready cash paid daily in this mill; come as many as want eight annas a day."[77] The usual practice of holding back wages by employers and the use of wage arrears as a way of exercising control over workers was no longer viable. Workers could literally choose the terms on which they worked. In many Mumbai mills, in fact, workers put in fewer hours at higher wages. In Kanpur, too, the 'scarcity' of labor during the plague years prized open the labor question, leading to an inquiry into questions of labor supply. Fremantle, the official in charge of the inquiry, stressed the need to make work in the mills 'attractive' in order to draw labor. Ideas around housing, educational facilities for children of workers, social security, and pension and provident fund schemes proposed by Fremantle have to be located in the exceptional circumstances of the plague years.[78]

If the turn of the twentieth century saw the opening up of the labor question and a loosening of the forms of control employers had previously exercised over labor,[79] today we see the creation of a new normative that can allow employers to exercise their already strong private powers with greater impunity. Many state governments, for example, Uttar Pradesh, Madhya Pradesh, and Gujarat, responded to the crisis by bringing in a series of ordinances to suspend and dilute labor laws.[80] Faced with collective opposition by ten trade unions and an intervention by the International Labour Organization urging the government to uphold its commitments to international conventions on the protection of labor rights, the labor ministry had to make a public announcement that the dilution of laws by state governments would not be allowed.[81]

---

[77] Aditya Sarkar, *Trouble at the Mill*: 294.

[78] Selwyn Howe Fremantle, "The Problem of Indian Labour Supply," *Journal of the Royal Society of Arts* 57, no. 2947 (1909): 510–524.

[79] Aditya Sarkar, *Trouble at the Mill*: 293–300.

[80] Amended laws to allow an extension of working hours and an exemption from provisions of the Factories Act, which give workers employment security. See also Shyam Sundar and Rahul Suresh Sapkal, "Changes to Labour Laws by State Governments Will Lead to Anarchy in the Labour Market," *Economic and Political Weekly* 55, no. 23 (June 2020).

[81] By August however, the Uttar Pradesh government, in contravention of the Centre's notification announced the suspension of certain laws. See Deepa Jainani, "UP Cabinet empowers govt to suspend certain provisions of crucial labour laws," *Financial Express*, August 12, 2020, https://www.financialexpress.com/industry/up-cabinet-empowers-govt-to-suspend-certain-provisions-of-crucial-labour-laws/2052154/, accessed September 02, 2020.

In recent weeks, however, we see a rush to put in place reforms that erode the already tenuous basis of protective labor legislation. This is a sign of the times we are living in. Globally, the erosion of a language of rights and citizenship is pushing labor onto the margins of public discourse. It is true that the bulk of the informal labor force in India was never covered by any protective laws. Yet, the present codes formally exclude a vast majority from the ambit of law by redefining the terms under which industrial establishments come within the purview of regulation.[82] According to the Industrial Relations Code passed in the Parliament, all establishments employing under three hundred workers are to be exempt from the regulations of the code. This allows the employers to relocate units, fragment and atomise the work force, hire and fire at will, and escape all norms that govern working conditions, trade union activity, dispute resolution, working hours, and health and safety norms. In addition, the government reserves the right to exempt any new factory – even the large ones – from any or all of the provisions of the code, if it deems it necessary for encouraging production. These wide discretionary powers of the government to grant exemptions disempower the workers, and strengthen the arbitrary power of capital.

If labor laws previously had no real meaning for a large majority of workers in India even earlier, the increased 'formal' powers of employers over employees now weaken them further.[83] What was not possible within the realm of the legal before becomes legal with the new normative. Despite the previous limits of the law, it did open up possibilities for workers to press for rights using a language of citizenship, and appeal to the formal law.[84] The reforms today signal a removal of the idea of regulation from the realm of imagination. While practice may be different from what is codified or held up as an ideal, the destruction of the ideal itself radically transforms labor regimes.

For the vast numbers of migrant workers doing varieties of 'informal' work, the pandemic, the lockdown, and its aftermath has been a cataclysmic moment. The strictures on mobility, together with the sudden closure of borders controlling exit and entry between states – even if temporary – have adversely impacted the already fragile economy within which large numbers of migrants live and work. Circular movements between the urban and rural, and the rural and rural have been crucial to strategies that have sustained life and livelihood for a vast majority. The restraints on mobility have eroded structures that were essential to the social reproduction of the labor force. Cash remittances from migrants in the cities to their rural households, and harvest-time work in the villages forged ties — economic and affective —between the urban and the rural. Mobility also allowed those living precariously to hold on to alternative visions of a better life, or a less bad life, even in the face of disappointment and crushed hopes.

A downward trend in the economy and a perceptible decline in opportunities for employment in urban areas were visible long before signs of the pandemic appeared early this year. Available data for the period between 2011 and 2018 point to falling employment in agriculture and in manu-

---

[82] Under the provisions of the Factories Act of 1948, a manufacturing unit was categorised as a factory if it employed more than ten workers and any part of the manufacturing process used power, and twenty workers if it did not use power, https://labour.gov.in/sites/default/files/TheFactoriesAct1948.pdf, accessed September 22, 2020. The revised codes raise these thresholds to twenty and forty workers respectively. See M. R. Madhavan, "Dilution without Adequate Deliberation: on Labour Laws," *The Hindu*, September 22, 2020, https://www.thehindu.com/opinion/op-ed/dilution-without-adequate-deliberation/article32663006.ece#:~:text=The%20Industrial%20Disputes%20Act%20of,raise%20it%20further%20through%20notification, accessed September 23, 2020.

[83] For an insightful piece on questions around law and regulation see Prabhu Mohapatra, "Unravelling the Puzzle," *Seminar* 669 (May 2015): 63–67.

[84] Rina Agarwala, "Using Legal Empowerment for Labour Rights in India," *The Journal of Development Studies* 55 (2019): 409–419.

"On the Track" April 2020: When the roads were barricaded after the lockdown to stop the reverse migration from the cities, workers walked on the railway tracks, risking their lives. Some thirteen exhausted workers sleeping on the tracks were run over by a goods train near Aurangabad.

facturing industries and an overall decline of around 9.1 million in the total workforce.[85] Figures from the labor bureau show a decline of 12.8 million jobs between 2013 and 2016.[86] Even sectors like construction and the brick kiln industry, which would usually absorb a large number of short-term migrants, showed a decline of 5.3 million between 2013 and 2016.[87] Despite a blockage of employment opportunities in both rural and urban areas, circular migration continued with large numbers of migrants moving between the rural and urban, and the rural and rural, allowing precarious labour to survive difficult times. These chains of circulation are now suddenly fractured.

We are still living the pandemic and the uncertainties of a situation that is changing rapidly. There is a slow trickle back of migrant workers, with some finding work again. Economic activity will no doubt resume, but a resumption on new terms, under the shadow of regulations that deny labor rights. In contrast to 1897, when labor contractors were out on the streets, luring workers back to the mills, there is now a reversal, with employers free to 'hire' and 'fire' as they please. Returnee migrants today are confronted with crippling vulnerabilities.

85 Jayati Ghosh, "While India was busy celebrating its 'ease of doing business' ranking, its real economy tanked," *Quartz*, August 05, 2019, https://qz.com/india/1681259/indian-gdp-growth-slump-shows-ease-of-doing-business-not-enough/#:~:text=While%20India%20was%20busy%20celebrating,ranking%2C%20its%20real%20economy%20tanked&text=Work%20in%20progress.&text=Suddenly%2C%20it%20seems%20like%20everything,%E2%80%94and%20now%2C%20economic%20growth, accessed May 05, 2020.

86 Radhicka Kapoor, *Waiting for Jobs*, ICRIER Working Paper no. 348 (Delhi: Indian Council for Research on International Economic Relations, 2017).

87 Radhicka Kapoor, *Waiting for Jobs*.

In public memory, the present pandemic will remain a moment of heightened visibility of migrant workers; the sheer numbers out on the streets and highways in cities gave them a visibility they never had in the past. Paradoxically, it also marks a moment of erosion and repression of rights. If the post-plague years saw the making of the social body of workers as a collective, and their struggle for new norms of work, today we see an attempt to dismember that body and deny them all claims to protection. How the workers confront the new situation and create new solidarities is to be seen. In the crush of migrants on the streets and highways, at railway stations and bus stands, one can see signs of helplessness and despair, as well as a powerful assertion of notions of self and dignity in the face of hunger and joblessness.

Being 'Relevant to the System' is Female

Larissa Rosa Corrêa and Paulo Fontes

Maids in Brazil: Domestic and Platform Workers During the COVID-19 Pandemic

COVID-19's first fatality in Rio de Janeiro was an impoverished sixty-three-year-old black woman. The domestic worker, whose name was never revealed by the press or official bodies, would travel over 120 kilometers every week from her working-class community to the city's South Zone to work in a family house in Alto Leblon, the most upscale neighborhood in Rio. She was contaminated by her employer, who had just returned from a trip to Italy and did not release the maid from service. She was the second official death in Brazil, and on the day of her death the country registered 291 confirmed cases and 8,819 suspected cases. A week earlier, Brazil's president, Jair Bolsonaro, had minimized the disease by stating that "the destructive power of the coronavirus" would be "overstated."[1]

Two and a half months later, another death would shock part of the country. With schools closed due to social isolation policies determined by city halls and states (but discouraged by the federal government), black domestic worker Mirtes Santana de Souza had to take her five-year-old son Miguel to the house where she worked, in a luxurious condominium in the city of Recife, in northeast Brazil. Despite social isolation measures, Mirtes was not released from her job. One day, she left Miguel with her employer while she walked her employer's dog, and her employer quite negligently left the child unsupervised in the elevator, with the scene captured by the building's video surveillance system. Miguel climbed to a higher floor of the building, ended up losing his balance on a parapet, and fell from a thirty-five-meter height, dying shortly thereafter. On that brutal June 2, Brazil had already reached 31,199 officially registered deaths and 555,383 confirmed cases of COVID-19 (these numbers were suspected to be much higher, due to underreporting). A month earlier, when asked about the ballooning death toll in the country, Jair Bolsonaro replied, "So what?" And he added, employing a pun on his middle name, "my name's Messiah, but I can't work miracles."[2]

On August 7, a video began to frantically circulate on Brazilian social networks. It shows a young black delivery worker approached in an absurdly violent manner by a white man living in a deluxe condominium in Valinhos, a town in the interior of the state of São Paulo. Yelling and screaming, the customer complains about an alleged delay and says, "You're jealous of this here. Boy, listen here, you're jealous of these families here, you're jealous of this here [pointing out to the skin of the arm]. You'll never have it! You're semiliterate. You piece of trash, how much do you make per month, huh? You probably don't even have a place to live!" The young delivery worker reacted with dignity, in an exemplary class-struggle quarrel: "Of course I've a place to live. Did you get yours because you worked or because your father gave it to you?"[3] The episode caused outrage and

---

1 AFP Miami, "Bolsonaro says virus threat is 'overstated'," *France 24*, March 10, 2020, https://www.france24.com/en/20200310-bolsonaro-says-virus-threat-is-overstated, accessed August 01, 2020.
2 Tom Phillips, "'So What?': Bolsonaro Shrugs Off Brazil's Rising Coronavirus Death Toll," *The Guardian*, April 29, 2020, https://www.theguardian.com/world/2020/apr/29/so-what-bolsonaro-shrugs-off-brazil-rising-coronavirus-death-toll, accessed August 10, 2020.
3 "Entregador sofre ofensas racistas em condomínio de Valinhos; VÍDEO," *G1*, August 07, 2020, https://g1.globo.com/sp/campinas-regiao/noticia/2020/08/07/entregador-registra-boletim-de-ocorrencia-apos-sofrer-ofensas-racistas-em-condominio-de-valinhos-video.ghtml, accessed 10 August, 2020.

protests. The following day, President Jair Bolsonaro remained silent as the country reached the tragic milestone of 100,000 deaths from COVID-19, with more than three million people infected.

The cases described here are painfully illustrative of how the pandemic has even more strikingly revealed the deep social inequality in a country already sadly known for its huge gap between rich and poor. It has also widely exposed how closely these inequalities are related to the worlds of labor and social markers of difference such as race, gender, regional origin, and generation. The pandemic hit the country amid a deep political, economic, and moral crisis, which, worsened by the health crisis, will bring consequences still difficult to predict.

Similarly to his idol, Donald Trump, far-right President Jair Bolsonaro (in office since January 2019) underestimated the impact of the coronavirus pandemic. Advocating negationist and anti-scientific policies, he came into conflict with his own ministers of health – he discharged two ministers before appointing a military officer to the post, who has been in charge for months despite the declared "provisional character" of his position. The president also developed contentious relationships with the governors and mayors who were in favor of more effective social isolation policies, with the scientific community in general, and with the World Health Organization itself.

Bolsonaro has created a narrative according to which the measures to prevent the disease are incompatible with, and opposed to the good functioning of the country's economy. He has emphasized the idea that only the "privileged ones" could stay at home. Traders and especially the "poor" population (he almost never uses the word "workers"), who are massively dependent on the informal economy, which has been aggravated by the chronic unemployment that has been plaguing the country since 2016, would need to work and "go out on the streets." His minister of economy, the ultra-neoliberal "Chicago boy" Paulo Guedes, only reluctantly accepted the proposal from the opposition and approved by the Congress to create an emergency aid program of 600 Brazilian real (around 110 US dollars) per month for the unemployed and those working in the informal economy. The aid, initially granted for three months, has been extended and already distributed to about fifty million people.

The Bolsonaro administration's management of the health crisis was initially rejected by most of the population, but the economic crisis and the exhaustion regarding social isolation measures have played to his approach. The president's approval rating had been declining since he took office and fell further in the first months of the pandemic, when the health crisis was added to a political crisis triggered by the resignation and withdrawal of support of important political allies. However, Bolsonaro retains the resilient support of nearly one third of the electorate. Paradoxically, the same emergency aid proposed by the opposition and the labor movement (and which has encouraged important discussions about a program for a permanent universal basic income) seems to have contributed to Bolsonaro's increased popularity, albeit possibly temporary, among the most impoverished sectors of the population, compensating for a relative loss in his popularity among the middle and upper sectors, the more educated, and also his traditional constituency.

The cases mentioned in the opening paragraphs of this essay also highlight, on another note, the pandemic's unexpected effect of affording visibility to types and forms of work that have otherwise remained historically invisible. Obviously, health professionals have gained prominence, as we have seen across the world. In the Brazilian context, however, domestic workers and delivery app workers have achieved surprising notoriety.

Domestic Workers

Between at least the end of March and the beginning of May 2020, social isolation resulted in most middle- and upper-class families being at home, many of them without their maids or day laborers, who were isolated in their own homes. It was somehow a historic moment. These families, many for the first time in their lives, had to maintain and clean their homes, assist disabled and ill members, and handle children and elderly care without any external help. Social networks were flooded with reports of the difficulties and the efforts involved in the accomplishment of these tasks.

For a moment, there was an implicit and sometimes explicit recognition that domestic work and workers are essential to the functioning of society and the daily lives of millions of people. This perception, however, seems to have quickly disappeared. Many housekeepers did not even stop working during the peak of social isolation, and it was not long before a significant number of them were compelled to return to work at their employers' residences.

The relationship of dependence established by the middle and upper sectors of Brazilian society towards hired domestic work has a structural character. According to official data from the Brazilian Institute of Geography and Statistics (IBGE) for 2019, Brazil has the largest number of domestic workers in the world, with nearly 6.3 million workers. Few professions have such a defined social profile: ninety-seven percent of them are women, and domestic work alone is the biggest employer of women. Most of these workers are Afrodescendants, and a large proportion are migrants from the northern and northeastern regions, the most impoverished areas of the country.

As several studies have shown, domestic work is directly connected to the long history of black slavery in the country and to the ways in which the historical process of post-abolition, between the late nineteenth and early twentieth centuries, relegated black men and women to the most subordinate and precarious roles in the labor market.[4]

Domestic work is permeated with customary notions of paternalism, informality, and the 'privatization' of social relations within the home, traditionally considered outside the scope of the norm and state regulation of labor relations. Thus, in the 1930s, when the Getulio Vargas administration enacted a broad labor legislation, domestic workers were not included in the legal system of social protection. They were not – it was said – workers with rights, but rather part of the family, supposedly counting on the patriarchal protection, affection, and benevolence of those who would welcome them.

In fact, the history of domestic employment in Brazil is also intrinsically related to the history of childhood and family relationships. For several decades it was common, for instance, that middle- and upper-income white families 'took care to raise' a poor and black girl who, in return for the 'benevolence' and the 'opportunity' would be responsible for the household chores and the care of the home. On the one hand, reports of gratitude and affection between housekeepers and families are recurrent; on the other, blunt narratives of abuse by employers are equally common, and the sexual initiation of white teenagers with their employees was until recently part of a certain 'male folklore,' even finding a place in the national literary canon.

The economic growth resulting from the import-substitution industrialization strategy and the intense migration from rural to urban regions experienced by the country since the 1950s – more than thirty million people left the countryside and migrated to cities between 1950 and 1980 – did

---

4 Recently, domestic workers have gained some prominence in the agenda of Social History of Labor in Brazil. See for example: Flavia Fernandes de Souza and Maciel Henrique Silva, eds., "Trabalho doméstico: sujeitos, experiências e lutas." Special Dossier, *Mundos do Trabalho* 10:20 (2018).

not bring a decrease in domestic employment rates. Quite the opposite. There was a significant expansion of formal urban employment, particularly 'manual labor' in industries, transport, and civil construction, but this type of work had more of a masculine profile. Meanwhile, sectors that traditionally employed women on a large scale (such as the textile and food industries) gradually shrunk. In part, female work was transferred to the service sector, with an emphasis on domestic employment, which increasingly absorbed mostly poor, black, and migrant women.

It was during this period that domestic workers began to organize themselves and fight for their rights. The first union struggles date back to the 1930s, but it was not until the 1960s and 1970s that domestic workers – influenced by Catholic sectors of the so-called Liberation Theology, other union groups, and feminist organizations – would set up associations and put pressure on authorities and political leaders. At the height of the military dictatorship in the early 1970s, government sectors realized the political potential of this movement, and granted a few labor rights to domestic workers. While rarely implemented, these rights served to boost a growing social identity among militants, that would create leaders such as the famous black member of parliament and activist Benedita da Silva. They would also play an active role in the fight for the re-democratization of the country and later for a new constitution in 1988. Despite these efforts, the constitution once again did not grant full rights to domestic workers, but did allow unions to be created; they have proliferated in the country in the last three decades.

It was not until the Workers' Party administrations (2003–2016) that domestic workers acquired full labor citizenship from a legal point of view. In 2012, a constitutional amendment enacted by President Dilma Rousseff – the famous "PEC das Domésticas" – regulated the eight-hour working day and the possibility of receiving overtime payment, in addition to all other labor rights for domestic workers. The law sought to create mechanisms for the formalization of labor relations, in addition to fighting abuse. Received as a victory, the package was the culmination of a process of empowerment and dignity.

Not by chance, this moment was echoed in cultural phenomena. One of the most popular soap operas on Brazilian television in that period had as protagonists three housekeepers aware of their rights, and one of 2015's most commended movies – *The Second Mother* (*Que Horas Ela Volta?*) – tells the story of a domestic worker, a northeastern migrant in São Paulo whose daughter had access to a college education thanks to her commitment and the public policies launched by the government. But the law also provoked strong reactions. Many partly blame the law for the discomfort felt by the middle classes toward the Workers' Party administration. In 2016, with the massive support of the middle sectors, President Dilma Rousseff was overthrown by an impeachment process with a very precarious legal basis, a sort of parliamentary coup. Michel Temer, the vice president, took over the government, and one of his first measures was to propose wide-ranging labor reforms, approved by the Congress, that removed and weakened these historic rights, including those of domestic workers.

Platform Workers

Social isolation and seclusion during the pandemic also brought platform workers providing delivery and transportation services to the forefront of the public debate. This type of work has been widespread for some years in Brazil, particularly in large cities. Several companies such as Uber, in the urban transport sector, and I-food, Uber-eats, and Rappi, for the fast delivery of food, pharmaceuticals, and supermarket purchases, among others, have become well-known brands. Even amid the economic crisis, they have been among the most profitable sectors: according to the Brazilian

Association of Bars and Restaurants (ABRASEL), the so-called delivery market in Brazil generated about two billion dollars in 2018.[5]

The pandemic scenario has further boosted this economic sector. Delivery services were officially declared essential and have expanded in geometric progression. In the city of São Paulo alone, the download of delivery apps increased by seven hundred percent between March and April 2020.[6] However, the expansion of these services did not correlate with better working conditions and wages for delivery workers; in fact, quite the opposite.

The health and economic crisis, combined with an increase in demand, enabled companies to recruit even more delivery workers, actually lowering remuneration and increasing the already precarious nature of the work. According to a survey carried out by the University of Campinas (UNICAMP) and the Federal University of Parana (UFPR), about sixty percent of delivery workers stated that their income had decreased since the pandemic. In addition to the drop in pay, the survey pointed to a significant deterioration in working conditions. Nearly fifty-seven percent of delivery workers said they worked more than nine hours a day, six or seven days a week. Most of them also reported having received no assistance from companies to reduce the risks of contamination during the pandemic.[7]

This picture, however, is not surprising. In recent years, delivery workers have become a symbol of the 'precarization' of work in the country. Circulating on their motorcycles and rental bicycles, thousands of young people, mostly Afrodescendant men living in the urban peripheries, started to mark the landscape of large cities. Many have been the victim of traffic accidents, which has forced the establishment of specific mobility policies in cities like São Paulo, for instance. The deepening of the economic crisis since 2015 and the growth in unemployment combined with neoliberal reforms in labor legislation have made this type of job the only option for thousands of people. Recently the profile of delivery workers has changed, with increasing participation seen among women and older men.

Along with app drivers and telemarketing operators, delivery app workers would come to represent a supposed new type of labor relations in the country. Sociologists and scholars studying this topic have articulated concepts, sometimes controversial, such as 'uberization' and 'precariat,' in relation to their understanding of this phenomenon.[8]

Companies, governments, and, in turn, a large part of the media, seek to deny these people the status of workers – and, therefore, the corresponding labor rights. According to this rhetoric they would rather be 'entrepreneurs,' owners of their own microbusinesses that, in partnership with larger companies, could thrive and grow. The ideas of 'freedom' and 'autonomy' (also linked

5 "Delivery movimenta R$11 bilhões por ano," *Abrasel*, March 12, 2020, https://abrasel.com.br/noticias/noticias/delivery-movimenta-r-11-bilhoes-por-ano-enquanto-franquias-de-alimentacao-diversificam-a-oferta-de-produtos, accessed August 10, 2020.

6 "Downloads de aplicativos de delivery crescem 700% durante a quarentena em São Paulo," *Mercado & Consumo*, June 4, 2020, https://mercadoeconsumo.com.br/2020/06/04/downloads-de-aplicativos-de-delivery-crescem-700-durante-a-quarentena-em-sao-paulo, accessed 10 August, 2020.

7 Ludmila C. Abílio et al., "Condições de trabalho de entregadores via plataforma digital durante a COVID-19," in Silvio B. Neto and R. Clarissa Schinestsck, eds., *Dossiê COVID-19* [= special issue *Revista Jurídica Trabalho e Desenvolvimento Humano* 3 (2020)]: 1–21.

8 See, among others, Ludmila. C. Abílio, "Uberização: a era do trabalhador just-in-time?" *Estudos Avançados* 34 (April 2020): 111–126; Henrique Amorim and Felipe Moda, "Trabalho por aplicativo: gerenciamento algorítmico e condições de trabalho dos motoristas da Uber," *Revista Fronteiras: Estudos Midiáticos*, 22 (2020): 59–71; Ruy Braga, *A rebeldia do precariado: trabalho e neoliberalismo no Sul global* (São Paulo: Boitempo, 2017).

to the very notion of 'mobility' implied by the use of cars, motorcycles, and bicycles) are widely associated with a culture of 'entrepreneurialism' that marks social relations in this new digital age. Despite the concealment of precarious labor conditions and the evident relationships of dependence between the workers and the companies, this is a seductive discourse that resonates with the wishes and ambitions of many.

However, the situation generated by the pandemic has brutally exposed the precarization and the exploitation to which delivery workers are exposed. Certain expressions of associativism carried out in recent years by the so-called "motoboys" were articulated within some informal networks and ended up generating a surprising wave of mobilization among delivery workers. The same cellphones and apps used by the companies to control them were used by the workers to organize and combat the dispersion and isolation typical of these working relationships. It is crucial to note that many of these networks of sociability are anchored in a language identified with hip hop and the celebration of black culture, quite common among the youth from the suburbs of several cities in the country.

On July 1, a large number of delivery workers across the country participated in a large-scale strike called "Apps Brake" ("Breque dos Apps"), to demand better pay and working conditions. The movement's proportions and strength surprised the Brazilian urban population. Images of thousands of workers on their characteristic motorbikes and bicycles, taking to the streets in different cities and protesting with a mixture of anger and festivity, were printed on newspaper websites and quickly disseminated by WhatsApp and other social media, almost announcing the birth of a new type of collective actors. Large parts of the population sympathized with the movement, leading the delivery app companies to realize the damage caused to their image. They immediately launched a television advertising campaign, depicting themselves as "humane" and "supportive" companies to their "collaborators" and excellent "entrepreneurs."

The articulate and politicized discourse of the delivery workers' leaders also drew attention: although they recognized the potency of the 'entrepreneurism' argument among their bases, they also started fighting it and claiming the identity of worker for their category. They have demanded inclusion in the legal code of Brazilian labor relations, the Consolidation of Labor Laws (CLT), which is the only remaining body of labor rights in the country. At the same time, these workers are advocating the establishment of cooperatives that use the same technological resources as large companies, making it possible to compete within the delivery market.

Amid the COVID-19 pandemic, domestic workers and delivery app workers have resisted precarization and have generated new forms of resistance and repertoires of collective action. Surprisingly for many, however, these future-oriented discourses and practices are not disconnected from the past. On the contrary, these groups repeatedly claim to belong to a historical lineage of resistance perpetrated by black people, women, and workers. In a moment of invisibility and attack on the very concept of labor, the history of workers is triggered as a founding element of identities, collective action, and a project for the future. As rapper Paulo Galo, an emerging leader of delivery workers in São Paulo, tells us:

> I don't give up the workers' struggles (...), there were many and many rights the workers have won (...), a beautiful story. If uberization is an unfolding of the industrial revolution, delivery workers are an unfolding of factory workers. We are an unfolding of the history of laborers. We are the factory workers of our time. So, for us, these struggles are connected.[9]

---

9 Paulo Roberto "Galo" da Silva Lima, interview by Paulo Fontes and Dulce Pandolfi, *Rádio Cidadania*, Universidade da Cidadania – UFRJ, July 24, 2020, audio, episode 11, 22:00, https://anchor.fm/radiocidadaniaufrj/episodes/Rdio-Cidadania---Episdio-11---Paulo-Galo-Entregadores-Antifascistas-eh6dao.

Bridget Kenny

Coronavirus Conjunctures: Waged Work, Wagelessness, and Futures in South Africa

I live in Johannesburg, a city with deep inequalities that manifest as its harsh yet heady edginess. There is no pastoral wool to pull over Jozi's[10] eyes. It is from this place that I write of three interconnected 'coronavirus conjunctures' that locate our present and its grim futures. The virus has wound its way into the South African terrain in ways that intensify existing rifts. Hunger and wagelessness have increased; those in employment, such as service and care workers, have faced further precariousness; and young people at school and university have seen their futures contorted. Still, there are lineaments threading outward as people adapt to the changes that in fact reproduce already-known relations and conditions.

On the eve of the pandemic shutdown, South Africa was already nervously predicting an unprecedented increase in unemployment and recessionary conditions. The year began with sobering calculations of the shrinking economy. Indeed, in the first quarter of 2020 the economy had contracted by two percent and the (official, narrow) unemployment rate had expanded to 30.1 percent, even before lockdown.[11] Stock-makers and takers offer newer predictions that GDP will be down by as much as ten percent by December, exacerbated by COVID-19. As the Minister of Finance put it in late June in his supplementary budget address, he expected "the largest contraction [of the economy] in nearly ninety years."[12] The IMF approved a 4.3 billion dollar emergency loan to South Africa in late July.[13] South Africa had already introduced austerity measures in mid-2019, and the Minister of Finance has continued on this path in adherence to future possible demands. This macroeconomic picture sets the scene for the everyday experiences of coronavirus.

On March 27, 2020, President Cyril Ramaphosa announced a countrywide strict lockdown (later to be called Level 5). This included no mobility unless you were an essential service worker. Residents were meant to be contained to the parameters of their own homes, not allowed outside, including for exercise, except for the most basic of errands, such as getting food or medicine. Already the lockdown conditions posed contradictions of inequality – the suburban middle class has large properties and yards while informal settlement dwellers live multiple people to a few small rooms with the neighbors closely abutting. In fact, many could not feasibly 'distance' themselves from others.

The police and later the army (the South African National Defence Force) patrolled townships for those breaking lockdown conditions. Within the first week of lockdown, police had arrested more than two thousand people for infractions of the regulations for the new State of Disaster, and

10 Informal name for Johannesburg

11 "South Africa's Recession Deepens as First Quarter GDP Sinks 2 Percent," *BusinessTech*, June 30, 2020, https://businesstech.co.za/news/finance/412009/south-africas-recession-deepens-as-first-quarter-gdp-sinks-2/, accessed August 11, 2020.

12 Marianne Merten, "Tito Mboweni Outlines the Budget to Weather the Storm, COVID-19 and Head Off Bankruptcy," *Daily Maverick*, June 24, 2020, https://www.dailymaverick.co.za/article/2020-06-24-tito-mboweni-outlines-the-budget-to-weather-the-storm-covid-19-and-head-off-bankruptcy/, accessed August 11, 2020.

13 The loan was granted under its Rapid Financing Instrument (RFI). Danny Bradlow, "The IMF's $4bn Loan for South Africa: The Pros, Cons and Potential Pitfalls," *Daily Maverick*, July 30, 2020, https://www.dailymaverick.co.za/article/2020-07-30-the-imfs-4bn-loan-for-south-africa-the-pros-cons-and-potential-pitfalls/, accessed August 11, 2020.

by June 1, over 230,000 people had been arrested, mostly for issues such as "being outdoors without a permit or possessing alcohol and/or cigarettes."[14] The sale of both of the latter was banned. Alcohol sales were reopened (and then shut again) under the logic that a ban prevented accidents and violence that would monopolize hospital beds and health care workers. Cigarettes were a different matter – with many claiming the rationale had more to do with the corrupt relationship of some African National Congress (ANC) top party officials with illegal cigarette smugglers (and indeed, the markets for both have gone underground).[15] While overall crime has fallen, especially violent crime, reported incidents of police brutality have increased, with at least ten people having died as a result of police actions by June, including the well-publicized case of Collins Khosa, who the police detained for suspicion of having alcohol in his front yard. The family accused the police of brutally beating up Khosa, who later died from his injuries.[16]

Thus, was our boundary drawn with normal life. And yet, it was also clear how these new conditions exposed the ordinary everyday continuities in a city like Johannesburg. As urban studies scholars recently wrote, cities like Johannesburg are places which "cannot be so clearly divided into 'before' and 'after' the pandemic, and where 'crisis' and the 'everyday' are not so neatly separable."[17]

From the first and strictest Level 5 lockdown, we are now at Level 3, in which more industries have opened, schools, particularly for transition grades, have restarted with a phased approach for other grades, and exercise is allowed. Unlike in Europe, our partial reopening has occurred with the upswing of our coronavirus curve. Level 3 has seen limitations gradually relaxed, such that now churches can meet with up to fifty congregants, mass transport (called 'kombi' taxis) can run with health measures in place, restaurants can serve customers with social distancing, and spas and hair salons can open, although still people are not allowed to meet with friends or extended family.

South Africans are used to adjusting to ceremonious national 'stages' of difficulty because for years now we have been socialized to the phases of 'load-shedding,' planned interruptions to electricity supply on rotating shifts. These range from Stage 1 to Stage 8, we alarmingly found out in late 2019, when the power company Eskom jumped suddenly from Stage 4 (the previous maximum) to an unheard-of Stage 8. '#Stage8' trended on South African Twitter, and its humorists quipped that "Eskom has more stages than your relationship" and "'#Stage8' is when Eskom goes house to house and takes all your candles." Thus, when the presidency announced that lockdown would also have its levels, South Africans were already savvy to the dictates of gradualized prohibition and its attendant future-directed hope of easing.

Still, the schizophrenic euphoria of slowly reopening while cases and deaths mounted produced a strange dissociation in many. As of mid-August, the total cases of COVID-19 were nearly 573,000, with the total deaths reported as being over 11,200. Over thirty-four percent of those cases

---

14 Katie Trippe, "Pandemic Policing: South Africa's Most Vulnerable Face a Sharp Increase in Police-Related Brutality," *Africa Source*, June 24, 2020, https://www.atlanticcouncil.org/blogs/africasource/pandemic-policing-south-africas-most-vulnerable-face-a-sharp-increase-in-police-related-brutality/, accessed August 13, 2020.
15 Jacques Pauw, "Tobacco Trade Bred Industry with 'Criminality, Political Links Embedded in DNA'," *News24*, May 31, 2020, https://www.news24.com/news24/analysis/analysis-tobacco-trade-bred-industry-with-criminality-political-links-embedded-in-dna-20200531, accessed August 03, 2020.
16 Katie Trippe, "Pandemic Policing".
17 Gautam Bhan, Teresa Caldeira, Kelly Gillespie, and Abdou Maliq Simone, "The Pandemic, Southern Urbanisms and Collective Life," *Society and Space Magazine*, August 03, 2020, https://www.societyandspace.org/articles/the-pandemic-southern-urbanisms-and-collective-life, accessed August 03, 2020.

are now located in Gauteng Province, where Johannesburg is located. Level 3 was introduced to assist the economy but, as it was, people slowly realized the health impacts. The middle class either began to go about their days 'taking precautions' or they bunkered down. For those who had to return to their physical spaces of work via mass transportation, such as many service workers, or for those who had no income and had to hustle, the parameters of the limits increasingly have meant less and less. The lockdown has only called out the existing contradictions within South Africa's highly skewed economy of sedimented racial capitalism.

Wagelessness and Hunger

First, increased unemployment has hit the poorest South Africans, and especially (black) women. Hunger has increased to alarming levels. The Coronavirus Rapid Mobile Survey (CRAM), a nationally representative panel survey of ten thousand South Africans, based on follow-up telephone interviews with household members already participating in the National Income Dynamics Study (NIDS), reported its first results in mid-July, from interviews conducted in May about retrospective conditions between February and April 2020.[18] The survey found an eighteen percent decline in employment from February to April 2020, accounting for some three million jobs. Further studies of the data found a thirty-three percent decline in income among adults, including both unemployment and furlough. Job losses were concentrated among the lowest earners in the economy. Of the approximately three million jobs lost, the survey reported that two million of these had been held by women, that is, two of every three jobs lost were by women. Women also lost more hours than men of those who maintained jobs, and overall experienced a greater decline in earnings, by twice as much. Black workers reported a forty-three percent chance of losing their jobs, compared with seventeen percent for white workers. To further their vulnerability, while many who lost their jobs are in households in receipt of a government welfare grant, as many as thirty percent of the newly unemployed or furloughed do not reside in households receiving any government support.

Before lockdown, twenty-one percent of households reported running out of money for food in the month, with some 2.5 million households having inadequate access to food and another 0.9 million households with severely inadequate access.[19] In the recent survey, forty-seven percent of people responded that they ran out of money to buy food in April, and twenty-one percent of respondents reported that someone in their household had gone hungry in the last seven days.[20] Furthermore, food intake among the poor is often already of low value nutritionally because of the consumption of high amounts of processed foods, which in turn has been linked to health risks such as diabetes, high blood pressure, and heart attack, which are critical risk factors for COVID-19 here.[21]

18 Nic Spaull et al., "NIDS-CRAM Wave 1 Synthesis Report: Overview and Findings," NIDS-CRAM Working Paper, July 15, 2020, https://cramsurvey.org/wp-content/uploads/2020/07/Spaull-et-al.-NIDS-CRAM-Wave-1-Synthesis-Report-Overview-and-Findings-1.pdf, accessed July 15, 2020: 4.
19 Solidarity Fund and Genesis, "Sustainably Addressing Hunger Through Food Production: Initial Findings" (Johannesburg: Solidarity Fund and Genesis, 2020): 3.
20 Nic Spaull et. al., "NIDS-CRAM Wave 1 Synthesis Report": 5–6.
21 Department of Agriculture, Forestry and Fisheries, "National Policy on Food and Nutrition Security" (Pretoria: DAFF, 2014): 9–15.

In general, working class and poor South Africans rely on purchasing food through formal retailers and informal traders or 'spaza' shops, making food security highly dependent on income.[22] While the CRAM-NIDS survey results related to the period just before an emergency temporary (means-tested) COVID-19 grant – the Social Relief of Distress grant of 350 rand (approximately twenty US dollars) per month – was first released, there have since been reports of problems with people qualifying and with delays in the disbursement of the grant.[23] Thus, key state measures of relief may be woefully inadequate. The hungry find new routes to beg for food and resources: "Asking some food, please!" rings out daily in my neighborhood of Kensington, signaling new and now ordinary rhythms, like a town crier punctuating each afternoon to alert middle-class residents of the proximity of need.

In what Achille Mbembe has called the 'necropolitics' of postcolonial places, the vast abandonment of scores of Johannesburg city residents as a structural feature of our political economic disciplinary apparatus indeed seems to have left many to their own devices.[24] But of course, the social relations that produce such wagelessness also reproduce the long-standing devaluation of much waged labor in South Africa, for instance that which has only now become recognized in these contexts as properly essential: the service and care work that keeps the economy going. The precarious many not only labor to materialize food distribution networks throughout South Africa, but they also share households and income with the unemployed. Their return to their jobs for a scarce wage also has brought coronavirus health concerns closer to everyday anxieties for many.

Service Workers and Precarious Lives

Since Level 5 lockdown, food retail workers have been at work. Yet many supermarkets have had to close temporarily due to staff testing positive for COVID-19.[25] Early on, several supermarkets in Cape Town became hotspots for the (super)spreading of coronavirus, traced from middle-class customers to workers to townships and between provinces, as workers returned from Cape Town to the Eastern Cape.

Health care workers across the country have complained of not having proper supplies of personal protective equipment (PPE). The health care system was already stretched and the extra burden of COVID-19 patients have hit some provinces' hospitals particularly badly, as an exposé of Eastern Cape hospitals brought to light.[26] Health care workers have noted understaffing and the psychological effects of overwork and unsafe conditions.[27] Doctors and nurses have died from

---

22 Solidarity Fund and Genesis, "Sustainably Addressing Hunger Through Food Production": 6.

23 Sandisiwe Shoba, "Basic Income Grant on the Table for South Africa's Unemployed Poor," *Daily Maverick*, July 14, 2020, https://www.dailymaverick.co.za/article/2020-07-14-basic-income-grant-on-the-table-for-south-africas-unemployed-poor/, accessed August 13, 2020.

24 Achille Mbembe, "Necropolitics," *Public Culture* 15 (2003): 11–40.

25 Shani, Reddy, "The COVID-19 Realities of Frontline Staff in SA Retail Stores and their Coffee Shops," *Daily Maverick*, May 13, 2020. https://www.dailymaverick.co.za/article/2020-05-13-the-covid-19-realities-of-frontline-staff-in-sa-retail-stores-and-their-coffee-shops/, accessed August 12, 2020.

26 Andrew Harding, "Coronavirus in South Africa: Inside Port Elizabeth's 'Hospitals of Horrors'," *BBC News*, July 15, 2020, https://www.bbc.com/news/world-africa-53396057, accessed August 13, 2020.

27 Tiyese Jeranji, "Healthcare Workers' – Often Unheard – Plea for Government Help," *Daily Maverick*, June 25, 2020, https://www.dailymaverick.co.za/article/2020-06-25-healthcare-workers-often-unheard-plea-for-government-help/, accessed August 10, 2020.

working without protection. Community health care workers, too, have filled the gap in continuing to provide care for working class township residents without receiving PPE or much support at all.[28]

Service workers, such as retail workers, health care workers, municipal workers, and teachers, have all raised the issue of not having proper protective gear. The union in the retail sector, the South African Commercial Catering and Allied Workers Union (Saccawu), has defended workers' access to PPE, such as masks and face shields. While regulation stipulates the provisioning of PPE to frontline workers engaging with the public, the union said that there was little monitoring capacity by government and that compliance from some retailers was a problem. The union has received many complaints from members about inadequate protections.[29] Thus, service workers have borne the burden of intensified health risks to carry out their jobs.

Furthermore, the Commission for Conciliation, Mediation and Arbitration (CCMA) reported that between lockdown and the end of June, it has handled 1,800 cases of retrenchment, a 156 percent increase in cases from 2019 in only the three months of April to June. Of those, the retail sector was hit the hardest, with some 23,000 jobs to be lost.[30] As another important ameliorative intervention, the state set aside unspent money from the Unemployment Insurance Fund for temporary employer/employee relief to try to prevent retrenchments, but still retrenchments across sectors are expected to increase. Thus, for many workers the pressure on jobs they hold, too, is intensifying.

Informal traders often provide cheaper and easier access to food for many. They were initially prohibited from operating during lockdown until there was an outcry. While the government allows them to trade now, it requires them to have a license, which not everyone has been granted.[31] Thus, informal workers, in particular, even though they provide more affordable access to fresh produce than supermarkets for many working class South Africans, have faced particular struggles in continuing to operate and thereby securing income.[32]

Tithi Battacharyiya speaks of the way that COVID-19 has exposed the essential labor of care to economies around the world.[33] While Wall Street bankers are at home, the service of health care workers, food retail clerks, sanitation workers, cleaners, and teachers continues, often at great risk to these generally low waged workers. The unpaid reproductive labor, those 'life-making activities' of cooking, cleaning, nurturing, raising, and educating those we care about, has also become more visible as people are held together in living spaces. In South Africa, as in other places, already-high

28 Arnold Tsunga, Tatenda Mazarura, and Mark Heywood, "The Implications of COVID-19 on Workers' Rights: A Regional Overview," *Daily Maverick*, June 19, 2020, https://www.dailymaverick.co.za/article/2020-06-19-the-implications-of-covid-19-on-workers-rights-a-regional-overview/, accessed August 14, 2020.

29 Jarita Kassen, "Saccawu Says No COVID-19 Oversight Mechanism in Place for Retail Workers," *Eyewitness News*, May 11, 2020, https://ewn.co.za/2020/05/11/saccawu-says-no-covid-19-oversight-mechanism-in-place-for-retail-workers, accessed August 14, 2020.

30 Sarah Smit, "Possible Lockdown Retrenchments are Already Soaring," *The Mail & Guardian*, June 29, 2020, https://mg.co.za/business/2020-06-29-possible-lockdown-retrenchments-are-already-soaring/, accessed August 14, 2020.

31 Dennis Webster, "Not all Joburg's Street Traders are Trading," *New Frame*, May 18, 2020, https://www.newframe.com/not-all-joburgs-street-traders-are-trading/, accessed August 12, 2020.

32 Michael Rogan and Caroline Skinner, "The COVID-19 Crisis and the South African Informal Economy: 'Locked Out' of Livelihoods and Employment," NIDS-CRAM Working Paper, June 15, 2020, https://cramsurvey.org/wp-content/uploads/2020/07/Rogan-Covid-crisis-and-the-South-African-informal-economy.pdf, accessed August 14, 2020.

33 Sarah Jaffe, "Social Reproduction and the Pandemic, Interview with Tithi Bhattacharya," *Dissent*, April 2, 2020. https://www.dissentmagazine.org/online_articles/social-reproduction-and-the-pandemic-with-tithi-bhattacharya, accessed April 17, 2020.

incidences of gender-based violence have shot up under lockdown, as the contradictions of these relations bubble up. The intertwined waged and unpaid labor of care and service sustains economies during the pandemic, then, in ways that reveal how capitalist relations rely on, yet obscure, these primary forms of work, as well as how such labor cuts across divided geographies of home and workplace, and, in Johannesburg, suburb, township, and urban center.

That coronavirus has exposed these articulated conjunctures is a feature of our present. It both uncovers such everyday divides and somehow sutures them together in a manner that invokes an insistent call for futures that can attend to such everyday 'normal' states of contingent endurance.

Futures?

Rehilwe Mooketsi, 'Man rushing to work', May 12, 2020.

This photograph was taken in May 2020 by Rehilwe Mooketsi, one of my third-year students. She took it when the lockdown was eased to Level 3. It is shot from the window of her (private) university residence in Braamfontein, the neighborhood surrounding Wits University. Such private university residences have proliferated recently and expanded as student protests called out campus housing shortages. As a result, qualifying students receive rental income via the national student loan program. This private accommodation thus serves poor and working-class black students who are the recipients of government funding, mostly through loans, to assist students to pay university fees. The property owners receive market rates for these rentals. With Level 3, students were allowed to return to these private residences (while still not able to return to campus). Many who could return, did, as their home context made it difficult to continue learning while the university moved to 'online' teaching.

The picture portrays the labor of a municipal cleaner, called a sanitation worker in other places, tidying the streets. She bends over to clear the rubbish by the curb wearing her bright yellow safety jacket, and an ordinary garbage bag wrapped around her skirt for protection against dirt. Crews of women workers clean the streets manually. In the early 2000s they were subcontracted out to a private firm, but over the past twenty years workers have fought to be insourced on the better wages and conditions of public sector workers. This cleaner has returned to work with Level 3 to tend to the city's streets. Another man rushes past her and through otherwise empty streets to return to his workplace, as interpreted by Mooketsi. While the street cleaner wears a mask, the running man does not. The photograph also represents the distance between people, then, lengthening as the man jogs past the stooped cleaner in the grey quietness of the times. From the window of the university residence, higher up yet still taking in the street view, Mooketsi observes these relations and the history of their articulations: the (black) woman's low-paid cleaning work keeping an entire city operating, a (black) man's presumed anonymous job, urgent only in its labor, and she, the next generation, waiting for and anticipating what is next.[34]

My daughter is seventeen, and in her 'Matric' year of high school. This is the last year (grade 12) before graduating. In South Africa it is defined by pressurized national exams, for which all 'learners' are prepared over the entire period of high school. National results are published every year in the newspapers, and every year there is a scandal about some feature of the exam paper being leaked, which becomes symptomatic of the decline of national standards and the global uncompetitiveness of the nation. The Matric year is, then, a national rite of passage, which seemingly teaches young people, regardless of their class background, that punitive learning, rote pedagogy, and presumed abstract (yet highly unequal) conditions are the deeply rutted ground from which each individual must claw herself up and out. The results of these national exams determine the first step into adulthood. They determine whether a student can proceed to university.

While my daughter goes to a privileged school in Johannesburg organized to channel the next generation of university entrants, the existing stress of a school year has obviously been compounded by the uncertainties of COVID-19, of shutdown and reopening and shutting down again, of (partial) online learning and partial face-to-masked-face returns for Matrics. For her and the other middle-class kids preparing for university, their future is slowed. For working-class kids, whose schools have been unable to continue, their next year recedes into an even more distant horizon. The everyday battle of keeping going becomes common and, yet of course, even more differentiated. Furthermore, the young yearn for the optimism of delusional neoliberal futures, but instead return to a deep melancholy for what is certainly lost but too hard to mourn just yet: the lost senior year, but also the very possibility of a future of jobs and bigger contributions as the measures of adulthood.[35]

University students, whom I teach and who have been sent back to their myriad homes across the city, the province, and the country, remain tied into, albeit tenuously, a place beyond this one. These young people also have quite different levels of what is euphemistically termed 'access' to learning online. In fact, we are teaching remotely rather than 'online,' partly because of the 'digital divide' preventing many students from connecting to the internet, but also because of a range of difficulties of home environments. One student eloquently expressed how he had become an 'indigent' member of the university community. He was beginning our second semester, which started

34 Henri Lefebvre, "Seen from the Window," in *Rhythmanalysis: Space, Time and Everyday Life* (London and New York: Continuum, 2004): 27–37.
35 Lauren Berlant, *Cruel Optimism* (Durham: Duke University Press, 2011).

in July, after having barely scraped through the first semester, which ended in June. He has had scarce access to any course material because where he lives has been without any power for weeks. The lapses in electricity are a regular experience across the country, as we noted. While the economic slowdown exacerbated by lockdown has meant that regular 'load-shedding' has actually tapered (since there is less drain on the grid), the electricity company in many working-class areas has purportedly switched off power as a punitive measure – a stand against 'illegal connections' of electricity, the practice where informal (and dangerous) riggings run the current from a working box directly into other people's households. This student tried to explain that even with university support to connect to online platforms, he had no electricity and therefore no means of participating. Often students would travel to an internet café to try to find access, which involved having to pay, or to friends or family members, meaning travelling across areas during lockdown, to get their cellphones charged. Many students have been using only their cellphones as their main device to learn from, including for writing assignments.

Yet internet access has been only one problem. Hunger, cramped residences, noise, reproductive labor demands, family members losing jobs, and then, eventually and more recently, illness from the disease itself have affected the households to which our students returned. Learning plans have not been flexible enough to account for the range of experiences that have exacerbated existing inequalities – which over the past five years had fueled student protests around high fees and for demands to decolonize the university; that is, to base learning from students' lived experiences of racism and class inequalities, the precise conditions that now meet them head on and that they must solve, seemingly on their own. The future for them is also tentative. They want to finish their degrees, but they have become a locus of all of the contradictions in this society – the pressure to change this place with structural racism deeply girded to every aspect of social relationships.

My students push forward with their plans to apply for honors degrees. Mooketsi wrote about the role of black women in the social imaginaries of care that reproduce the space of the city. She also understands that she needs to take care of her mother and her daughter. That she sees these relations in the same frame is testament to one of the effects of coronavirus: entanglements have become that much clearer and survival that much more urgent. Perhaps because of the continuities of coronavirus times with the everyday lives of so many, 'normal' has not changed as much as the jarring temporality of lockdown might presume.[36] The intricacies of everyday life and its normalized violence in Johannesburg, indeed, articulate in this conjuncture, tying together the wageless with the labor of food distribution and the care of the home-bound student.

There are some new ventures: for instance, emergent networks, which responded to calls for food relief, bridged the gap left by the state. Churches, charities, activist groups, and community residents have organized to coordinate supply lines to get food from small-scale farmers to small logistics and transport operators to energized community teams, who identified vulnerable households. The C19 People's Coalition is one such initiative but there are many other local-level initiatives throughout the country. They build on volunteers and donations of cash and kind, which cut across race and class divisions. A surge of interest in homestead and collective food gardens has coalesced new networks of diverse organizations and individuals as well, connecting producers and consumers in localized 'food flows.'

---

36 Dionne Brand, "On Narrative, Reckoning and the Calculus of Living and Dying," *The Star* (Toronto), July 04, 2020, https://www.thestar.com/entertainment/books/2020/07/04/dionne-brand-on-narrative-reckoning-and-the-calculus-of-living-and-dying.html, accessed July 04, 2020.

If there is a future, then, it is in how ordinary South Africans endure these times. We are on the cusp of a future that portends much of the same but where perhaps one learns that with no safety nets, we must create our own next bridges.

Bahru Zewde

Lending Style to the Unseemly: COVID-19 and Mask Design in Ethiopia[37]

Introduction

COVID-19 has many faces. One of them is the faceless mask. What had once been a peculiarity of East Asian countries has steadily assumed global dimensions. The virus that began in the Chinese city of Wuhan has now reached every corner of the world. Records of infections and deaths are being superseded by the day. First it was Italy and Spain that bore the brunt of the pandemic. Then it was the turn of the United Kingdom. Currently, commensurate with its global stature, the United States has taken the unmistakable lead, followed by Latin America and India. The United States and Brazil, the two countries headed by presidents with the most skeptical view of the virus (and an almost pathological aversion to the wearing of masks), have suffered the most.

The African Experience

Africa was spared the early depredations of the virus. It was as if Nature, cognizant of the continent's poor health infrastructure, had shown mercy on it or given it more time to prepare for the inevitable onslaught. Yet, some countries, such as Egypt and South Africa (particularly the latter), have already witnessed a high number of infections. Ethiopia initially had one of the lowest rates, but cases have been growing since June 2020. Various explanations have been adduced for the relatively low rate of infection in Africa. They include the relative youth of the population, the hot climate, and the low degree of mobility. Government responses have varied. Some, like South Africa, have instituted total lockdown for a limited period of time, including a ban on the sale of alcohol to minimize social interaction. Most countries have opted for partial shutdowns in consideration of the large sectors of the population whose survival depends on daily returns from the informal economy. The president of Madagascar has been touting a locally produced herbal potion

---

[37] This essay is based on two interviews with owner and CEO of Miss.T.Cal, Tsion Bahru, on June 28 and July 19, 2020, and the following sources: "20 People Who Came up with Incredible Face Mask Designs," *deMilked*, 2020, https://www.demilked.com/creative-diy-face-masks/, accessed June 26, 2020; Abiy Ahmed, "If COVID-19 Is Not Beaten in Africa, It Will Return to Haunt Us," *Financial Times*, March 25, 2020, https://www.ft.com/content/c12a09c8-6db6-11ea-89df-41bea055720b, accessed July 13, 2020; Afomya Tesfaye, "Exploring the History and Artistry of African Masks," *NOVICA*, https://www.novica.com/blog/exploring-history-artistry-african-masks/, accessed June 25, 2020; Arkebe Oqubay, "Ethiopia's Unconventional COVID-19 Response," *EABW News*, May 29, 2020, https://www.busiweek.com/ethiopias-unconventional-covid-19-response/, accessed July 15, 2020; "COVID-19 in Africa: No Room for Complacency", *The Lancet*, Editorial, May 30, 2020, https://www.thelancet.com/journals/lancet/article/PIIS0140-6736(20)31237-X/fulltext, accessed July 15, 2020; *COVID-19 Situation Report, March 13-June 7. Ethiopian Health Data*, Trisha Greenhalgh et al., "Face Masks for the Public During the COVID-19 Crisis," *British Medical Journal*, April 9, 2020, https://doi.org/10.1136/bmj.m1435, accessed June 25, 2020, *Federal Negarit Gazette of the Federal Democratic Republic of Ethiopia*, April 20, 2020, Regulation No. 466/2020, "History of Venetian Masks," *Magic of Venezia*, http://magicofvenezia.com/history-of-venetian-masks/, accessed June 25, 2020, and Mimi Alemayehu, "Ethiopia Battles the Pandemic and Its Economic Consequences," *Center for Strategic and International Studies (CSIS)*, June 10, 2020, accessed July 12, 2020.

as the ultimate cure, drinking it himself in public to drive his point home. The country was even able to export its product to some gullible African countries. But that did not save the island from witnessing a rise in infections in July.

The Ethiopian government response to the pandemic has been more proactive than reactive. The undeclared motto has been "better to err on the side of caution rather than lassitude." The first case of the virus, a Japanese professional transiting from Burkina Faso to his home country, was not detected until March 13, two days after the World Health Organization (WHO) officially designated the virus a global pandemic. But already on January 27, the Ethiopian Ministry of Public Health had set up the Public Health Emergency Operation Center (PHEOC) under the auspices of the Ethiopian Public Health Institute, successor to the Ethiopian version of the Pasteur Institute. Over the following months, the two institutions worked in tandem not only in taking measures to mitigate the virus but also in educating the public and keeping it adequately informed of the latest developments. The minister, Dr. Lia Taddesse, has assumed almost iconic significance with her steady and composed daily briefings on the progress of the pandemic.

The early precautionary measures were necessitated by the size of the country's population (over 100 million), the crowded nature of its capital (Addis Ababa), and the fact that its airport is effectively the gateway to Africa. These measures included the closing of schools and universities, the shutting down of nightclubs and similar entertainment centers, the prohibition of sporting, religious, and similar public gatherings, the closing of all international borders, the suspension of Ethiopian Airlines flights to over eighty destinations, the imposition of a mandatory fourteen-day quarantine for all incoming international passengers, and the postponement of the general elections initially scheduled for August 2020. On March 25, the Nobel Laureate prime minister, Abiy Ahmed, wrote an op-ed in the *Financial Times* calling for a concerted global initiative to combat the pandemic and its injurious economic and social effects, especially for Africa. He argued: "We can defeat this invisible and vicious adversary – but only with global leadership. Without that, Africa may suffer the worst, yet it will not be the last. We are all in this together, and we must work together to the end."

The government began to take more robust measures with the proclamation on April 8 of a state of emergency for a period of five months. The ministerial regulation that followed on April 20 imposed a host of restrictions to ward off the virus as well as to ease the burden imposed on the public by the pandemic. These included a ban on meetings of more than four people, a moratorium on all redundancies and evictions of tenants or the raising of rents, a reduction of passenger numbers on public transport vehicles by fifty percent (with a corresponding compensatory tariff raise), and the mandatory wearing of face masks in public places. The penalty for the violation of the regulations ranged from terms of imprisonment to rather implausible fines of 1,000 to 200,000 Ethiopian birr (roughly 28 to 5,700 US dollars).

Implementation of these measures was stringent, especially in the early phase. The chief culprits for large gatherings in confined spaces were the joints for chewing the mildly exhilarating plant called *khat* and for smoking shisha, both of which are generally consumed communally. Yet, at a time when the government had released prisoners as part of the effort to control the spread of the pandemic, detention was not always a viable option. Nor could many people afford the stiff monetary fines, having become even more impoverished by the lack of gainful employment. So, police sometimes resorted to shaming transgressors. On one occasion, for instance, they rounded up people not wearing masks and made them squat for hours in public. As the rate of infection rose in May and June, businesses refused to provide their services unless customers were prepared to wear masks and be subjected to body temperature testing. They also had either to clean their hands with their own sanitizer or wash their hands in the outfit provided.

The Contentious Issue of Masks

Wearing masks is not that uncommon. History provides many examples of mask-wearing. However, the major difference between the past and the current situation is that, then, they were worn out of volition rather than compulsion. Also, those masks were designed to cover the entire face whereas coronavirus masks cover only the mouth and nose. Leaving aside the Halloween masks that are an annual occurrence, we have the celebrated Venetian masks that had their heyday in the glorious days of the Republic of Venice in the fifteenth and sixteenth centuries. They had the dual purpose of concealing one's identity while performing acts of promiscuity and of leveling down the classes. They became particularly popular during the annual Venetian Carnival, a street pageant with a decidedly hedonistic tinge.

In Africa, masks have an even deeper meaning. They have long been almost ubiquitous on the continent, although probably most evident in Western Africa. They are very often great works of art, designed in multiple shapes and adorned with bright colors. This made them desirable targets during the colonial era for massive relocation to Europe, where they now constitute the prized possessions of many museums. Arguably the biggest haul was made during the famous Dakar-to-Djibouti expedition led by the French ethnologist Marcel Griaule between 1931 and 1933. Most of these masks ended up in the Musée de l'Homme in Paris, now relocated to the new Musée du Quai Branly.

Contemporary versions of these historic masks are to be found in many an African household for their artistic value. But, originally, these masks were worn not so much for decoration as to create a bond with the spiritual world and ancestors in order to steer the community in times of crises or significant landmarks. The wearing of the mask is invariably attended by a performance during which the wearer goes into a trance.

Unlike these historic masks, the face masks necessitated by COVID-19 (and similar earlier pandemics) have no social function. They are worn to reduce the spread of the virus. Hence, they are shrouded in ambivalence. There is still no unanimity about the medical utility of face masks. The WHO, the highest body in charge of global health, initially delivered conflicting messages. Medical opinion is also hardly conclusive. Opponents of wearing masks argue that, apart from their unproven efficacy, they might even aggravate the situation by inducing self-contamination through constant tampering and by instilling a false sense of security. However, on the basis of trials that were conducted, an article in the *British Medical Journal* of April 9, 2020, concluded somewhat cautiously that "they could have a substantial impact on transmission with a relatively small impact on social and economic life." More and more, the wearing of masks has come to enjoy universal acceptance. So much so that those who do not wear them are shamed or even become victims of 'mask rage.'

In the political realm, the wearing or not wearing of masks has assumed an ideological status. Donald Trump and his followers appear to have equated the wearing of masks with capitulation to the virus. The same goes for Brazil's president Jair Bolsonaro, who famously called the virus "a little flu." In the early days of the pandemic, there were some fantastic demonstrations in the media of improvising face masks out of T-shirts and other personal effects. Why one would have to resort to such an exercise when ready-made face masks were available for a modest price is inexplicable. More understandable are the various efforts to inject life and verve into what is without doubt a dour experience. Some of these try to rehabilitate the smile, which was perhaps the single greatest casualty of the face mask. Others design masks that almost literally merge into the face.

Face Masks in Ethiopia

As indicated above, the Ethiopian Council of Ministers regulation of April 20, 2020, made the wearing of face masks mandatory. Article 4, Sub-Article 6 of the regulation stipulated: "Any person who is found at banks, marketplaces, transport depots, in public transit, shops, pharmacies, places where public services are provided, or any other public space where a large number of people are found is required to put on a cover on his nose and mouth." Even though there are few reports of the strict application of the draconian sanctions provided for in the ministerial order, public observance of the regulation has increased steadily, particularly as the figures for infections and deaths showed a significant increase in June and July. At the time of writing, it is highly uncommon to see people not wearing face masks in the public arena. If there are transgressions, the culprits tend to be men, much more than women. Yet, as in many other countries, there has been some bizarre conduct associated with mask use, such as covering the chin rather than the mouth and nose, or letting it dangle from one ear. People enter bars and restaurants with face masks but take it off as soon as they are seated with friends and begin savoring their meals and drinks. Others make extra effort to make their face masks attractive and personalized. That is where fashion design comes in. It is in this context that the Miss.T.Cal story unfolds.

Miss.T.Cal and Mask Design

Miss.T.Cal is the name of an apparel design company launched by the Ethiopian fashion designer Tsion Bahru in January 2019. The name is a playful blend of the *mystical*, for which she has always had an abiding fascination, and her name, Miss T(sion). With an MBA in international business and international marketing from a British university, she had no problem finding a job at Heineken Ethiopia, rising to the position of sales automation manager within a couple of years. But her association with the corporate world, which she found incompatible with her personality, proved short-lived. She chose to follow her passion for art and set up the apparel design company in January 2019. She started with swimwear and soon moved into full-fledged apparel. Two fashion show events that she organized – the first in August 2019 (christened the 'Diva Collection') and the second in February 2020 ('Harlem Nights') – planted her brand on the Addis Ababa fashion landscape. No sooner had she organized the second event than the specter of the COVID-19 pandemic began to cast its shadow over her fledgling business.

The two weeks following the detection of the virus in Ethiopia in mid-March were ones of despondency. As is to be expected, demand for her products dropped; people were preoccupied with surviving the pandemic and had little appetite for fashion. The general sense of apprehension meant a decline in all activity. What changed the situation for her were her avid following of global developments in the fashion industry and a fruitful discussion with her mother, who urged her to go into mask design. Social media had helped her company grow; social media showed her the way out of her temporary predicament. Indeed, this was a time when almost all people engaged in the garment industry (from the small tailor to the large-scale entrepreneur) were moving in this direction. Even street vendors and hawkers had shifted from their traditional wares to selling cheap imported masks, displaying their items covered in plastic either on the ground or, in the more sanitary-conscious cases, hooked on temporary stands.

Artistically speaking, masks are a rather unattractive proposition to both the producer and the wearer. The basic mask with which she started the business was not compatible with her artistic taste. Nor was it that lucrative, as it had to compete with the more established garment shops, which could easily produce in mass. That is when she shifted to producing more fashionable masks, injecting the Miss.T.Cal brand into the design. Waking up early to the market potential of fashionable masks, she charted her own path to relative success. The technical part of mask design, she claims, is basic, although she brought her own style and vibe, what she calls the Miss.T.Cal brand, into it. More decisive was the entrepreneurial skill and the customer networks that she transferred from her fashion design. In numerical terms, the technical part represents about thirty percent of the input, whereas seventy percent is down to her entrepreneurial and marketing skills.

The new direction of her business has entailed an increase in personnel, from one sewer to three. It has also meant a lot more work, a change from the sedate hours of fashion design. With the rise in demand for masks, working hours started early in the morning and ended late in the evening, often including weekends as well. The pandemic threat created yet another opportunity in terms of space, as she could now afford to move to a shop offering more space in a more congenial neighborhood thanks to the discount in rent induced by many businesses being forced by the slump to vacate their rented space. She continued to outsource the embroidery of emblems and trademarks that clients wished to have on their masks. As the price of even the smallest embroidery machine was expensive and its operation would also involve additional personnel, it made a lot of business sense to outsource rather than do it in-house. The cost of outsourcing was very low (about five percent of the total). Masks, which are ordered in bulk, also cost less than designer dresses.

As would be expected, the most significant impact of the transition has been the expansion of clientele. Previously, her clients were almost all women. Now, the base has diversified to include men and kids. In terms of the age profile of clients, formerly they were fifteen to thirty-five years old. Now, the range is between the ages of two and fifty. Kids are the company's favorite clients because they are the least demanding; they are happy as long as the mask is colorful. An added bonus is that they keep losing their masks, necessitating fresh orders! In terms of class, the clients could be classified as middle class and above. An equally novel development has been the appearance of corporate orders, which are all the more lucrative because they are in bulk. Companies that have ordered in bulk either for their staff or for promotional purposes include: a dentist, a furniture company, a burger joint, an entertainment medium, a big liquor supply store, and the branch office of Al Jazeera.

With regard to emblems embroidered on the masks, the most popular is the Lion of Judah. This was the Ethiopian royal emblem in imperial times; for many Ethiopians, too, it has become a national symbol. Contrary to expectations, the Rastas, who venerate the former Emperor Haile Sellassie and a sizable number of whom have settled in Ethiopia, are not among the clients for this particular brand, presumably because they could not afford it. Other popular designs include the Golden Swan, Spider-Man, and other comic characters for kids. Of late, scarf masks (bandanas) have become the craze and they have lent themselves to all sorts of artistic refinements. Corporate clients naturally want to have their logos emblazoned on the masks. Football fans wish to brandish their favorite clubs. Among them are the Walias (the Ethiopian national team), Manchester United, and, more recently for a group of expatriates working for an energy company, the English champion Liverpool FC.

Thanks to social media and alumni connections, there have been orders from abroad as well, notably from neighboring Djibouti, where a number of Lycée alumni ordered two hundred masks. A few masks have been sent to the United States and links are being established with Lycée alumni in Mali and Senegal. A major challenge in this regard has been shipment costs, especially for a business which is not yet well established.

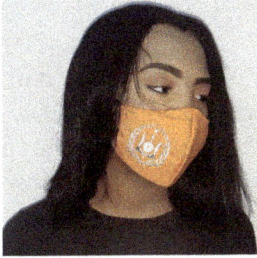

"Djibouti National Emblem"

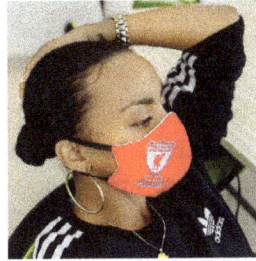

"Champion Liverpool FC"

"Royal Furniture Masks"

"Bandana and Hijab"

"Spiderman Mask"

"Bandana I."

"Bandana II."

"The Lion of Judah" (with a matching T-shirt bearing the image of Emperor Haile Selassie)

As we all know, the 'new normal' induced by COVID-19 could suddenly be disrupted by even more abnormal occurrences. In the United States, the Black Lives Matter protests following the callous killing of George Floyd made a mockery of all the social distancing precautions that had been put in place. Ethiopia had its own version of the even more abnormal in late June, when the country was plunged into chaos in the wake of the assassination of the popular Oromo singer, Hachalu Hundessa. Oromo youth from districts adjoining Addis Ababa stormed the capital to mourn the slain singer and wreaked havoc on lives and property in the process. This was duplicated across different sites in the Oromia region. The government sensed a veritable insurrection and shut down the internet for two weeks. Social media, which was allegedly being used to incite inter-ethnic and inter-religious conflict by opponents of the government, was deemed to be the chief medium for such agitation. This inevitably affected the production and sale of masks, which had relied significantly on social media. Recourse had to be made to individual telephone and text messages, which was quite time-consuming and not as rewarding in terms of sales. Where social media disappeared, social networks came to the rescue. The fact that there were sufficient personnel to attend to the mask production meant that the owner could concentrate on managing telephone calls and text messages. Tsion described the way she met these challenges – first the pandemic and then the internet shutdown – as "managing to escape while the whole world was ablaze behind my back."

Conclusion

Few events have tasked humanity in recent years the way COVID-19 has done. Hardly any country has escaped its clutches. Quite apart from its obviously devastating effect on public health, with millions of infections and hundreds of thousands of deaths, the social and economic fallouts are manifold. And, at the time of writing, the end is not yet in sight. In Africa, where a substantial portion of the population lives from hand to mouth, the social distancing that is so essential to avoid the spread of the virus is hardly feasible. Masks have thus assumed special significance as the best way of minimizing the contact that helps spread the virus. Although they have their doubters, they are increasingly gaining universal acceptance. Yet, masks have the singular effect of universally leveling down. It is to escape this oppressive sense of anonymity that people search for more personalized and customized masks. And that is where businesses like Miss.T.Cal came in. They catered to this understandable human urge. At the same time, they managed to weather these difficult times, giving normal work a new dimension in abnormal times.

Shutter Release I. Current Issues in the World, Told Visually

Maurice Weiss
Black Ward

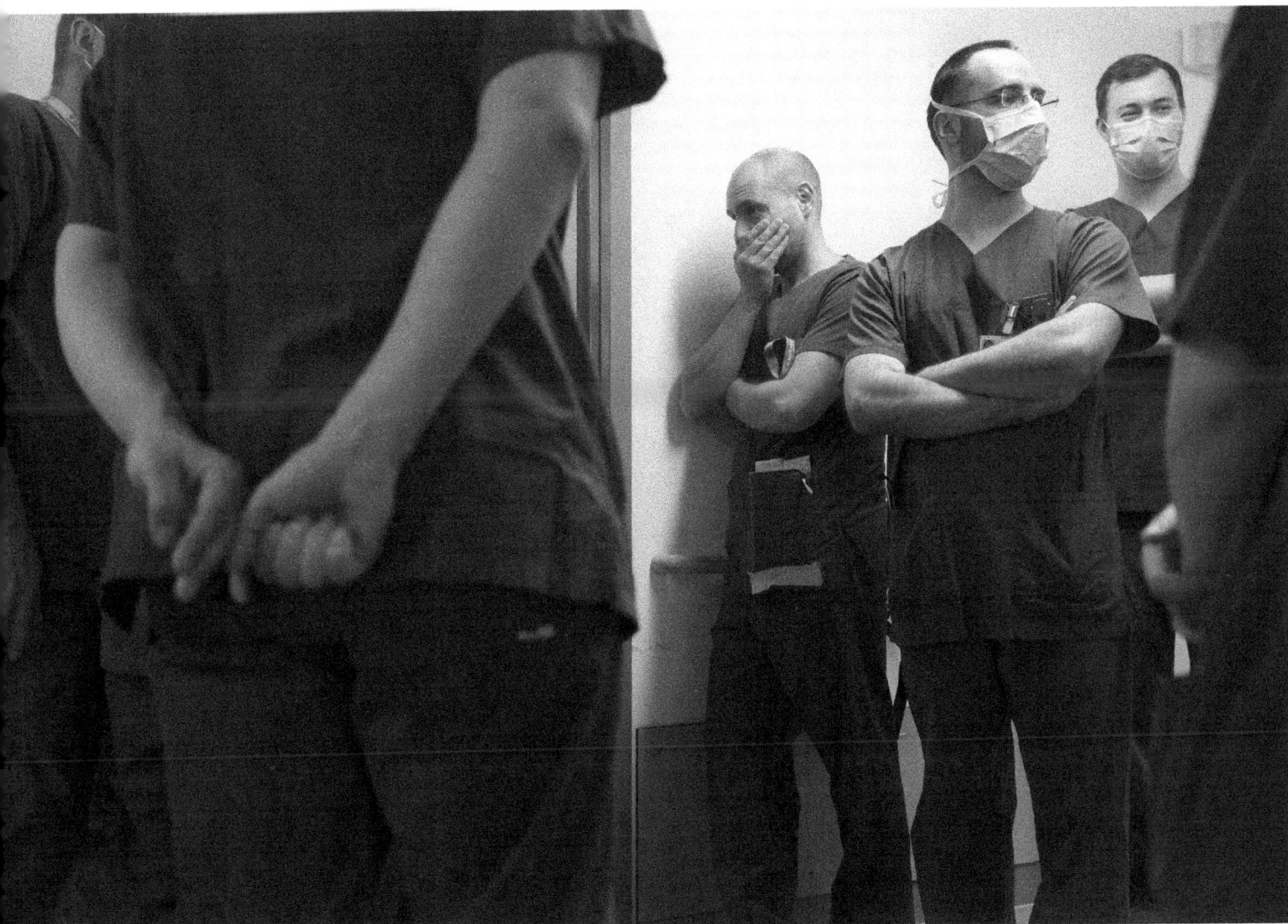

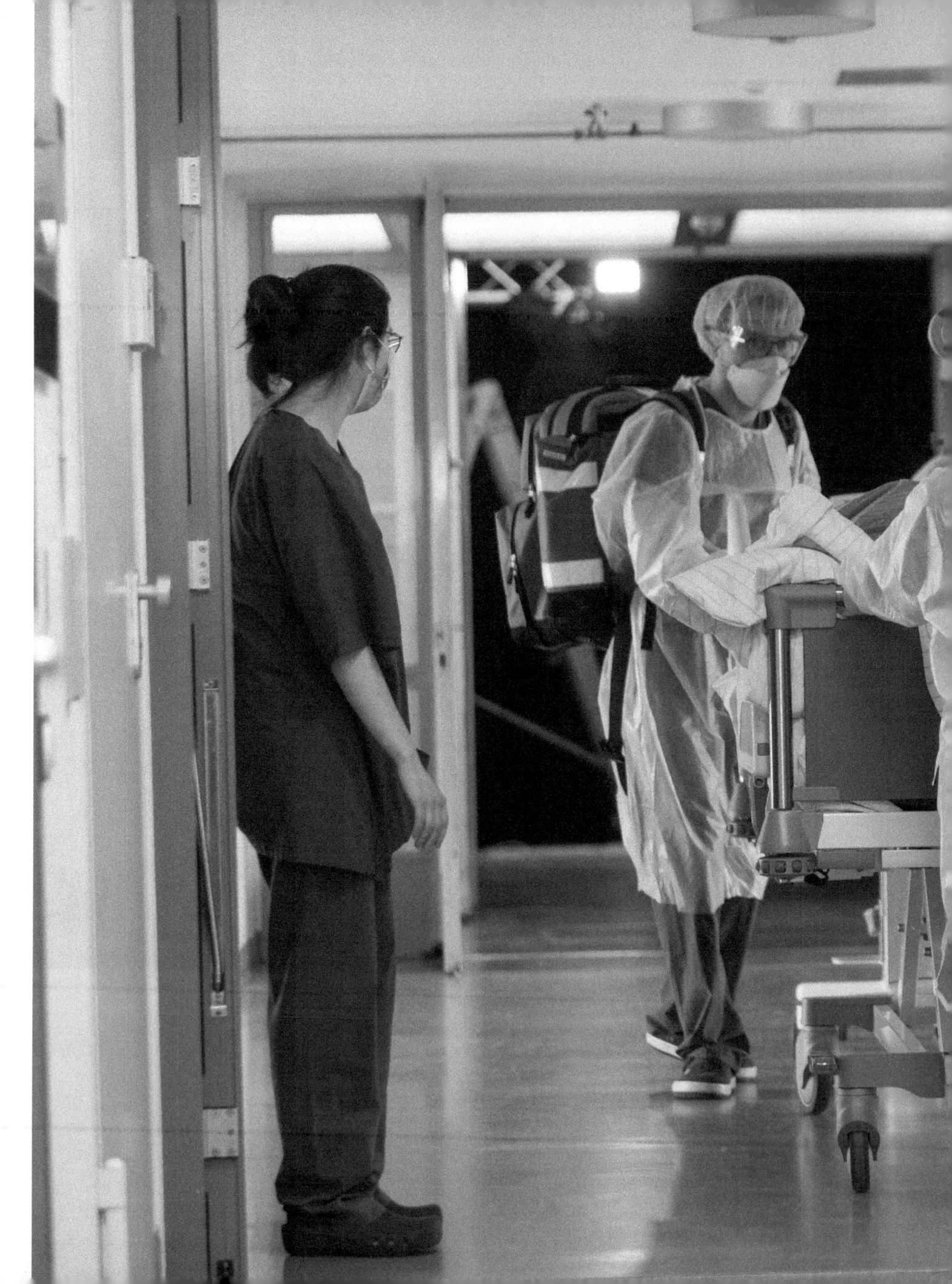

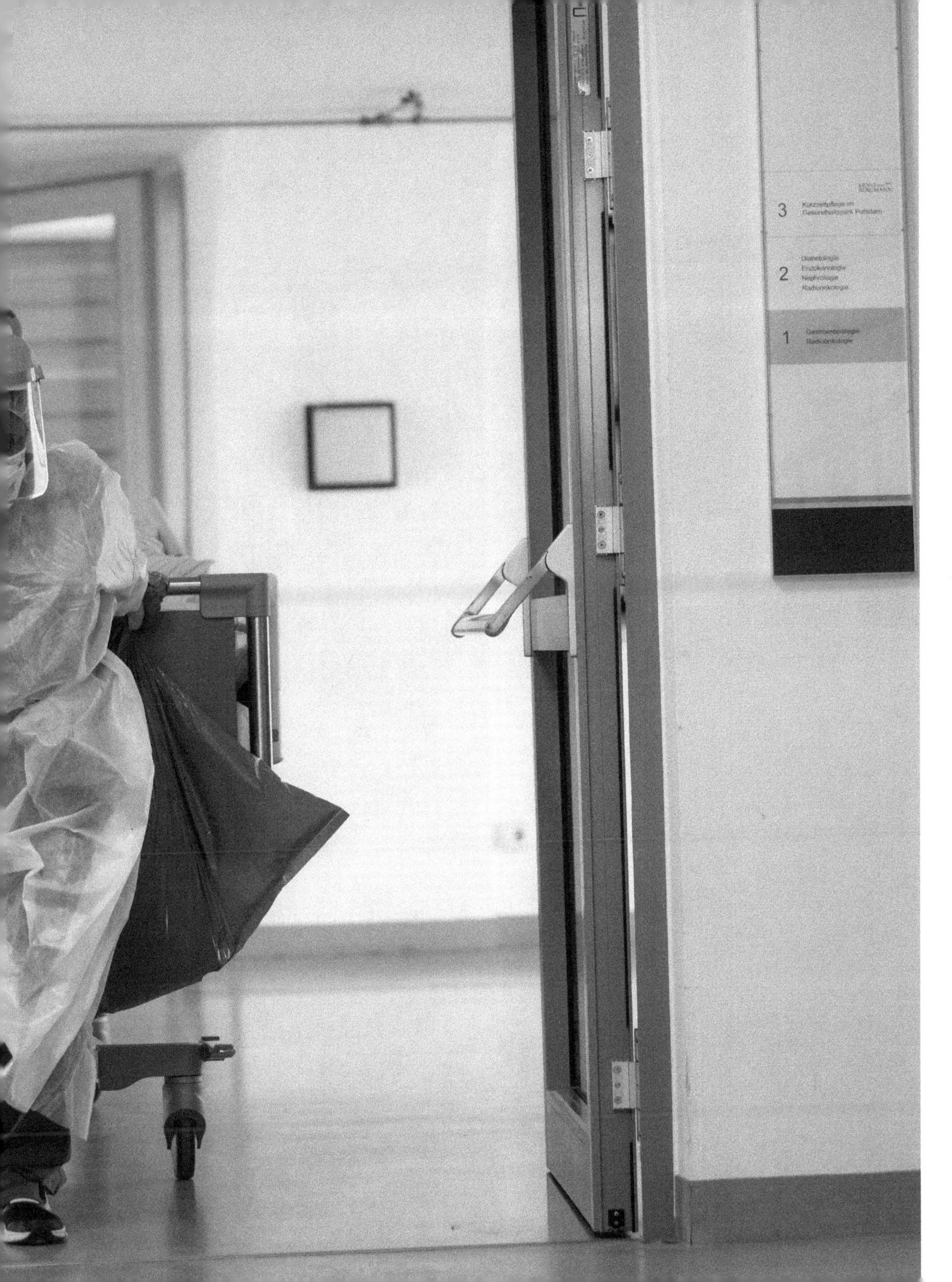

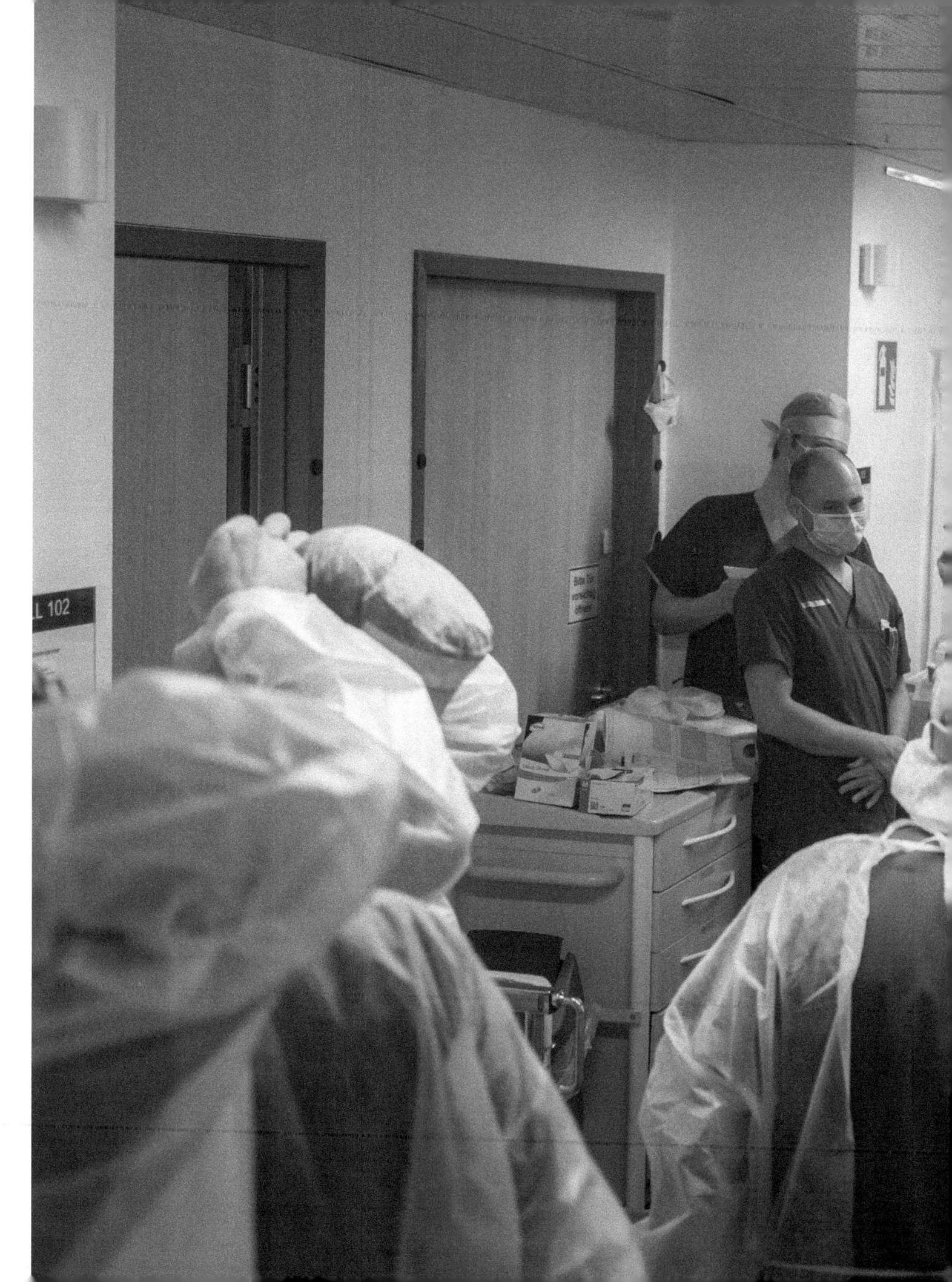

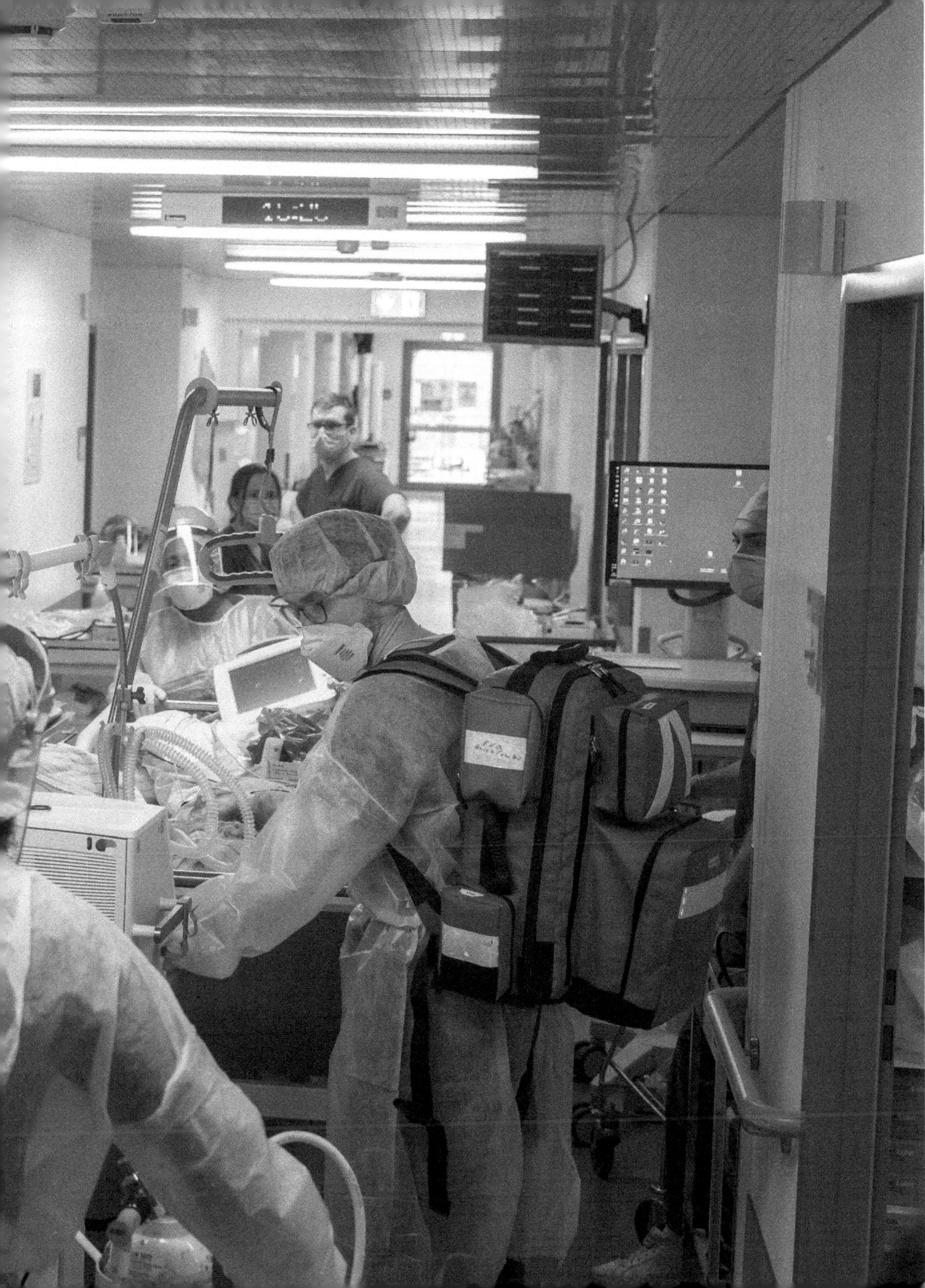

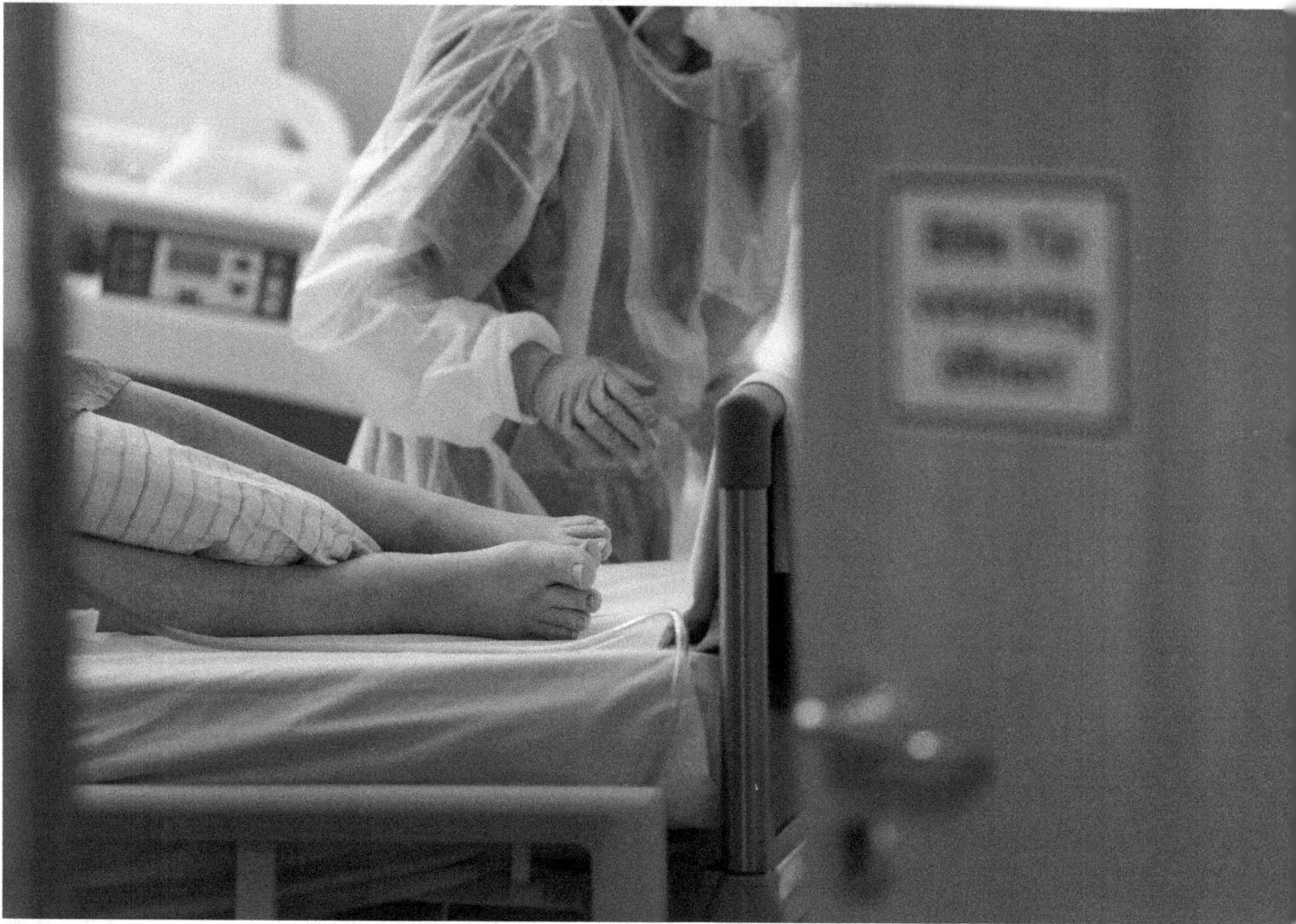

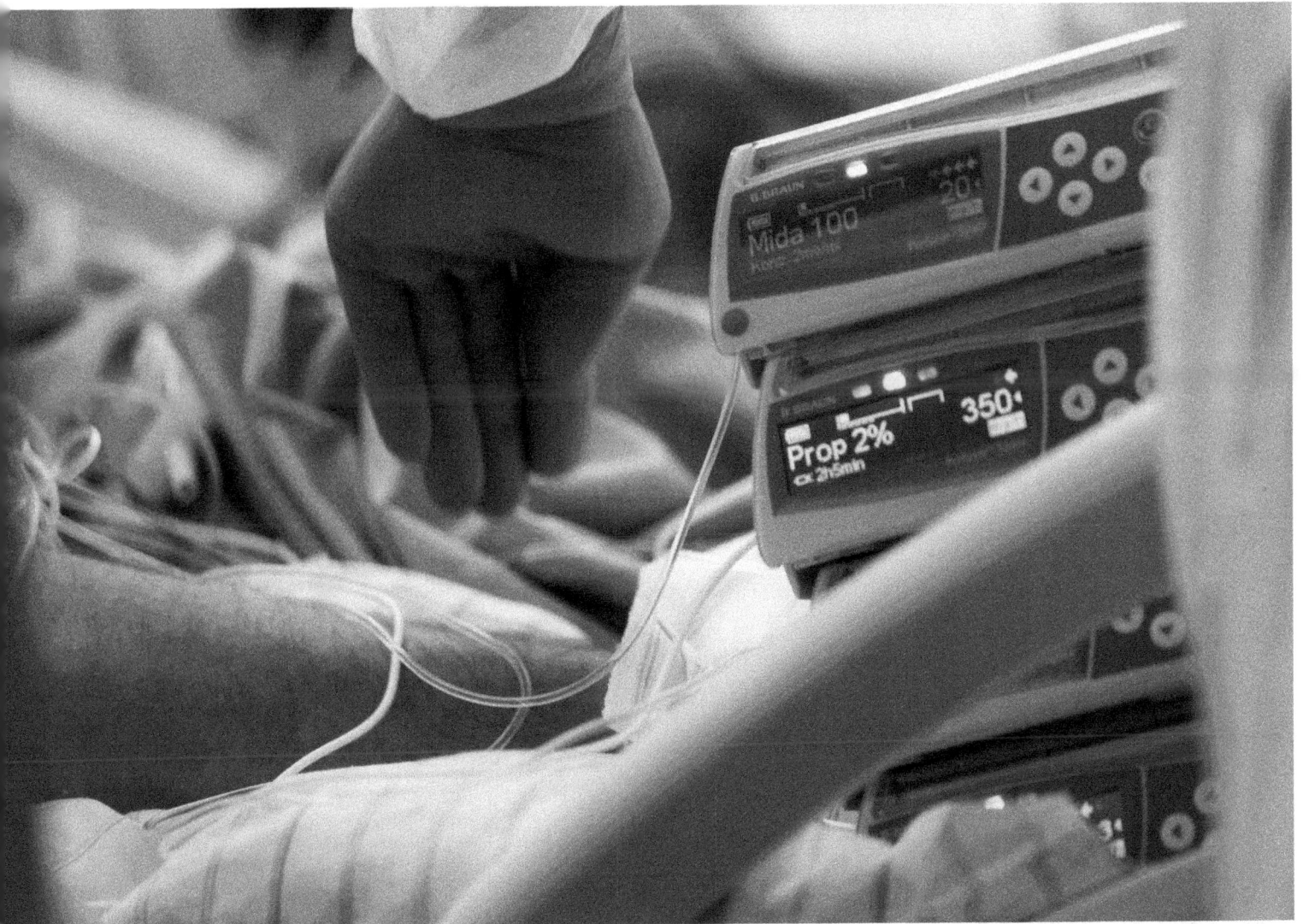

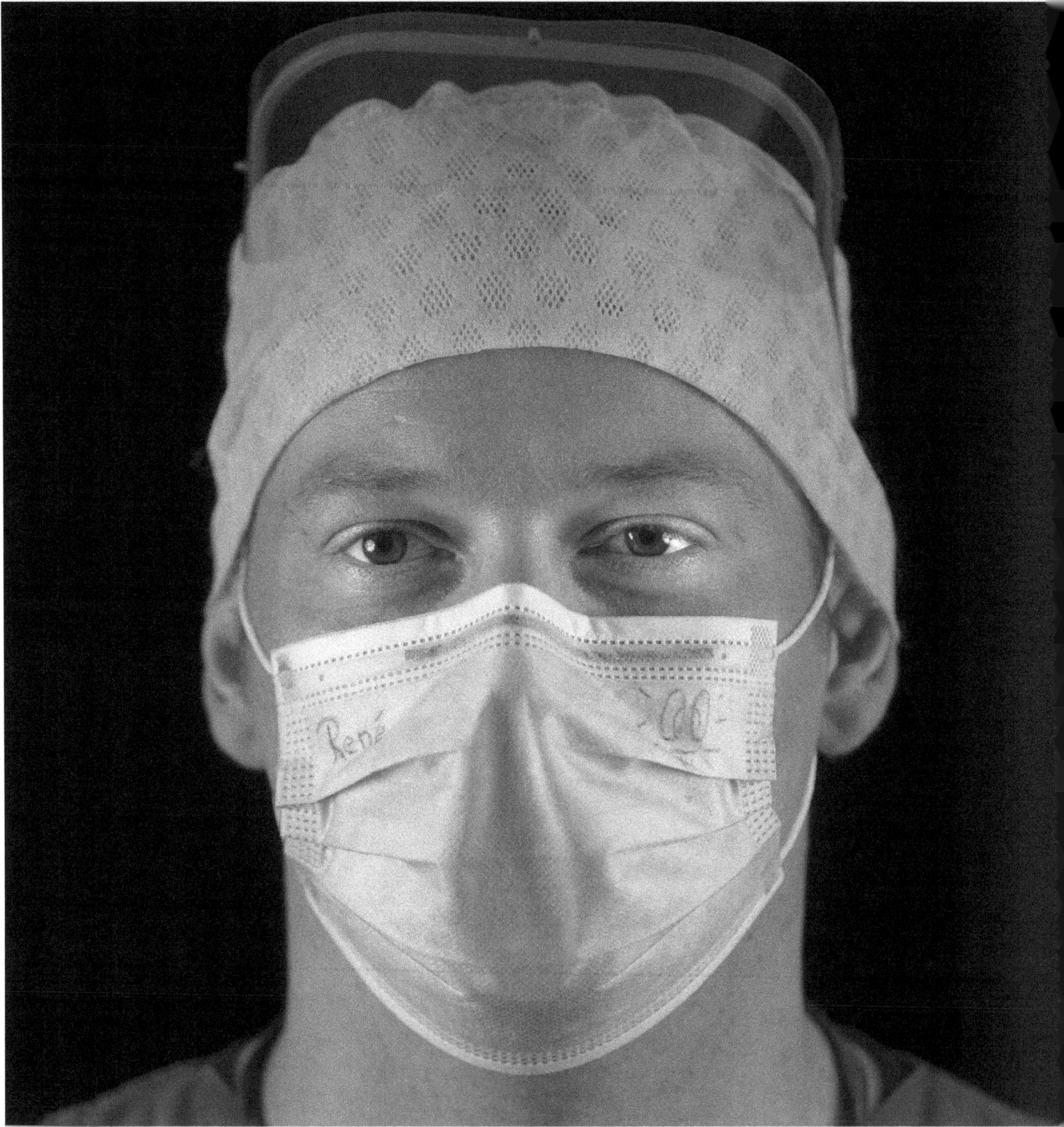

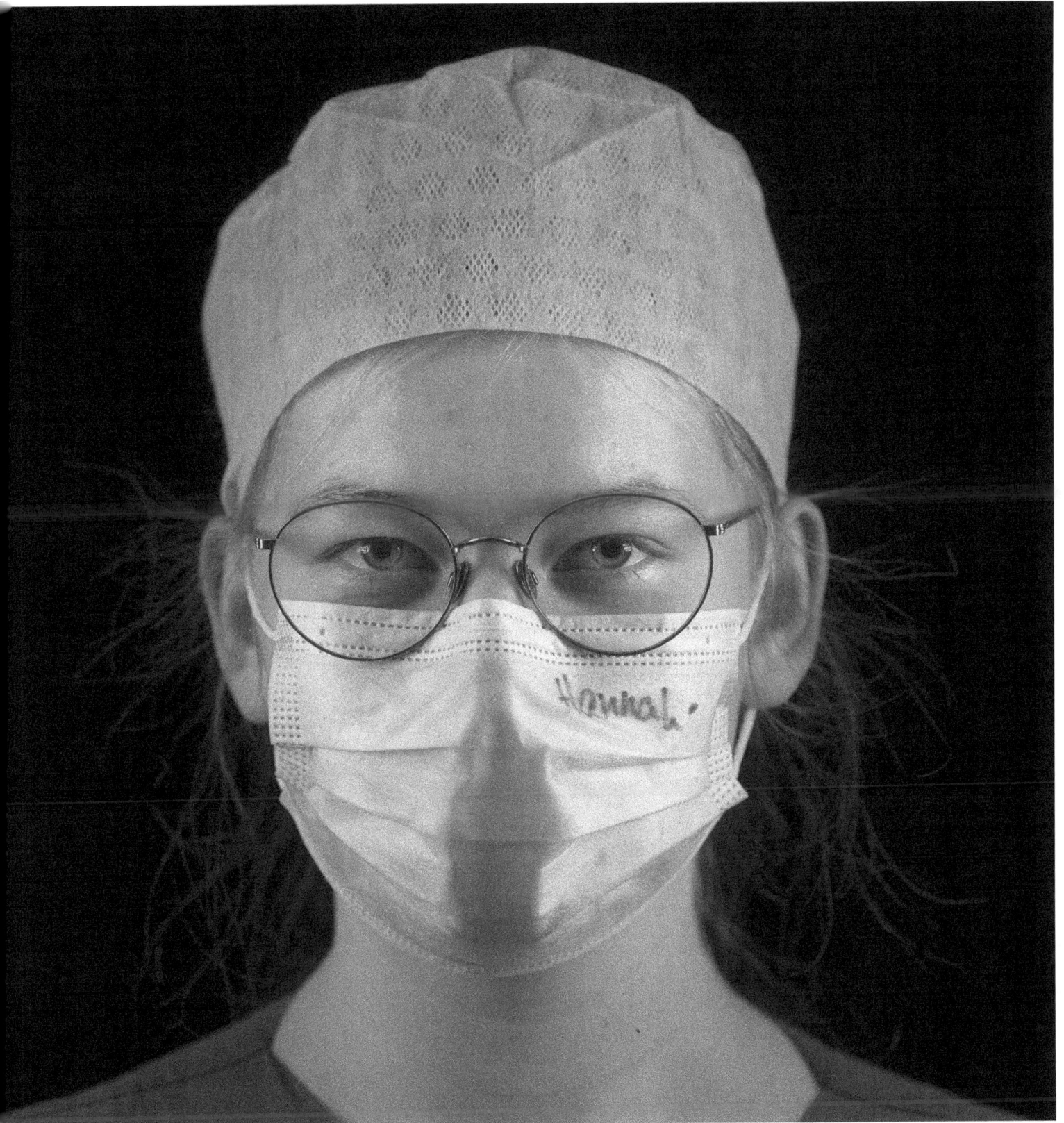

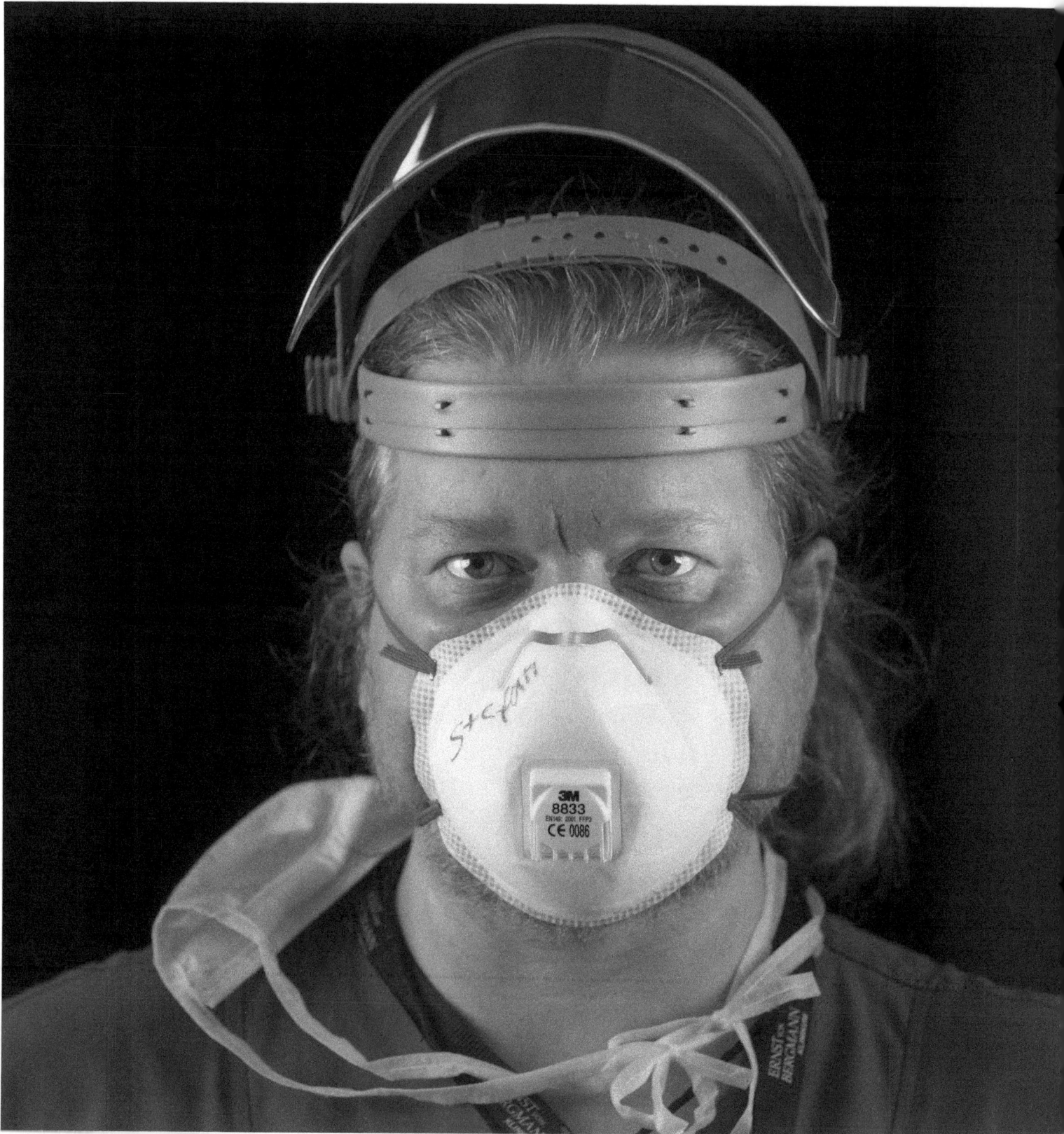

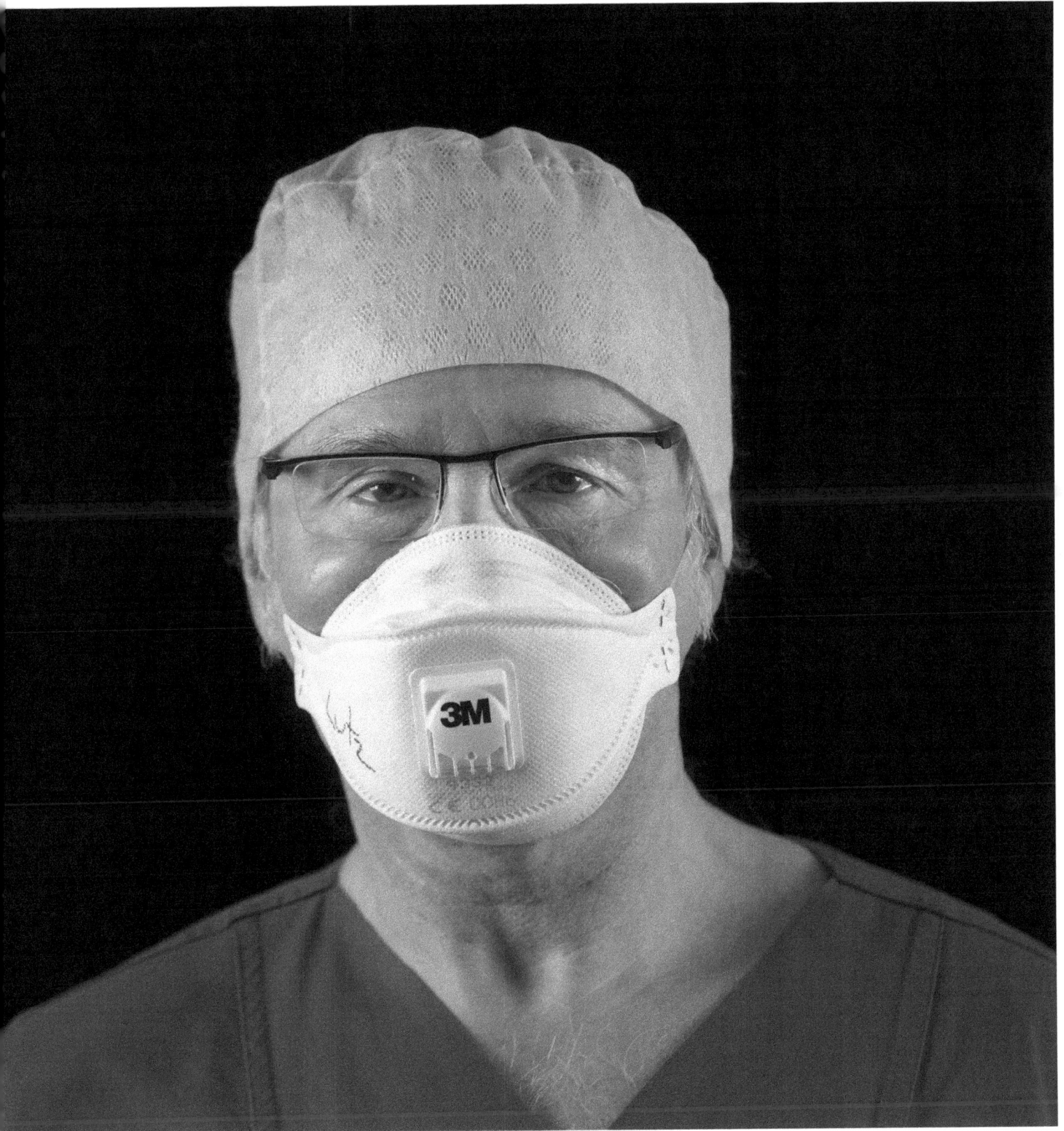

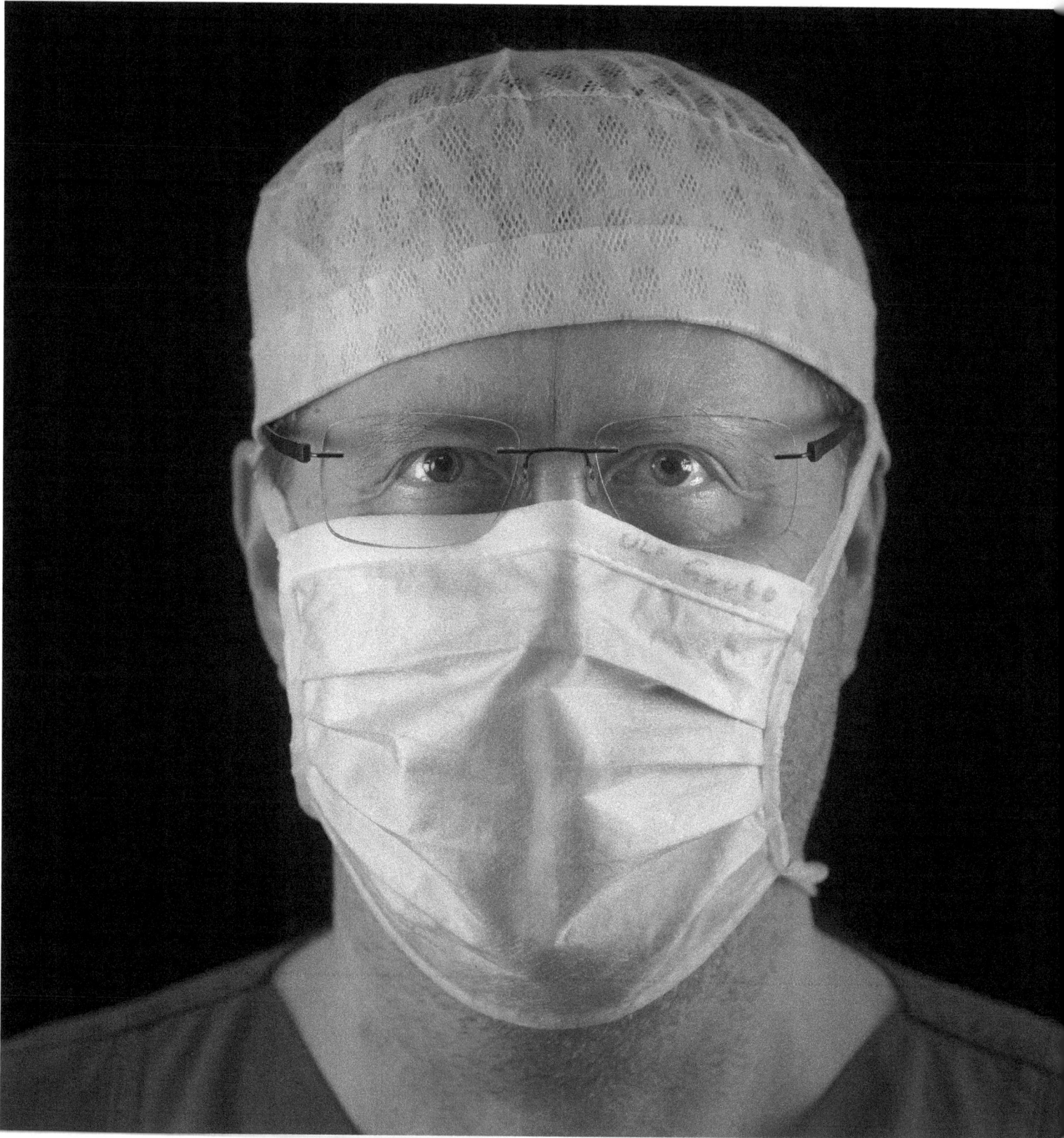

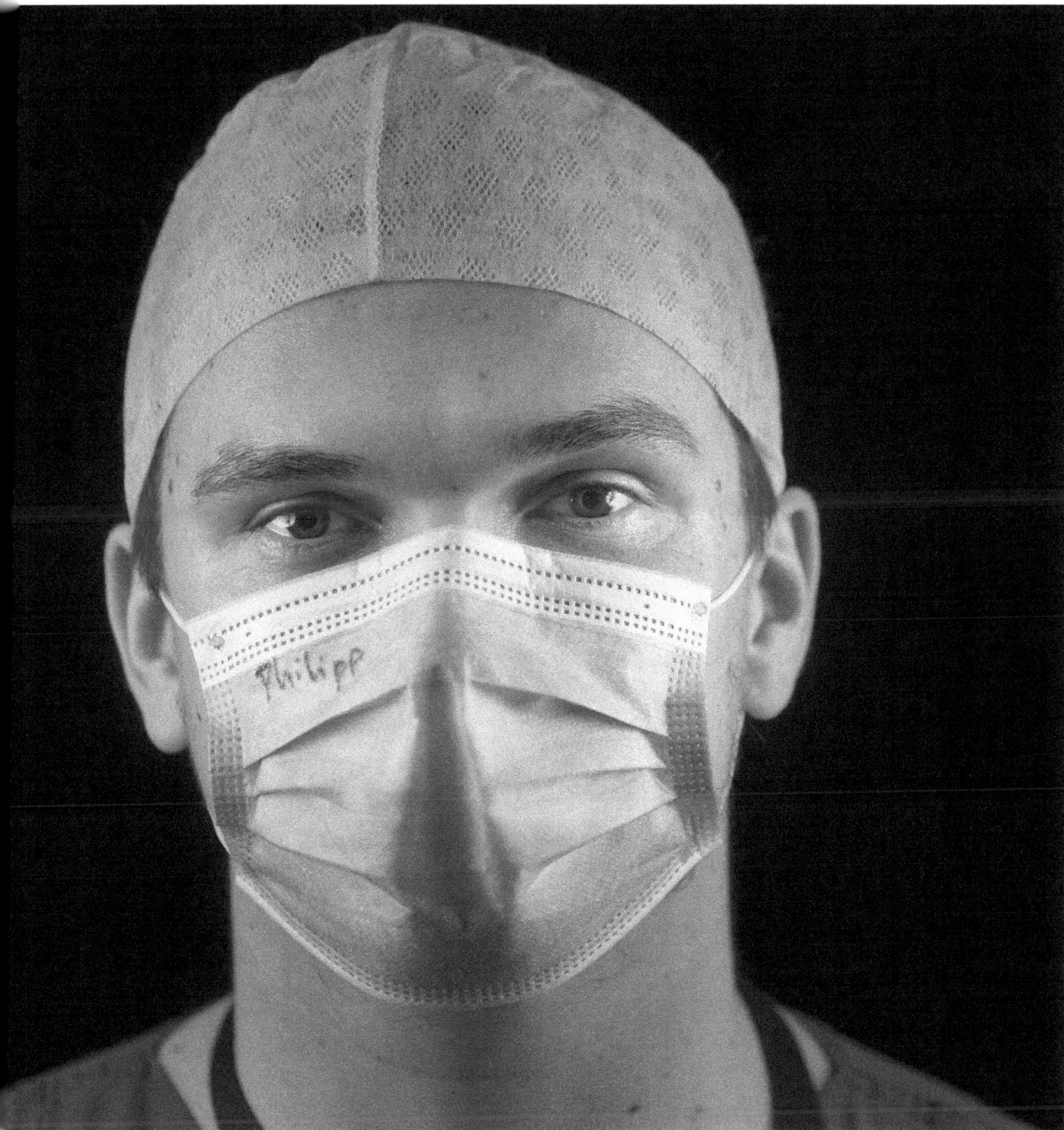

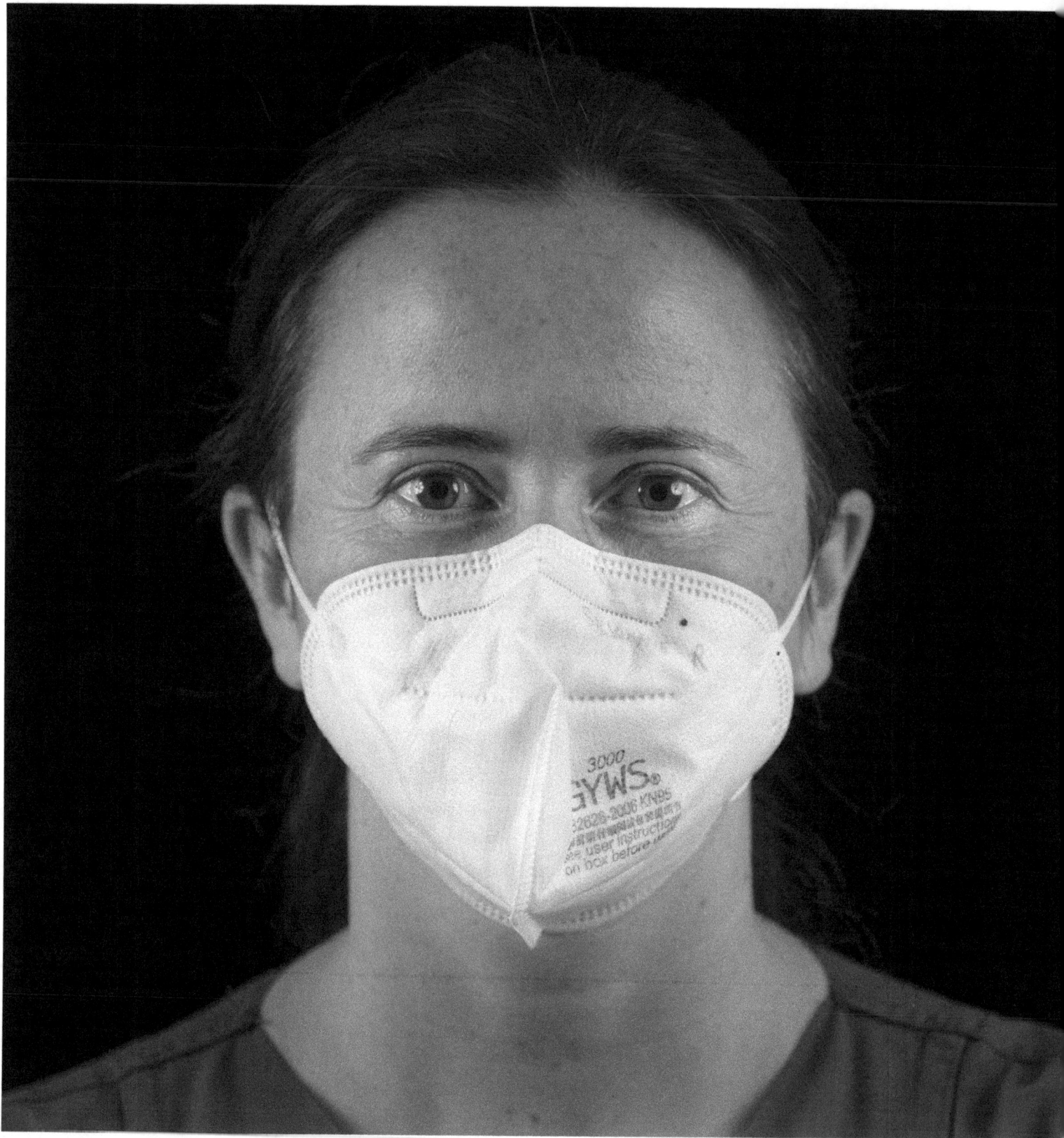

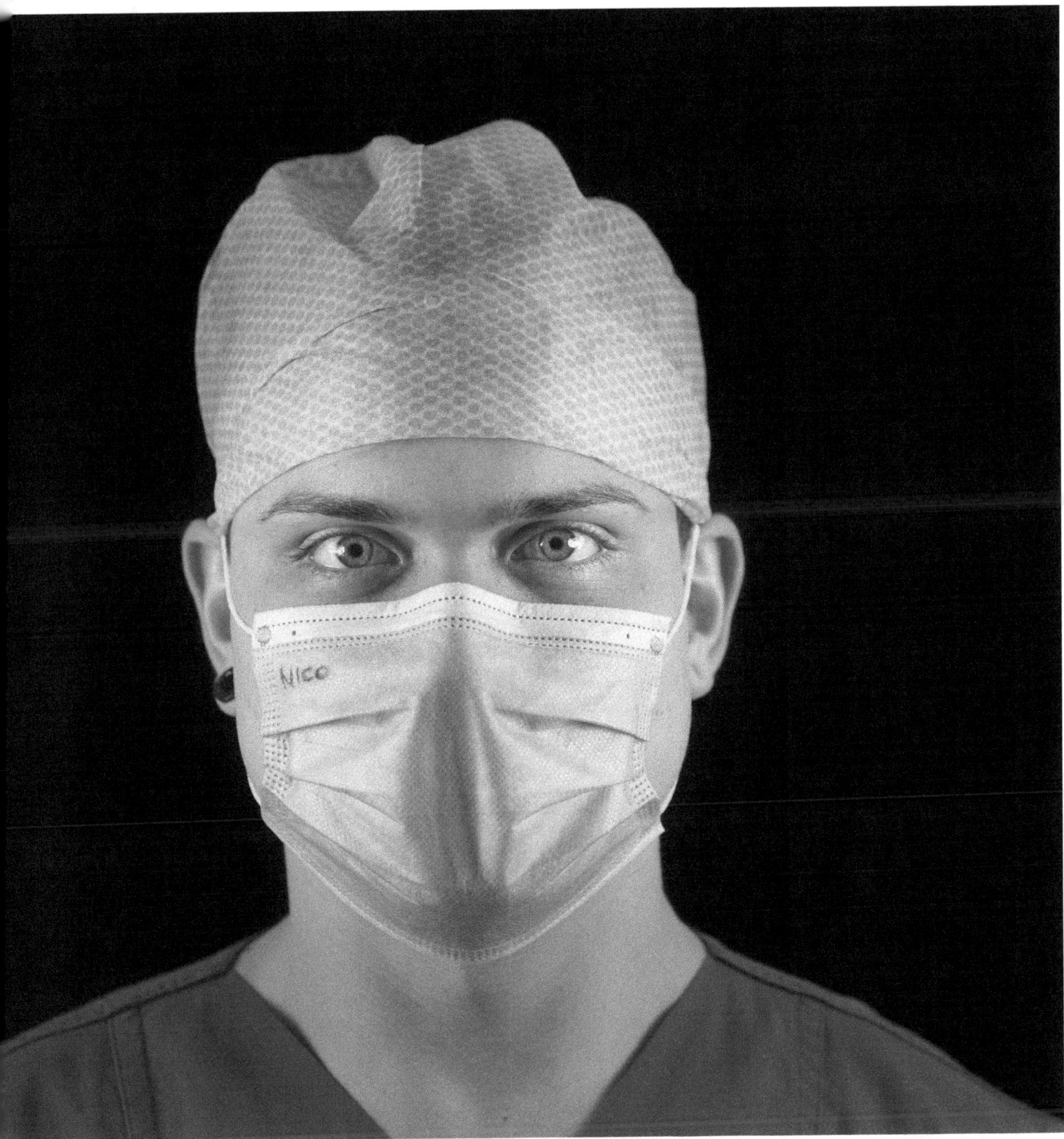

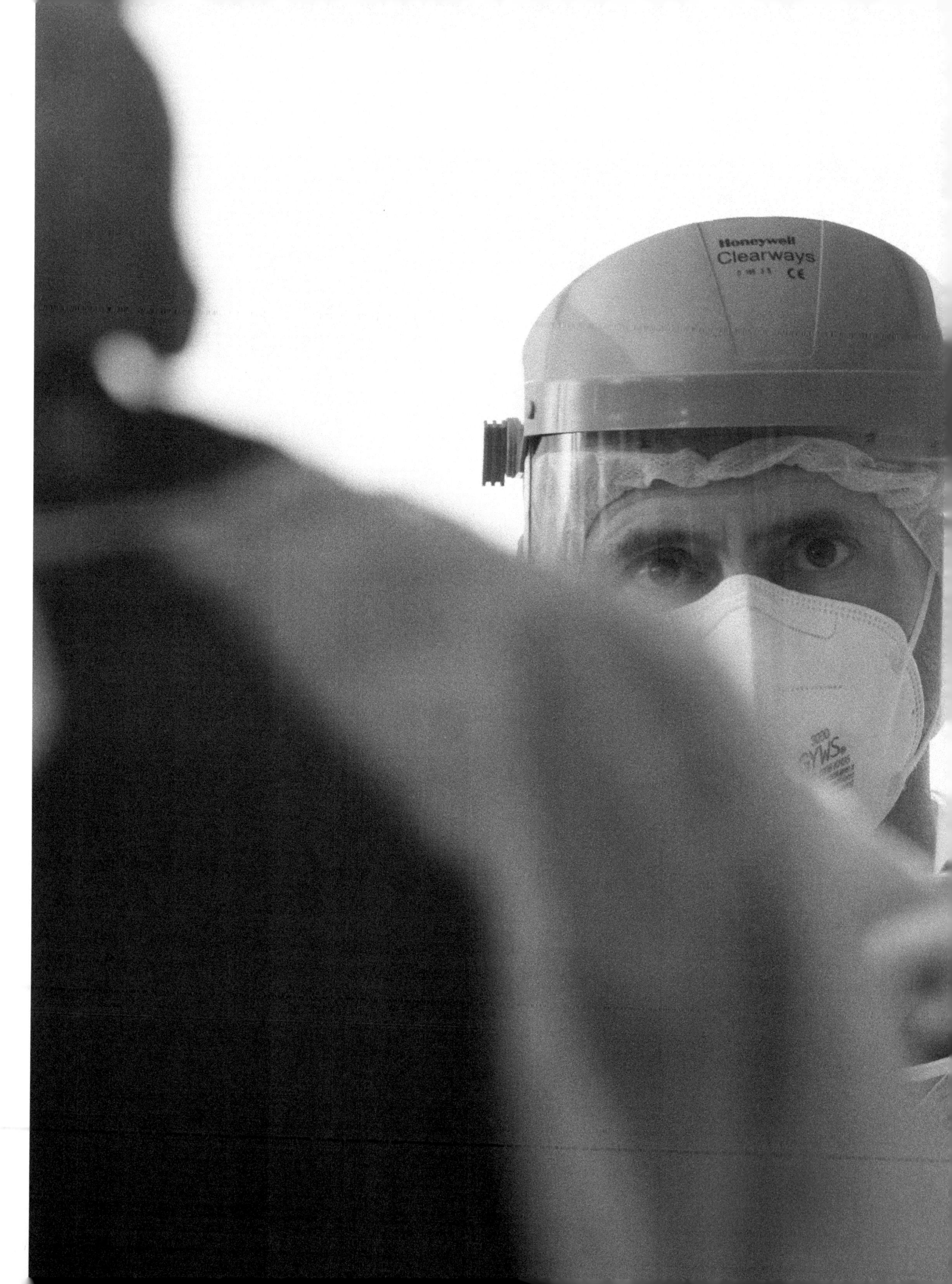

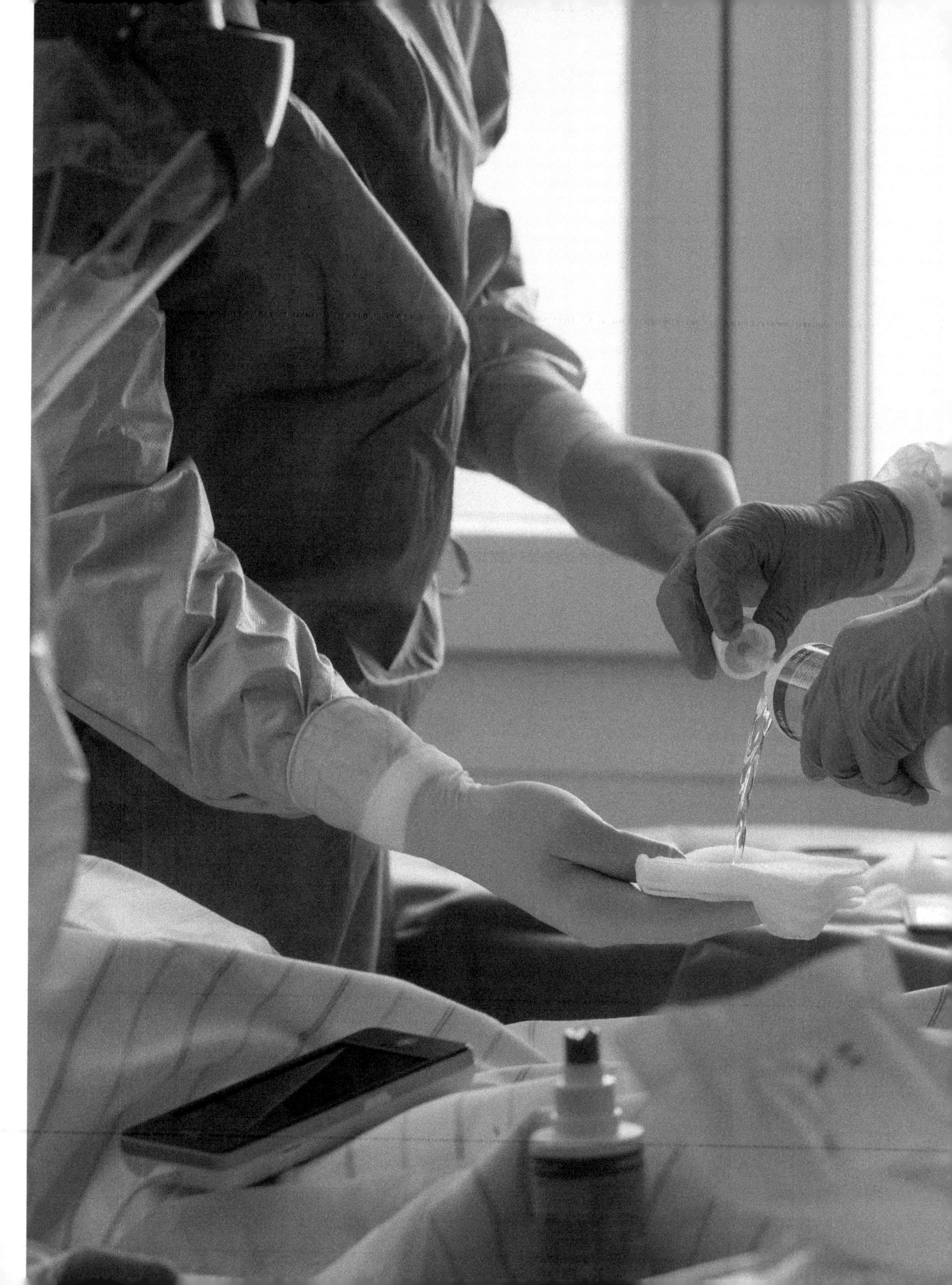

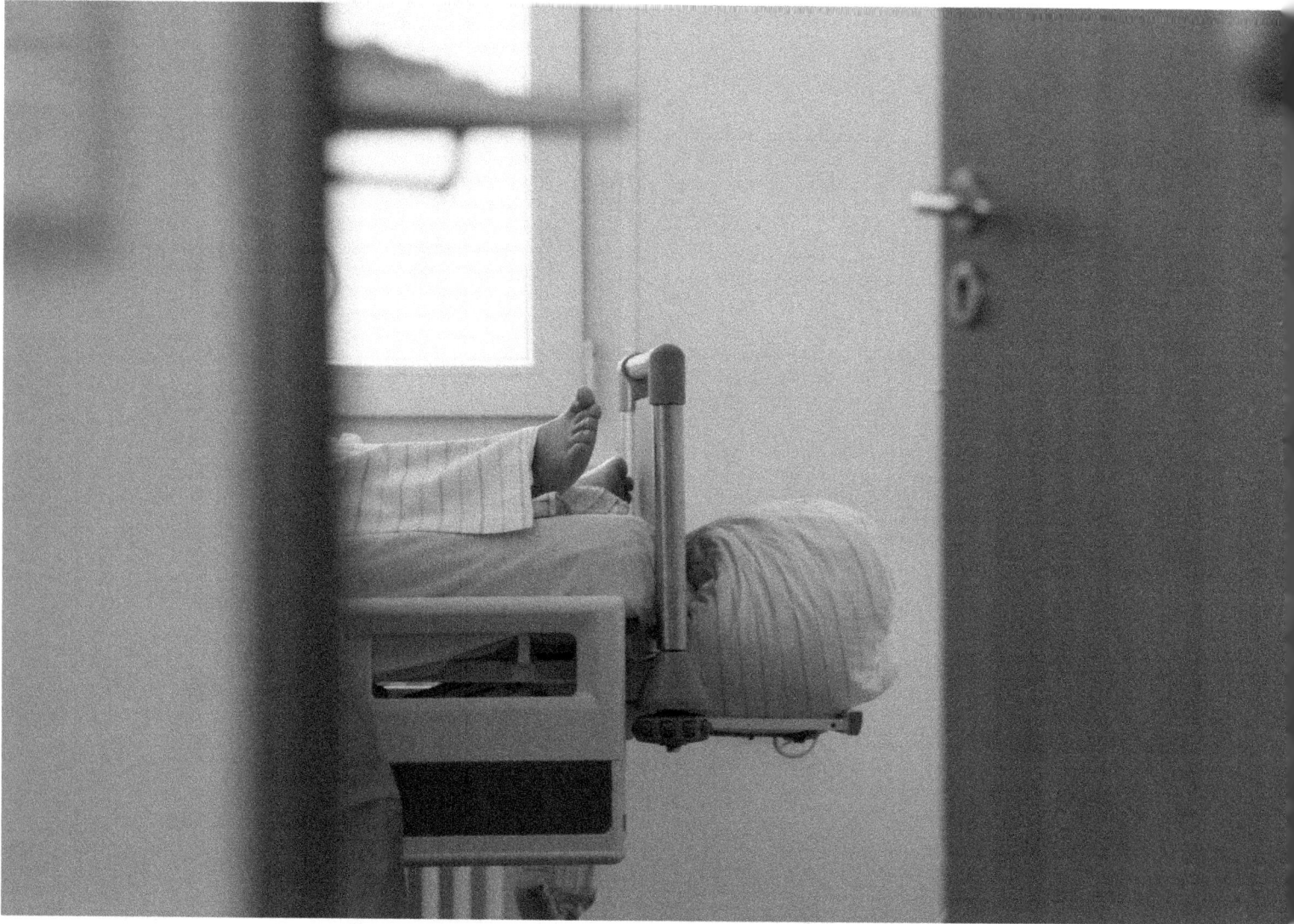

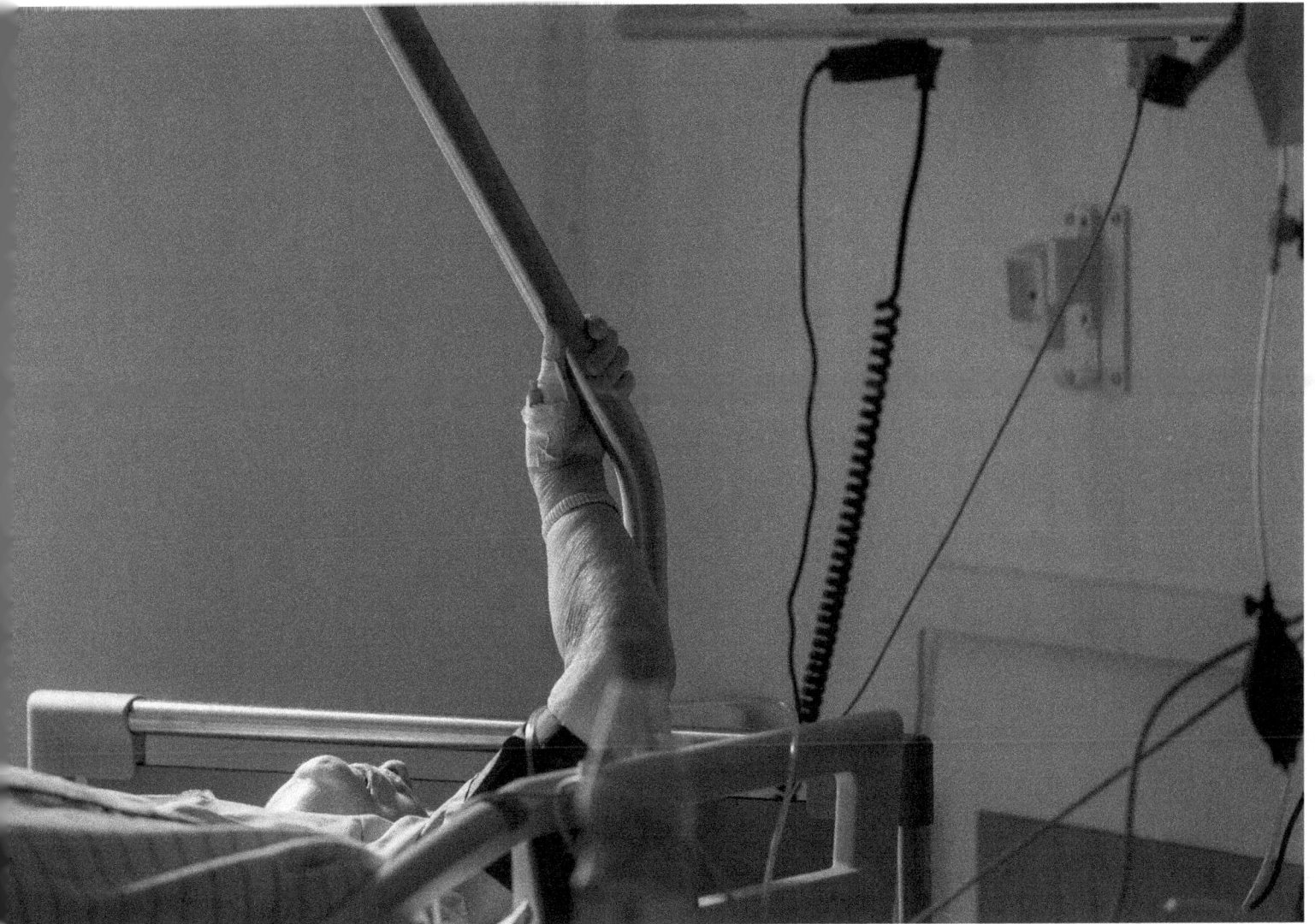

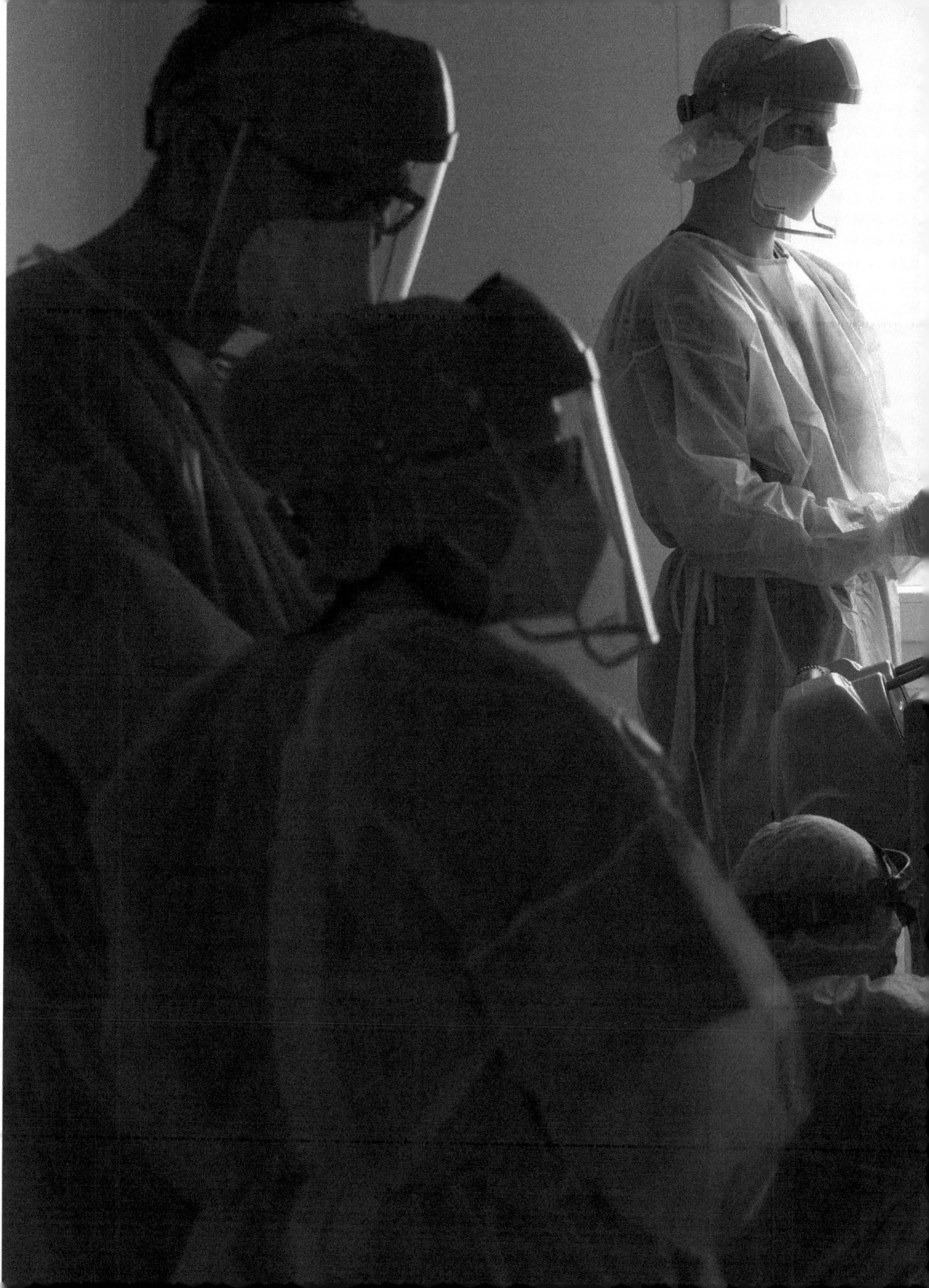

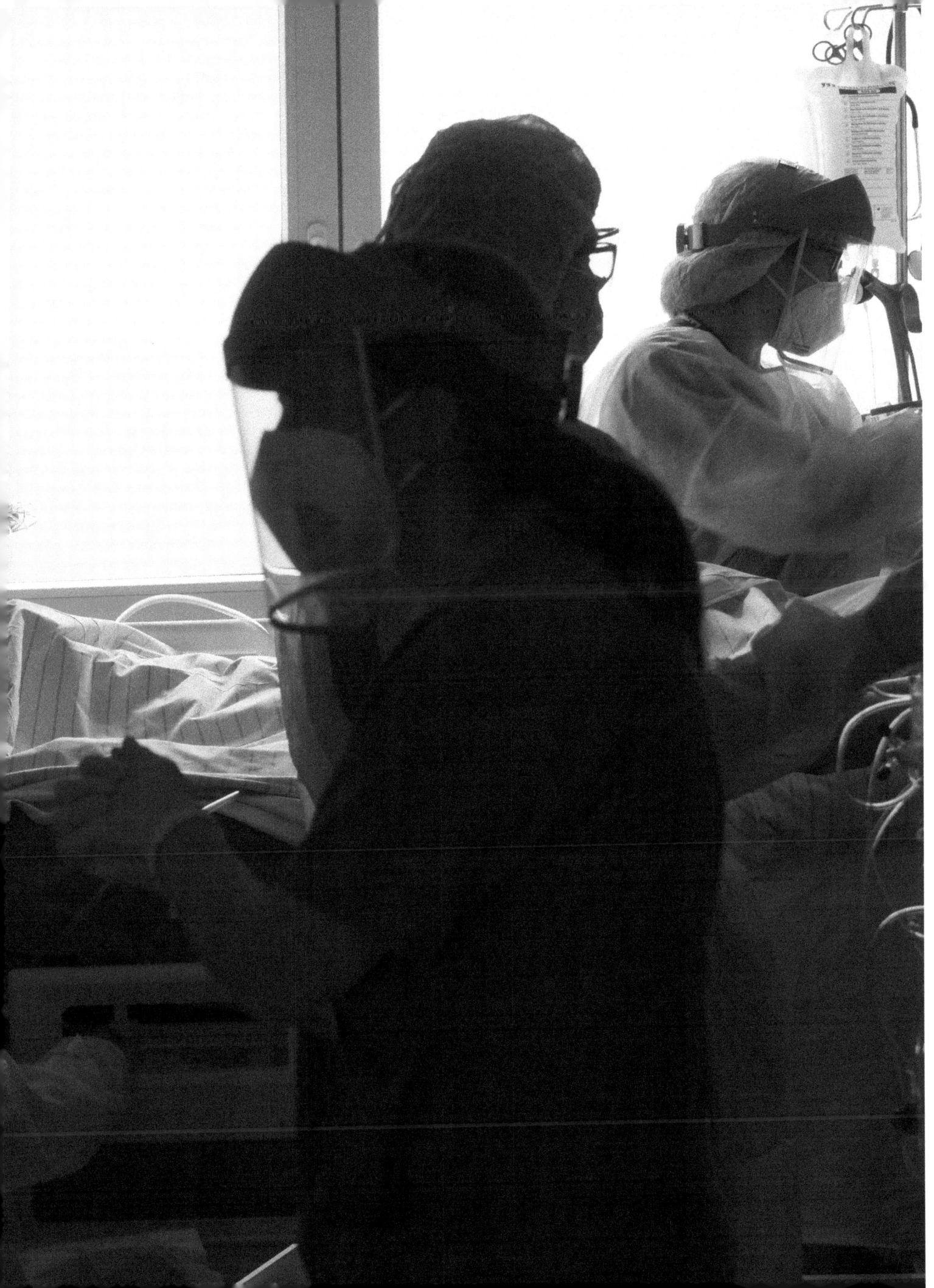

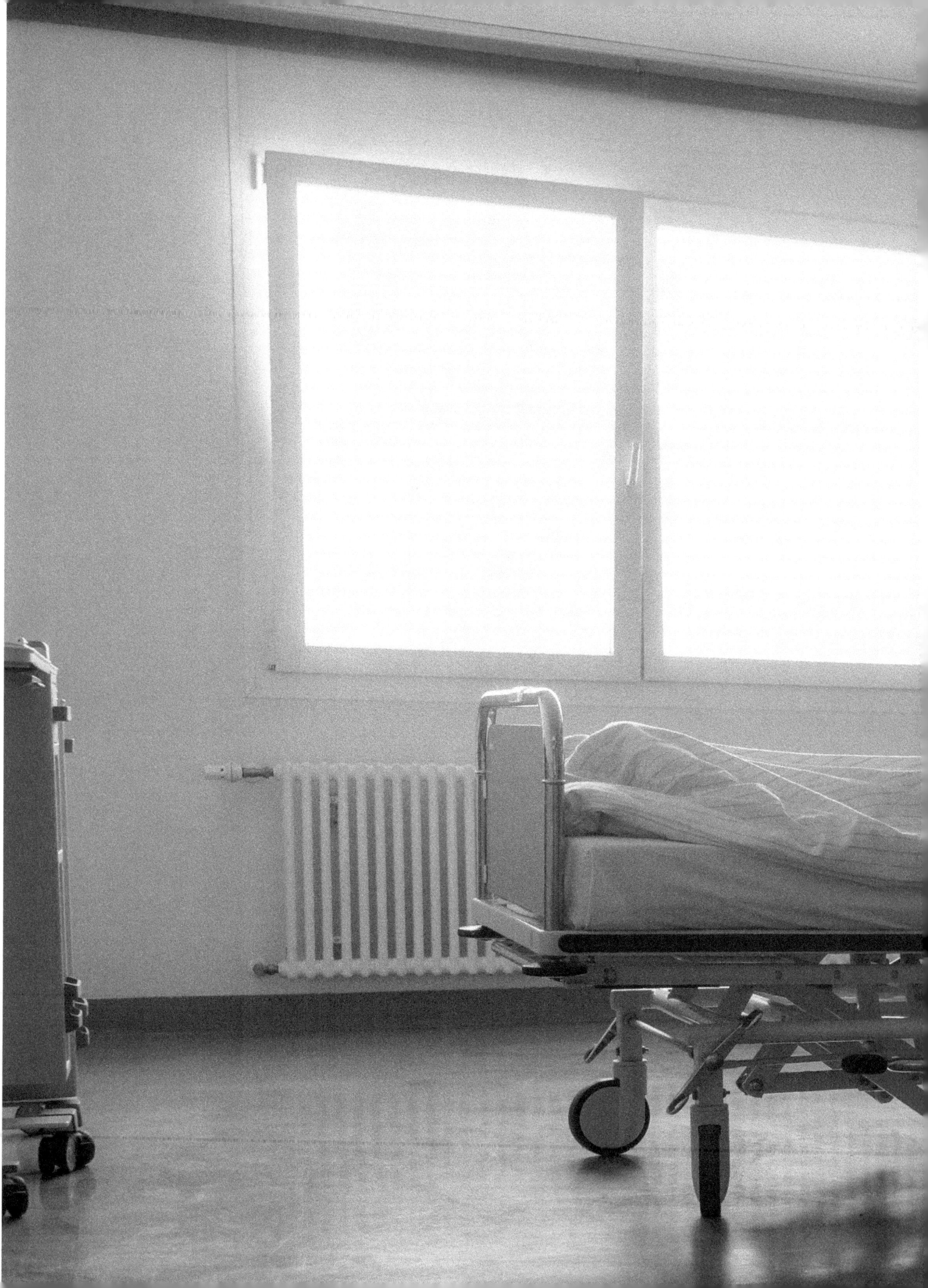

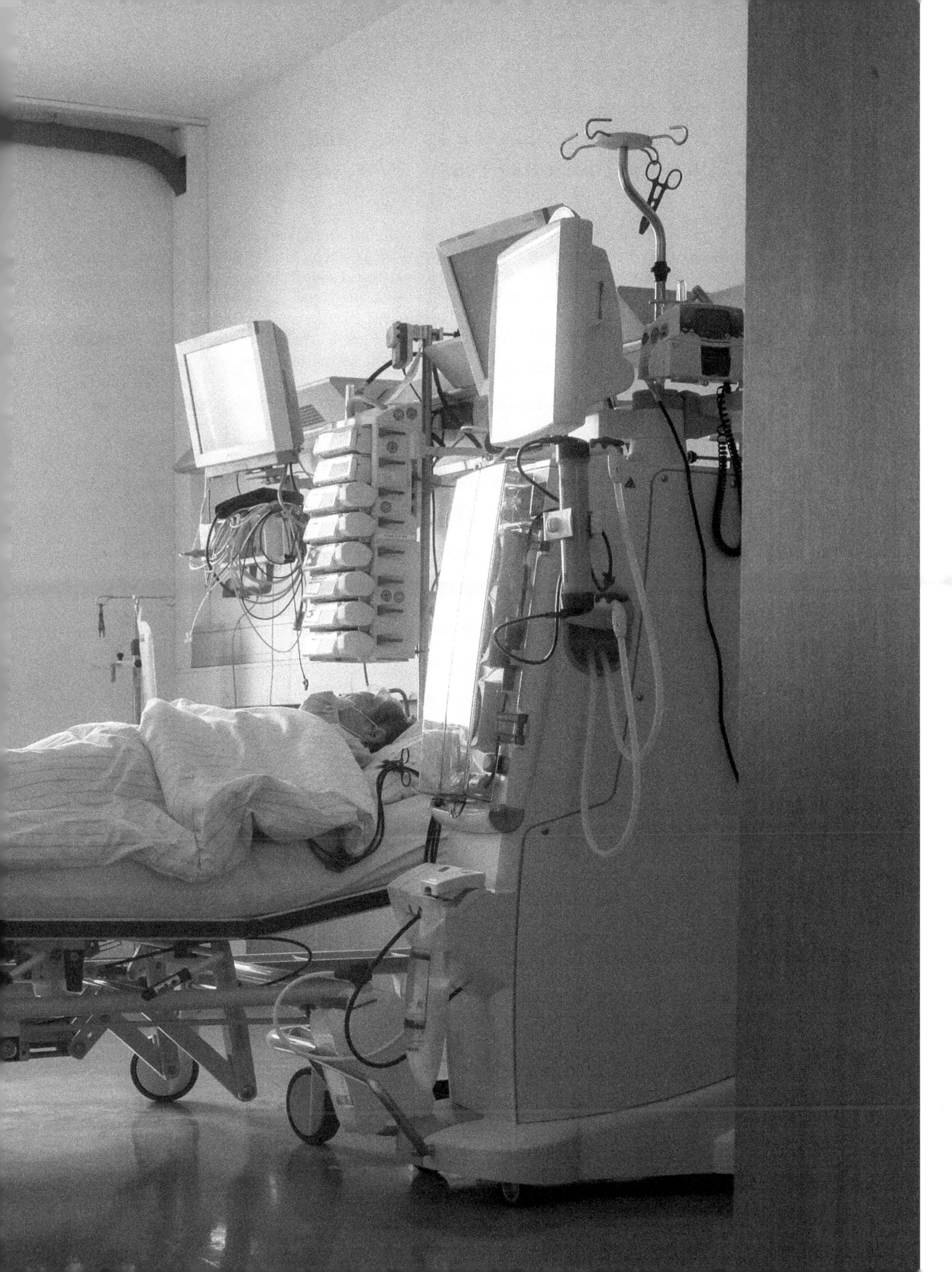

Maurice Weiss, with Felicitas Hentschke

"Why are People Dying in Our Hands?" was a Question that was Present Everywhere – An Interview

Maurice Weiss is a successful documentary photographer, filmmaker, and artist. He is a member of *Ostkreuz*, a Berlin-based agency run by twenty-two photographers. In all the years that cohorts of fellows have been coming to re:work, he has been responsible for their portraits. These portraits have become a brand mark of our center.

In the middle of lockdown, when all the streets in Germany seemed to have been swept empty, when little was known about coronavirus but all measures to fight it were being taken, he accepted a commission for the weekly magazine *Der Spiegel*. With his colleague, Jonathan Stock, he followed a medical team working at a clinic in Potsdam, Germany, which would be quickly expanded into a coronavirus clinic. The clinic made headlines for its many sudden deaths, dubbed the "Black Ward." The piece by Stock and Weiss was published under the same title in April 2020.[1]

We asked him if he could imagine putting together a contribution for this book from the material he collected at the clinic. We also asked him if he could use his visual language to tell us something about the work of the medical staff – the doctors, nurses, and volunteers – in this state of emergency; how they tried to help infected people with inadequate equipment and little knowledge about how coronavirus was spread. The result is an impressive picture of the challenges facing this medical team. He contrasts a lack of material with an overwhelming load of technical equipment, behind which those affected by COVID-19 virtually disappeared. With his camera, he captured the helplessness and exhaustion of the staff, but also their courageous commitment.

In this interview we asked him not only about the "Black Ward," but also in general how he approaches coronavirus in his work and how coronavirus affects his work.

When we think about certain global moments in history – the first moon landing, or the 9/11 attacks on New York – most people who witnessed these defining events still vividly remember where they were and what they were doing at the time. Coronavirus is a different kind of event, more a kind of phase that comes with drastic measures and consequences for each and every one of us and that will remain in the collective consciousness for a long time. You were in Berlin, at home with your family. How did coronavirus affect your daily life and work?

A letter from our son's school was our first contact with coronavirus. That was on March 11, 2020. Some teachers at his school had been infected with COVID-19 while skiing in Austria, so our seventeen-year-old son had to stay at home in quarantine for two weeks, along with a thousand fellow students. Shortly after, when features and other jobs were called off, the *corona effect* hit me personally. My colleagues and I started to feel uneasy. We were wondering what we would still be allowed to do, and how we could respond to this event, the coronavirus. There's nothing more challenging than attempting to capture in images the disappearance of everyday life and the

---

1 Jonathan Stock and Maurice Weiss (Photos), "The Black Ward. Infected Doctors, Dead Patients, the Public Prosecutor's Office Checks: In the Ernst von Bergmann Clinic in Brandenburg, the Situation Apparently Got Out of Control. What Exactly Happened – a Log," *Der Spiegel*, April 17, 2020, 1:56 pm, htps://www.spiegel.de/panorama/ernst-von-bergmann-klinikum-in-potsdam-die-schwarze-station-a-00000000-0002-0001-0 000-000170518572, accessed September 15, 2020.

sudden silence descending on a large city. My family and I took to escaping to the countryside every weekend. We went on long bike rides exploring remote parts of Brandenburg, taking along a picnic and trying to stay away from people.

What was your experience with coronavirus in Germany? As someone who is also at home in France, did you compare coronavirus policies in both countries?

It was the first warm days in Berlin. In my neighborhood there is a café where, in the spring, everyone meets at about five o'clock for a kind of aperitif. The regular guests were now divided. Surprisingly, it was the middle-aged men in particular who continued to meet – until mid-March, encouraging each other by insisting that coronavirus couldn't be worse than a normal flu. My other neighbors became extremely cautious and either stopped coming altogether or avoided close contact with other people. Thanks to my experience with pandemics in Asia and Africa, right from the beginning I refused to believe that COVID-19 was merely another flu. And very soon, even my not-so-careful neighbors began to follow the new rules.

But aside from this very personal experience, I was surprised at how quickly people in Berlin became disciplined – apart from the panic buying in supermarkets and brawls over rolls of toilet paper during the initial phase of the lockdown. I still remember telephone calls with my Italian friends in Milano. They were warning me that everything was a lot worse than we could imagine in Berlin. And my friends in Paris were shocked about the strict and determined approach taken by Macron and his government, with high fines for breaking the new regulations. In my small village in the Pyrenees, with a couple of hundred inhabitants, the same rules applied as in Paris. They watched with a certain degree of envy how each state in Germany was adopting individual restrictions according to the number of local coronavirus cases.

How did it come about that you were asked to document the Ernst-von-Bergmann hospital in Brandenburg?

The assignment to document the coronavirus ward of the Ernst-von-Bergmann hospital in Potsdam came via the *Spiegel's* picture editors. With a lot of luck and thorough research, Jonathan Stock, a *Spiegel* reporter, had gained the confidence of one of the senior physicians at the clinic and was invited to cover events on the ward for three weeks. My task was the images. There was some discussion on the potential risks associated with this assignment due to my age. But in the end, the two of us decided to go ahead.

I sourced protective suits and acquired some masks for us from a paint shop. A friend had ordered millions of face masks from China and had a couple at home that he gave me. We hoped that this would allow us to visit the ward and save us from being turned away. Personal protective equipment was almost impossible to get hold of at the time, and we knew that they wouldn't be able to spare us anything from their stocks.

When we arrived at the hospital, the press officer briefed us on the health risks, regulations, and restrictions. After that we were allowed to move around freely. The only remaining question for us was how this would affect us personally. How should we protect ourselves and our families? To avoid infecting loved ones, some of the hospital staff had even moved out of their homes. We then developed our own routine: we took many more showers than usual, changed clothes when moving between locations, and disinfected our equipment. In this regard we were no different from the rest of the staff at the hospital.

At first the idea was to document the set-up of the specialized coronavirus wards. Expecting a 'wave' of infections similar to the one witnessed in Italy in early March, all available equipment, even equipment that was no longer in use, beds, and other medical instruments were gathered together. There were three coronavirus wards, a white ward for mild cases, where people were brought mainly to be isolated, a grey ward for more severe cases requiring more intensive medical care, and a black ward, where patients were fighting for their lives. This was the ward we were on.

The staff here had received special training. All of us were very worried because we didn't know how dangerous the virus would be for us. Little was known about how the virus spreads and its clinical course. We quickly became part of the team and were allowed to be on the ward whenever we wanted. We attended all team meetings and discussions. But I didn't take pictures there. I felt it was important to collect as much background information as possible. The rest of the time the two of us split up and only met to talk about specific issues. We also shared advice or called each other whenever something was happening that seemed potentially relevant to both of us.

Interestingly, at the time neither of us believed that getting infected would actually impact our health. We just thought that at least then we'd be immune. While I didn't get infected, Jonathan did. He told me I was lucky. He said that no one would want such an ugly disease. Since then I've become even more cautious.

When you were taking your pictures, did you already know the kind of story you were going to tell? When working, do you already have pictures in your mind that you would like to take? Are you sometimes surprised when in the end everything is very different from how you thought it would be?

Usually I approach stories intuitively. My favorite term in this regard is serendipity, or 'cultivated coincidence.' The idea is to understand the issues and the complexity of a situation, to remind myself that my knowledge is often piecemeal, and take a step back from my prejudices, expectations, and fears. If you manage to maintain such a state of mind throughout an entire job, meaningful pictures will usually emerge on their own. The main thing is to take your time and be patient. People open up in front of your camera, you learn to see problems and feelings through the eyes of the protagonists, and learn to separate right from wrong without being misled by clichés and sensationalism. Often people were grateful to be able to speak with us. And we learnt a lot about the mood, the breadth of the issues they were struggling with.

One of these coincidences involved a soldier in the French foreign legion who had volunteered to help on the ward. He had completed his training in my home town, Perpignan, so we immediately had a connection. We got along very well. He took me everywhere, even to the storerooms for equipment and supplies. And because his colleagues liked and trusted him, when they realized that he trusted us, we were welcomed wherever we went with him. His presence really opened doors for us.

Another coincidence, albeit less positive, was the lack of face masks and other personal protective equipment. Face masks were marked with the names of the people that were using them so they could be re-used the next day. Working with coronavirus patients requires a lot of staff. I gradually realized how important the names on the masks were because they enabled the team to communicate with each other. Because their faces are covered – their eyes are all you get to see – and the team members hardly knew each other, the names on the masks became a crucial means of communication.

A photo essay tells a story through pictures. What is your story?

At the time, the events we were witnessing at the hospital were breaking news, conveying the potential extent of the coronavirus disaster. Our focus was on how serious the situation was. Today, we know a lot more about the virus and we have been through this first wave of the crisis once already. Now, we are seeing the situation with new eyes, we feel differently, and our interest in the story unfolding at the hospital has shifted.

This is why I chose different pictures for this book than for the report in the *Spiegel*. Luckily, I was able to collect a lot of material, which allowed me to shift the focus and create a second photo series – without a commentary to support them. The people looking at these pictures will always see them through the lens of their own experiences and personal context: back in March, nobody knew much about the virus. Today, there is an incredible wealth of information and many people have experienced it personally in some way. We're beginning to understand and live with the virus, which is why it's not surprising that our individual perspectives are evolving and the same photos are beginning to tell new stories again.

I began compiling the photo series for this book three months after the pictures were taken. I, too, see the pictures differently now from how I did then. Pictures I initially discarded have become more interesting. And others that I thought were worth publishing then I now find too biased. For example, at the time, we thought it was important to include a number of pictures from the hospital's morgue. Today, knowing that the pandemic in Germany was comparatively mild and that Italy, Spain, and of course countries like the United States and Brazil are now suffering outbreaks of a very different quality, these pictures feel overly dramatic. Including them would distort the course of the outbreak in Germany.

In hindsight, the struggle for equipment, appliances, and drugs created an important momentum – the scarcity of masks, disinfectant, the high demand for ventilators, the shortage of beds, and the lack of staff, the capacity of staff to improvise. I admired the team for their endurance, their capacity to improvise and their courage. They put themselves at risk of becoming infected even though it was still completely unclear how bad the virus really was. My story therefore also talks about the team, the ties between them, their relationships with the patients, the virus, and the risks, their profession, and the confidence each of them had in their abilities. As we are still in the midst of the COVID-19 pandemic, I prefer to show these pictures in black and white. I'm convinced that the bleak yellow-green hospital colors that we see in the daily news only distract us from focusing on the work of the medical staff. In other words, the eyes of the hospital staff are easier to see in black and white photos.

What did you know about the people whose work you were portraying?

Initially nothing, but after three weeks, I was part of the team. Launching into such an assignment, it's important to earn people's trust. I depend on them to share their knowledge and experience with me and give me hints. This is the only way for me to do my work well. But I also want to avoid exploiting them and so I try to give them something in return based on the modest options at my disposal. One of the senior physicians asked me to document a new tracheostomy procedure. I have allowed the team use the images free of charge – as a thank you in exchange for their trust.

How do you work when you are shooting a story? Do you see what's important immediately?

The staff at the clinic was working around the clock. They were all exhausted and tense. "Why are people dying in our hands?" was a question that was present everywhere. On the coronavirus ward itself there weren't that many people dying. Deaths surged because the hospital administration decided to reorganize the wards and move people from one ward to another. This allowed the virus to spread throughout the hospital. Smear infection was considered the most plausible path of transmission at the time, and airborne transmission seemed unlikely. The hospital management failed to contain the outbreak, and the tabloids dubbed the hospital the "Black Ward" or "Clinic of

Death." The immediate victims of this badly researched and one-sided press coverage were the hospital staff. On top of the extra working hours and fears of becoming infected, they now were facing heavy criticism from their friends and families. As journalists, we were angry. Tabloid newspapers and television talk shows repeatedly asked me whether they could use my pictures. I refused, and I continue to refuse. I refused to release my pictures, because I had seen firsthand that the hospital staff were doing everything they could, to help patients. As I see it, the staff we worked with did not deserve the smear campaign that was unleashed upon them. Initially, the hospital was intended to admit patients during the coronavirus wave, in a special department. As deaths increased in other wards the entire hospital had to close.

At first, I coped well with working in an environment where people were fighting for other people's lives. When I take photos, I need to be focused. There are so many decisions I have to take at once that I block out any emotional responses. I can't let the unfolding events get to me. But once I've wrapped up the job, my experiences eventually do catch up on me and leave behind their scars.

You are a political person, you shoot stories for newspapers and magazines, photograph politicians and document their work. You travel the world to document defining events as they happen. You captured the fall of the Berlin Wall; in 2016, you visited the European borders to follow the so-called refugee crisis, and in 2017 you made a film about the 2015 attack on the Bataclan theatre in Paris. It doesn't surprise us at all that during the lockdown in Germany you decided to document a coronavirus hotspot. What is it that drives you?

That's a difficult question. It's a mix of curiosity and the desire to understand social and political contexts. I firmly believe that photography as a language with its own rules and syntax has something to add to texts. Especially in situations where words are simply not enough, images can spark people's interest in understanding complex issues. Photography has its roots in the Enlightenment, an era driven by a longing to understand the world, at the center of which stands the human being. It's about humans.

Thus, photography in Europe is deeply humanistic, a small tool to reflect the human condition. I feel bound to this tradition. The Enlightenment would be inconceivable without Renaissance paintings. Images are a key element of our culture: they create an 'image of humankind,' they create memories. The responsibility of someone who 'makes images' is as great as that of someone who writes books. Today it's photographers that create images of our world, and today's high-speed technology has significantly increased their responsibility of photographers. But that's another matter.

Social media, too, has made photography an important means of communication and often also of propaganda. An important part of my work in recent years has been to search for images that capture democratic processes. As politics is usually expressed in words, being able to understand and contextualize images is becoming more and more crucial, and making proper and sensible use of photography in the political arena remains an enormous challenge, in particular when it comes to countering the rise of populism across Europe.

You have been involved with re:work since 2009 and completed the portraits of all of our fellows. You have spoken with all of them, asked them about their research. This way you have learnt a lot about the history of work. You also contributed photos to the fifth volume of this book series, "To Be at Home. House, Work, and Self in the Modern World," with an impressive selection of photographs from your archive. You told us once that you would like to work on a long-term portrait of a researcher. What would that consist of? Would it focus on an issue related to the global history of work?

Digitalization has radically redefined journalistic and documentary photography. For decades, our collective visual memory was financed nearly exclusively by publishers and their editors. This is now fundamentally changing. Photographers hardly or only rarely have the means to produce meaningful visual narratives. At the same time, however, during exhibitions we feel that the public actually has a strong need for such narratives. At re:work I have repeatedly met talented researchers who spend years exploring exciting issues that I believe it would be worthwhile for a photographer to document. My hope is that images can be a tool to make these issues more readily accessible to a larger and broader public. To me it wouldn't make a difference whether I was documenting steel workers in China or gold miners in South Africa. Their work, how they interact with other workers, their tools, their rhythms of work and rest, hierarchies, and the spaces that define working conditions can be identified and described for any kind of work. Let's get started!

Do you have a favorite picture? Which picture from the series would you choose if you had to, and what would its title be?

My favorite picture is the one where you see a doctor holding huge amounts of equipment (photograph no. 19), which he seems to be offering as a kind of religious sacrifice. Or the photo of the young nurses about to embark on their first real test, risking a glimpse of the world outside (photograph no. 1), also tells a story I feel is important.

The Health System in Which We Live

Marcel van der Linden
Nurses[1]

Nurses' Day is celebrated annually around the world on May 12, Florence Nightingale's birthday. In 2020 – Nightingale's bicentennial – the holiday received much more attention than usual. Across all continents, officials and celebrities were extolling the virtues of those women and men who were risking their lives during the coronavirus pandemic to save COVID-19 patients under very difficult circumstances. Residents under lockdown in Spain, Italy, and elsewhere stood on their balconies or at their windows to offer mass applause to health care workers. *The Hindu*, the Indian daily, praised the nurses, "who have been rendering commendable service in fighting the dreaded coronavirus." The pope released a message saying, "At this critical moment [...] we have rediscovered the fundamental importance of the role being played by nurses and midwives." Britain's Prince Charles informed social media that the royal family wanted "to join in the chorus of thank yous to nursing and midwifery staff across the country and indeed the world." Yo Yo Ma, the famous musician, posted the Sarabande from Bach's *Cello Suite No. 3* on his Twitter page with the following message: "This is for the health care workers on the frontlines. Your ability to balance human connection and scientific truth in service of us all gives me hope." And the World Health Organization (WHO) designated 2020 the Year of the Nurse and the Midwife.

Naturally, millions of health care workers appreciated these laudatory words and gestures. But the critical voices were not far behind. It soon became clear that many nurses were working under unacceptable conditions, lacking facilities for undisturbed sleep; without clear guidelines or any influence on decision-making. Robert Mardini, the director-general of the International Committee of the Red Cross, emphasized a further problem: "It's heartening to see many communities praise and thank nurses, but it's distressing that other nurses face harassment, stigmatization, and even attack."

A Global View

According to the WHO, the global nursing workforce is 27.9 million, of which 19.3 million (sixty-nine percent) are professional nurses, 6.0 million (twenty-two percent) associate professional nurses, and 2.6 million (nine percent) who are not classified either way.[2]

Generally, health care workers are much respected. Every year, Gallup, the advisory company based in Washington, DC, asks a representative sample of the United States population: "How would you rate the honesty and ethical standards of people in these different fields?" Nurses are consistently seen as the most trustworthy profession. Table 1 summarizes a few of Gallup's results.

1 Special thanks to my companion Alice Mul, who is not only a political scientist but, more importantly, a baccalaureate nurse. The article was finished at the end of July 2020.
2 *State of the World's Nursing 2020. Executive Summary* (Geneva: WHO, 2020): 3.

Table 1: Professions rated "very high," United States, 2010–19 (percentages)

	2019	2015	2010
Nurses	85	85	81
Medical doctors	65	67	66
High school teachers	49	60	67
Police officers	54	56	57
Clergy	40	45	53
Bankers	28	25	23
Members of Congress	12	8	9
Car salespeople	9	8	7

Source: Gallup's annual honesty and ethics of professions ratings.

The working and living conditions of nurses differ enormously – between countries, and sometimes even within countries. For a start, their incomes are very unequal. Even among the rich countries, salaries vary widely; in the OECD they range from 28,000 to 114,000 euros per year.[3] Elsewhere health care workers are extremely poor. The distribution of nurses is very uneven too. The density of nursing personnel varies from 0.7 per 10,000 population in Guatemala and 1.2 in Guinea to 175.4 in Switzerland and 182.2 in Norway (Figure 1).[4]

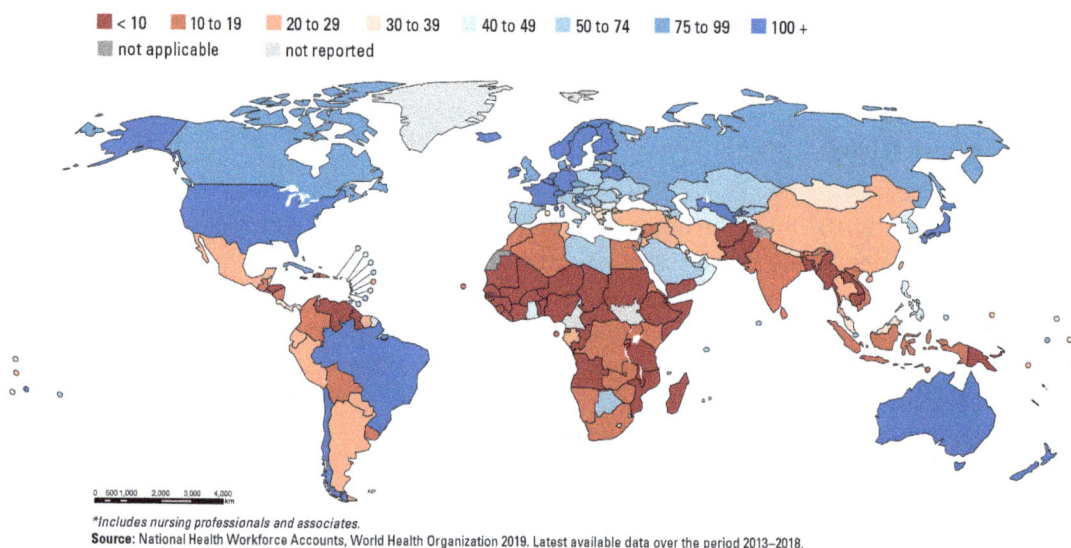

Figure 1   Density of nursing personnel per 10 000 population in 2018

■ < 10   ■ 10 to 19   ■ 20 to 29   30 to 39   40 to 49   ■ 50 to 74   ■ 75 to 99   ■ 100 +
■ not applicable   not reported

*Includes nursing professionals and associates.
Source: National Health Workforce Accounts, World Health Organization 2019. Latest available data over the period 2013–2018.

---

3 Nina Jerzy, "In diesen Ländern verdienen Krankenschwestern am meisten," *Capital*, July 21, 2020.
4 Source: Map quoted after: *State of the World's Nursing 2020.*

The density of medical doctors is also uneven, but with a divergent geographical distribution: Cuba is located at the world's top (84.2), Somalia at the bottom (0.2).[5] Consequently, the nurse-to-physician ratio varies enormously from country to country, and in large parts of the world there is a significant shortage of both nurses and physicians. In sub-Saharan Africa there are five times as many nurses as physicians, while the ratio of both physicians and nurses to the population is low. In India, by contrast, the overall ratio of physicians and nurses to the population is low in comparison with many other low- and middle-income countries, but there are only 1.5 nurses for each physician. In China, the ratio is 1:1. According to the health economist Jack Needleman, such differences "clearly reflect variations in how care is organized and delivered, the relative role of physicians and nurses, and perhaps the relative cost of, or historic capacity for, educating physicians versus nurses. Countries with low nurse-to-physician ratios may be missing opportunities to expand access and services faster and at lower cost."[6]

Table 2: The global distribution of medical doctors and nurses/midwives in 2018

Region	Density of medical doctors (per 10,000 population)	Density of nursing and midwifery personnel (per 10,000 population)	Nurse-to-physician ratio
Africa	3.0	10.1	3.4
Americas	24.0	83.3	3.5
Southeast Asia	8.1	17.9	2.2
Europe	34.1	81.3	2.4
Eastern Mediterranean	10.1	14.5	1.4
Western Pacific	18.8	36.3	1.9
Global	15.6	37.6	2.4

Source: World Health Statistics 2020 (Geneva: WHO, 2020), p. 64, plus calculations by the author.

Rise of the Medical Hierarchy

A global view reveals huge differences in the position of nurses, but also that, even in the richest countries, few are really well rewarded or enjoy good working conditions. For a better understanding of these facts, we need to dive into the past. The position of nurses has undergone major and regionally uneven changes over time.

For many centuries there have been women and men who devoted an important part of their lives to the care of the sick and old. In the Islamic world, Rufaidah bint Sa'ad is a well-known name; she was an early follower of the prophet in the eighth century. As a doctor's daughter, she trained other nurses and set up hospital tents in times of war. In the Christian world, nuns some-

5 *World Health Statistics 2020* (Geneva: WHO, 2020), Annex 2, Part 3.
6 Jack Needleman, "Nurses, the Costs of Healthcare, and the Pursuit of Value in Health Care," in Lindsey Williamson, ed., *Nurses: A Voice to Lead Nursing the World to Health* (Geneva: International Council of Nurses, 2020): 33–34.

times performed similar tasks – and later also knightly organizations such as the Maltese Order. In large parts of the world, relatives and servants took care of the sick. In case of illness, the Chinese emperor was tended to by his prime minister and members of the royal family.

It was in Europe that important changes began to take place. First of all, medical science developed rapidly from the eighteenth century onward. It became, for example, common practice to measure body temperature in patients, which was estimated by putting a hand on the chest or the inflamed area. A little later the importance of hygiene also became clearer. The end of the nineteenth century saw a development in the science surrounding pain relief and antiseptics. The role of nursing also gradually changed. Hygienic treatment, in which nursing care supplemented medical procedures, became more important. Because the conditions for this could not be guaranteed at home, care moved to the appropriate institutions – also for the wealthy. This stimulated the growth of hospitals. Important innovations seem to have mainly taken place in Britain, with pioneers such as Elizabeth Fry and Florence Nightingale, and in Germany, where the deaconess clinic in Kaiserswerth-Düsseldorf was founded by the local pastor Theodor Fliedner. New, 'modern' forms of nursing increasingly tried to incorporate scientific insights. It was no longer just about wound care or washing patients, but also about administering medication and care plans, monitoring diets, and recording vital statistics.

Second, the social composition of nursing staff changed. During much of the nineteenth century, it was mainly upper-class ladies who were interested in innovative nursing – both Fry and Nightingale, for instance, were from wealthy backgrounds. But the number of available ladies was limited and soon women from the lower classes also had to be recruited to work as nurses. Many ladies did not like this. In the 1880s in England, the then most highly developed country, a number of upper-class nurses, led by Ethel Bedford Fenwick, started campaigning for the introduction of a register. This would codify the difference between trained and untrained nurses – an obvious thought, because over the years there had been a proliferation of hospitals with very diverse training courses. But, according to Mark Bostridge:

> Mrs Bedford Fenwick and her cohorts had another major goal in mind. They wanted to exclude working-class nurses, and make nursing a profession for ladies only. Under their plan, nurses in training would be paid no salary, and would be charged the sum of five guineas to be examined in writing, certificated, and, finally, registered. In this way they hoped to deter those they viewed as undesirable from entering the profession while, at the same time, encouraging middle-class entrants, with a liberal education 'and a refined home training.' Enhanced social status was a clear aim of those lobbying for registration. They hoped to achieve parity with the medical profession.[7]

A complicated power struggle thus took place. The doctors, relying on increased medical knowledge, aspired for full control of their patients. The 'ladies' considered themselves as equals of the doctors, had great difficulty in subordinating to them, and wished to distinguish themselves from the lower-class nurses. The lower-class nurses, however, viewed nursing not only as a vocation but also as a livelihood. A long and mostly silent battle arose around these issues, and this was not limited the United Kingdom. Nurses began to be subject to national regulation in an increasing number of countries, starting with New Zealand in 1901. In the following decades many other countries followed. But there were also paid nursing courses that enabled working-class women to become registered health workers. The 'proletarianization' of the nurses also promoted the consolidation of the medical model, whereby the nurse is a manual worker who helps the doctor and

---

7 Mark Bostridge, *Florence Nightingale* (Harmondsworth: Penguin, 2009): 502–503.

is allowed to make very few decisions herself. In this way a new health care hierarchy developed. At the top were the medical doctors, who supervised a group of assistants, the nurses, consisting of an upper layer (registered nurses) and a lower stratum (non-registered nurses).

This health care hierarchy spread around the world from the late nineteenth century. It was introduced in a wide variety of social relationships. In Senegal, for example, until after World War I, all nurses had been military men because:

> French wars of conquest of West Africa in the nineteenth century gave rise to the need for medical auxiliaries to assist army surgeons and doctors and to administer care to sick and wounded soldiers. As the ranks of the colonial military mostly comprised African recruits, so too did this early corps of medical assistants. Thus, men formed the core of both the nursing and the medical professions from an early stage.

It was only in the 1920s and 1930s that female nurses and midwives began to appear.[8] In other parts of the world it has long been inconceivable that 'Ladies' would take care of the sick outdoors. In Imperial China, young women could only leave the house with a chaperon; it was impossible for them to take care of patients outside their family. Nursing was only done by lower-class women, who were often illiterate. The president of the Chinese Nurses' Association recalled the late 1930s: "I was told by one of the older nurses that it was necessary to mark the bottles so that all nurses would understand, for example, an eye would be drawn on the zinc sulphate solution, indicating eye medicine, and a hand on the lysol solution bottle, indicating its use for washing hands."[9] In addition, traditional Chinese medicine was still influential (and remains so today). It took a long time before nursing became a real profession. At the time of the founding of the People's Republic in 1949, there were 183 nursing schools and 32,800 nurses in China.[10] Even today, the country has only 26.6 nurses per 10,000 inhabitants. That is a small number compared with, for example, Germany (132.4) or the United States (145.5).

Transformation of the Medical Hierarchy

Two developments disrupted the medical hierarchy in the course of the twentieth century. The first we may call registration and specialization. The technical knowledge of doctors grew in leaps and bounds, and as soon as a new technique had become routine and had to be applied often, it was taught to nurses. For example, intramuscular injections, blood pressure measuring, intravenous injections, or the application of an infusion. And because not every nurse had access to all knowledge, specialization gradually took hold. Today, the differentiation of functions is impressive. The Canadian Nurses Association currently distinguishes twenty-two practice areas, including cardiovascular, critical care, emergency, gastroenterology, peri-anesthesia, and psychiatric and mental health nursing. This increasing specialization has naturally promoted professional awareness. As such, organizations were established early on to develop ethical standards; they also lobbied, dealt

8 Jonathan Cole, "Engendering Health: Pronatalist Politics and the History of Nursing and Midwifery in Colonial Senegal, 1914–1967," in Patricia D'Antonio, Julie A. Fairman and Jean C. Whelan, eds., *Routledge Handbook on the Global History of Nursing* (London and New York: Routledge, 2013): 114–130, at 117.
9 Evelyn Lin, "Nursing in China," *The American Journal of Nursing* 38 (January 1938): 1–8, at 3.
10 Francis K.Y. Wong and Yue Zhao, "Nursing Education in China: Past, Present and Future," *Journal of Nursing Management* 20 (2012): 38–44, at 39.

with public relations, and provided education and training: for example, the American Nurses Association (1896), the Dutch Nosokomos (1900), the German Berufsorganisation der Krankenpflegerinnen (1903), and the French Association Nationale des Infirmières Diplômées (1924). The educational level of nurses increased dramatically, especially after World War II. Symptomatic was the introduction in the 1960s in the United States of so-called clinical specialists: nurses with a Master's degree who are experts in evidence-based practices.

The second development was the enormous expansion of health care. There is much debate about the causes, but the facts are clear. Health care expenditure as a proportion of gross domestic product has risen rapidly virtually everywhere. According to the WHO, it is approximately six percent in middle-income countries, seven percent in low-income countries, and ten percent in high-income countries. The strongest growth within OECD countries occurred in the United States, where the share has risen from 4.8 percent in 1960 to 14.7 percent in 2003; a close second was Switzerland (from 4.8 percent to 11.3 percent) (Figure 2).

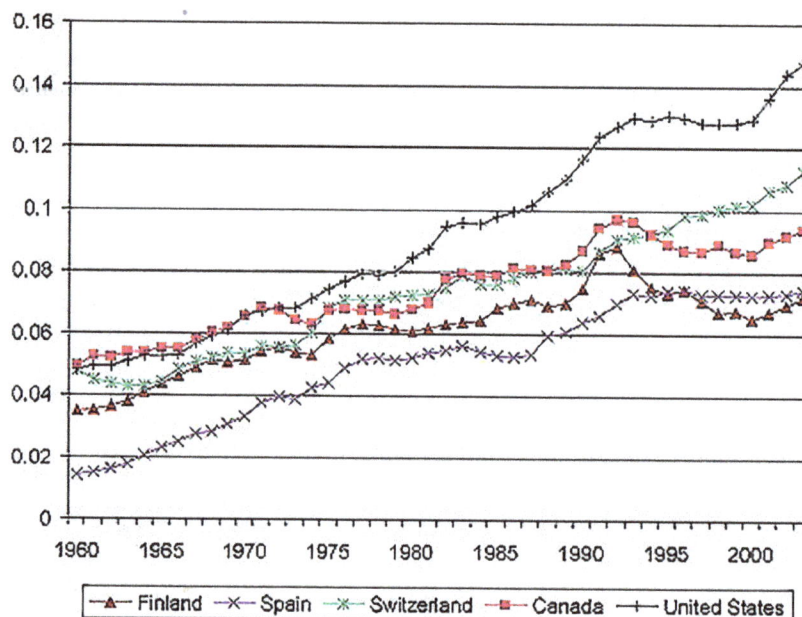

Figure 2: Health care expenditure as percentage of gross domestic product, 1960–2003

Source: OECD Health Data 2005 CD ROM.

But this expansionary trend was undermined from two sides. The fabulous growth of health care has, of course, been accompanied by sizeable investments in medical equipment; wages are often by far the largest cost item, with the cost of nurses being the most significant. This is even more true for poor countries than for rich countries. In response, nurses' wages are reduced, with their workloads increased, their working hours reduced, and tasks transferred from registered nurses to non-professional nursing staff. It goes without saying that this does not improve the working conditions for nurses, nor the quality of health care. At the same time, the influence of market thinking has increased considerably since the 1980s. As a result, in many countries the number of hospital beds has declined, for example, in the United States from 889,600 in 1985 to 641,395 in 2010, and in

Germany from 665,565 in 1991 to 497,182 in 2017.[11] This was made possible through a drastic reduction in the average length of stay per patient.

Nurses' work is frequently arduous and underpaid, especially following recent economic changes. One consequence of this is a shortage of nurses in many parts of the world. Globally, it is estimated that this amounts to between six and nine million nurses. The uneven distribution of prosperity across the world is reflected, among other things, in the fact that large numbers of nurses are lured from the poor countries to the wealthy, so that the health care situation in the poor countries deteriorates even further. Developed nations have seen a sixty-percent increase in the number of foreign-educated health care professionals since 2010.[12] "While nurse migration affects different countries in different ways, there is a troubling pattern of growing disparity in which poor nations with the fewest nurses are losing them to wealthy countries with the most nurses. As numerous reports have noted, developing nations often publicly fund nurse education, making the loss of nurses to wealthy countries in effect a massive public subsidy from the poorest to the richest areas of the world."[13]

But there is also another consequence: the combination of registration and specialization on the one hand and numerical growth on the other had an unintended result: nurses became trade unionists. "The historical trend among registered nurses has been a shift away from narrow 'professionalism' toward unionism, that is, a realization by at-the-bed staff nurses that, like all other employees, their working conditions must be protected and their rights nailed down by unions in collective bargaining."[14] Any of the old professional organizations that were not converted into unions simply lost influence. This development began hesitantly in the 1950s, when nurses were typically difficult to organize because they assumed that unionization would inevitably lead to hospital strikes. Moreover, the idea "that a hospital worker might desert her 'calling' and leave a patient on the operating table to join a picket line was a frightening prospect to both patients and the community at large."[15] Despite these obstacles, the trend toward unionization has continued. Today, of the 630 organizations currently affiliated with Public Services International (PSI) in Geneva, there are now 230 unions representing health workers, with approximately seven million members; eighty percent of these are nurses.

---

11 Neil A. Halpern et al., "Critical Care Medicine in the United States 1985– 2000: An Analysis of Bed Numbers, Use, and Costs," *Critical Care Medicine* 32 (June 2004): 1254–1259; Neil A. Halpern et al., "Trends in Critical Care Beds and Use Among Population Groups and Medicare and Medicaid Beneficiaries in the United States: 2000–2010," *Critical Care Medicine* 44 (August 2016): 1490–1499; Verena Kreilinger, Winfried Wolf and Christian Zeller, *Corona, Kapital, Krise: Für eine solidarische Alternative in Zeiten der Pandemie* (Köln: Papyrossa, 2020).

12 Joan Zolot, "International Nurse Migration," *The American Journal of Nursing* 119 (2019): 16, https://doi.org/10.1097/01.NAJ.0000559791.78619.8b.

13 Patricia Pittman, Linda H. Aiken, and James Buchan, "International Migration of Nurses: Introduction," *Health Services Research* 42 (June 2007): 1275–1280, at 1275.

14 Herman Benson, "Unionization of the Nurses in the U.S.: Worker Power, Autonomy, and Labor Democracy," *Working USA* 13 (June 2010): 297–307, at 302.

15 Susan Reverby, "Hospital Organizing in the 1950s: An Interview with Lillian Roberts," *Signs* 1 (1976): 1053–1063, at 1054.

Coda

Just over a century ago, in February 1918, the Spanish Flu broke out, an unprecedented pandemic that infected a third of the world's population within two years. Estimates of the death toll range from seventeen to fifty million. The nurses' efforts were heroic everywhere. Dr. Basil Hood of London's Charing Cross Hospital wrote afterwards: "Each day the difficulties became more pronounced as the patients increased and the nurses decreased, going down like ninepins themselves."[16] However, it was not the nurses but the doctors that were especially praised. Probably partly due to the recent consolidation of the 'modern' medical hierarchy, the work of nurses during the great flu pandemic of 1918-19 remained largely "invisible and subordinate."[17]

This brings me back to my starting point. Many nurses also sacrificed themselves for their patients during the current pandemic. In July 2020, Amnesty International estimated that at least three thousand nurses had died from COVID-19, with the caveat that this number was likely to be a significant underestimate due to underreporting.[18] The International Council of Nurses (the worldwide umbrella organization) during its biennial (this time, virtual) meeting on June 19, 2020, pointed out how risky the work of nurses has become during the pandemic:

> Large numbers of nurses have become infected with COVID-19 and many have sadly died, and a lack of sufficient amounts of appropriate, high-quality personal protective equipment was reported in every region of the world. In some countries, nurses have only been issued with gloves and masks when nursing COVID-19 patients, despite the known risks and recommendations that protective visors and gowns are essential in such situations.[19]

As a result, nurses are often perceived as public health hazards themselves. That is why they are confronted with aggression and violence in their communities. A recent comment in *The Lancet*, one of the leading medical journals, says:

> Since the beginning of this pandemic, headlines have also captured stories of health care personnel facing attacks as they travel to and from health care facilities. Nurses and doctors have been pelted with eggs and physically assaulted in Mexico. In the Philippines, a nurse was reportedly attacked by men who poured bleach on his face, damaging his vision. Across India, reports describe health care workers being beaten, stoned, spat on, threatened, and evicted from their homes.[20]

But even under these difficult circumstances, nurses' collective self-confidence seems to have grown over the past hundred years. Amnesty's researchers reported at least thirty-one countries witnessing "strikes, threatened strikes, or protests, by health and essential workers as a result" of unsafe working conditions.[21] The balance of power in health care is shifting.

---

16 Mark Honigsbaum, "'Nurses Fell Like Ninepins': Death and Bravery in the 1918 Flu Pandemic," *The Guardian*, April 05, 2020.

17 Laura Almudéver Campo and Ramón Camaño Puig, "Enfermeras y practicantes durante la epidemia de gripe de 1918: Análisis a través de la prensa española," *Cultura de los Cuidados* 52 (July-September 2018): 109–118, at 117.

18 Regular updates can be found at: https://flourish.studio/covid/.

19 "Virtual Meeting of World's Nurses Highlights Importance of Unity, Solidarity and Collaboration in the Face of Covid-19 Pandemic," *International Council of Nurses*, July 15, 2020, https://www.icn.ch/news/virtual-meeting-worlds-nurses-highlights-importance-unity-solidarity-and-collaboration-face, accessed August 14, 2020.

20 Donna McKay et al., "Attacks Against Health-Care Personnel Must Stop, Especially as the World Fights COVID-19," *The Lancet*, May 20, 2020: 1–2.

21 *Exposed, Silenced, Attacked: Failures to Protect Health and Essential Workers During the Pandemic* (London: Amnesty International, 2020): 20.

London School of Economics Department of Anthropology's Covid and Care Research Group[22]

Changing Care Networks in the United Kingdom

It is a truism to point out that the COVID-19 pandemic (and the United Kingdom government's response to it) has brought major disruption to everyday life. It has also, however, exposed and intensified existing fault-lines in society. The relationship between paid and unpaid labor, and the need to better recognize and reimburse the latter, long a key concern of feminist theorists and activists especially in relation to work within the household, has been one key issue of focus in our research. As parents with children have had to add childcare and home schooling to their work portfolios, there are reports of women in both middle-class and poorer households doing the lion's share. Meanwhile, as low-paid workers in the National Health Service (NHS), 'care' sector, and essential/key workers – often hailing from communities of recent or not-so-recent immigrants – have had to continue to work, other, higher-paid workers (not deemed to be 'key') have been able to stay safe by working at home; pre-existing inequalities between classes have been laid bare in ever-starker fashion. Pre-Covid, even after a decade of austerity, certain aspects of care for families in the low-paid category were undertaken by a 'mixed economy' of welfare.[23] This combined state welfare facilities, often provided at local level, with services rendered by charities staffed both by volunteers and salaried officers, while welfare payments known as 'universal credit' were delivered centrally by the Department of Welfare and Pensions. Now, in the time of coronavirus, these services have been thinned out, while lockdown has truncated informal sources of support in social relationships, making them difficult to draw on in times of need. This has caused anger and distress, and in some cases trauma. Whether people feel that the lockdown has been necessary or not, many of those in the low-paid sectors feel as though their situation – and suffering – is invisible to the government. Multiple forms of disadvantage emerge from this threat to the ties that bind people to each other.

Background

The COVID-19 pandemic, while having profound impacts on everyone in the United Kingdom regardless of race, class, gender, or region, has been and will be more severe for some communities than others. COVID-19 has brought inequalities of wealth and opportunity into sharp relief, rendering visible the social, economic, and political divisions – at national, regional, and local levels – that prevent the formation of a more equitable society. Those who are losing out, in terms of both economic losses and health and mortality, are communities whose members have historically experienced poverty, inequality of opportunity, and discrimination over the past decades of

22 LSE Department of Anthropology's Covid and Care Research Group – Authors for purposes of citation: Laura Bear, Deborah James, Nikita Simpson, Eileen Alexander, Jaskiran K. Bhogal, Rebecca E. Bowers, Fenella Cannell, Anishka Gheewala Lohiya, Insa Koch, Megan Laws, Johannes F. Lenhard, Nicholas J. Long, Alice Pearson, Farhan Samanani, Milena Wuerth, Olivia Vicol, Jordan Vieira, Connor Watt, Catherine Whittle, Teodor Zidaru-Barbulescu.

23 Hugh Cunningham and Joanna Innes, eds., *Charity, Philanthropy and Reform, from the 1690s to 1850* (London: MacMillan, 1998).

austerity policy in the United Kingdom. They include, but are not limited to, members of black, Asian, and minority ethnic groups (commonly glossed as BAME). However, many in these communities have accustomed themselves to doing without state support, and have formed robust mutual help and other forms of organization. Some have also come together to support each other in new and improvised ways as a result of the crisis, but in ways that lockdown has rendered unstable and precarious.

The research undertaken by LSE Department of Anthropology's Covid and Care Research Group, through online and telephone interviews with community leaders (including faith leaders, trade union representatives, and advisers), community groups, and individuals in four broad sites (London, the Midlands, the Northeast, and Scotland), sought to identify the effects of these new forms of disadvantage on caring processes within and beyond the household. We aimed to explore, among other things, how government policies aimed at responding to the pandemic are generating new forms of inequality (intensified social divides, stigma, social isolation, and discrimination), and how pre-existing and new care networks are responding to these in order to sustain life (through caring labor, financial aid, social support, and the like). Such networks of care – which cross-cut categories of class, ethnicity, and region – comprise formal interactions with the state, third sector, and civil society organizations as well as informal interactions with kin, friends, neighborhoods, and communities.

Our research was animated by a feminist substantivist approach[24] together with an interest in the increasing importance of care,[25] economies of advice,[26] and the third sector.[27] It pays attention to how care in society is configured, and how unpaid, informal care networks of households, families, and communities sustain productive, economic life, often in complex interaction with the vestigial remnants of older state-driven welfare schemes, access to which requires the expenditure or effort, empathy, and care. This approach challenges the division between the domestic and public spheres of society, and the boundedness of the economic domain.[28] In bringing our findings to the attention of policy-makers at national and local levels, we have sought to make it clear how the local solutions being generated by communities – in interaction with other actors – might, and should be, amplified, thus building on solutions already in place rather than inventing new ones.

---

24 Laura Bear, Karen Ho, Anna Lowenhaupt Tsing, and Sylvia Yanagisako, "Gens: A Feminist Manifesto for the Study of Capitalism," *Cultural Anthropology*, March 30, 2015, https://culanth.org/fieldsights/gens-a-feminist-manifesto-for-the-study-of-capitalism#:~:text=%20Gens%3A%20A%20Feminist%20Manifesto%20for%20the%20Study,of%20Gender%2C%20Race%2C%20Sexuality%2C%20and%20Kinship%0AA...%20More%20, accessed August 09, 2020; Nancy Fraser, "Can Society Be Commodities All the Way down? Post-Polanyian Reflections on Capitalist Crisis," *Economy and Society* 43:4 (2014): 541.

25 Ana P. Gutiérrez Garza, *Care for Sale: An Ethnography of Latin American Domestic and Sex Workers in London* (Oxford: Oxford University Press, 2018); Victoria Lawson, "Geographies of Care and Responsibility 2007," *Annals of the Association of American Geographers* 97 (2007): 1–11.

26 Insa Koch and Deborah James, "The State of the Welfare State: Advice, Governance and Care in Settings of Austerity," *Ethnos*, February 24, 2020, https://www.tandfonline.com/doi/full/10.1080/00141844.2019.1688371, accessed August 09, 2020; Deborah James and Insa Koch, "Economies of Advice," in Mark Aldenderfer, ed., *Oxford Research Encyclopedias: Anthropology* (Oxford: Oxford University Press, 2020).

27 Catherine Alexander, "Third Sector," in Keith Hart, Jean-Louis Laville, and Antonio David Cattani, eds., *The Human Economy, a Citizens' Guide* (Cambridge: Polity Press, 2010).

28 Diane Coyle, *Markets, State, and People: Economics for Public Policy* (Princeton: Princeton University Press, 2020).

Policy and the Domestic Arena

We start with the arena – much-contested by feminists for half a century – of the household.

The succession of new social distancing guidelines and economic policies implemented by the government were modelled on two assumptions. First, heteronormative and middle-class conceptions of the nuclear family have led to unintended consequences, such as the exclusion and/or stigmatization of single-parent households, multigenerational households without access to online resources, and single men. Second, the assumption that the 'economy' operates – independently of households – according to the rules of the free market, and is 'disembedded' from social and moral life, has resulted in a push to 're-open the economy' and allow people to return to paid work before allowing them to engage in unpaid caring work *between* households. As one member of our team observed, it is as though 'money disinfects.' Conversely, relationships based on care, neighborhood, and kinship are treated as though they are contagious, even indicative of danger.

To elaborate: the role of unpaid caring labor in sustaining economic and social life has been side-lined even more than it is under normal circumstances. Traditional gender roles have been reinforced by policies that do not account for such informal care. Households have had to absorb care for the elderly, children, the disabled, and those with special needs, without the support of public institutions such as schools, community centers, and social support services. The inability of households, under lockdown, to access informal networks of care through kin, friends, and neighbors has forced many to fill the gap by using paid care, and left others unable to meet their needs. Meanwhile, these needs are intensifying as the return of increasing numbers of citizens to the workplace heightens the care deficit in households during working hours. The choice to prioritize re-opening of the 'economy' has produced newly intensifying inequalities between households who, in order to return to work, are able to pay to replace their caring labor at home, in the form of nannies, care workers, or cleaners, and those who cannot. This latter group risks loss of income, indebtedness, and loss of employment.

The ideological and discursive divide between the domain of the household and the public domain has thus become more visible and salient in the public imagination. As a result, the work of the household in sustaining economic life is further obscured. When certain groups – such as single parents and mothers in nuclear households unable to pay for care – are then prevented from returning to the workforce, they face financial difficulty and mental distress. (The lack of support from kin and formal care networks has been particularly difficult for new mothers). Parents have been reluctant to take their children to the hospital, or unable to access support from formal support services such as general practice clinics, nurseries, and community centers.

In addition to their struggles to gain or retain access to formal and informal networks of care, previously (and now newly) disadvantaged households have experienced difficulties in accessing vital necessities including schools, the internet and IT resources, and food. Significant effects – on mental health and wellbeing, education, income, nutrition, and domestic violence levels – have been widely documented. Schools previously provided key services to families, ranging from referral to social workers, domestic violence services, and special needs support, but such provision has been discontinued with their closure. Greater responsibility has been placed on parents to attend to the educational and emotional needs of their children while they are unable to go to school or nursery; a burden that has largely fallen on mothers, including those with poor literacy or IT skills. The division of roles along gender lines, in households that previously had two working parents, has intensified, which has affected the way employers see their female employees. Partners of key workers, or of employees who are now returning to work as lockdown eases, face particularly heavy care burdens during working hours.

Single parents, most often single mothers, have faced particularly severe challenges in reconciling the demands of work with those of the family. They have often been forced to choose between paid employment and childcare, foregoing income or compromising the needs of their children. In one case a single mother, who, was already in a precarious situation in good times, was forced to stay at home with her children, unable to leave them even to go shopping. She was likely to lose her job. Many report being forced to make similarly complex calculations of risk in attending to the needs of their children, balancing risk of exposure to COVID-19 with the need to access food banks, medical help, and social care services for themselves or their children. There have been reported rises in calls and referrals to childcare support services by single-parent families, particularly single mothers and pregnant women who are refugees or asylum seekers. With extended family networks truncated, single parents are unable to access respite care or informal sources of food provision for their children. Respondents to a survey reported feeling increasingly distant from non-relatives, including friends, colleagues, and partners living outside the home. The breakdown of child maintenance payments means some partners are not required to pay child support, leaving one parent without an income. Nor does state welfare provision necessarily ameliorate the problem. The lag in Universal Credit and other benefit payments has had a particularly egregious effect on single-parent households.

In the case of multigenerational households, especially those stretched for resources, the lockdown has resulted in a 'squeezed middle' – with middle-aged women providing physical and financial support to both their elderly relatives and children. Multigenerational households, especially in BAME communities where such living arrangements are more common, and particularly in deprived communities where there is overcrowding of spaces, have tended to be stigmatized as vectors of transmission. In the case of households where dependence is more common, such as those containing elderly or disabled members, the lockdown has truncated networks of personal care. This means that many people providing such care (most often women) have become isolated, unable to access respite care. In the case of single-person (male) households, individuals experiencing financial stress have been likewise isolated from sources of emotional, financial, and physical care, whether this be because they are ashamed of asking for support or remote from networks that might provide it.

To contextualize these in-the-household effects, we move on to sketch some of the broader parameters, focusing especially on the changes to state welfare provision noted earlier.

Care Provision

Under lockdown, state interactions with vulnerable people, and the third sector activities which during the austerity era had already begun to replace these,[29] have been stripped back. Besides central areas of concern, such as food provision, help for domestic violence, child protection, and mental health, other activities that usually mediate, cushion, or replace caring interactions with the state have dwindled. In parallel, those formerly relying on such systems have experienced a sense of stigma about accessing services that render visible their experience of poverty, violence, or deprivation. For example, distanced queues for social welfare or food banks make people visible, and a visit from a social worker is more carefully observed by neighbors. The sense of stigma is

---

29 Insa Koch and Deborah James, "The State of the Welfare State."

particularly acute for men, especially from migrant communities, for whom the role of breadwinner and the value of work is important to a sense of self-worth. Hence, even where care has not been stripped back, the idea of being a recipient of welfare or charity is perceived as degrading and shameful.

Parents have experienced intensified disadvantage as a result of the closure of public spaces such as schools, libraries, and children's centers, which formerly provided referral, advice about, or mediated access to social services as well as face-to-face support to parents (including free school meals). Schools, engaging in a process of trial and error to keep the children of poorer families fed in lockdown, with some inviting families to collect food from school, then decided that this contradicted 'stay at home' guidelines. Shielding families were left under-served. The move to food vouchers was welcomed since this empowered families to choose their own food for their children but parents reported that it was often difficult to use them; vouchers have been impossible to cash in, recipients face long wait times on welfare websites, or have difficulty in securing slots for delivery of groceries from allocated stores. The closure of public spaces has also affected referral systems for individuals experiencing domestic abuse. Many are unable to access public spaces such as schools or libraries, women's groups, or the technology that is needed to reach out for help or to be contacted by professionals. Some schools and other social services have tried to compensate for not seeing service users or students by making phone calls or home visits, or asking to see the pupil when delivering food, to maintain welfare monitoring. While those about whom there were existing welfare concerns or known vulnerabilities have been contacted by service providers, problems have gone unnoticed for those developing new mental health problems or experiencing new social or relational problems in the household during lockdown.

As schooling has gone online, strengths and weaknesses have been exposed. The latter have come to the fore, in particular, because of the digital inclusion gap. Children in economically disadvantaged households have poorer access to technology and the internet, and schools worry about the challenges of later 'closing the gap' between advantaged and disadvantaged scholars after lockdown. Supporting education at home has been more difficult for parents with poor literacy or IT skills, or those who are learning English. Parents living in temporary housing or other overcrowded spaces, particularly women who have left abusive households, are likewise finding it difficult to support their children in education.

Institutional care interventions are a site of increasing distress. More children are being taken into care, and, during lockdown, have been forbidden from having regular face-to-face contact with their parents while their case is under consideration: a situation particularly acute for women who have recently given birth. Falling into the economically disadvantaged bracket, most parents in this situation lack access to digital platforms to interact with their children via technology, where this might otherwise have been arranged.

These developments, reaching back to before the lockdown, need to be seen from a long-term perspective. For ten years prior to lockdown, the government's austerity policies saw care provision at local level thinned out.[30] It is certainly true that local, community-based initiatives came into being to substitute for these, particularly among those seeking to evade state gaze. As noted in the next section, for example, new collaborations between the local state and the third sector have filled the gap left when state provision and funding was withdrawn. Nevertheless, disparities in funding allocated to these authorities have exacerbated inequalities between boroughs, with wealthy ones more able to support the ecosystem of service provision than their more deprived counterparts. The

---

30 Deborah James and Insa Koch, "Economies of Advice."

latter are often those that have experienced higher COVID-19 caseloads and excess deaths. Small grants given out by local authorities were important and well-received, but limited and often insufficiently targeted to meet the needs of communities. Many local charities and social enterprises, such as in the case outlined below, were unable to access the Coronavirus Small Business Loan Scheme, as their 'rateable value'[31] was above the threshold. Grassroots services are often funded voluntarily by their communities and unable to access local authority grants, which has threatened their long-term sustainability. Social workers and other support staff are not permitted under statutory regulations to refer people to such services, despite the fact that they often meet the needs of vulnerable service users better than formal services do. Meanwhile, paid-for care is beyond their means. There is thus a risk that local authorities become dependent on informal care providers to meet the service gap, without adequately compensating them.

With this patchy set of provisions, it is perhaps hardly surprising that families in minority communities, already suspicious of state welfare arrangements, social workers, and the like – and now even less likely to be benefitting from whatever such officers normally supply – have come increasingly to mistrust state bodies. Especially those with the in-between status that forbids them access to public funds ('No recourse to public funds'; NRPF),[32] as well as refugees who are in the process of being resettled and unsuccessful asylum seekers, report that they are stuck in limbo, fearful that accessing charitable or local authority services will make them visible to the state. In addition, engagement with government information and guidelines is informed by existing relationships of trust and mistrust, with a lack of clear messaging from government sources meaning that people have little understanding of social distancing guidelines and government policy changes. It is under these circumstances that many, already involved in neighborhood and community systems of care, have intensified that involvement.

State or Community? A 'Mixed Economy of Welfare'

Grassroots community support services, often informal, cultural, or faith-based and local, have been of critical importance in supporting isolated families, providing culturally-specific information, and advice in navigating welfare, health, and financial support. Particularly those marginal communities with poor English and IT literacy, who do not engage with mainstream media outlets and who thus receive information on epidemiology in a mediated way, have come to rely on these interpersonal interactions with community networks, gatekeepers, or trusted advisors. Such local responses, however, are not routinely as simple and binary as the above account may suggest. The cards do not always fall in a manner as simple or predictable as pro- or anti-state; pro- or anti-community. To illustrate the complex interaction of factors that mean a 'mixed economy of welfare'[33] remains a prominent pattern in the United Kingdom, we highlight two cases in particular.

The first is from Leicester, the site of the United Kingdom's first localized lockdown and which became notorious for the working conditions in its garment factories. Here, the Highfields Community Centre, for forty years serving one of the most deprived areas in the city with a predominance of BAME groups, continued to give support to local residents and newly-arrived asylum seekers alike.

31 Basis for calculating business rates.
32 This status is imposed on certain categories of people for whom the permission to remain in the United Kingdom is contingent on being prohibited from accessing certain defined public funds, especially welfare benefits.
33 Hugh Cunningham and Joanna Innes, eds., *Charity, Philanthropy and Reform, from the 1690s to 1850.*

The decade of austerity, during which the local authority (starved of support by central government) cut funding by half a million pounds, forced the center to rely instead on grants from bodies such as Children in Need and the Lottery Fund (the increasing prevalence of this kind of 'patchwork funding'[34] has been a common pattern around the country during the austerity decade). Since the lockdown in March, the center has been closed. In a demonstration of the poorly-thought-through character of central government provision with its conditionalities, they were unable to access the government business support as their value was calculated as being above the rateable value. Nonetheless, the center kept going; it soon started a food parcel delivery service and has seen the demand double. This service enabled staff to keep in touch with vulnerable users, including young people, the elderly, and the unemployed who belong to a local 'jobs club.' Accessing a small grant, they also sent out community workers wearing personal protective equipment to persuade parents who are reluctant to send their children back to school or nursery, reasoning that failure to do so would lead to further disadvantage in the longer term. In addition, they are considering seeking funds for summer schools using creative methods to help children make up for lost time in education and lack of psychosocial support.

The second case is from Kensington and Chelsea, the borough that in 2017 saw the disastrous Grenfell fire destroy a high-rise council building and kill seventy-two people. Here, the building of community networks in response to that incident proved resilient in helping to provide protection and care in the face of the pandemic. The mismatch between government policy and the advice of the World Health Organization and health specialists in countries already responding to the virus encouraged some local charity leaders to begin joint preparations for the effects of a likely lockdown. In part as a result of the fire, there was already a spirit of community cooperation across faiths and across denominations within faiths. Showing that not all government officers were mistrusted, "local charities were assisted by a trusted NHS worker at their first meeting, at which he noted the difference between his advice as an official, and his advice as a citizen." The organizers reached out to "trusted statutory leaders in both the local authority and health authority" – including officers from Public Health England and from West London Clinical Commissioning Group as well as representatives from key charities and the voluntary sector – on the basis of their "integrity, honesty, and diligence." The pandemic response was thus "based around a multi-sectoral group that trusted each other from the start and were open to challenging 'business as usual.'"[35] One of those involved was the CEO of the Al Manaar Muslim Cultural Heritage Centre, which was already offering multilingual telephone advice (in Arabic, English, Berber, French, and Turkish). To help elderly people who were housebound because of vulnerability or infection, they teamed up with various charities. In addition, realizing that the mosque – closed for prayers during lockdown – was an important asset/resource, they started using it as a distribution hub for food distribution.

Conclusion

The two cases detailed here demonstrate the salience of observations about the importance of third sector and/or locally generated initiatives in the face of state withdrawal and state-driven auster-

---

34 Alice Forbess and Deborah James, "Innovation and Patchwork Partnerships: Advice Services in Austere Times," *Oñati Socio-Legal Series* 7:7 (2017), http://ssrn.com/abstract=3056205, accessed August 09, 2020.
35 Michael Ashe, Testimony to Parliament, 2018, https://committees.parliament.uk/writtenevidence/8142/pdf/, accessed August 09, 2020.

ity. Both to offset these longer-term processes and to help cope with the belated, patchy, and often inadequately communicated measures taken by the United Kingdom government to counter and control the spread of the COVID-19 pandemic, activities that are informal – and often voluntary and unpaid – intensify to fill in for the thinning of state services, as is the case with other "economies of advice."[36] Care, in turn, entails "the construction of new forms of relationships, institutions, and action," which may (but do not always) "enhance mutuality and wellbeing."[37] Paid and unpaid work, market and nonmarket, formal and informal, neoliberal and redistributive here coexist in a tight embrace.

"A Right to Care." Original illustration by Maggie Li, 2020.

---

36 Deborah James and Insa Koch, "Economies of Advice."
37 Victoria Lawson, "Geographies of Care and Responsibility 2007."

Preben Kaarsholm
Scares and Possibilities: The COVID-19 Emergency, the Disruption of Globalization, and the Reinvention of the Welfare State

The COVID-19 pandemic and responses to it have exposed dramatically the inherent contradictions of globalization. The pandemic has been an unprecedented global emergency, presenting the whole world with attacks from the same strand of coronavirus, thus signaling homogenization and universality. But while it was possible to contain earlier attacks from coronaviruses such as SARS in 2002–4 through international efforts coordinated by the World Health Organization (WHO), the response to COVID-19 has been diffuse and subject to fierce political contestation. This essay will discuss this contradiction through the lens of the impact of the pandemic and responses to it in Denmark and its Scandinavian neighboring countries. I shall point out some of the unprecedented threats occasioned by the pandemic, as well as some of the possibilities for radical change and realignment, which have presented themselves suddenly and unexpectedly. My essay will address in particular how the emergency has affected work conditions and labor regimes, and what kind of prospects for the future this may entail.

The WHO, the 'China Virus,' and Scandinavian Health Authoritarianism

The WHO declared the COVID-19 outbreak a pandemic a pandemic on March 11, 2020, during a period that was already undergoing some of the greatest upheavals in world hegemony since the end of World War II in 1945 and of the Cold War in 1989. China's rise to global power has coincided with the disintegration of the US-Western Europe consensus centering on NATO; we have seen challenges to European unity presented by Brexit and the rearrangement of global political geography into – on the one hand – fortresses of peace and – on the other – vast territories of permanent conflict, proxy wars, and displacement of populations. The planet faces unprecedented levels of risk in the face of climate change, and of the difficulties in reaching international agreement on measures to counter it.[38] Never has the need for global governance been greater, and never has the crisis of international institutions been so severe.

The WHO was established in 1948 as an important ingredient in the system of multinational institutions established around the United Nations to consolidate postwar development and to counter the threats of epidemics in the aftermath of World War II. The COVID-19 pandemic has turned it into a battlefield for the control or undermining of multinational governance. China – where the pandemic originated – has made significant investments into the WHO as part of a more general ambition to increase its influence over multinational institutions. On the other hand, the

---

38 Will Steffen, et al., "Trajectories of the Earth System in the Anthropocene," *Proceedings of the National Academy of Sciences of the United States of America* (PNAS) 11:33 (August 14, 2018); Anon., "Briefing Climate Change," *The Economist*, September 21, 2019.

United States has pursued a longer-term strategy of disengagement from United Nations institutions (UNESCO being one example), as well as from institutional innovations aimed to promote transitional justice and the universalization of human rights such as the International Criminal Court. In the aftermath of the initial panic, the COVID-19 emergency has offered itself as a showpiece of Chinese mastery and strategical superiority and of the incapacity of the United States to recognize and contain the spread of the pandemic.

For China, this is an opportunity to demonstrate the superiority of authoritarianism, disproving the assumptions of modernization theory that growth and capitalism require liberalism and democracy, and that "all good things go together."[39] On the United States side, distancing itself from the political bias of the WHO has helped justify the libertarian and denialist response applied by the United States, as well as by the United Kingdom and Brazil, to what President Donald Trump insists on calling the 'China virus.'[40] WHO recommendations in the early days of the COVID-19 pandemic in March and April 2020 also involved criticism of Danish and Scandinavian policies vis-à-vis the pandemic. The Danish counterargument was that the WHO recommendations of mass testing and containment through physical isolation were not relevant for Scandinavia at that point, because testing capacity was too low for it to be effective. Only mitigation and the slowing down of the spread of the virus would make sense and be acceptable.[41]

The policy responses by the three Scandinavian welfare economies have been different, and a lot has been made of the differences between the Danish-Norwegian and Swedish approaches, especially in the early days of the pandemic. This was particularly so, because the differences in policy contradicted traditional stereotypes of a centralist and authoritarian Sweden as against more easy-going Denmark and Norway. These stereotypes have a certain amount of historical foundation in different trajectories of democratization and designs for state-society interaction. In all three countries, however, social democratic and labor parties with strong links to trade unions and workers' organizations have been prominent since the 1930s, and have been initiators and guardians of welfare state and mixed-economy frameworks.

A stereotypical view of Sweden (at least within the confines of exchanges of mutual prejudice among Scandinavians) has been as the land of political correctness, where all things good and righteous do indeed go together. It is part of this view that righteousness should be policed through the silencing of incorrectness and by far-reaching interventions by government and experts into private spheres and citizens' behavior. Though racist and anti-immigrant discourse has a strong presence in Swedish society, it has so far been kept out of respectable parliamentary collaboration, and traces of racism are vigorously policed in the historical representations of museums and in children's literature. Sexism and gender discrimination are not tolerated, and the gender-neutral third-person pronoun "hen" is promoted as an alternative to traditional masculine and feminine usage.

---

39 Seymour Lipset, *Political Man: The Social Bases of Politics* (Garden City: Doubleday, 1960), ch. 2; Cf. Walt Whitman Rostow, *The Stages of Economic Growth: A Non-Communist Manifesto* (Cambridge: Cambridge University Press, 1960) and Daniel Lerner, *The Passing of Traditional Society: Modernizing the Middle East* (Glencoe: Free Press, 1958).

40 On Trump, China, and the history of the WHO, see James Meek, "The Health Transformation Army," *London Review of Books* 42:13, July 02, 2020, https://www.lrb.co.uk/the-paper/v42/n13/james-meek/the-health-transformation-army, accessed September 06, 2020.

41 Esben Schjørring et al., "WHO kritiserer Danmark igen og igen – men taler altid pænt om Kina," *Altinget*, April 4, 2020, https://www.altinget.dk/artikel/who-kritiserer-danmark-igen-og-igen-men-taler-altid-paent-om-kina?SNSubscribed=true&ref=newsletter&refid=ekstra-lordag-4-4&utm_campaign=altingetdk%20Altinget.dk&utm_medium%09=e-mail&utm_source=nyhedsbrev, accessed August 28, 2020.

By contrast, Norway and Denmark have been seen through matching stereotypes as softer and less uncompromisingly righteous than Sweden. In the Danish-Norwegian setting, democracy has had a less centralized history, with grass-roots movements, civil society agendas, and folk high schools playing more prominent roles. Consequently, traditions of state paternalism are seen as less rigorous than in Sweden, and – in contrast to Sweden – xenophobic and anti-immigrant political parties have long been considered respectable enough for parliamentary collaboration in both Denmark and Norway.

The COVID-19 pandemic and the political responses to it seemed to overthrow many of these stereotypical assumptions. When the pandemic struck, all three countries were ruled by minority governments – the Social Democratic Party in Denmark, a Right Party-Left Party-Christian People's Party coalition in Norway, and a Social Democratic-Green Party coalition in Sweden. All three governments were fragile in the sense of being dependent on the support of other parties, known to be volatile. In Norway, the xenophobic Progress Party had recently seceded from the governing coalition, and in Sweden, the red-green minority government was formed against the background of a four-month period of political stalemate between September 2018 and January 2019, when no government could be agreed upon with the necessary parliamentary support. The COVID-19 emergency brought political consolidation to all three Scandinavian countries, at least for a period, and in Denmark perhaps most spectacularly so.

The image of a progressive, female Danish prime minister has been popularized internationally through the television series *Borgen*, and on March 11, 2020, the Social Democratic prime minister, Mette Frederiksen, seized the moment, and – flanked ceremonially by heath experts and line ministers – announced wide-ranging interventions and restrictions in Danish public life.[42] This was an emergency measure, based on what became the magical formula of "sundhedsfaglig ekspertise"– health science expertise and consultation – but the prime minister assumed full responsibility for it as an urgent political intervention, even if it might later turn out to have involved judgment errors. Danes who had been used to living closely with each other now had to adjust their behavior and learn to "stand together by keeping distance." Schools and universities were closed, as were libraries and cultural and sports facilities. All public employees "not in critical functions" were sent home, and private enterprises were encouraged also to let their employees work from home as much as possible. Public transport was restricted, limitations were placed on visits to hospitals and nursing homes, and public gatherings of more than one hundred people were prohibited. Foreign travel was restricted and reinforced border controls introduced. Mette Frederiksen ended her address by stating that, "We must do everything we can to look after the Danes. To look after Denmark. To look after each other." The objective of this was not containment along Chinese lines, and a proper 'lockdown' has never been on the agenda in Scandinavia. The aim was 'mitigation' – to keep casualty figures low and the spread of the pandemic at a rate where hospital and health capacities were not overstretched, as had been the scenario in Italy and Spain.

This early and determined declaration – with its nationalist and populist ingredients – had a powerful impact, and was a difficult act to oppose. An equally determined announcement followed on March 15, 2020, of a "three-part agreement" between the Social Democratic government, the Danish trade unions, and the employers' organization on state provision of wage compensation for workers who were sent home, so that they would not lose their jobs. Subsequently, on March 19, the finance minister announced an agreement between all the parties in the Danish parliament to

42 Her speech can be found at https://www.stm.dk/_p_14916.html, accessed August 29, 2020; For the television series *Borgen*, see https://www.imdb.com/title/tt1526318/, accessed August 29, 2020.

make available an extensive financial support package to keep the Danish economy afloat in the face of the COVID-19 emergency.[43] By May 2020, COVID-19 interventions were estimated to amount to around 200 billion krone, which would bring the Danish government budget deficit to nearly 300 billion Danish kroner – approximately 43 billion US dollars.[44]

Norway followed a similar line of caution to that adopted by the Danish government, adding the radical measure of restricting citizens' rights to travel to their mountain cottages, even for skiing during the Easter holidays – a sacrosanct ritual of Norwegian national culture. Sweden, however, chose a different path that was much less restrictive in terms of movement and kept primary schools, public institutions, businesses, and even cafés and restaurants open. Health authoritarianism in Sweden also had a different public face. While Denmark and Norway made a point of basing interventions on political decisions, taking advice from health expertise into account, politicians in Sweden to a larger degree stood aside and let health experts make the decisions and announce publicly what would be the best approach. This brought to the fore Anders Tegnell as 'state epidemiologist,' representing Sweden's Public Health Agency, who by now has become world-famous as the spokesperson of the Swedish 'open' way of addressing COVID-19.

What was particularly striking about the Swedish way compared with the Danish and Norwegian approaches was the stated objective of letting the open society contribute to the building of herd immunity to the COVID-19 virus, combined with that of taking the economic cost of possible closures of institutions and enterprises into account.[45] There was not really a disagreement between the three countries at the time, concerning the necessity of reaching herd immunity. At the onset of the pandemic, it was the general assumption that – in the absence of a vaccine – herd immunity could only be reached with the gradual spread of infections through the population. The disagreement was over the speed and violence with which infections might be allowed to spread, and what levels of deaths and casualties could be tolerated.

The outcome was that Sweden ended up with dramatically higher death figures than Denmark and Norway, something also caused by serious neglect in the protection of nursing homes and the elderly population. As of August 30, 2020, COVID-19 deaths came to 5,891 in Sweden (in a population of 10.3 million), 624 in Denmark (in a population of 5.8 million), and 264 in Norway (in a population of 5.4 million).[46] At the same time, the expected impact on immunity and the economy have not materialized. A study carried out at the beginning of May 2020 showed that only 7.3 percent of those tested in Stockholm had developed antibodies against COVID-19, with only five percent at a

---

43 The March 15 and March 19, 2020, announcements from the Ministry of Finance can be found at https://fm.dk/nyheder/nyhedsarkiv/2020/marts/regeringen-og-alle-folketingets-partier-er-enige-om-omfattende-hjaelpepakke-til-dansk-oekonomi/ and https://fm.dk/nyheder/nyhedsarkiv/2020/marts/trepartsaftale-skal-hjaelpe-loenmodtagere/, both accessed August 29, 2020.

44 DKK 294 billion more exactly, according to the overview presented by the Ministry of Finance on May 25, 2020 – https://fm.dk/nyheder/nyhedsarkiv/2020/maj/statens-nettofinansierings-og-finansieringsbehov-for-2020/, accessed August 29, 2020.

45 Anders Tegnell kept arguing long into the pandemic that Swedish policy would lead to levels of herd immunity, which other countries would necessarily have to strive towards by different means later. See Richard Milne, "Architect of Sweden's No-Lockdown Strategy Insists It Will Pay Off: Epidemiologist Anders Tegnell Says Other Countries Could Face Big 'Second Wave'," *Financial Times*, May 8, 2020, https://www.ft.com/content/a2b4c18c-a5e8-4edc-8047-ade4a82a548d, accessed August 30, 2020.

46 See Johns Hopkins University COVID-19 Interactive Map, where country figures are updated continuously, https://www.arcgis.com/apps/opsdashboard/index.html#/bda7594740fd40299423467b48e9ecf6, accessed 10 September 2020.

national level.[47] In terms of economic impact, OECD figures indicate a worse outcome for growth and employment in Sweden than in Denmark and Norway.[48]

The differences between the measures of health authoritarianism had very practical impacts, leading to travel restrictions between the three countries. The bridge between Sweden and Denmark was not closed for good – in spite of the long-standing ambitions of radical nationalist and xenophobic Danes.[49] Nevertheless, movement across the bridge slowed down as border controls, immigration checks, and travel restrictions were introduced. For a long time, this was enforced asymmetrically, meaning that Danes could commute freely to their holiday homes in the south of Sweden, while Swedes could only enter Denmark if they subjected themselves to a two-week quarantine. The free flow within and amalgamation of the Copenhagen-Malmoe region into a Bay Area-like unified space under the banner of European unity and globalization came under threat, and it remains to be seen how permanent the disruption will be.

Health Authoritarianism, Xenophobia, and the Reinvention of the Danish Welfare State

Such re-fragmentation has obviously also affected growth and has – together with increasingly draconic anti-immigration and refugee policies – halted the development of a prospering cross-border labor market in the Copenhagen-Malmoe region. In this sense, health authoritarianism may be seen as contributing to new strands of protectionism as far as the labor market and employment are concerned. Labor market protectionism has, however, been significantly countered by European Union open-market obligations. In spite of the slow-down produced by border controls, the movement of labor across both the Danish-Swedish and the Danish-German border, and between Denmark and Poland has continued with few restrictions throughout the COVID-19 pandemic period. This in spite of occasional outbursts of scapegoating with Polish workers coming to Denmark portrayed – alongside Somali immigrants and asylum seekers – as possible carriers of infection. I shall come back to this below.

The COVID-19 emergency has exposed the vulnerability of migrant and informal laborers as members of a global reserve army. This was flashed across media screens in the images of home-

---

47 Asbjørn Goul Andersen, "Sverige følger sin helt egen corona-strategi – men hvor længe?," *Videnskab.dk*, June 6, 2020, https://videnskab.dk/kultur-samfund/sverige-foelger-sin-helt-egen-corona-strategi-men-hvor-laenge, accessed August 30, 2020. See also "Immune Responses and Immunity to SARS-CoV-2," *European Centre for Disease Prevention and Control (ECDC)*, https://www.ecdc.europa.eu/en/covid-19/latest-evidence/immune-responses, accessed August 30, 2020. This shows only marginal differences in the immunity figures for Sweden, Denmark, and Norway.
48 As for projected change in GDP during 2020, the OECD by June 2020 gives minus 6.7 percent (single-hit scenario) and 7.8 percent (double-hit scenario, i.e. with impact from a second pandemic wave) for Sweden, 5.8 percent and 7.1 percent for Denmark, and 6 percent and 7.5 percent for Norway. See "OECD Economic Outlook, June 2020: The World Economy on a Tightrope," *OECD*, 2020, http://www.oecd.org/economic-outlook/june-2020, accessed August 30, 2020. For unemployment forecasts, the OECD gives the following figures for the three countries for the fourth quarter of 2020 in a single- and double-hit scenario respectively: Sweden 11 percent and 13.4 percent, Denmark 7.2 percent and 8.8 percent, Norway 5.5 percent and 7 percent. See "Unemployment Rate Forecast," *OECD*, 2020, https://data.oecd.org/unemp/unemployment-rate-forecast.htm, accessed August 30, 2020.
49 The symbolism of the bridge across the Øresund is explored brilliantly in the 2011 first season of the TV series *Broen*, which has won international acclaim and was a Danish-Swedish co-production. See https://www.imdb.com/title/tt1733785/, accessed on August 30, 2020.

less migrant laborers forced to leave Indian cities at the declaration of lockdown, or being arrested in South African shack settlements for breaking restrictions on movement to queue for food and shopping.

The pandemic has brought into view how Europe, too, is affected by informalization and by the transnational disaggregation of work processes and the undermining of trade unions through individualized contract labor. This happened in the exposure of the Tönnies slaughterhouse outbreak in Gütersloh in June 2020, when COVID-19 was shown to have spread through the miserable and congested living conditions of the Polish, Bulgarian, and Romanian '*Kolonnen-Arbeiter*,' who had no contractual or trade-union protection.[50] In Denmark, this was addressed in an indignant newspaper commentary by a worker employed at the Danish Crown abattoir in Horsens – the biggest slaughterhouse in Denmark with more than 1,300 employees – who argued that the 'slave-like' working conditions in Germany represented a threat to workers internationally. He also described how his German colleagues at the slaughterhouse in Horsens were willing to commute six hundred kilometers by car every day to be able to work under a Danish labor regime, which was regulated in a different way.[51]

Not long after, in early August 2020, a similar outbreak of COVID-19 occurred at a Danish Crown slaughterhouse in Ringsted, where the majority of those infected were Polish workers under Danish union contracts, but accommodated in conditions not dissimilar to their Gütersloh Tönnies colleagues.[52] It also emerged that the Danish Crown abattoir brand was not so Danish after all, as its production processes were disaggregated in complex ways across several plants and national borders. At the same time, it turned out that Danish Crown operates its own slaughterhouses in Germany, including one in Essen producing pork for the Chinese market, which had had to be closed down temporarily in June 2020 because of Chinese worries about importing COVID-19-infected pork. Danish Crown is also involved with German partners in a major joint-venture slaughterhouse enterprise in Lower Saxony, again fully embedded in a German labor regulations framework.[53]

The differences between the Scandinavian/Danish and the German model are therefore becoming difficult to uphold, and it seems that 'slave-like conditions' can also be accommodated within the Danish framework. This is a challenge for the Social Democratic Party's project for the revival of the welfare state, for the support of which it has sought to capitalize on in its successful

---

50 "More Than 1,300 Coronavirus Cases in Meat Factory," *General-Anzeiger* (English edition), June 22, 2020, https://ga.de/ga-english/news/more-than-1300-coronavirus-cases-in-meat-factory_aid-51778017, accessed August 31, 2020.
51 Frank Vestergaard, "Slagteriarbejder fra Horsens: Slavelignende forhold hos vores tyske naboer er blevet normalen. Og kan komme til Danmark" [Slaughterhouse worker from Horsens: Slave-like conditions among our German neighbors have become the norm. And may come to Denmark], *Politiken*, June 28, 2020, https://politiken.dk/debat/art7837985/Slavelignende-forhold-hos-vores-tyske-naboer-er-blevet-normalen.-Og-kan-komme-til-Danmark, accessed August 31, 2020; This was echoed in the Danish trade-union media, see e.g. Nicolai Søndergaard, "Slagteriarbejder: Slavelignende forhold i Tyskland presser os i Danmark," *Fødevareforbundet NNF*, June 29, 2020, https://www.nnf.dk/nyheder/2020/juni/slagteriarbejder-slavelignende-forhold-i-tyskland-presser-os-i-danmark/, accessed August 31, 2020.
52 "Coronavirus Digest: Danish Abattoir Closed Over COVID-19 Cluster," *Deutsche Welle*, August 8, 2020, https://www.dw.com/en/coronavirus-digest-danish-abattoir-closed-over-covid-19-cluster/a-54492986, accessed August 31, 2020.
53 "Corona Outbreak in Essen Called Off," *Danish Crown*, June 29, 2020, https://www.danishcrown.com/en/contact/media/news/corona-outbreak-in-essen-called-off, accessed August 31, 2020; On the Westcrown slaughterhouse in Osnabrück, of which Danish Crown owns fifty percent, see Peter Rasmussen, "Hver tredje ansat smittet: Danish Crown ramt af corona-udbrud i Tyskland," *Fagbladet 3F*, 18 May 2020, https://fagbladet3f.dk/artikel/danish-crown-ramt-af-corona-udbrud-i-tyskland, accessed August 31, 2020.

COVID-19 interventions. This revival has had a strongly traditionalist and even nostalgic ring, seen for example in the flagship political promise to introduce special early retirement public pensions for worn-out blue-collar laborers. In essence, this is a modest attempt to roll back some of the reductions in pensions and retirement support schemes, which have been introduced over the last decade of conservative-liberalist government. It is being promoted, however, in a vigorously elaborated discursive framework, which reintroduces notions of class and images of what a worker is, and which seems more concerned with bringing back the past than addressing the future.[54]

At the same time, together with the boost received from its resolute public health interventions, the Social Democratic Party has gained strength by stealing some of the fire from the populist xenophobic right in Danish politics. This applies in particular to the Danish People's Party, which in recent years has competed with Social Democrats over welfare agendas – a competition that seems for the time being to have been more or less completely neutralized.[55] The prime minister has recently spoken in emotional terms of the need to safeguard fearful Danes against attacks from 'immigrant youth' on Copenhagen commuter trains. In addition, at the beginning of August 2020, Social Democratic councilors in the country's second-largest city, Aarhus, were vocal in calling for 'cultural' interventions against Somalis immigrants and asylum seekers, among whom there was recently a much-debated 'hotspot' virus outbreak. It was subsequently agreed to make information on COVID-19 precautions available in the Somali language to help address the problem.[56]

The Social Democratic minister for immigration, Mattias Tesfaye, has been an unflinching upholder of strict immigration controls and repatriation of undocumented migrants and unsuccessful asylum seekers, and within the European Union, Danish Social Democrats have opposed refugee quotas for member countries and the adoption of a common European policy on refugees and immigration

The party's position has been expressed forcefully also in more populist terms by Rasmus Stoklund, a young and aspiring MP and political scientist, who has made his career through the Dansk Metal trade union, and who is currently the Social Democratic spokesperson for immigration and integration. In 2016, Stoklund published a book explaining that – to win voters back from the Danish People's Party or the Liberals, who were then in minority government - the Social Democrats should align itself with the Danish People's Party, rather than fight its xenophobia. Social Democrats must address and take seriously the fears and insecurities that globalization has imposed on 'ordinary people.' The best way to do this would be to secure jobs for Danish workers and to restrict immigration.[57]

---

54 The Danish worker in this simulacrum is a white, male brewery worker in his sixties called Arne, who has worked for decades, contributed through his tax paying to the building of the welfare state, and who is regularly embraced on television by the prime minister; see the Social Democratic Party website's presentation of its campaign called 'Lille land, stor retfærdighed' ('Small Country, Big Justice'), https://www.lille-land.dk/retfaerdighed/, accessed August 31, 2020.

55 In August 2017, support for the Social Democrats and the Danish People's Party amounted to respectively 25.5 percent and 19.2 percent; By August 2020, the corresponding figures were 32.4 percent and 7.3 percent; VoxMeter for Ritzau, https://voxmeter.dk/meningsmalinger/, accessed August 31, 2020.

56 Christina Nordvang Jensen, "Professor om smitte i somaliske kredse i Aarhus: 'Det er social ulighed og ikke etnicitet, der er problemet'," *DR Nyheder*, August 11, 2020, https://www.dr.dk/nyheder/indland/professor-om-smitte-i-somaliske-kredse-i-aarhus-det-er-social-ulighed-og-ikke, accessed September 05, 2020.

57 Rasmus Stoklund Holm-Nielsen, *Til blå Bjarne: en debatbog om Socialdemokratiet, globaliseringen og fremtiden* (Copenhagen: Skriveforlaget, 2016). 'Blå Bjarne', to whom the book is addressed, is a fictional blue-collar worker, who has shifted his support from the Left to more rightist parties, and whom Social Democratic policies must aim to win back.

Like the prime minister, Stoklund has also made a point of stating in public media that areas of Copenhagen with a majority Muslim immigrant population must not be allowed to become unsafe for Danish citizens.[58] Most recently, he has criticized a government-commissioned research report produced by Roskilde University colleagues of mine, who argued that policies to address 'negative social control' among young Muslim immigrants might require Arabic and other foreign language skills as well as insights into the teachings of the Qur'an: "I can promise with absolute certainty that a report like this will never be used as the foundation for Social Democratic interventions against negative social control."[59]

Pension reforms, retirement age, and immigration policy relate to each other closely. The demographic trends that form the basis for arguments in favor of raising the age of retirement are exacerbated by anti-immigration policy. The paradoxical conundrum of being faced with a combined threat of unemployment and a lack of available labor power could be addressed rationally through an alternative policy of regulated immigration, perhaps from selected partner countries, as well as through a more humane policy toward refugees and asylum seekers. At the moment, such an alternative seems as far as it could possibly be from the policy of the Social Democratic Party. The party sees its commitment to an anti-immigration policy and discourses of anti-Muslim feeling as a significant contribution to the strong position that the party has consolidated through COVID-19 health authoritarianism.

Prospects for a New Deal?

Denmark and the Social Democratic Party are thus at a crossroads. The limited extent of the negative impact on growth and employment indicated in the OECD figures quoted above appears to have been a highly successful result of the early, resolute, and comprehensive interventions by the Danish Social Democratic government, including the extensive financial injections to boost the economy and keep unemployment at bay. Suddenly, since early March 2020 and the onset of the pandemic, Keynesianism and economic policies of debt financing, public investments, and multiplier effects have become respectable and possible. This comes after a long drought of so-called neoliberalism, where state coffers have been treated like a family household budget, and state budget deficits seen as the road to national ruin. The question now is whether this will be the beginning of a great re-awakening of a New Deal era, and how the new level of extensive state interventionism into the economy will be managed. Will the interventions through loans and aid packages be used to re-establish as far as possible a pre-COVID-19 status quo, and primarily save existing enterprise structures from collapse? Or will they be used pro-actively to re-structure the economy and employment, and used to further other urgent and more long-term challenges of counteracting climate change, environmental degradation, and the growth in global inequalities and the exploitation of labor? How will work conditions and labor regimes be affected by the cor-

---

58 This followed episodes around New Year's Eve, when fireworks were thrown at passers-by in the streets of Nørrebro; See Sebastian Abrahamsen, "Socialdemokratiets nye hardliner: For mange med ikkevestlig baggrund opfører sig dårligt," *Information*, January 15, 2020, https://www.information.dk/indland/2020/01/socialdemokratiets-nye-hardliner-ikkevestlig-baggrund-opfoerer-daarligt, accessed September 5, 2020.

59 Rasmus Stoklund, "S til RUC-dekan: Du forsvarer pinlig og absurd rapport med stråmænd," *Altinget*, September 3, 2020, https://www.altinget.dk/forskning/artikel/s-svarer-ruc-dekan-du-opstiller-en-straamand-i-forsvar-for-pinlig-rapport, accessed September 5, 2020.

poratist instruments of governance that have been introduced? How will job-sharing, extensions in the possibilities of working from home, and further disaggregation of production processes affect workplace cultures and labor organization?

These are among the big questions for the immediate future. The 2021 budget proposed by the Social Democratic government – designated a "corona budget" – provides an indication of what may be expected, as well as what will be possible in terms of parliamentary support. It contains a "war chest" of 9.2 billion krone – approximately 1.4 billion US dollars – that will be "kept in reserve for the re-starting of the Danish economy and to meet special challenges occasioned by COVID-19. This reserve is added to the numerous interventions introduced since the spring of 2020, and will be used to safeguard Danish jobs and employment and for health services, vaccines, and economic rehabilitation."[60] This does not sound like a declaration of Keynesian revolution, but rather as of one of returning as far and as soon as possible to a pre-COVID-19 status quo.

A more radical departure would require fundamental changes in both Danish national and European Union frameworks for state expenditure and deficit financing. A Danish 'budgetlov' agreed upon by a broad parliamentary majority in 2012 stipulates that the annual deficit in government budgets cannot exceed half a percent of GDP, and European Union regulations impose a restriction of three percent of GDP on deficits in member states' national accounts, and do not allow public gross debt to go beyond sixty percent of GDP. To pursue further the possibilities opened up by the COVID-19 emergency interventions of economic stimulus would require a new consensus to revise such limitations in order to enable massive investments in, for example, climate change countermeasures. A Keynesian revolution proper would mean that such investments were made by governments also to provide new radical welfare and anti-inequality reforms. This would require political visions of a transnational nature, for which Danish Social Democrats, trade unionists, and the labor movement are not yet prepared, and for which parliamentary backing would be so far unthinkable.

In any case, within the perspective of Danish Social Democratic visions, welfare is prioritized over climate change intervention – red is valued above green. This may well become the most important battlefield on the Left of Danish politics and within trade unions and the labor movement in the immediate future. Endeavors to avoid unemployment and place limitations on retirement age and on reductions in public pensions will make public expenditure dependent on a continued growth in GDP. Though interest rates are negative and likely to remain so for some time, debt repayments will also contribute to the need for continued growth, and a green prospect of zero growth or even reductions in growth to halt global warming will be extremely unlikely. The best-case scenario that can he hoped for as an agreed political agenda for a Social Democratic government, basing itself on support from the Left, would therefore be one of green growth, job-sharing, and technological innovation.

This could boost hopes of a Danish national salvation, though from a broader perspective it might contribute only marginally to global solutions. But we are still waiting for the Social Democratic government to point out what exactly will be the way forward to accomplish something like this.

---

[60] Government of Denmark press briefing, "Finansministeren præsenterer forslag til finanslov 2021," https://www.regeringen.dk/nyheder/2020/forslag-til-finanslov-for-2021/, accessed September 05, 2020.

Yoko Tanaka
State Dysfunction in a 'Fortunate' Japan

Compared with humanity's long history of powerlessness against the onslaught of infectious diseases, we do have some means of fighting COVID-19. We have the medical means of testing, isolating, and treating; while limiting contact to prevent infection, we have the economic means to enable people to sustain their livelihood. In both cases, how these are deployed by the state will be a critical factor determining the social damage caused by the virus.

Japan, with its relatively few infections and deaths, may have had the good fortune of being spared the colossal devastation by COVID-19. However, this good fortune is not necessarily the result of appropriate and successful policies. On the contrary, in spite of the state retaining exclusive control over virus-fighting measures, the hollowing-out of state functions and limitation of services has frustrated and endangered the Japanese public.

Despite the fact that the fight against coronavirus demanded incredible amounts of work, the state has delegated all responsibilities to the overworked and longsuffering frontline workers. Cutting the budget and reducing personnel in health services and allocating only a piddling amount of support for medical care only exacerbated the situation. In addition, public assistance to support workers and companies who were facing economic hardship was insufficient and not allocated quickly enough. The state's reluctance to provide financial support to frontline workers resulted in a whole host of dysfunctions in the battle against the virus and led to widespread public suffering.

This essay explains how, instead of enjoying the 2020 Summer Olympics in Tokyo, the Japanese people have been enduring stressful days under a government bungling its coronavirus response.

Japan's Mysterious Pandemic Success

The first case of COVID-19 in Japan was confirmed on January 16. It spread quickly on a cruise ship anchored in Yokohama in February and reached its peak between late March and early April with a new infection rate of around five to seven hundred people a day. The infection rate began to decline after a state of emergency urging people to stay home as much as possible was declared in Tokyo, Osaka, and five other heavily populated prefectures on April 7, and expanded to the entire country on April 16. On May 25, when the state of emergency was lifted, 17,000 people were confirmed to have been infected, and 846 people had died.

The relatively few infections and deaths were chalked up to Japan's "mysterious pandemic success." "Crushingly crowded public transport. The world's oldest population. A huge outbreak on a cruise ship. A state of emergency without penalties. It sounded like a recipe for a coronavirus catastrophe."[61] "Yet with among the lowest death rates in the world, [...] everything seems to be going weirdly right."[62] The widespread use of masks, the custom of bowing rather than shaking

---

61 Jake Sturmer and Yumi Asada, "Japan Was Feared to Be the Next US or Italy: Instead Their Coronavirus Success Is a Puzzling 'Mystery'," *ABC News*, May 23, 2020, https://www.abc.net.au/news/2020-05-23/japan-was-meant-to-be-the-next-italy-on-coronavirus/12266912, accessed August 14, 2020.
62 Wiliam Sposato, "Japan's Halfhearted Coronavirus Measures are Working Anyway," *Foreign Policy*, May 14, 2020, https://foreignpolicy.com/2020/05/14/japan-coronavirus-pandemic-lockdown-testing, accessed August 14, 2020.

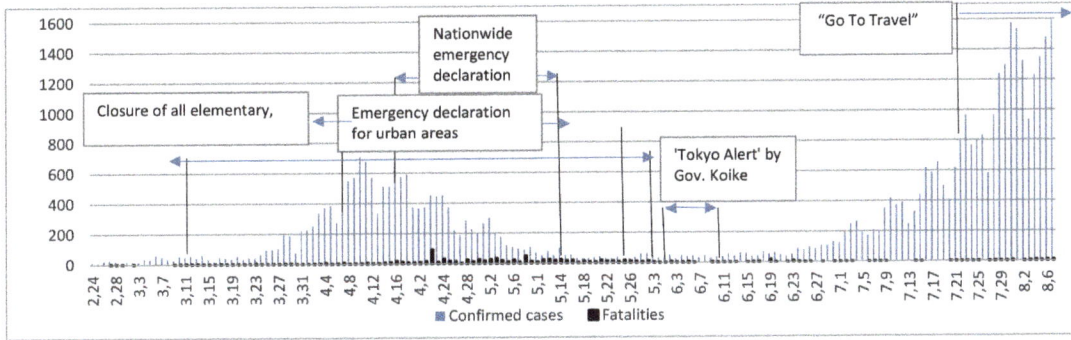

Figure 1: Trends of confirmed COVID-19 cases and fatalities in Japan and countermeasures[63]

hands or hugging, generally high standards of personal hygiene, and the removal of shoes when entering homes have all been held up as possible explanations for Japan's low infection rate.[64]

To be sure, when compared with the other G7 nations, the COVID-19 infection and mortality rates have been overwhelmingly low in Japan (Figure 2). The prime minister, Shinzo Abe, has used this fact to boast of the "Japan model." However, this assessment is misleading – the infection and mortality rate has been low across all Asia-Pacific countries, including China, Korea, and New Zealand. Among these countries, Japan's mortality rate is by no means admirable (Figure 3). This phenomenon cannot be accounted for by theories of Japanese exceptionalism, such as the high value afforded to cleanliness in Japan.

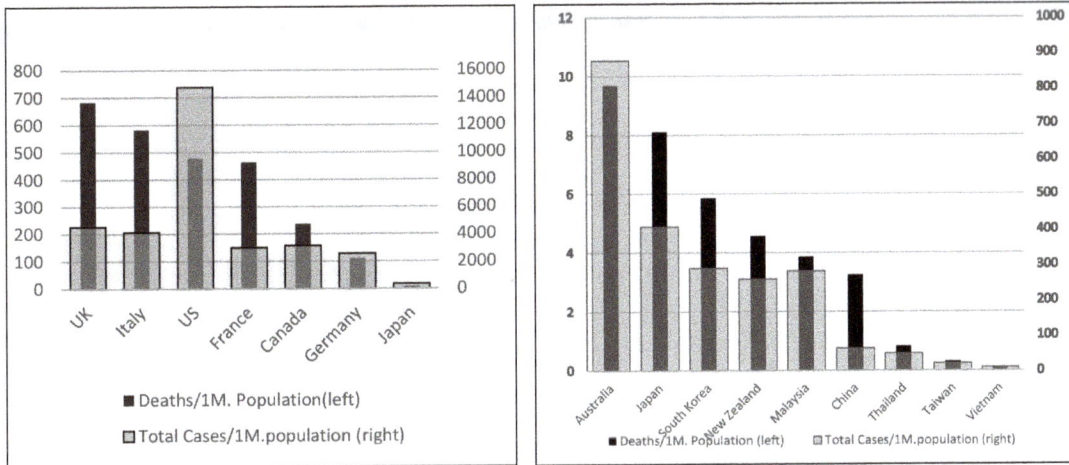

Figure 2 & Figure 3: Deaths and total confirmed cases of COVID-19 per million people in G7 countries and in Asia-Pacific countries (August 7, 2020)[65]

---

63 Source: Ministry of Health, Labor and Welfare (MHLW), "Situation Occurring Within the Country," https://www.mhlw.go.jp/stf/covid-19/kokunainohasseijoukyou.html, accessed August 09, 2020 (厚生労働省「国内の発生状況など」).

64 Justin McCurry, "From Near Disaster to Success Story: How Japan Has Tackled Coronavirus," *The Guardian*, May 22, 2020, https://www.theguardian.com/world/2020/may/22/from-near-disaster-to-success-story-how-japan-has-tackled-coronavirus, accessed August 14, 2020.

65 Source: "Coronavirus (COVID-19) Cases," *Our World in Data*, https://ourworldindata.org/covid-cases#world-maps-confirmed-cases-relative-to-the-size-of-the-population, accessed August 08, 2020.

The reason for the wide divergence in mortality rates between Europe and the United States and Asia is currently being studied: the yet-unknown 'Factor X.' Researchers have put forward various hypotheses including virus variants, genomic immunity, and differences in natural immunity. For example, that many Japanese people, even if they are infected, are asymptomatic or suffer only mild cases from which they recover through natural immunity. Many patients do not make antibodies – some scholars have deduced that the incidence rate is two percent among Japanese patients but twenty percent in Europe and the United States (the positivity rate for antibody tests is 12.3 percent in New York, 16.7 percent in London, and 0.1 percent in Tokyo).[66] In any case, Japan's low mortality rate cannot be attributed to prudent government action.

Medical Measures

You Can't Get a PCR Test in Japan

Japan's distinctive and baffling medical response to this infectious disease has been a policy of suppressing PCR (polymerase chain reaction) testing to the greatest possible extent – indeed, more than any other developed country, and as a near global anomaly (Figure 4).

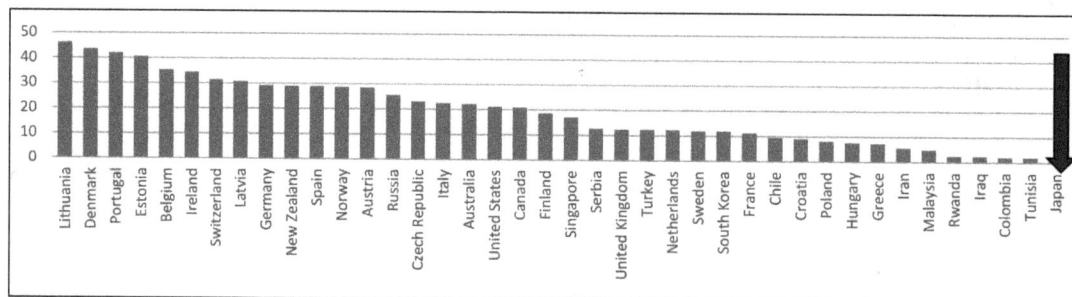

Figure 4: Total tests per 1,000 population in 40 countries (end of April 2020)[67]

In August, Japan's testing rate is ranked 159th among 215 countries; fewer tests have been conducted in Japan than in Uganda, Pakistan, or Libya.[68] Many people who request a test are unable to receive one. The official death toll, in turn, is limited to those whose death has been confirmed through testing.

On April 3, the United States Embassy in Tokyo announced, "The Japanese government's decision to not test broadly makes it difficult to accurately assess the COVID-19 prevalence rate," and advised American citizens to return to the United States.[69] Shigeru Omi, vice-chair of the Novel

---

66 Akiko Osaki, "COVID-19: The Reason for the Low Rates of Death and Severe Disease in Japan," *Toyo Keizai*, July 17, 2020, https://toyokeizai.net/articles/-/363402, accessed August 14, 2020 (大崎 明子「新型コロナ、日本で重症化率・死亡率が低いワケ」東洋経済新報社).

67 Source: "Coronavirus (COVID-19) Testing, Total tests performed relative to the size of population," *Our World in Data*, https://ourworldindata.org/covid-testing, accessed 14 August, 2020.

68 "Reported Cases and Deaths by Country, Territory, or Conveyance," *Worldometers*, https://www.worldometers.info/coronavirus/#countries, accessed August 08, 2020.

69 "Health Alert – US Embassy Tokyo," *US Embassy & Consulates in Japan*, April 3, 2020, https://jp.usembassy.gov/health-alert-us-embassy-tokyo-april3-2020, accessed August 14, 2020.

Coronavirus Expert Panel told the Diet, "No one knows what the actual number of infected people is – it could be ten times, fifteen times, or twenty times."[70]

In February, the Ministry of Health, Labor and Welfare (MHLW) had severely restricted the criteria for undergoing a COVID-19 consultation and receiving a test. Eligibility was limited to people such as returnees from China or those who had had close contact with returnees, those with fevers of 37.5 degrees or higher lasting for four days or longer accompanied by fatigue or trouble breathing, the elderly, and those with chronic illnesses.[71] Anyone showing symptoms was supposed to call the Consultation Center for Returnees and Exposed Individuals at their local public health center in order to get tested, but it was nearly impossible to actually get through, "even if you called all day long."[72] And even if their call was answered, they could not get tested unless they met all the criteria described above. As a result, only six percent of those who called the consultation center actually went on to receive a coronavirus test[73] – at a top-secret location. Physicians lamented: "I consulted the public health center about a number of patients I suspected were infected and they didn't accept a single one."[74] With the increase in the number of cases resulting from community transmission as well as infections within medical facilities, many have demanded more testing.

Social Divisions Surrounding PCR Testing

Yet, powerful forces working to suppress testing made it difficult to get tested or even advocate for expanded testing. The dominant opinion in Japan is that PCR testing should not be increased. The political clout of the groups blocking expanded testing, including medical bureaucrats, physicians, and a faction of the Japan Medical Association concerning infectious diseases, is extremely powerful and influential. These forces have made claims such as: "Infections spread more in countries conducting more tests," Increasing the number of tests will lead to a breakdown of the medical system," "'The PCR Religion' in Japan is the human disaster," "Testing causes trouble for other

70 "Vice-chair Omi: Number of True Cases 'Could be 10 or 20 Times Higher'," *Nihon Keizai Shimbun*, May 11, 2020, https://www.nikkei.com/article/DGXMZO58959520R10C20A5CC1000, accessed August 14, 2020 (「実際の感染者数「10倍か20倍か分からず」尾身副座長」日本経済新聞社).
71 MHLW Department of Health Division of Tuberculosis Infection, "Regarding Goals for Consultation and Diagnosis of COVID-19 Infection," February 17, 2020, https://www.mhlw.go.jp/content/10900000/000596978.pdf, accessed August 14, 2020 (厚生労働省健康局結核感染症課「新型コロナウイルス感染症についての相談・受診の目安について」).
72 Yasushi Inoue, "'If I Was the Source of the Coronavirus Infection...' Mounting Anxieties About the Difficulty in Asking Questions About COVID-19, Much Let Alone Getting Tested," *Tokyo Shimbun*, April 15, 2020, https://www.tokyo-np.co.jp/article/17167, accessed August 14, 2020 (井上靖史「「自分がコロナ感染源だったら...」検査どころか相談すら困難. つのる不安」東京新聞).
73 MHLW, "Case Numbers for Consultation on Symptoms, etc. at Consultation Centers for Returnees from Abroad and Exposed Individuals," March 31, 2020, https://www.mhlw.go.jp/content/10900000/000623322.pdf, accessed August 14, 2020 (厚生労働省「帰国者・接触者相談センターの症状等に関する相談件数」).
74 Naoki Kazuma and Mariko Tsuji, "The Darkness Preventing Person After Person from Receiving a PCR Test. The Preoccupation With Cluster Containment Leaves Frontline Workers Exhausted," April 29, 2020, *Toyo Keizai Online*, https://toyokeizai.net/articles/-/347451, accessed August 14, 2020 (風間 直樹・辻麻梨里子「PCR検査『全然受けられない人』を続出させる闇. クラスター対策への拘泥が現場を疲弊させる」); Rupert Wingfield, "Tokyo Hospitals are 'Hard Pressed Due to Infected Patients,' Inside the Facilities Dedicated to Treating the Novel Virus." *BBC News Japan*, April 24, 2020, https://www.bbc.com/japanese/video-52392925, accessed August 14, 2020 (「東京圏の病院は「感染患者でひっ迫」新型ウイルス専用治療室の内部」BBC).

people around you," "Testing is a waste of medical resources," "Laboratory technicians are very limited," and "Testing is inaccurate and more tests lead to more mistakes."[75]

This discourse was reflected in policymaking, when, as late as July, the state-run Committee for Novel Coronavirus Disease Control argued that, "even if we increase the number of tests, only a few people will test positive and it will do little to prevent spread of the infection," "test sensitivity is seventy percent and those with false negatives will spread the infection," "the cost of the test (manpower, goods, and capital) is enormous," and "it is problematic to hospitalize the one percent of false positives."[76]

Meanwhile, those calling for increased testing became the target of harsh criticism both by the mass media and on social media. Concerned about how few tests were being conducted in Japan, Masayoshi Son, CEO of the telecommunications giant SoftBank, announced on March 11 that he would offer free PRC tests to one million people, while Hiroshi Mikitani, CEO of the online shopping giant Rakuten, announced on April 20th that his company would begin selling PCR test kits online. Both men were subjected to severe criticism online and ended up backtracking on their offers.[77] Universities such as the University of Tokyo have the capacity to conduct over 100,000 tests a day using fully automated testing equipment, but these facilities were closed down by order of the education ministry. A University of Tokyo professor who tried to conduct tests in these facilities was buffeted by the "swirl of obstruction."[78]

---

75 Riko Muranaka, *The Novel Coronavirus Has Made Clear Japan's Weaknesses: Infectious Disease as National Defense* (Tokyo: Kodansha, 2020)（村中璃子『新型コロナから見えた日本の弱点. 国防としての感染症』光文社）; Yuko Matsuura, "Why the Certificate of Non-Infection Through PCR Testing Is Only Disadvantageous," *Asahi Shimbun*, March 08, 2020, https://digital.asahi.com/articles/ASN373G9WN36ULBJ01G.html, accessed August 14, 2020 (松浦祐子「『PCR検査で非感染証書』デメリットだけの理由を聞く」朝日新聞); Kimiyoshi Tsukazaki, "The Reason Why You Should Not Receive the PCR Tests Irresponsibly," *DIAMOND online*, March 13, 2020, https://diamond.jp/articles/-/231539?page=2, accessed August 14, 2020（塚崎公義「新型コロナの検査を安易に受けるべきでない理由」ダイヤモンドオンライン); Hiroaki Baba, "Expansion of PCR Testing for the Novel Coronavirus Should Be Undertaken Carefully: The Danger of False Results," *Japan Center for Economic Research*, April 15, 2020, https://www.jcer.or.jp/blog/baba-zonoakira20200415.html, accessed August 14, 2020 (馬場園明「新型コロナ、PCR検査拡大は慎重に. 誤判定がもたらす危険性」日本経済研究センター); Jun Sasaki, "Are PCR Tests Really Necessary?" *Yushokai Medical Corp.*, May 11, 2020, https://www.yushoukai.org/blog/pcr, accessed August 14, 2020（佐々木淳「本当にPCR検査は必要か？」医療法人悠翔会).
76 Subcommittee on Covid-19 Contagion Counter-measures, "Basic Strategy and Thoughts on Testing System," July 16, 2020, https://www.cas.go.jp/jp/seisaku/ful/kensa_senryaku.pdf, accessed August 14, 2020 (新型コロナウイルス感染症対策分科会「検査体制の基本的な考え・戦略」).
77 "Why Mr. Son Rolled-Back 'Providing PCR Tests at No Cost'," *Mainichi Shimbun*, March 12, 2020, https://mainichi.jp/articles/20200312/k00/00m/040/140000c, accessed August 14, 2020 (「孫正義さん『簡易PCR検査無償提供』はなぜトーンダウンしたのか」毎日新聞); "Rakuten Test Kit Sales Temporarily Halted, Resurgence of Conflict with Medical Association behind the Scenes," *NewsSocra*, May 02, 2020, https://news.yahoo.co.jp/articles/b30bb3cf7612e6d357647c-d571e5f6dbc77d2d7e, accessed August 14, 2020 (「楽天の検査キット販売一時中止、背後に医師会との対立再燃」ニュースソクラ).
78 Tatsuhiko Kodama, "'Infection is 10 Times Reported Rate': Government Expert Panel Following Unspoken Orders of Government is 'Nonsense'," *Japan National Press Club Interview*, July 03, 2020, https://www.m3.com/open/iryoIshin/article/793969, accessed August 14, 2020 (児玉龍彦「『感染者は報告の10倍』、行政官に忖度する専門家会議『意味がない』」日本記者クラブ会見).

Handling by Closed Administrative Organizations

Why has Japan continued to suppress testing in this way? One reason is that the handling of COVID-19 measures has been strictly limited to certain administrative organizations involved in the management of infectious diseases.

It began on January 28, when the government declared COVID-19 to be a designated infectious disease under Japan's Act on the Prevention of Infectious Diseases. This designation removed COVID-19 measures from the jurisdiction of general health care infrastructure and placed them under the exclusive control of administrative organizations: Division of Tuberculosis and Infectious Diseases Control in the MHLW Health Service Bureau, the National Institute of Infectious Diseases (NIID), the Regional Institute of Health, public health centers, and Designated Specified Infectious Disease Medical Institutions. These organizations formed a kind of strong-tied community of experts, which resembles the scientific community of atomic energy.[79] Some of their representative members were to lead the committee guiding the government response to the virus.

PCR tests were here positioned as "aggressive epidemiologic surveys to be conducted by the NIID" at the public expense, with all the data integrated to NIID. This plan did not include other testing channels such as private hospitals, universities, or testing companies. Regarding this monopolization of testing and associated data by the NIID, former MHLW minister Yoichi Masuzoe commented: "NIID's predecessor was incorporated into the Imperial Japanese Army. Suppressing information is in its DNA."[80] The decision-making process behind the measures have not been released to the public, purportedly to allow for "frank discussion" of the topic (Figure 5).

Physicians remained unable to order COVID-19 tests even after they began to be covered by insurance on March 6. Testing within medical facilities was only permitted through epidemiologic surveys by the NIID and relied on time-consuming subcontracting agreements and acceptable facility conditions. Drive-through testing sites, simple outdoor testing facilities, and fever clinics were not budgeted for at all. As a result, except in a few cases where they were independently established by hospitals or local municipalities, these kinds of testing channels did not become widely available in Japan.

Because the law required anyone testing positive to be hospitalized regardless of their symptoms, hospital beds were quickly filled by patients with mild symptoms, leaving seriously ill patients unable to receive inpatient treatment. In order to be able to treat the seriously ill patients, it was critical to test as little as possible and thus suppress the numbers of those testing positive. From April, those with mild symptoms were allowed to recover in hotels or at home, but with insufficient accommodation, the pressure to not expand testing only increased.

---

79 Masahiro Kami, "The 'Infectious Disease Clique' That Monopolizes Funds and Information: Novel Coronavirus and Clinical Research," *Welfare and Wellbeing*, July 07, 2020, Jijitsushin, https://www.jiji.com/jc/v4?id=202007skkm30001, accessed August 14, 2020（上昌広「資金と情報を独占する『感染症ムラ』. 新型コロナウイルスと臨床研究」時事通信社).
80 Masuzoe, Yoichi, "Why at This Time are There Not More PCR Tests?," *Japan Business Press*, July 25, 2020, https://jbpress.ismedia.jp/articles/-/61433?page=2, accessed August 14, 2020（舛添 要一「なぜこの期に及んでもPCR検査は増えないのか」日本ビジネスプレス).

Figure 5: Minutes from 2nd meeting of the Novel Coronavirus Government Expert Panel (February 19, 2020: pp. 28–32)[81]

Overcapacity and Overwhelmed

The situation may have turned out differently if the state had allocated sufficient funds and personnel to this channel. Unfortunately, however, Japan has been hollowing out its public organizations responsible for public hygiene, health, and welfare for the past thirty years. The budget and the staffing for public health institutes have been reduced, and medical facilities and hospital beds for infectious diseases have been cut. The number of public health centers, which were once exemplary institutions of public health and hygiene, was reduced by half during the post-1990s administrative reforms. It was not only that the number of personnel were reduced; fifty-three percent of MHLW employees were also transformed into low-wage, non-regular workers on short-term contracts.[82] It was this hollowed-out public organization that was then entrusted with the entire pandemic response.

Even with staff working until late at night, these public health centers, which served as the points of contact for COVID-19 countermeasures, were soon overwhelmed.[83] "The telephone counseling line would ring off the hook from the morning. In addition to testing requests and questions about potential infections, we also get calls about disinfecting in businesses and from mothers asking about how to take care of their kids while schools were closed." Staff, donning personal protective equipment, transport patient testing samples and arrange for hospitalization or treatment at a hotel if a person tests positive; they drive the patient to the facility and then disinfect the inside

---

81 The cabinet office in response to an information disclosure request on February 25, 2020. The cabinet office says redacted notes were "the portion of the record that would not hamper the frankly exchange of opinions or unduly impair the neutrality of decision making," (April 28, 2020). Source: "Stenographic Record of the Second Novel Coronavirus Expert Meeting Released Black as Coal," *Oshidori Mako & Ken Portal*, April 28, 2020, http://oshidori-makoken.com/?p=4601, accessed August 14, 2020 (「新型コロナ、第二回専門家会議の速記録、真っ黒で開示」); "Redaction Thick as Black-Painted Walls Prevents 'Verification' of Meeting Notes from Novel Coronavirus Expert Meeting," *Fuji News Network*, August 21, 2020, https://www.fnn.jp/articles/-/76291, accessed August 21, 2020 (「 新型コロナ専門家会議の発言録 "検証"阻む黒塗りの壁」).

82 Cabinet Bureau of Personnel Affairs, "Statistics on Condition of Clerical Employees for Public Servants in Office," https://www.e-stat.go.jp/stat-search/files?page=1&layout=dataset&kikan=00000&stat_infid=000031646160, accessed August 14, 2020 (内閣官房「一般職国家公務員在職状況統計表」).

83 "Public Employees Fighting COVID-19 at Ministry of Health, Labor and Welfare 'Covid Headquarters:' Health Care Centers on the Ground," *NHK News Web*, April 2, 2020, https://www3.nhk.or.jp/news/html/20200402/k10012363911000.html, accessed August 14, 2020 (荒川真帆「コロナと闘う公務員たち. 厚労省「コロナ本部」、現場の保健所は」).

of the vehicle. Staff are also responsible for visiting the site where the infection occurred, taking contact histories, and tracking close contacts. They have to write up reports, to be faxed to the local municipality, check on numerous patients who have been either hospitalized or are undergoing in-patient treatment twice a day by email, or telephone to ask about any sudden changes in their physical condition.

"We are doing all of these tasks with just over ten staff members. If one of our team collapses, it's over." Thus, the responsibility for the whole process of infection control – from testing to follow-up to quarantine to treatment – has been borne by a small number of workers in public health centers. Staff are overwhelmed: no matter how hard they work, there is no improvement in sight.

Medical Care Limited by Lack of Support

Health care facilities are also facing a crisis because the state will not allocate funds to hospitals. According to a survey by the Japan Hospital Association, two-thirds of hospitals nationwide were operating at a financial deficit in May.[84] This figure rises to eighty percent for hospitals accepting COVID-19 patients and ninety percent for hospitals in Tokyo. The deficit is caused by decreased profits related to fewer hospital visits and delayed operations, combined with the increased cost of implementing infection-prevention measures. The government tripled their payment points for COVID-19 patients, but this still did not cover the shortfall. "Without emergency subsidies to hospitals, it will be impossible to adequately respond to new outbreaks in the future. We should be very concerned about the collapse of medical care in the region," the Hospital Association announced in June. Kyoto University Hospital could not even cover the cost of a negative pressure chamber; it resorted to crowdfunding in July to raise the thirty million yen (285,000 US dollars) needed for the construction.[85]

This cash crunch has affected health care workers. They have worked day and night under incredibly stressful working conditions to save patient lives. As a tragic antithesis to the United Kingdom's "Clap for Carers," Japan has seen the widespread harassment of health care workers and their families. Health care associations have reported stories such as that "the children of health care workers at a hospital with coronavirus outbreaks are bullied at school," and "day care facilities bar the children of doctors and nurses."[86]

---

84 Japan Hospital Association, All Japan Hospital Association, Japanese Association of Medical Care Corporations: "Emergency Inspection of Hospital Operating Conditions Due to Expansion of COVID-19 Infections," June 05, 2020, http://www.hospital.or.jp/pdf/06_20200605_01.pdf, accessed August 14, 2020（日本病院会・全日本病院協会・日本医療法人協会「新型コロナウイルス感染拡大による病院経営状況緊急調査(追加報告)」).

85 Susumu Miyamoto, "On Implementing Crowdfunding," *Kyoto University Hospital*, https://www.kuhp.kyoto-u.ac.jp/relation/crowdfunding20200710.html, accessed August 14, 2020 (宮本享「 クラウドファンディング（寄附募集）の実施について」京都大学医学部附属病院).

86 Japanese Nursing Ethics Association, "Appreciation for Medical Professionals Fighting COVID-19," April 03, 2020, http://jnea.net/9.html（日本看護倫理学会事務局「新型コロナウイルスと戦う医療従事者に敬意を」); Japan Medical Association, "For a Correct Understanding of the COVID-19 Contagion," August 08, 2020, http://www.med.or.jp/people/info/people_info/009162.html, both accessed August 14, 2020 (日本医師会 「新型コロナウイルス感染症の正しい理解のために」).

Beyond the physical and mental burden, economic damage has also occurred. About one-third of hospitals announced further cuts to staff summer bonuses.[87] One egregious example is the Tokyo Women's Medical University Hospital: when accepting COVID-19 patients resulted in the hospital running a budget deficit of three billion yen (28.5 million dollars), it announced that it would not pay summer bonuses to any of its doctors, nurses, medical technicians, or administrative staff – bonuses that had averaged 600,000 yen, approximately 5,700 US dollars, the previous year.

Staff deplored this decision: "I cry when I think about how we don't even receive gratitude when we have been working ourselves to death. The nurses I work with are losing motivation and there are many who want to quit" (female nurse in her thirties), "My salary in May was only sixty percent because of leave. I won't even get a bonus and I'm in the red just from rent and utility expenses. I can't repay my student loans or even have enough money for food" (woman in her twenties).[88]

As health care workers saw their livelihoods increasingly threatened, medical staff at Funabashi Futawa Hospital went on strike in June – a rare scene in Japan – to protest the decision to cut bonuses.[89] At Eiju General Hospital in Tokyo, a crowdfunding campaign raised 47 million yen (450,000 US dollars) to provide cash payments to workers. Government aid failed to reach deficit-ridden hospitals and exhausted health care workers quickly enough as Japan headed into the next season of rising infection rates.

Economic Measures

The Effects of Stay-at-home Advisories and Business Closure Requests

State mismanagement has not been limited to medical measures. The government has shown extreme reluctance to agree to any financial expenditure to support those who are facing serious problems because of COVID-19. Because the economic measures were sometimes abrupt – and, more often, too little too late – many people fell into crisis without receiving any help from the government for months. The public's feelings of abandonment are reflected in the approval ratings of the Abe administration – the longest-serving administration in Japanese modern history – which had plunged to thirty-four percent by August.[90]

In terms of strategies for reducing contact, Japan bucked the global trend of lockdown measures and adopted the lax policy of only urging people to stay home and requesting businesses to close voluntarily. The only national policy implemented across the country was the sudden closure of all elementary, junior high, and high schools on March 2. This drastic measure, an idea of one

87 "30 percent of medical institutions to cut summer bonuses, additional resignations feared," *NHK News Web*, July 13, 2020, https://www3.nhk.or.jp/news/html/20200713/k10012511731000.html, accessed August 14, 2020（「医療機関の3割で夏のボーナス引き下げ 退職者増えるおそれも」）.
88 "The Health Care System Is Already Collapsing! The Crisis of Nurses Quitting in Mass After Having Their Bonuses Cut or Reduced," *J-CAST*, July 19, 2020, https://www.j-cast.com/kaisha/2020/07/19390279.html?p=all, accessed August 14, 2020「これはもう医療崩壊だ！ ボーナス「引き下げ」「ゼロ」で看護師が大量退職の危機」J-CAST）
89 "Doctors Strike in Protest of 'Bonus Cuts Due to Corona-Caused Revenue Loss' and Demand the 'State to Help'," *J-CAST* , July 13, 2020, https://www.j-cast.com/2020/07/13390058.html?p=2, accessed August 14, 2020（「医師らのストにエール。『コロナ減収でボーナスカット』に『国は支援を』」）.
90 "Cabinet Approval-disapproval Rate," http://www.nhk.or.jp/senkyo/shijiritsu/, accessed August 14, 2020.

of Abe's aides, was implemented without consulting the minister of education and left schools all over the country in a state of chaos.

On April 7, Prime Minister Abe declared a state of emergency in Tokyo, Osaka, and five other urban areas, expanding it nationwide on April 16. This emergency order, however, only urged people to stay home, to refrain from the 'three Cs' – closed spaces, crowds, and close-contact – and to reduce social interaction by seventy to eighty percent. Tokyo requested the closure of exhibition facilities and venues for large-scale commercial, recreational, educational, sports, and cultural gatherings from April 11, and for smaller businesses to implement measures to prevent infection and restaurants to close at 8pm. As a result of the level of cooperation with which the Japanese public responded to these directives, infection rates passed their peak and the nationwide emergency declaration was lifted in stages between May 14 and May 25.

Unfortunately, however, even these lax stay-at-home advisories and business closure requests had a devastating impact on employment rates and livelihoods. Figure 6 shows employment figures for April 2020 compared with the same month of the previous year.

Here you can clearly see the impact of COVID-19 on work in Japan. First, although there was a minimal increase in unemployment, workers taking leave (those not working for a month after being told not to come back to work) increased by approximately six million.

Second, the breakdown of the six million employees on leave reveals high numbers of women (sixty percent), non-regular workers (fifty percent), and the self-employed (twelve percent). By industry, the proportion of those on leave in the customer-facing service industries is conspicuously high; the food and hospitality sectors have seen the largest proportion of those on leave, followed by wholesale and retail, manufacturing, education, life services, and entertainment.

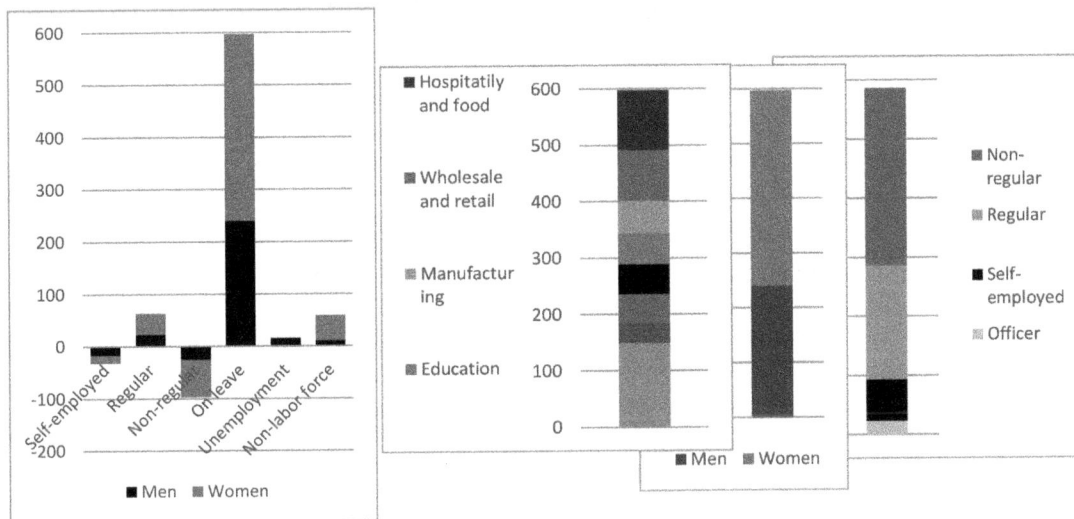

Figure 6: Changes in employment structure (from April 2019 to April 2020)[91]

91 Source: Ministry of Internal Affairs and Communications, Labor Force Survey, 2019-2020, https://www.stat.go.jp/data/roudou/rireki/gaiyou.html#ft_tsuki, accessed August 14, 2020 (総務省「労働力調査(基本集計)」).

Third, among the reduced 970,000 non-regular workers, 710,000 were women. At the same time, 480,000 women newly joined the "non-labor-force population" (people not seeking work), a phenomenon thought to have resulted from the mass closure of elementary, junior high, and high schools across the country, which obliged women to stay at home in order to take care of their children.

The impact on employment and livelihoods has been significant for non-regular workers, small businesses in the service industry, and women, rather than for the regular office workers who could flexibly switch to teleworking instead of taking leave. What kind of measures, then, did the Japanese government implement in response to this economic distress?

Fish Coupons, Two Masks, and a Travel Campaign

In March, countries around the world were taking various measures in response to the virus, including city-wide lockdowns and penalties for breaking quarantine. Governments were planning and implementing various economic relief measures such as cash payments to citizens, benefits for small businesses, salary subsidies, rent moratoriums, and large-scale business loans. In late March, millions of Germans breathed a sigh of relief as the German government provided substantial benefits to small and medium-sized enterprises, and freelancers.

Meanwhile, in Japan, policymakers were discussing meat and fish coupons. The ruling Liberal Democratic Party (LDP)'s Agriculture and Forestry Division was behind the plan to shore up demand for the high-end Japanese beef and high-end fish flooding the market due to falling numbers of overseas tourists. After a barrage of criticism, these coupons were removed from the list of emergency relief measures in late March.

In their place was the now-infamous *Abenomask* initiative. On April 1, Prime Minister Abe announced that he would distribute two small gauze masks to every family in Japan, on the advice of his aide. This was taken as an April Fool's joke, derisively dubbed the *Abenomask* ('Abe-no-mask' translates as 'Abe's mask'), and ridiculed on social media.[92] The government's announcement on April 7 that it would be spending 46.6 billion yen (around 440 million US dollars) on the distribution of masks as part of its emergency relief measures was widely denounced as critics questioned, "Why not spend that money on testing and medical treatments?"

Few households actually received their *Abenomask* during the period when there was a shortage of cheap masks. *Abenomask* distribution was completed at the end of June, by which time ordinary non-woven masks were once again widely and cheaply available.

At the end of April, the government approved a gargantuan 1.35-trillion-yen or 13-billion-dollar budget to promote domestic tourism. As part of this 'Go To Travel' campaign, the government would cover fifty percent of domestic travel expenses up to 20,000 yen (190 US dollars) per person per night. The start of the campaign was oddly moved forward on July 22, when a single-day record

---

92 Travis Fedshun, "Coronavirus Measure in Japan of Two Masks Per Home Taken as April Fool's Joke, Mocked as 'Abenomask'," *Fox News*, April 02, 2020, https://www.foxnews.com/world/coronavirus-japan-abenomask-april-fools-joke-outbreak-mask-per-home; Gearoid Reidy, "From Abenomics to Abenomask: Japan Mask Plan Meets With Derision," *Bloomberg*, April 02, 2020, https://www.bloomberg.com/news/articles/2020-04-02/from-abenomics-to-abenomask-japan-mask-plan-meets-with-derision; Elaine Lies and Linda Sieg, "Two Masks, No Lockdown: Japan PM's Latest Coronavirus Step Riles Social Media," *Reuters*, April 2, 2020, https://www.reuters.com/article/us-health-BN21K0CQ, all accessed August 14, 2020.

of 795 new COVID-19 cases were confirmed in Japan. Go To Travel was met with widespread criticism for promoting movement at a time when people were being urged to exercise self-restraint. In response, the government announced that the campaign would exclude travel to and from Tokyo, leaving travel agents and travelers alike confused. In the first two weeks of the campaign, the number of new COVID-19 infections shot up to 1,354 per day and spread to previously unaffected areas of the country. While the national government was encouraging people to travel, local governors were begging them to stay at home, leaving the public at a complete loss.

Funds Falling Short

The government did eventually do more to help those suffering from job losses, though too little too late.[93] The first relief measure, in late April, was a fixed one-off payment of 100,000 yen or 950 US dollars to all residents. However, it took an extremely long time to actually arrive. As late as August, residents in parts of Tokyo and Osaka had still not been paid. This delay provoked a troubling incident in May, when an unemployed thirty-nine-year-old man appeared at the city hall, directed a knife at himself, saying, "I have no more food to eat. I'll die if I can't get the money right now."[94]

The second relief measure came in May, in the form of subsidies to sustain small and medium-sized enterprises and freelancers in crisis. Where monthly sales had dropped at least fifty percent against the previous year, they were promised twelve months' worth of the shortfall up to a maximum of two million yen (19,000 US dollars), to be paid within two weeks. However, this payment also arrived too late. Many people waited for months without receiving the funds. Hashtags such as "#sustainabilitysubsidiesnotpaid" began trending on Twitter, with users posting tweets such as, "Applied on May 9, still no money on June 17. I consulted with my husband and decided it was time to close the business. We have been neglected and ridiculed by our country and feel terrible."[95]

The third measure involved interest-free and unsecured loans through the Japan Finance Corporation and private financial institutions, from May onward. However, many struggling businesses were deemed risky creditors and denied loans as a result; many companies who managed to get loans saw the money quickly run out on rent and personnel expenses. In response to a public outcry, a housing security benefit system was finally launched on July 14.

The only relief package that has functioned since March is the welfare fund loan system, providing 100,000 to 200,000 yen (950 to 1,900 US dollars) to households struggling with living expenses and helping to partially stave-off homelessness.

---

93 Emi Urabe, Takyou Yuko, and Nohara Yoshiaki, "Sluggish State Coronavirus Assistance, Purportedly the 'World's Largest' Economic Countermeasure, Fails to Reach Members of the Public," *Bloomberg News*, June 24, 2020, https://www.bloomberg.co.jp/news/articles/2020-06-23/QCDASHDWLU6901, accessed August 14, 2020 (占部絵美他「政府コロナ支援は国民に行き渡らず．もたつく『世界最大』の経済対策」ブルームバーグ).

94 "'I'll Die, if You Don't Give Me the Benefit Money Right Now,' Why Did a Man Point a Knife at Himself at the Service Counter? Loneliness, Poverty and Misunderstanding," *Mainichi Shimbun*, July 04, 2020, https://mainichi.jp/articles/20200703/k00/00m/040/341000c, accessed August 14, 2020 (「『給付金、今すぐくれないなら死ぬ』なぜ男性は窓口で自分に包丁を向けたのか．孤独と貧困と誤解と」毎日新聞).

95 Tweet of 'asamichan', July 17, 2020, https://twitter.com/asamich71979546/status/1273133723844780032, accessed August 14, 2020.

The Reality of Leave Allowances and Employment Subsidies

Far more important than these benefits is the subsidy system that supports the immense number of workers on leave. The Employment Adjustment Subsidy was developed after the oil shock and the financial crisis of 2008 and is financed from the unemployment insurance system. The government subsidizes the leave allowance that employers are required to pay to workers (specified as sixty percent or more of workers' wages) if they are forced to reduce operations due to a change in economic circumstances. The government supplements two-thirds of this allowance for small and medium-sized enterprises and half for large enterprises, up to a maximum of 8,330 yen or 80 dollars a day for up to one hundred days per year.

From mid-April, the subsidy rate increased to seventy-five percent for large enterprises and one hundred percent for small and medium-sized enterprises, on the condition that the employer did not terminate any employment. Additionally, the daily wage limit was raised to 15,000 yen in June. Furthermore, the limit on eligibility for unemployment insurance to those having worked for six or more months was also lifted. This change meant that many non-regular workers such as part-time and dispatch workers were now also eligible. In theory, this system would enable all workers to maintain their employment, protecting both their livelihood as well as that of business owners.

The reality of this system, however, is quite different. First, many workers are simply not paid a leave allowance. Some businesses are unaware of their obligations in this respect, especially for non-regular workers. Second, although the leave allowance is specified as sixty percent or more of the worker's salary, the amount they receive is actually much lower.[96] The formula for determining leave allowance – salary ÷ number of calendar days (30) x days on leave (22) x 60 percent – results in forty-four percent of the salary, which, minus tax and insurance, could end up being less than thirty percent of average salary.

Third, employers who do pay a leave allowance have a very difficult time in applying for an employment adjustment. There is a wait of over one month for a meeting with the Labor Bureau. Those who try to apply are faced with a complicated system requiring myriad document submissions. Many become frustrated to the point where their "hearts are breaking," and end up abandoning their application.[97]

Fourth, even if an employer does manage to get through the application process, it takes the bureau at least two months to make a decision. As of the end of April, only 282 of 2,500 applicants had been paid, out of the 200,000 employers who had consulted the office since February.[98] The public's point of contact to the Labor Bureau, job-placement offices called Hello Work, were said to have gone into "melt down" due to serious personnel issues – much of the personnel are

---

96 "How Much Leave Allowance Do I Get? Actually Less Than Half of My Wages!" *Zeimo*, May 22, 2020, https://zeimo.jp/article/31326, accessed August 14, 2020 (「休業手当はいくらもらえるの？実は給与の半分以下！」ゼイモ).

97 Kengo Ichihara and Taira Godo, "With 200,000 Employment Adjustment Subsidy Consultations, Applicants' 'Hearts Are Breaking'," *Asahi Shimbun Digital*, April 30, 2020, https://digital.asahi.com/articles/ASN4Z3HBDN4XPTIL03K.html, accessed August 14, 2020 (市原研吾、後藤泰良「雇用調整助成金相談20万件．申請者「心折れそうに」」朝日新聞).

98 Hiroaki Mizushima, "It is Almost Impossible to Use Employment Adjustment Subsidies! Difference Between the System and Reality," *Yahoo! News*, April 29, 2020, https://news.yahoo.co.jp/byline/mizushimahiroaki/20200429-00175816/, accessed August 14, 2020 (水島宏明「『雇用調整助成金』ほとんど使えない！『制度と実際の乖離』」ヤフーニュース); Satoshi Tanaka, "Payment of Japan's 'Employment Adjustment Subsidy' Comes Too Late: Learn from Germany's Rapid Payment System That Protects Workers," *Toyo Keizai Online*, April 11, 2020, https://toyokeizai.net/articles/-/343663, accessed August 14, 2020 (田中理「日本の「雇用調整助成金」は支給まで遅すぎる．労働者を守るドイツの迅速な支給制度に学べ」東洋経済).

non-regular workers and the total number of staff is entirely insufficient in order to fulfill a multitude of tasks, with the prevention of fraudulent applications made a high priority.[99] The process was simplified in mid-May, made available online in June, and permitted workers to make a direct application for leave allowance; this only increased the confusion for applicants and Labor Bureau employees alike. Unfortunately, many business owners as well as workers had seen their cash holdings vanish in the meantime.

The State and Workers During the Resurgence of COVID-19

The number of new COVID-19 infections in Japan remained low until mid-July, and despite remaining anxieties, daily life began returning to normal. Exhausted workers in health centers, hospitals, and other frontline facilities were able to catch their breath, and the number of workers placed on leave, which had reached almost 6 million in April, dropped to 2.36 million in June. From June to July, the quantity of payments as well as the amount paid in delayed sustainability benefits and employment adjustment subsidies finally increased, developments which, to a certain extent, helped many people maintain their jobs and livelihoods. It appeared that the most harrowing days of the crisis may finally have come to an end.

Since the middle of July, however, the number of COVID-19 cases has significantly increased within Japan again. Since infection and mortality rates in Japan have remained low, it is possible that Japan will escape the devastating harm the virus has wrought in other regions of the world.

Nonetheless, the fact that the government, whose response to the crisis can hardly be called swift or appropriate, has shown little change in its position or attitude toward the disaster has left dissatisfaction and anxiety among the public. Over these past few months, the state has continued its reactive approach of delegating life and livelihood-saving responsibilities to those working with very limited resources, depending on these workers' tenacity and sense of personal responsibility to get the job done. The state dysfunction evinced by the government's inability to make necessary reforms in order to move swiftly and proactively in a crisis augurs more human suffering in possible pandemics to come.

---

99 Nobuhide Kiuchi, "The Problem of Personnel Shortages at Job-Placement Offices 'Hello Work' Heightens the Risk of a Worsened Employment Situation," *Nomura Research Institute*, June 17, 2020, https://www.nri.com/jp/knowledge/blog/lst/2020/fis/kiuchi/0617, accessed August 14, 2020 (木内登英「雇用悪化リスクを高めるハローワークの人手不足問題」野村総合研究所).

Thwarted Youth

James Williams

Learning in Lockdown: Studying and Teaching in Wales during the Coronavirus Pandemic

Introduction

Institutions, workplaces, and daily practices were disrupted and transformed as coronavirus (COVID-19) spread across the world in 2020. Education and schools were a workplace and area of public life that were affected significantly in an attempt to slow the speed of the infection. 188 countries implemented country-wide school closures in 2020. Ninety-four percent of the world's children faced disruption in their learning. The Brookings Institute has calculated a global economic impact of school closures to be over ten trillion dollars.[1] While the impact of school closures is likely to be greater and more prolonged in the global south, as anthropologist Jean Comaroff writes, "Affluent Western countries have not been spared the wrath of the pandemic [...] Their fate has been worsened by their sense of their own invulnerability, their stubborn ideological commitments."[2]

This essay describes the closures of secondary schools across Wales and the United Kingdom in March 2020 and the challenges of migrating teaching and learning from classrooms to computer screens. Both endeavors proved politically controversial and highly detrimental to children's learning. The essay, written at a time when debates around schools were ongoing and unfinished, also considers the impact of school closures on secondary school pupils and teachers. While some research has been conducted into the impact of school closures on children, very little research has been conducted into the impact of school closures and the transformation of teaching as a professional practice on teachers. The essay suggests some avenues for further exploration as the impact of the pandemic on public education becomes clear.

Closing Schools in Britain

The United Kingdom was the last country in Western Europe to implement country-wide school closures in March 2020 in an attempt to curb the spread of coronavirus. Schools in Italy, the European country initially hit hardest by the pandemic, closed first on March 5 (schools in northern Italy closed two weeks earlier). Schools in Greece, Albania, Romania, and Czechia closed next. Schools in the Republic of Ireland were closed on March 12. By March 12, the day the director general of the World Health Organization named Europe the "new epicenter" of the pandemic, fourteen European countries had fully closed their schools and nine had partially closed them. By March 16, all European countries bar Sweden, Belarus, and the United Kingdom had fully closed their schools.

For many in the United Kingdom in March, following news of school closures in Europe and alarmed by growingly dire national headlines and health figures, school closures seemed

1 George Psacharopoulos, et al. "The Covid-19 cost of school closures," The Brookings Institute, April 29, 2020, https://www.brookings.edu/blog/education-plus-development/2020/04/29/the-covid-19-cost-of-school-closures/, accessed August 15, 2020.

2 Jean Comaroff, "When the virus makes the timeline," *Social Anthropology* 28 (2020): 245–246, 245.

inevitable. Yet even as late as March 17, despite the number of confirmed COVID-19 cases in the United Kingdom passing two thousand and the number of reported deaths reaching seventy-one, the prime minister, Boris Johnson, was adamant that British schools would not shut. Accused of "playing roulette with the public" by the editor-in-chief of *The Lancet*,[3] Johnson's position on schools confused and unsettled the public. Keeping schools open appeared to be at odds with a raft of government announcements that emphasized the pandemic's seriousness: rationing in supermarkets; a three-month moratorium on home mortgage payments in anticipation of a surge in unemployment; postponing elections; news that the Queen had retreated to Windsor Castle to self-isolate indefinitely; a surprise announcement of a 3.2-million-pound fund (4.1 million US dollars) to accommodate all homeless people; an outbreak of COVID-19 in parliament.

Johnson reversed his position on the afternoon of March 18, the day the United Kingdom death toll passed one hundred. He announced his decision to close schools "from March 23 until further notice" from 10 Downing Street as the British education secretary, Gavin Williamson, made a synchronized statement in parliament. From March 23, Williamson explained, schools were to be repurposed as childcare centers for vulnerable children and the children of 'key workers' – children whose parents work in the health service, core public services, supermarkets, etc. Public examinations in May and June were canceled. Teachers were charged with providing distance learning for pupils at home. Speaking alongside Johnson, Sir Patrick Vallance, the government's chief scientific adviser, said the closures were "not because schools are dangerous places for children," but to "put some brakes" on the transmission of the virus and ensure NHS (National Health Service) hospitals did not surpass capacity. Scientists were openly querying the value of school closures as a public health measure, Vallance explained, noting that "the vast majority of children and adolescents experience mild symptoms in response to SARS-CoV-2 infection" and that school closures were unlikely to reduce COVID-19 deaths overall by more than two to four percent.[4]

As well as reacting to public pressure and scientific advice, the government's decision was also influenced by domestic politics. Johnson's statement came some hours after the governments of Wales, Scotland, and Northern Ireland announced imminent school closures in their nations and region. The Welsh education minister, Kirsty Williams, spoke first that morning (March 18) announcing school closures in Wales, followed by the first minister of Scotland, Nicola Sturgeon, moments later. Education, like health and policing, is a devolved matter in the United Kingdom. The governments of Wales, Scotland, and Northern Ireland make decisions over schools and schooling entirely independently of London. Responding to public and teacher concerns more quickly, Welsh, Scottish, and Northern Irish politicians demonstrated leadership and clarity on the matter of schools by acting ahead of London. They appeared to take pleasure in upstaging the British prime minister, and enjoyed boosts in public approval for doing so. This ignited tensions that would escalate during the months that followed – concerning the management of the pandemic overall, but also reflecting divisions in the United Kingdom that have widened since the 2016 Brexit referendum.

---

3 Richard Horton, *The Covid-19 Catastrophe: What's Gone Wrong and How to Stop It Happening Again* (Cambridge: Polity Press, 2020).
4 Neil M. Ferguson et al., "Impact of non-pharmaceutical inventions (NPIs) to reduce Covid-19 mortality and health-care demand," https://doi.org/10.25561/77482, accessed August 15, 2020.

Locking Down Society

A full United Kingdom 'lockdown' was announced on the afternoon of March 23. "Stay at home" SMS messages were sent to all United Kingdom mobile telephones. For the next six weeks, all residents of the United Kingdom were unable to leave their homes except for health visits, essential work and shopping, and one hour of daily outdoor exercise. Confirmed cases of COVID-19 peaked two weeks after schools were shut (35,711 for the first full week in April), with the highest weekly death toll reported the week after (6,399). As case numbers soared, vociferous debates unfolded concerning the lack of personal protective equipment in hospitals and the safety of elderly residents in nursing homes. Led by the opposition Labour Party, criticisms that the government was "too slow to lock down" began to surface (in which the closure of schools was central), a miscalculation the prime minister appeared to acknowledge in a BBC interview at the end of July 2020.

Schools in the United Kingdom closed their doors to teachers and pupils on Friday, March 20. From March 23, a new form of teaching and learning began for most school teachers and pupils. Children received codes to access online classrooms, began streaming recorded or live lessons on their computers and smart phones, and completed home-packs of work sent out by schools under parental supervision. Teachers drew on their professional skills and creativity to deliver lessons from afar, aware of the challenges most pupils would face completing work without their teachers and peers nearby. Teachers I interviewed for this essay were particularly mindful of balancing learning and wellbeing when school closures began. They described pupils becoming anxious in the weeks before schools closed and feared that overly demanding home learning and the social isolation produced by school closures would heighten this. Teachers accordingly devised activities to engage children positively alongside formal learning: live-streamed exercises lessons; reading and writing competitions; TikTok dance challenges.

Schools and schooling moved out of the news headlines once learning in lockdown began. Online learning started well for many children. In fact, teachers told me how some of the children excelled in this new environment – working more independently; using technology to learn more extensively; interacting with teachers and classmates in new ways. Parental engagement was initially high, even if some parents found home schooling a challenge. (This was more a source of humor than despair or concern at the start of the lockdown. Entertaining videos of exasperated parents struggling with their children's homework were shared widely on social media). Questions about schools and education featured infrequently in the televised daily news briefings between media, medics, and ministers in late March and April. Tensions between governments created by the timing of school closures dissolved temporarily as England, Wales, Scotland, and Northern Ireland moved into the lockdown together.

With time, however, concerns arose about the quantity and quality of lockdown education. Pupil engagement in home learning waned very, very quickly: a once novel way of learning turned tedious. Parents started to struggle to motivate their children to learn at home, which entailed exposing children to excessive hours of screen time. A much greater number of pupils lacked computers or access to internet connections than was first anticipated and the laptop computers governments had promised to loan to these children took months to arrive. Staffed by teachers, childcare 'hubs' for the children of key workers and vulnerable children were poorly attended. Teachers expressed concern for pupils who were not participating in online learning and pupils who were not attending school centers despite their eligibility. Several teachers I interviewed described schools losing contact completely with pupils from particularly challenging family backgrounds. More serious concerns arose around online safety, children's mental health and physical wellbeing, the education of children with special learning needs, and the increase in domestic violence reported during the period of lockdown. In the first month of school closures, the charity Childline noted a twenty percent increase in telephone calls from children reporting neglect and physical, sexual, or emotional abuse in their homes; London's Metropolitan Police reported an eleven percent increase in domestic abuse in April and May.[5] Rapid research conducted by social scientists and educational organizations documented school closures increasing educational inequality.

The Challenges of Reopening Schools

At the start of May, debates turned to schools reopening, which proved a much more formidable challenge than closing them. Prolonged school closures risked "scarring the life chances of a generation of young people," wrote the Royal College of Paediatrics and Child Health, a point every teacher and teaching union representative I spoke with supported. Many parents were unable to return to work while schools stayed shut, and grandparents, at higher risk in relation to the virus, were shielding at home and unable to help with childcare responsibilities. The United Kingdom once more risked falling behind other European countries, even though it had reduced the reproductive rate of coronavirus to comparable levels by this time. Denmark had started reopening schools from April 15 and schools in the Netherlands, Belgium, Finland, and Austria had opened in early May, all without reporting a subsequent increase in COVID-19 community transmission. Pressed on the subject in press briefings and in parliament, the government expressed its intention to ensure all schools reopen fully for face-to-face learning in September.

On May 11, Johnson announced, suddenly, a staggered reopening of schools in England beginning Monday, June 1. Three year-groups in primary schools would return to schools on June 1 and two year-groups in secondary schools would return on June 15. All pupils would return shortly after this date, so that every child would receive a full month of schooling before the summer holidays began in late July.

The announcement was met with near-universal criticism. There had been no prior consultation with school leaders and teaching unions. Teachers were bewildered that basic questions over how schools were to operate practically could not be answered: how would schools maintain social distancing between pupils and teachers? Would the school day need to be changed to accommodate safe 'bubbles' of pupils in small classrooms? How would schools staff their classrooms, if teachers were unwell or shielding at home, or had childcare responsibilities themselves? How could parents return to work if their children were each attending school on different days? Though teachers overwhelmingly supported prioritizing the return of particular year-groups of pupils when schools reopened (ninety percent), only eighteen percent of primary school leaders and thirty-seven percent of secondary school leaders felt school openings in June were feasible. Teaching unions asked for the scientific evidence that had informed government policy to be shared. Eventually published on May 22, the scientific evidence did not reassure teachers or parents: the government's scientific advisory group said the risk of coronavirus to pupils was "very, very small, but it is not zero" and that they were "uncertain" of the extent to which reopening schools might increase the spread of the virus. Union surveys found eighty-five percent of classroom teachers "did not think it would be

5 Ria Ivandic and Thomas Kirchmaier, "Home is not a safe place for everyone: Domestic abuse between partners increased during lockdown," https://blogs.lse.ac.uk/covid19/2020/06/30/home-is-not-a-safe-place-for-everyone-domestic-abuse-between-current-partners-increased-during-lockdown/, *accessed* June 30, 2020.

safe to return to school on June 1."[6] Parents expressed concerns around safety too. After being told that fines would not be imposed for non-attendance, fifty percent of parents said they would keep their children at home in June. (This proved an underestimate; over four-fifths of targeted pupils in England did not return to school in June). Over half of English local councils said they would not be able to open primary schools on June 1 in line with government guidance. Most English schools eventually managed to partially open during June – later than planned, on a restricted timetable and typically by rotating groups of children in schools at different times or on different days – but Johnson's original plan to reopen secondary schools in England to all pupils before the end of the school year was abandoned (on June 9).

The announcement to reopen schools in England coincided with a challenging period in the United Kingdom in which initial lockdown rules were eased – more shops were opened, restrictions on local travel were relaxed, and social distancing guidance changed concerning whom people could meet, and where and how. Despite attempting to reassert his authority as prime minister, Johnson's change of strategy – from 'Stay Home, Protect the NHS, Save Lives' to 'Stay Alert, Control the Virus' – was ridiculed as ambiguous. Most of these changes were rejected or delayed by the governments of Wales, Scotland, and Northern Ireland, leading to a period, still ongoing, in which the different United Kingdom nations had different guidelines in place for families and businesses. Face masks became mandatory in Scotland and England, for example, but not in Wales. Socializing in open spaces was permitted in Northern Ireland and England, but not in Scotland. The rules became so confusing as time passed – What are the rules for outdoor exercising in Scotland and England? How many people outside of your household can you meet in Wales or Scotland? – that newspapers had to publish diagrams explaining them to the public as they crossed internal United Kingdom borders. These changes all occurred before a national COVID-19 testing and tracing program had been established.

In Wales, Scotland, and Northern Ireland, plans to reopen schools on June 1 were rejected. The Scottish government explained that schools would remain closed until August. Northern Ireland opted to follow Ireland's timeline for schools and plans to open them on August 24. On June 3, the Welsh government announced that all schools in Wales would open on June 29. Described as 'Check in, Catch up, Prepare for Summer and September,' Welsh schools received flexible guidelines for three weeks of in-person learning. As part of this plan, Welsh teachers became a new priority group in an antibody-testing program. Welsh schools reported slightly higher attendance levels than English schools in late June when their schools finally opened, with over a third of pupils attending. Once again, the governments of Wales, Scotland, and Northern Ireland received public approval for their responses – for showing greater caution than the government in London, both on opening schools and in maintaining stricter lockdown policies.

At the time of writing, all schools in the United Kingdom are scheduled to reopen fully at the start of the next school year: late August for Northern Ireland and Scotland; early September for Wales and England. It remains uncertain as to whether this will happen.

---

6 Caroline Sharp, David Sims, and Simon Rutt, *Schools' Responses to Covid-19: Returning Pupils to School* (Slough: NFER, 2020).

The Impact of School Closures on Children

Aspects of how the coronavirus pandemic impacted pupils, teachers, and schools in Wales and the United Kingdom as a whole will be comparable elsewhere. Given that there have been no recorded cases of teachers catching coronavirus from pupils anywhere in the world and the likelihood of children and typically young and healthy teachers developing severe symptoms is low, the merits of deciding to close schools are likely to be debated for some time. In the United Kingdom, deaths in children from COVID-19 account for 0.03 percent of total deaths.

Rightly, of course, the focus of attention in the United Kingdom since March 2020 has been around how school closures and learning in lockdown have impacted children. Research and anecdotes reveal a varied and unequal experience for children across the United Kingdom. Data is highly inconsistent. One study found a majority of secondary school children completed two or three hours of schoolwork at home per day during the lockdown, while another reported most children completing five or more hours per day.[7] By socioeconomic category or local region, numbers vary considerably in terms of how much work children completed, children's access to a quiet work space at home, and parental support. "Children from the poorest fifth of homes are spending an average of 1.3 hours per day less on remote learning than children in the highest-income families."[8] The Education Endowment Foundation suggests that progress over the past twenty years "in closing the disadvantage gap is likely to be reversed as a result of the pandemic."[9]

The 'digital divide' among United Kingdom families posed particularly acute problems for children's abilities to engage and complete schoolwork from home, as well as to keep up and to maintain contact with peers and teachers. While the various departments of education in England, Wales, Scotland, and Northern Ireland achieved some success in providing laptops to the children who needed them, these were not always useful in households without sufficient internet access. A government-sponsored platform, Oak National Academy, for example, offered outstanding and free recorded lessons and worksheets for pupils to use, but these required unlimited broadband connections and home printers, which over 100,000 homes in the United Kingdom lack. One study found that a family relying on a mobile telephone to provide a child's laptop with internet access would cost a family 860 pounds (about 1,113 US dollars) per month in data to complete three lessons per day for a single child.[10]

Transforming Teaching: The Impact on Teachers

Much less consideration has been given to the pandemic's impact on teachers, who worked exceptionally hard before and since schools closed – staffing childcare centers for vulnerable and key

---

7 Ed Pennington, "The numbers behind homeschooling during lockdown," Children's Commissioner, June 11, 2020, https://www.childrenscommissioner.gov.uk/2020/06/11/the-numbers-behind-homeschooling-during-lockdown/, accessed August 15, 2020; Alison Andrew et al., *Learning during the Lockdown: Real-time Data on Children's Experiences during Home Learning* (London: Institute for Fiscal Studies, 2020).

8 Megan Lucas, Julie Nelson, and David Sims, *Schools' Responses to Covid-19: Pupil Engagement in Remote Learning* (Slough: NFER, 2020).

9 Education Endowment Foundation, Rapid Evidence Assessment Summary: Distance Learning, https://educationendowmentfoundation.org.uk/covid-19-resources, accessed August 15, 2020.

10 Amy Gibbons, "DfE fail means remote learning bill for poor," *Times Educational Supplement*, July 10, 2020.

workers' children while teaching classes and engaging with pupils online, as well as, in many cases, also managing their own children's home-learning. Teachers I interviewed spoke of personal and colleagues' struggles initially mastering new technology, clarifying expectations for pupils and parents (setting a realistic amount of work for children to complete at home each day), and setting boundaries at home between work and non-work. At the top of teachers' challenges, according to research conducted by teaching unions, was balancing teaching from home with their own childcare. Teachers also struggled becoming comfortable with their own isolation as members of a highly social profession; teachers missed their pupils and colleagues as much as pupils missed their teachers. Several teachers excelled at teaching in new formats and found the virtual platforms available creative and productive. School leaders I interviewed helped me to understand the largely unseen work that schools performed providing pastoral and other kinds of support to vulnerable children and families; maintaining continuity and structure was a theme in our discussions. Positively, teachers proved highly resilient during a time of crisis. Several experts have suggested that the quality of face-to-face teaching might improve as a result of the disruption: "The transferable problem-solving skills and reflective practice of analyzing home-learning in the eyes of a pupil could in fact strengthen in-class teaching and learning planning skills [...] Fifty-five percent of teachers agreed that distance teaching would have a positive impact on their future practice."[11]

While teaching unions have been challenged by politicians for constructively criticizing government plans, teachers – as other key workers in the United Kingdom, such as doctors, nurses, and carers – have been recognized positively by parents, pupils, and the public for their work during the pandemic. The difficulty and importance of teaching was grasped when parents attempted to teach their own children. Teachers I interviewed were humbled by kind responses they received from parents and pupils. Most, however, are concerned about possible future disruptions to schools in the event of a 'second spike' of the virus as winter approaches and by the challenges they expect to face next year: recovering pupils' lost learning time; minimizing the educational divides that grew during 2020; rectifying the behavior of children who have lacked the structure and discipline of school for six months. Teachers have much to teach universities and other organizations about the limits of virtual and blended learning as a means of instruction. Paradoxically, given the premium placed on ICT[12] in schools, many teachers reported young people beginning to resent continuous digital learning despite the ubiquity of technology in their everyday lives.

England in particular suffers continuously from teacher recruitment and retention in state schools, especially in secondary schools. One in five newly qualified teachers leaves the profession within two years; four in ten teachers leave after five years. Secondary school pupil numbers are expected to increase by ten percent between 2019 and 2023. Twenty-nine percent of schools in the most disadvantaged areas outside London and forty-six percent in the most disadvantaged areas inside London face difficulties filling vacant teaching posts. In 2020, however, far fewer teachers submitted resignations or applied for retirement than in previous years. Despite the high workload and poor pay, the two factors most cited for why teachers leave the profession, the unusually high retention of teachers in 2020 suggests that teaching is viewed as a secure career. Teaching has proven to be an unusual 'key worker' profession that has been able to migrate from the 'workplace' to the 'home' during the pandemic, albeit in an unsatisfactory form. Teaching complicates the pattern of less well-paid professionals (and women) being disproportionately hurt by the closing

---

11 Hannah Breeze, "The impact of Covid-19 on Early Career Teachers," June 04, 2020, https://www.thersa.org/discover/publications-and-articles/rsa-blogs/2020/06/early-career-teachers-covid, accessed August 15, 2020.
12 Information and communications technology

down of the economy.[13] As many individuals in the United Kingdom lost work or were placed on the government furlough scheme during the pandemic, teachers sometimes became the primary earners within households, challenging wider trends, too, given the gendered nature of the teaching workforce. Spring 2020 also saw a sharp increase in applications to teacher training programs from young graduates and others.

Conclusion

Two wider observations by way of a conclusion. First, the coronavirus pandemic and the closure of schools has reinforced the centrality of schools within British society: how important schools are in providing structure and stability in children's lives; how many British workers and families are dependent on schools for childcare provision. An underlying fragility in United Kingdom society was made visible when schools were closed or disrupted. Second, events since March have shown education to be a crucially political issue. Schools and schooling became a fissure along which United Kingdom politics were played out, especially in how its nations and regions (and local authorities in England) used education to assert power and express dissent. Scottish, Welsh, and Northern Irish politicians enjoyed public support for their cautious and consultative approaches to managing schools. Education has been used especially in Scotland to bolster support for Scottish independence, which soared during the pandemic. Though less prominent in Northern Ireland and Wales (twenty-five percent in Wales compared with fifty-four percent in Scotland), the Welsh parliament held its first ever debate for Welsh independence since Welsh devolution during the lockdown and Northern Ireland is shortly expected to hold its first 'border poll' since 1973 on reunification with the Republic of Ireland. Schools have become a new terrain in which the internal political and economic divisions within the United Kingdom are being played out, tensions exacerbated since the Brexit referendum.

Next Steps: A Coda

On August 13, A-Level examination results for secondary school leavers were published in England, Wales, and Northern Ireland. These grades determine pupils' university places. When all national exams were canceled in March, teachers and schools were required to submit predicted grades for their pupils to exam bodies, as well as a rank order of pupils by subject based on classwork, ability, and performance in mock exams. The United Kingdom government's Office of Qualifications and Examinations Regulation used the data to determine students' final grades.

While A-level grades were slightly higher overall, nearly forty percent of teacher predictions were downgraded by one, two, or three grades. Pupils from state schools in economically deprived areas were more than twice as likely to have had their marks downgraded than pupils from private schools and schools in wealthier areas. Devastated pupils and angry teachers shared their stories on television and radio programs as government ministers attempted to justify a "robust" and "fair" system that relied on an algorithm which calculated final marks based on a pupil's school's

---

13 Diane Coyle, "Why Did It Take a Pandemic to Show How Much Unpaid Work Women Do?" *The New York Times*, June 26, 2020.

past performance. To the outrage of teachers, parents, and students, ministers claimed that teachers had "inflated" the grades.

It is an understatement to write that the calculation of 2020 examination results (and the response by the government) has infuriated the education profession. A slew of teachers across the United Kingdom submitted their resignations on live television. As pupils took to the streets to protest, thousands of school leaders called for the firing of Gavin Williamson for mishandling the process: "Through no fault of their own, pupils have suffered enough disruption to their school lives. They have the unassailable right to successfully and fairly proceed with their future plans for university, A-level, vocational, and other vital future educational courses. This is currently in serious doubt unless decisive new action is taken." Similar results are anticipated next week when sixteen-year-olds receive their GCSE exam results, in which a similar algorithm has been used. More than two million predicted GCSE grades are expected to be lowered.

One of the challenges of writing about ongoing events is not knowing where the story will lead. The final impacts of closing schools on teachers and students in the United Kingdom during the coronavirus pandemic are far from clear. However, submitting this essay on August 15, the events of the past seven days have returned learning in lockdown to the forefront of public debate, reminding us that the impact of coronavirus on education and politics is as serious as its impact on health and the economy.

Mary Jo Maynes and Ann Waltner
Youth Transitions in the Time of COVID-19 and Political Uprising

When we think about young people in the context of the COVID-19 pandemic, our associations are often filtered through recurrent media frames. We have heard again and again that young people are less vulnerable to COVID-19 than their elders, but they may be asymptomatic spreaders. Or, that in regions where the virus has levelled off and then resurged, careless young people are responsible because of their partying in bars or in the streets. We'd like to tell a different story in this essay, one that emphasizes instead the particular burdens that the pandemic is placing on youth – burdens they experience in the present moment and which carry consequences that they will no doubt feel as they move through their lives. These thoughts are based on observations and reading; they reflect our particular positionality as residents of the Twin Cities of Minneapolis and Saint Paul, Minnesota, and as professors at the University of Minnesota. But much of what we have seen here has wider resonance as well.

The process of transition from youth to adulthood has varied widely across time and place. In our contemporary world this transition can occur relatively rapidly and at an early age for those youth who move into the full-time labor market in their teens and who may start a family or set up an independent household at around the same time. For others, who pursue advanced formal education or job training, or who have difficulties finding full-time work, the transition process can take a decade or more. For those coming of age during the COVID-19 pandemic, all bets are off. The ramifications of COVID-19 are wide and they will be long-lasting. Here we will look at a few specific dimensions of the current crisis in terms of their age-specific effects: the impact of the pandemic on education and career preparation; its consequences for transitioning into the workforce; levels of anxiety and depression related to COVID-19; and involvement in political protests that have occurred simultaneously with the pandemic.

Coming of Age in COVID-19 Times

We are already hearing about the "COVID-19 generation." Cohort effects have been noted in the past, of course – for example, for the Depression generation or the youth of the Sixties. But the impact of COVID-19 on the cohorts who are now in their teens and twenties promises to be especially marked. According to Cynthia Comacchio:

> This Covid spring is imprinting all those who are growing up and coming of age in its midst. COVID-19 is their generational marker, defining their cohort identity historically and through every stage that remains to the end of their lives [...] The majority of deaths are among seniors, testifying both to their greater physical fragility and to our disgraceful collective neglect. The majority of developmental impacts are among adolescents. Their outlook, their ideas, their world view, have been affected by this experience in ways that they will not 'outgrow.'[14]

---

[14] Cynthia Comacchio, "The Generation of 2020: Coming of Age in Covid-Time," *Active History: History Matters*, May 20, 2020, https://activehistory.ca/2020/05/the-generation-of-2020-coming-of-age-in-covid-time/, accessed August 24, 2020.

Other analysts, including several of our colleagues here at the University of Minnesota Life Course Center, have shared research that echoes this concern and points to a further one that is especially significant in political cultures like that of the United States, where there has long been an emphasis on 'career planning' and a belief that young people can shape their own futures. According to Richard Settersten and his collaborators, "The pandemic has underscored the reality that life's possibilities are limited [...] Differences by socioeconomic status are likely to be substantial in this regard because reduced control and choices already characterize the lives of those with few family resources."[15]

A recent report issued by the Social Science Research Council suggests that in a few short months, COVID-19 has undone a decade of progress in what they term "youth disconnection." This research has been looking at the proportion of Americans aged sixteen to twenty-four who are neither working nor in school. Since the study began, the proportion has been declining: "The number of teens and young adults disconnected from both work and school in the United States fell for the eighth year in a row, from a recession-fueled high of 14.7 percent in 2010 to 11.2 percent in 2018. The COVID-19 pandemic will cause youth disconnection rates to spike dramatically. We estimate that the number of disconnected youth will easily top six million and could swell to almost one-quarter of all young people [...] While it is clear that young people of all stripes will suffer, low-income people of color will be the hardest hit."[16]

Education Upended: Students' Experiences in Spring 2020

A recent life-course analysis of the impact of COVID-19 starts with the disruption of schooling:

> The United Nations' Educational, Social and Cultural Organization estimates that more than 180 countries from all continents enforced school closures during the pandemic, affecting over 1.5 billion students (ninety percent of the world's student population) at all levels of the education system. Only a handful of countries, such as Sweden and Taiwan, never closed schools. This experience quickly smashed the most basic of expectations in most countries around the world – that youth have the capacity to anticipate and control their educational futures.[17]

A survey of undergraduates at the University of Minnesota and several other large research universities that was conducted by the Student Experience in the Research University (SERU) consortium suggests some of the consequences. If most undergrads weathered the move to online learning and were able to complete most of their coursework, some sub-groups of students had a much more difficult time. The survey results show that first-generation college students faced far more challenges than did students with parents who had a post-secondary degree.

The survey of nearly thirty thousand undergrads, conducted between May and July of 2020, found that first-generation students, who comprised a quarter of respondents:

---

15 Richard A. Settersten, "Understanding the Effects of COVID-19 Through a Life Course Lens," *Advances in Life Course Research*, July 22, 2020, https://doi.org/10.1016/j.alcr.2020.100360, accessed August 24, 2020: 1040–2608.
16 Kristen Lewis, "A Decade Undone: Youth Disconnection in the Age of Coronavirus" (New York: Measure of America, Social Science Research Council, 2020), https://measureofamerica.org/youth-disconnection-2020/, accessed August 24, 2020.
17 Pamela Aronson, Arnaldo Mont-Alvao and Jeylan Mortimer, "Post COVID-19 Transformation of the Transition to Adulthood around the World," unpublished manuscript: 2–3.

were more likely than continuing-generation students to experience financial hardships during the pandemic, including lost wages from family members, lost wages from on- or off-campus employment, and increased living and technology expenses. They were nearly twice as likely to be concerned about paying for their education in fall 2020 [...] and more likely to experience food and housing insecurity.

Some of these added difficulties in adapting to online learning were related to their relocation from campus to home, where they experienced a "lack of adequate study spaces and lack of technology necessary to complete online learning" and were "less likely to be able to meet during scheduled virtual class times."[18]

Kriti Budhiraja, a PhD candidate in sociology at the University of Minnesota, happened to be doing research on equity and higher education in India when the pandemic struck and so we can compare these SERU findings about students in the United States with her observations in New Delhi. Budhiraja's own research – begun as an ethnography at Delhi University – had to be rethought: "With universities closing due to the pandemic, and most students in lockdown at home, these phone interviews are what allow me to continue my research," she reports. These calls were eye-opening. A call with one student was interrupted. A few minutes later he called back: "'The signal here is very bad,' he said, 'right now I'm on the roof, where the connectivity is still better.'" According to Budhiraja, this student and many others also had internet connectivity problems: "'There is simply no network at so many places!' He also informed me that a recent storm in his locality had resulted in electricity [poles] being down for two days. 'If uninterrupted power supply is an issue, how can we think of online exams?' he wondered."[19]

According to Budhiraja, a survey 1,500 Delhi University students revealed that "seventy-two percent cited poor connectivity as the reason for their inability to attend online classes [...] the reality is that most students from villages, small towns, and working-class neighborhoods in cities who apply to Delhi University pay their local cyber cafes to fill their online forms. Technological scarcity is still a barrier for many students."[20] While the argument here centers on the problem of moving to an online examination system, Budhiraja sees larger ramifications as well: "The divides of class, caste, region, and language that the remote examination brings into sharper relief do not disappear in the context of the on-site examination [...] However, everyday life in the public university offers a possible, if fragile, antidote to the workings of such inequities [...] The public university makes it possible to imagine infrastructures of sharing space and sociality that are, in many instances, unimaginable outside it."[21] Much was lost when instruction went online and students returned home. And as was the case for their American peers, many social inequities were multiplied off-campus.

18 Krista M. Soria, Bonnie Horgos, Igor Chirikov, and Daniel Jones-White, "First-Generation Students' Experiences During the COVID-19 Pandemic" (SERU Consortium, University of California - Berkeley and University of Minnesota: 2020), https://firstgen.naspa.org/report/first-generation-students-experiences-during-the-covid-19-pandemic, accessed August 23, 2020:1.
19 Kriti Budhiraja, "Why Remote Examination is Unfair to University Students," *Newsclick*, May 17, 2020, https://www.newsclick.in/Why-remote-examination-is-a-bad-idea, accessed August 23, 2020.
20 Kriti Budhiraja, "Why Remote Examination is Unfair to University Students."
21 Kriti Budhiraja, "Why Remote Examination is Unfair to University Students."

Transitions After Spring Semester 2020

Even more consequential, perhaps, than the spring mid-semester move to online classes were the interrupted plans for what was supposed to follow the semester's end – for all students, but especially for 2020 graduates. These interruptions affected plans for post-graduate education, first jobs, internships, and volunteer work. This became clear when Mary Jo Maynes asked undergraduate students in the two courses she taught in spring 2020 what their plans were for the immediate future, and how they had changed in the face of the pandemic. Maynes was teaching twenty-five undergrads in a senior capstone research course in history and an interdisciplinary course on child labor that was part of the university's 'Grand Challenges' curriculum. Remarkably, all but one of these students managed to fulfill course requirements – many in an exemplary fashion – despite the challenges involved moving to online instruction and often relocating as well. Among this hardworking and talented group, however, nearly everyone was facing the necessity of rethinking their plans for the summer and beyond.

Among the few whose plans weren't disrupted, Aaron[22] had been accepted onto a summer internship program that was going to convert to an online format. Similarly, Jeanine's new job was also converted to remote work. But most students' plans were in disarray. Caroline had assumed she would find a job for a year and then decide later about a graduate or professional program; as of May, her plans were uncertain. Hani's way of framing a similar situation was to declare that she was taking an uncertain 'gap year' before applying to graduate school. James and Pamela had both planned to start on the road to an education degree in the fall that involved student teaching. Both of them have temporarily put their plans 'on ice' – which, as the image suggests (See Figure 1) – is an appropriate metaphor for the aspirations of many of the graduates of the Class of 2020. Daniel decided to take extra summer classes to finish his degree early, but he had no idea what he would be doing after graduation. Jen had been accepted into graduate school but decided to defer for a year, rather than risking a cross-country move during the pandemic. She was hoping to find a temporary job. Taara had just learned that her summer pre-med program was cancelled. Anna's internship was also cancelled and so she will return home and hope to do conduct research from there. Lisa was supposed to do research abroad on a scholarship; instead, she will work on a farm and then hopes to return to Twin Cities in the fall to combine an altered plan of research and volunteer work. Alyssa will also be doing farm work, on her family's farm in Wisconsin. While both Lisa and Alyssa are actually happy to have the option of farm work, it is an understatement to say that it's not what they had been intending to do. Correy was planning to start a two-year stint in West Africa in the Peace Corps, but that, too, has been deferred to an uncertain point in the future. Teon was supposed to go back to a summer lab job in China; those plans, as of May, were also 'on ice.'

These Minnesota students' stories display the range of plans and dreams that have been disrupted by COVID-19. Settersten et al. underscore the potential long-term consequences of such interruptions: "One might expect to find the strongest long-term effects for the cohort of graduates whose immediate transition from school to work is hampered by the pandemic, particularly if it lasts a long time. This could result in a kind of 'lost generation' with shrinking opportunities in employment and truncated career and family formation, which would in turn have lifelong consequences."[23] Aronson et al., also examining the COVID-19 crisis from a life-course perspective with an emphasis on youth, remind us that the challenges of job market entry are not new in 2020:

---

22 Names have been changed here to protect student privacy.
23 Richard A. Settersten, "Understanding the Effects of COVID-19 Through a Life Course Lens": 6–7.

Figure 1. The Class of 2020 has had to put their plans on ice. *Original drawing by Rivi Handler-Spitz, based on stories from University of Minnesota 2020 graduates. Reproduced with permission of the artist.*

Over the last two decades, youth labor market prospects have deteriorated considerably around the world; youth unemployment reached higher levels in 2019 than during the Great Recession. The pandemic has further diminished young people's entry and establishment in the workforce. The International Labour Organization estimates that more than one in six young people lost their jobs during the pandemic, and those with jobs had their hours reduced by nearly twenty-five percent. In many countries, initial restrictions shut down major industries (e.g., restaurant and hospitality, the retail sector) that typically employ large numbers of young people [...] In the United States, the youth unemployment rate more than doubled between January 2020 (11.7 percent) and April 2020 (25.5 percent).[24]

Age-specific Levels of Anxiety and Depression

COVID-19 is taking a toll on mental health in general, but, here, too, the effects seem especially marked among young people for a variety of reasons, including the frustrating interruptions of the process of transitioning to adulthood. The SERU consortium mentioned earlier found unusually

---

24 Pamela Aronson et al., "Post-COVID-19 Transformation of the Transition to Adulthood around the World": 7.

high rates of depression and anxiety among undergraduate, graduate, and professional school students screened during the summer of 2020 at Minnesota, Berkeley, and other research universities. The consortium "used patient health questionnaires to screen 30,725 undergraduate students at nine research universities [...] and found that thirty-five percent of them were positive for major depressive disorder and thirty-nine percent for generalized anxiety disorder. The results show the negative mental health impact that the coronavirus pandemic has had on students, especially those who struggled to transition from in-person to remote instruction."[25]

These problems were not limited to students, but affected youth more generally, according to the United States Centers for Disease Control and Prevention. A survey conducted in late June 2020 showed that "the prevalence of anxiety symptoms was three times as high as those reported in the second quarter of 2019, and depression was four times as high." Moreover, these effects "were felt most keenly by young adults ages eighteen to twenty-four." According to Mark Czeisler, first author of the report, nearly sixty-three percent of respondents in this age group (compared with forty-one percent overall) "'had symptoms of anxiety or depression that they attributed to the pandemic' [...] Nearly eleven percent said they had suicidal thoughts in the month leading up to the survey, with the greatest clusters being among Black and Latino people, essential workers and unpaid caregivers for adults." Czeisler suggested that the rates were so high among young people "because now there are so many questions, especially for young people, about relative risk, duration of the pandemic and what their futures will look like."[26]

Another Response: Youth Involvement in Protests

Here in Minnesota, across the United States, and then globally, the COVID-19 spring was also the moment when a huge new wave of protests erupted in the wake of the brutal police killing of George Floyd in Minneapolis on May 25. We want to call attention to the generational dimensions of these protests. The video that documented the murder was taken by a seventeen-year old Black girl, Darnella Frazier:

> The camera had been rolling for twenty seconds when Mr Floyd, forty-six, uttered three more words that have now become a rallying cry for protesters, 'I can't breathe' [...] Ms Frazier was taking her nine-year-old cousin to Cup Foods, a shop near her home in Minneapolis, Minnesota, when she saw Mr Floyd grappling with police. She stopped, pulled out her phone and pressed record. For ten minutes and nine seconds she filmed until the officers and Mr Floyd left the scene; the former on foot, the latter on a stretcher.[27]

---

25 Greta Anderson, "Students Reporting Depression and Anxiety at Higher Rates," *Inside Higher Ed*, August 19, 2020, https://www.insidehighered.com/quicktakes/2020/08/19/students-reporting-depression-and-anxiety-higher-rates, accessed August 23, 2020. For full report, see: Igor Chirikov, Krista M. Soria, Bonnie Horgos, and Daniel Jones-White, "Undergraduate and Graduate Students' Mental Health During the COVID-19 Pandemic" (SERU Consortium, University of California – Berkeley and University of Minnesota: 2020), https://escholarship.org/uc/item/80k5d5hw, accessed August 23, 2020.
26 Jan Hoffman, "Young Adults Report Rising Levels of Anxiety and Depression in Pandemic," *New York Times*, August 13, 2020, https://www.nytimes.com/2020/08/13/health/Covid-mental-health-anxiety.html, accessed August 23, 2020.
27 Joshua Nevett, "George Floyd: The Personal Cost of Filming Police Brutality," *BBC News*, June 11, 2020, https://www.bbc.com/news/world-us-canada-52942519, accessed August 23, 2020.

Figure 2. Minneapolis, Minnesota, May 26: 'I can't breathe' protest held after man dies in police custody in Minneapolis. Protesters march on Hiawatha Avenue while decrying the killing of George Floyd on May 26, 2020, in Minneapolis, Minnesota. Stephen Maturen/Getty Images.

Frazier posted her video on Facebook. It went viral, and the rest is history. The outrage and protest that followed was notable in several ways: it was huge and immediate; it was cross-racial;[28] and young people were at the heart of it, in Minneapolis and beyond. This youth presence is documented in media stories and photos of the protests, beginning with the very first one in Minneapolis on May 26 (Figure 2). Journalistic accounts have made it clear just how crucial young people have been to the organization of the protests against racism and police violence. The opening story of a *New York Times* article about teenage girls leading protests featured Zee Thomas, a Black teenager from Nashville, Tennessee: "Ms Thomas had never been to a protest, let alone organized one. And yet five days later, with the help of five other teenagers, she was leading a march through her city, some ten thousand strong [...] The girls didn't know it at the time, but in cities across the country, legions of other young activists were doing something similar."[29] Some of these young women activists had had prior organizing experience. For example, nineteen-year-old Brianna Chandler has been active in the Sunrise Movement, a youth-led climate justice organization. And, as the *New York Times* reporter reminded readers, recent protests across a range of social justice

28 August Nimtz, "It's a Big Deal That the Outrage Expressed Over George Floyd's Death Was Massive and Multiracial," *MINNPOST*, May 28, 2020, https://www.minnpost.com/community-voices/2020/05/its-a-big-deal-that-the-outrage-expressed-over-george-floyds-death-was-massive-and-multiracial/, accessed August 23, 2020.
29 Interview by Jessica Bennett, "Teen Girls Fighting For a More Just Future," *New York Times*, June 26, 2020, Updated July 3, 2020 https://www.nytimes.com/2020/06/26/style/teen-girls-black-lives-matter-activism.html, accessed August 23, 2020.

movements have been notable for their leadership by teenage girls such as Malala Yousafzai and Greta Thunberg.[30]

At the University of Minnesota, President Joan Gabel announced just two days after the killing that "the University will no longer contract with MPD [Minneapolis Police Department] for law enforcement support during large events or for specialized services such as explosive detection [...] University students, staff, and faculty are day-to-day participants in the life of every community in this state, and we must act when our neighbors are harmed and in pain." Her decision and its speed came in response to a letter by the undergraduate student body president Jael Kerandi demanding that the university cease all partnerships with MPD. Kerandi also launched a petition on social media that drew thousands of signatures overnight.[31]

But it is important to note that, while the Floyd murder was the trigger for massive local and eventually global protests against racism, the response reflects political sentiments among youth that have been apparent for some time now, as well as growing organizational capacities among youth activists who were spurred to new levels of action in the context of COVID-19's disruptions of normal work and school routines and the fact that the pandemic's consequences visibly exacerbated pre-existing social, racial, and generational inequities.

The extent of youth organizing and involvement in the protests was underscored at a teach-in on "Protest and Policing" organized by an ongoing Interdisciplinary Collaborative Workshop (ICW) that includes faculty, students, and community leaders from the University of Minnesota and three Historically Black Colleges and Universities (HBCUs) – Spelman and Morehouse Colleges in Atlanta, Georgia, and Howard University in Washington, DC. Some of the most inspiring speakers at the teach-in were students and youth activists from the three cities involved in the ICW partnership. Twin Cities community activists included, for example, Rahhel Haile, a 2014 graduate of the University of Minnesota-Morris, who is the co-founder and executive director of policy and program at the Minnesota Youth Collective.[32] She and her organization are, in the words of the teach-in organizers, "dedicated to building the political power of young people without co-opting their movements. Combining grassroots and electoral justice work, her work with community members around political education on abolition and policy when defunding the police has intensified since George Floyd's murder."[33]

Haile was joined at the teach-in by Amber Jones, who graduated from the University of Minnesota-Twin Cities in 2015. She is currently the outreach coordinator for the Council for Minnesotans of African Heritage, an agency of the State of Minnesota. The teach-in organizers note that "Amber has done everything from leading community engagement initiatives in large institutions to build better relationships with African American communities, to organizing several policy and advocacy campaigns for systemic change at multiple levels of government. She is committed to increasing access & participation in social, economic, and political processes among communities of color; to cultivating the next generation of leaders; and to encouraging unity and self-determination among people of African descent."[34]

---

30 Jessica Bennett, "Teen Girls Fighting For a More Just Future".
31 Max Chao, "UMN Adjusts Relationship with MPD Following Death of George Floyd," *Minnesota Daily*, May 27, 2020, https://www.mndaily.com/article/2020/05/br-umn-changes-relationship-with-mpd-following-death-of-george-floyd-5ecf20a2b9653, accessed August 23, 2020.
32 https://www.mnyouthcollective.org/.
33 For a description of the collaborative, see the teach-in website : https://sites.google.com/umn.edu/icw-teach-ins-policing-protest/racial-justice-protests-and-social-change-july-29_1?authuser=0
34 Teach-in website.

Among the many other impressive activists from elsewhere speaking at the teach-in was Mary-Pat Hector. Hector is a recent graduate of Spelman College and a current graduate student at Georgia State University. "At twenty-two years old Mary-Pat Hector knows how to change the world. She began community organizing at the age of twelve years old. By the age of nineteen, she became the youngest woman and person of color to run for public office in the state of Georgia, losing by only twenty-two votes."[35] Hector is the program strategist at Rise, Inc, an organization that includes more than forty thousand students and supporters from colleges and universities across the nation.

These are challenging times for people of all ages, but especially, evidence suggests, for young people whose life-cycle transitions have been interrupted by COVID-19. Levels of unemployment and despair are even higher than they had been before 2020. But arguably, the COVID-19 spring and the contemporaneous act of police brutality that launched an uprising have also brought new forms of empowerment for many young people, and new confirmation of the deep-rooted injustices that had brought many of them to activism even before COVID-19 or George Floyd's murder. It is important to recognize these possible generational effects along with the others. As Jael Kerandi put it, when she thanked the signatories of her petition: "Never underestimate the power of your voice. This is for the mothers of George Floyd, Jamarr Clark, Philando Castile, and many others. Thank you to the two-thousand-plus signatories listed below, this couldn't have been done without you. The fight is not over, the marathon continues."[36] Her call within and across generations was echoed by Zee Thomas: "After the protest, I really couldn't sleep at all. I was on Twitter, as usual. And there was this one tweet from a mother. And I remember it so clearly, because I started crying. She said, 'I'm happy that my daughter will grow up in a world that these young girls will change.' And that's a moment where I felt really powerful, because my main goal, as a person and as an upcoming activist, is to make sure that people know that things will change. Eventually."[37]

---

35 Teach-in website.

36 Lucy Diavolo, "After Student Body President Demands, the University of Minnesota Announced It Will Cut Some Ties with Minneapolis Police," *Teen Vogue*, May 28, 2020, https://www.teenvogue.com/story/student-body-president-demands-university-of-minnesota-minneapolis-police-department, accessed August 23, 2020.

37 Jessica Bennett, "Teen Girls Fighting For a More Just Future."

Babacar Fall
Women's Empowerment Initiatives in the Sahel Challenged by COVID-19

Summary

One of the world's poorest regions, the Sahel, faces multiple challenges, including rapid population growth. Its demographic explosion is caused by several factors such as low levels of independence among women, poor access to education, and infrequent use of contraception in the region. The Sahel Women's Empowerment and Demographic Dividend (SWEDD) initiative was set up to respond to these challenges and improve the livelihoods of the population of the Sahel. It aims to "accelerate the demographic transition, to spur the demographic dividend, and to reduce gender inequality in the Sahel region." Against this backdrop, actions such as vocational training and support for economic initiatives have provided independence to out-of-school or unschooled adolescents and young women.

However, the lockdown measures and border closures implemented by countries to stop the spread of COVID-19 have led to a drastic drop in economic activity. Above and beyond the impacts on the economy and on public health, COVID-19 has also affected the capacity of the SWEDD project. The situation calls for new initiatives to strengthen women's resilience in the face of the pandemic, through measures that could include bolstering income-generating activities and dismantling the remaining legal obstacles that stand in the way of women's empowerment in most Sahel countries.

The Sahel is the world's youngest region, with fifty percent of the population under the age of fifteen. It is also one of the poorest and faces a range of challenges, from climate change and the surge of armed conflict to the lack of economic opportunities and poverty, all of which have effectively exacerbated the vulnerability of millions of people already dealing with climate uncertainty, malnutrition, and the resurgence of diseases.

Rapid population growth in the region has increased poverty and put pressure on the region's already scarce natural resources. This demographic explosion means that the economic efforts over the last two decades across most of the region may have driven annual economic growth up by around five percent. However, this economic growth never reached the general population; it has had little impact on the economic and social development in the region itself.[38]

The lack of economic opportunities, in particular for adolescents and young adults, combined with severely limited basic social services and non-existent social safety nets have seen populations become increasingly vulnerable to food insecurity, malnutrition, radicalization, and disease. High population growth remains the region's major challenge, with rates averaging 3.8 percent in Niger and 3.6 percent in Chad, compared with 0.3 percent in France and Germany in 2019.[39]

This makes it vitally important to substantially step up investment in creating jobs for young people, generating economic opportunities for girls and women, and developing women-led businesses. These are some of the objectives driving the United Nations Population Fund in its

---

38 Jean-Pierre Guengant, "La forte croissance démographique de l'Afrique freine son émergence," *Vie Publique*, September 03, 2019, https://www.vie-publique.fr/parole-dexpert/269994-croissance-demographique-de-lafrique, accessed August 18, 2020.
39 United Nations Population Fund, *State of World Population 2019: Unfinished Business - the Pursuit of Rights and Choices FOR ALL* (UNFPA: New York, 2019): 152–153.

current efforts to shore up funds from the World Bank, incentivize domestic investment and, above all, foster partnerships with the private sector.[40]

It is against this background that the Sahel Women's Empowerment and Demographic Dividend (SWEDD) initiative was developed in 2015 in six West and Central African countries (Burkina Faso, Côte d'Ivoire, Mali, Mauritania, Niger, and Chad). The initiative aims to address the challenges of high fertility rates, high maternal and neonatal mortality rates, and high dependency ratios, and to improve the livelihoods of the populations in the Sahel. The project consists of an integrated package of measures (education, literacy, skills development, health services including family planning, vocational training, and business support) to boost the independence of adolescents who have dropped out or have never attended school, as well as of young women.[41]

However, the COVID-19 pandemic now threatens to destroy all of the progress made to increase economic opportunities for women. The crisis also risks driving an even deeper wedge between the sexes. COVID-19 is severely affecting women and their economic status.[42]

This essay highlights the importance of women as a social group in the struggle against poverty but also as recipients of investment in vocational training and income-generating activities. It analyzes the effects of COVID-19 on initiatives developed to empower women in a number of SWEDD project countries (Burkina Faso, Côte d'Ivoire, Mauritania, and Niger).

The methodology is based on a review of the literature and an analysis of data from a short-term survey conducted by the regional United Nations Population Fund (UNFPA WCARO) with the support of the SWEDD project countries. The survey assesses the impact of the COVID-19 pandemic on the SWEDD project measures in each of the participating countries to enable the necessary steps to be taken to adapt these measures following the impact of the COVID-19 pandemic.

Women in the Sahel: Between Vulnerability and Poverty

Women are particularly exposed to poverty, discrimination, and exploitation. Gender-based sociocultural norms often condemn women to precarious and low-paid jobs. Social discrimination also limits women's access to land and loans. With their hands bound by domestic work, they often have little time to explore new economic opportunities, a situation that, in turn, limits women's participation in the development of economic and social policies.

Regarding education, a further challenge consists of keeping girls in school. Numerous factors continue to hinder access to education for girls. At the socioeconomic level, the main obstacles for girls remain their household responsibilities, participation in menial jobs, and early marriage. In addition, families are often poor and schools so prohibitively expensive – factoring in school supplies, meals, transport, and clothes – that families tend to send their sons rather than their daughters to school.

---

40 The World Bank, "Investing in Girls and Women's Empowerment in and Beyond the Sahel," May 28, 2020, https://www.worldbank.org/en/news/press-release/2020/05/28/investing-in-girls-and-womens-empowerment-in-and-beyond-the-sahel, accessed September 16, 2020.

41 United Nations Population Fund West and Central Africa Regional Office, "Sahel Women's Empowerment and Demographic Dividend (SWEDD)," 2016, https://wcaro.unfpa.org/sites/default/files/pub-pdf/SWEDD_ENG.pdf, accessed September 16, 2020: 14.

42 Kristalina Georgieva, Stefania Fabrizio, Cheng Hoon Lim and Marina M.Tavares, "The COVID-19 Gender Gap," *IMF Blog*, July 21, 2020, https://blogs.imf.org/2020/07/21/the-covid-19-gender-gap, accessed August 18, 2020.

Yet this situation is at odds with international efforts to increase the economic empowerment of women. These efforts primarily concern the Beijing Platform for Action and the Convention on the Elimination of All Forms of Discrimination against Women. The International Labour Organization, too, has adopted a number of gender equality conventions. In line with these principles, UN Women[43] promotes women's economic empowerment. The available socioeconomic data shows quite clearly that gender equality significantly contributes to economic and sustainable development.[44]

The reality is that investing in women's economic empowerment remains the most effective tool for promoting gender equality, eradicating poverty, and achieving inclusive economic growth. Women make an important contribution to the economy in every type of workplace – in companies, on farms, or in trade, women create value for the economy.

According to the United Nations Food and Agriculture Organization (FAO), reducing gender inequality should help us to achieve the three global objectives of eliminating hunger, promoting economic development (including the eradication of poverty), and sustainably managing natural resources.[45] Against this backdrop, the FAO has established an initiative to promote the economic empowerment of women in rural areas. This initiative encourages member countries to put programs in place to reduce poverty in rural areas and improve food security, thereby helping to ensure women and men profit equally from the benefits.

Many studies have shown that strengthening women's economic empowerment is an essential factor in laying the foundations for sustainable development. This implies adopting a comprehensive approach and making a commitment to gender-sensitive policies and programs. When women benefit from equal access to resources and services – land, water, technology, loans, banking, and financial services – their rights are strengthened, agricultural productivity is increased, and the economy grows.[46]

The SWEDD initiative aims to reduce the vulnerability of populations in their respective countries and to contribute to managing population growth with a view to capitalizing on the demographic dividend.[47] To this end, measures have been developed by SWEDD to empower girls and women and which allow the project to build on the transformative forces within Sahelian societies. Currently, 99,201 girls and young women are participating in empowerment programs. The concept of 'female entrepreneurship' takes numerous forms in each country. In Chad, 1,007 young girls received ITC-related vocational training as well as classes in how to drive and maintain farm machinery; 4,050 members of women's groups received modern assets for agricultural production; 3,549 women with profitable businesses received income-generating activity kits; and 5,996 women benefited from services in safe spaces. Niger has enrolled 500 young women in empowerment activities. Mali has conducted a series of training courses in income-generating activities and professions traditionally reserved for men (car mechanics, carpenters, electricians, and painters). In

---

43 United Nations Entity for Gender Equality and the Empowerment of Women

44 *UN Women*, https://www.unwomen.org, accessed August 18, 2020.

45 Food and Agriculture Organization of the United Nations, "Strategic Work of FAO to Reduce Rural Poverty," 2017, http://www.fao.org/3/a-i6835e.pdf, accessed August 18, 2020.

46 DAC Network on Gender Equality, "Women's Economic Empowerment: Issues Paper," *OECD.org*, April 2011, https://www.oecd.org/dac/gender-development/47561694.pdf, accessed August 18, 2020.

47 SWEDD receives funding from the World Bank, the United Nations Population Fund (UNFPA), and the West African Health Organization (OOAS).

Burkina Faso, 174 opinion leaders and women's association members in the project catchment area received training in entrepreneurial culture.[48]

The COVID-19 Effect and the Slump in Female Economic Activity in Sahel Countries

2020, considered a key year for the first phase of the SWEDD project in view of stepping up its activities to achieve the project outcomes, has been disrupted by the COVID-19 pandemic. The global outbreak and spread of the coronavirus (COVID-19) has also hit Sahel countries hard.

Beyond the alarming costs to human health and life with a total 30,158 confirmed cases and 594 deaths in six countries in the Sahel (Burkina Faso, Côte d'Ivoire, Mali, Mauritania, Niger, and Chad) as of August 18, 2020,[49] COVID-19 has also weakened the economies of the SWEDD project countries. This is mainly due to the measures taken to restrict the movement of people, such as the suspension of air and land travel between countries, social distancing, curfews, and/or the declaration of states of emergency – conditions that have always led and now indeed lead to economic downturn. Women are particularly affected by the devastating fallout of the crisis, because the vast majority work in harshly hit sectors in a region where the informal economy sustains around eighty-five percent of the population. In the face of these humanitarian and security challenges, Sahel countries have reacted differently to the impacts of COVID-19.

Lockdown measures and border closures for air and land travel enacted by nations to contain the pandemic have seriously disrupted production systems, thereby triggering, in most parts of the world, a brutal economic slump. Beyond its economic and health impacts, COVID-19 has had repercussions for economic initiatives led by young girls and women. This also applies to the SWEDD project.

A short-term survey was conducted in Burkina Faso, Mauritania, Niger, and Chad to assess the impact of COVID-19 on the SWEDD project. The objective was to identify the factors that limit the access of beneficiaries to the range of services offered by the project, and to determine viable options to ensure the continuity of services.

The survey shows that in Côte d'Ivoire 1,231 adolescents, young girls, and women benefit from economic support measures other than vocational training. The SWEDD administration revealed that the recipients of support for income-generating activities have stopped their activities during this period.[50]

In Mauritania, COVID-19 has also impacted efforts in the field of women-led economic activities. Out of a planned 2,500, only 233 adolescents, young girls, and women were able to actually benefit from vocational training during this period. Due to government measures to fight COVID-19, the beneficiaries of income-generating activities have had to stop working. On the basis of the

---

48 United Nations Population Fund WCARO/SWEDD, "Des expériences réussies dans la mise en oeuvre du projet SWEDD (2015–2018)," UNFPA WCARO: Dakar, 2019, http://www.projetswedd.org/wp-content/uploads/2019/05/SWEDD-Bonnes-Pratique-avril-2019-1.pdf, accessed August 18, 2020: 13, (Successful experiences in the implementation of the SWEDD Project (2015–2018).

49 European Centre for Disease Prevention and Control, "COVID-19 Situation Update Worldwide, as of 18 August 2020," https://www.ecdc.europa.eu/en/geographical-distribution-2019-ncov-cases, accessed August 18, 2020.

50 UNFPA, CEDEAO, and Banque mondiale, "Enquête rapide pour évaluer les effets de la maladie au nouveau coronavirus (COVID-19) sur le projet SWEDD," 2020.

data collected, every type of employment has been hampered for women by COVID-19 in one way or another. Among respondents not receiving any support from the SWEDD project, eighty-nine percent said that the COVID-19 crisis has impacted the implementation of project activities, compared with eleven percent who reported the opposite. In contrast, one hundred percent of respondents who had received support from the SWEDD project said that the COVID-19 crisis had impacted the implementation of project activities.

In Niger, all beneficiaries of economic interventions before COVID-19 who remain in the SWEDD programs declare that the crisis has affected the implementation of project activities. Out of those who did not benefit from measures before the COVID-19 pandemic, ninety-two percent state that COVID-19 has affected the implementation of projects as opposed to eight percent who say it has not. In general, the COVID-19 crisis has affected the implementation of project activities according to ninety-three percent of respondents, against seven percent who say that COVID-19 has not had any effect on project activities. Beneficiaries of economic support measures geared towards income-generating activities stopped their activities during this period. Beneficiaries of economic support point to the potential health threats as the key factor stopping them from running their activities at this time.

These difficult times, however, have also inspired innovation to ensure the continuity of services by generating employment in sectors such as sewing. Due to new demand for personal protective equipment, the manufacture of masks by girls in safe spaces has become an opportunity for developing new economic activities. In Niger, young girls following vocational courses in tailoring and fashion design have been taught to make masks. The CFSM center for vocational design and patternmaking training for adolescents (Centre de Formation Professionelle en Stylisme Modélisme) located in Niamey has adapted to meet the demand for masks. The center has been equipped with modern sewing machines as part of vocational training for young girls in safe spaces. It has been offering the young girls training in fashion design and patternmaking since 2017. During the COVID-19 crisis, the UNFPA placed an order for masks to be distributed among women's groups and health care personnel in hospitals and clinics. Some 300 girls now work producing masks and earn 300 CFA francs (circa 0.5 US dollars) a piece. They have committed to saving their earnings so as to be able to afford their own sewing machines within a few months. By supplying the UNFPA with masks, the sewing workshop provides continuous work.

Promoting women's economic independence therefore contributes primarily to women's full participation in the future of their societies and supports sustainable development. Today, women in the Sahel are severely affected by poverty. A situation that is the result of social inequalities and a lack of opportunity that further exacerbates their vulnerability. Women's economic empowerment is strongly connected to the question of gender equality. Indeed, equality will only be possible when men and women have the same economic opportunities.

Today, the COVID-19 pandemic is putting a strain on women's economic empowerment. Response measures such as lockdowns and closing large markets and borders to slow infections have caused a downturn in economic activity, with women being the main victims. Numerous income-generating activities have come to a grinding halt, threatening to throw high numbers of women who successfully joined the job market back into poverty.

As a consequence, steps need to be taken to strengthen the resilience of women in the face of the pandemic. To achieve this, there is an urgent need to protect jobs and lift all legal barriers that still stand in the way of women's economic independence.[51]

---

51 Kristalina Georgieva et al., "The COVID-19 Gender Gap."

Shutter Release II. Current Issues in the World, Told Visually

Ellen Rothenberg

'This is Ridiculous,' Voting as Labor During COVID-19: A Report from the United States

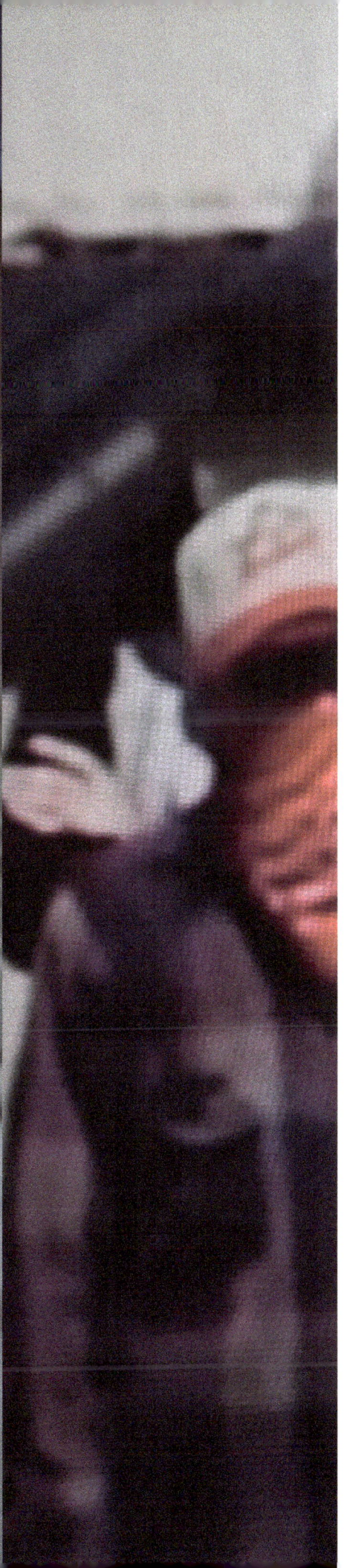

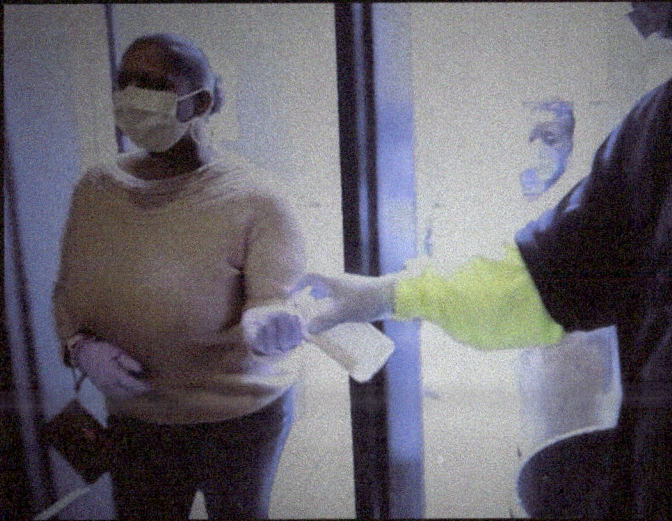

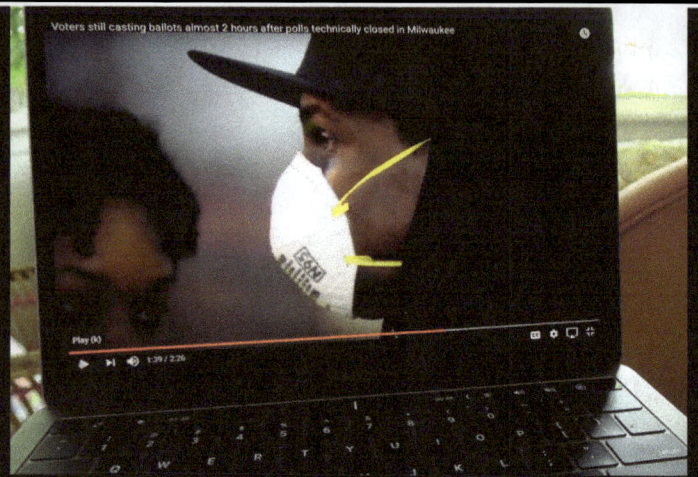

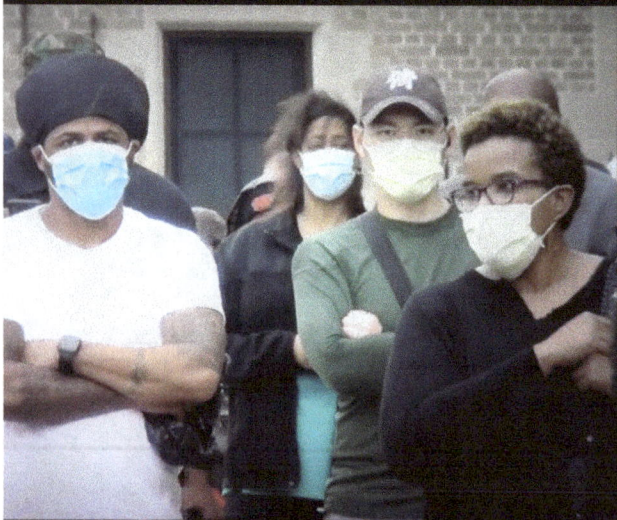

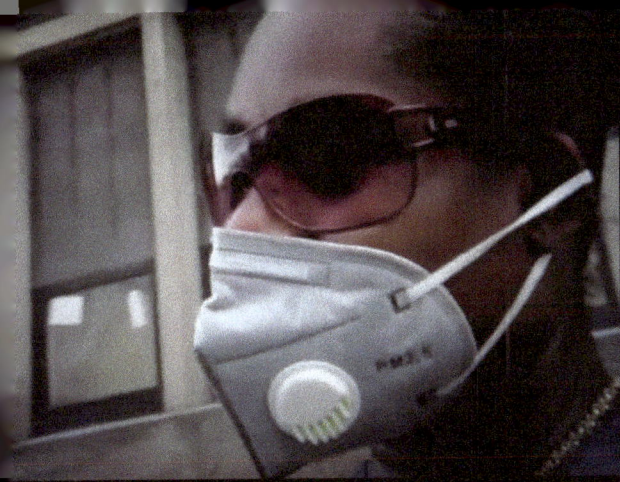
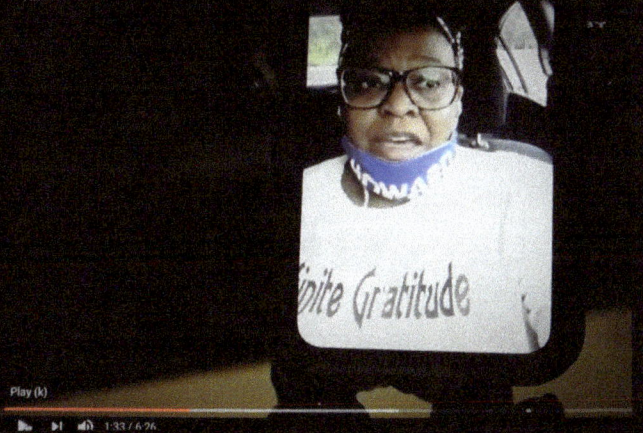

11alive.com

Play (k)   1:33 / 6:26

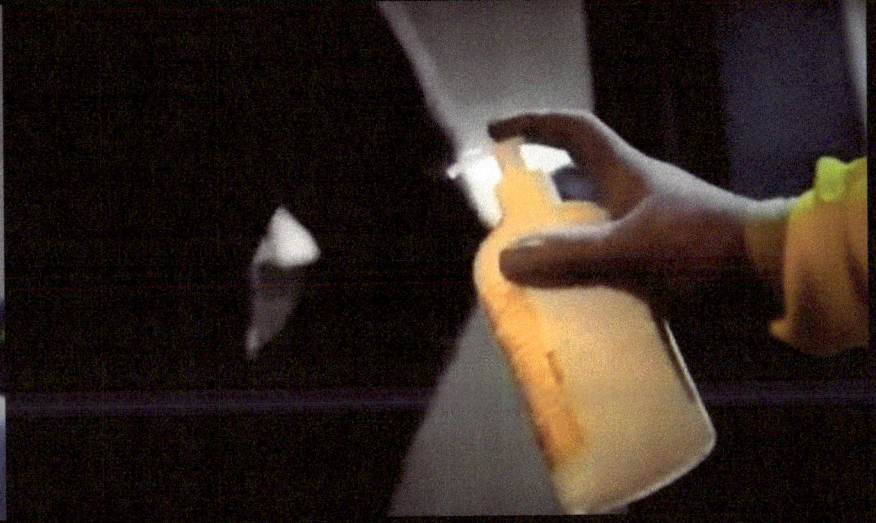

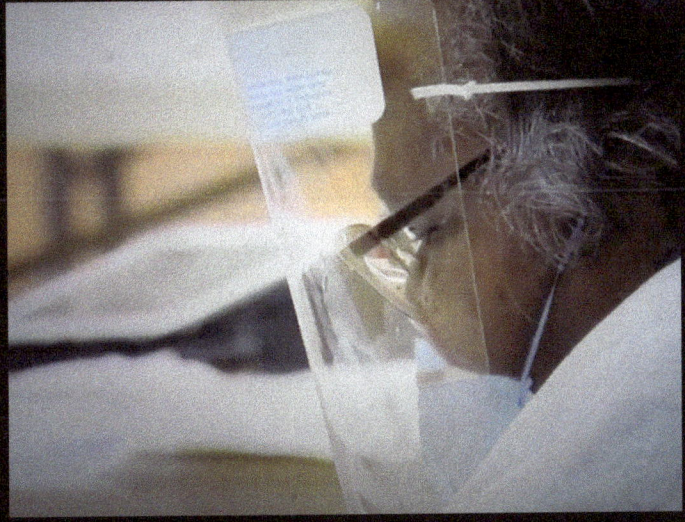

POLL WORKER

STAY 6 FEET
AWAY FROM ME

THANK YOU!

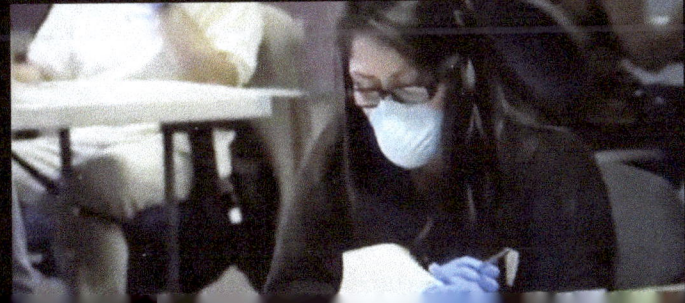

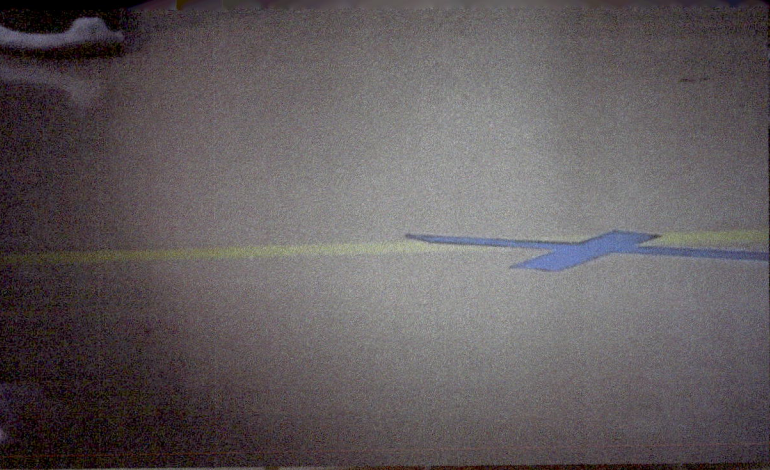

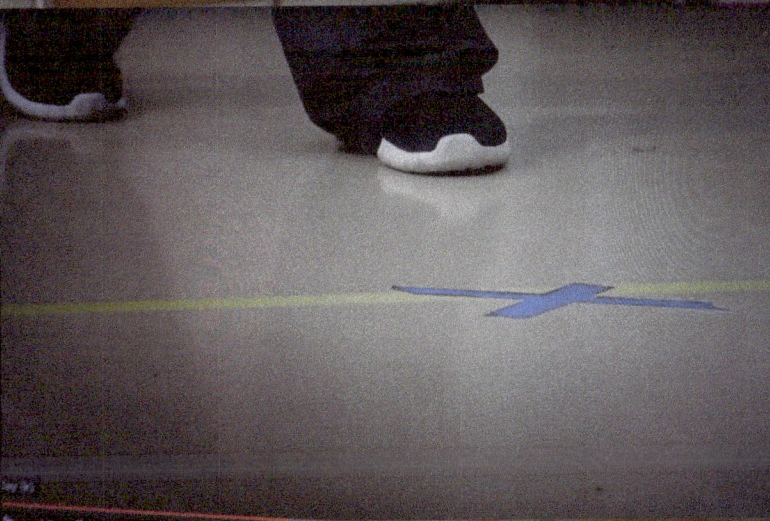

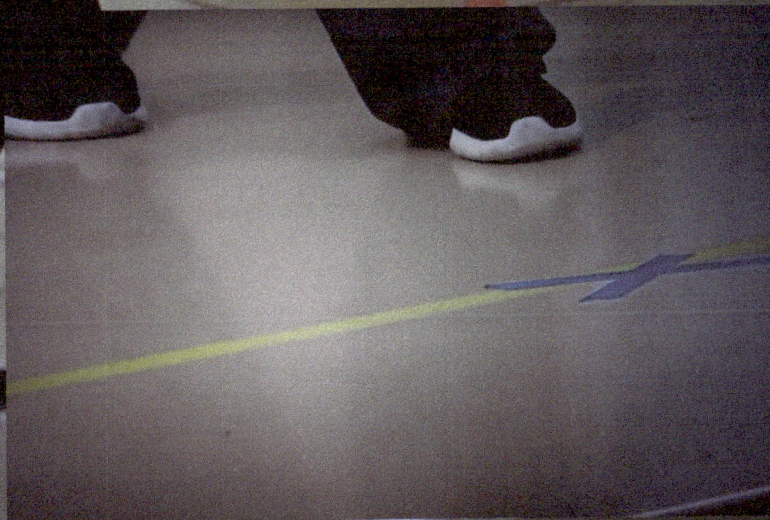

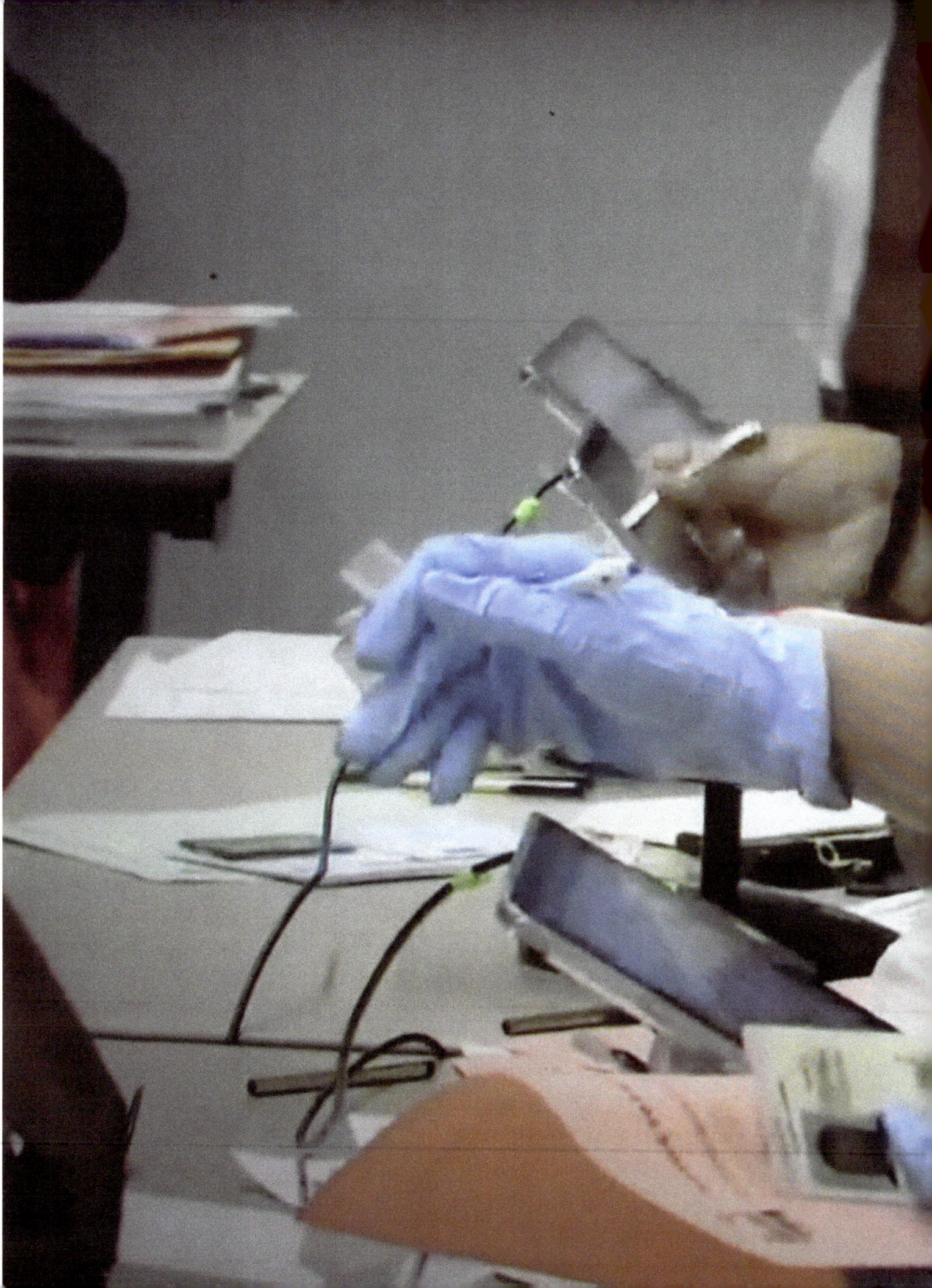

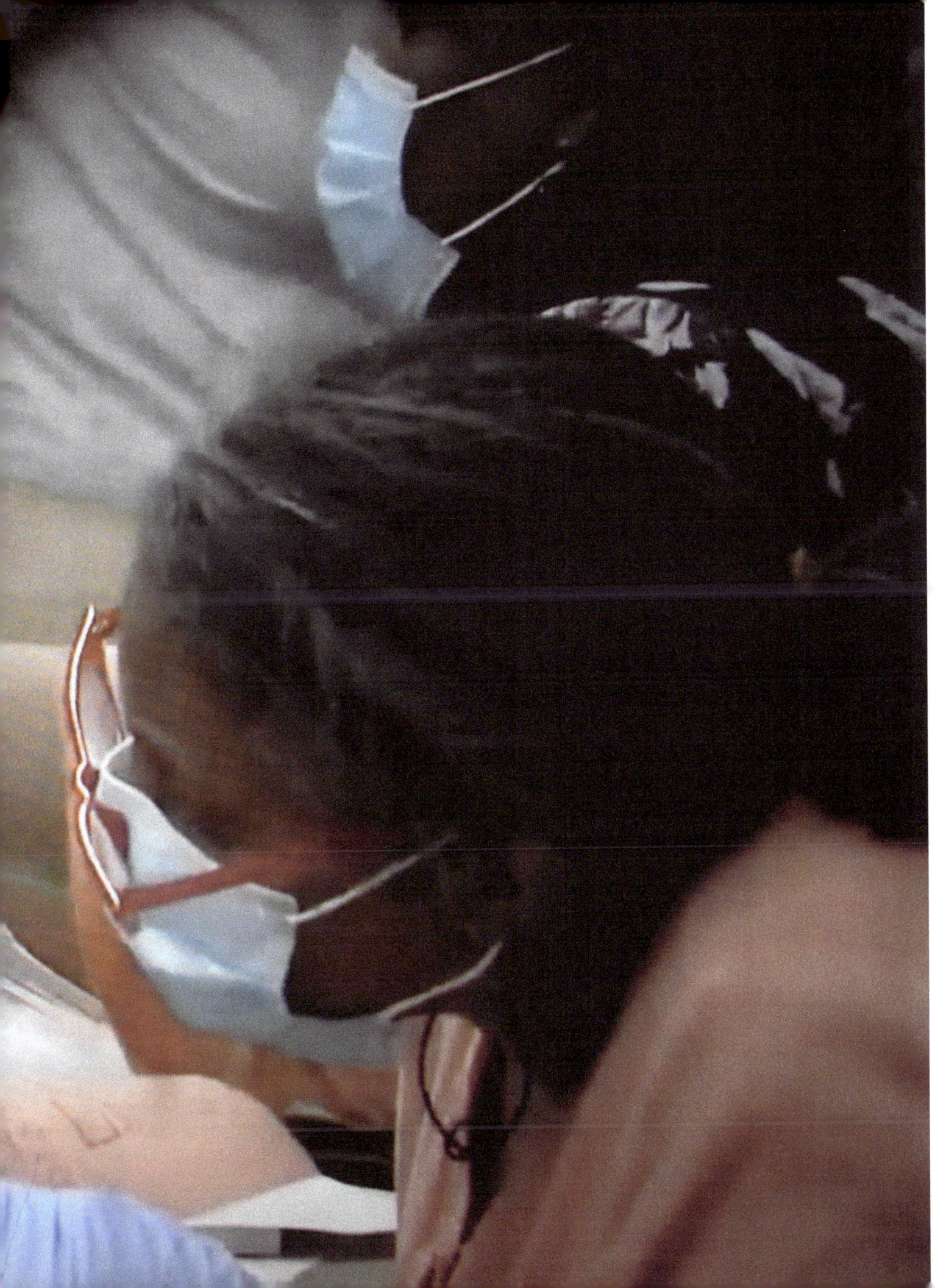

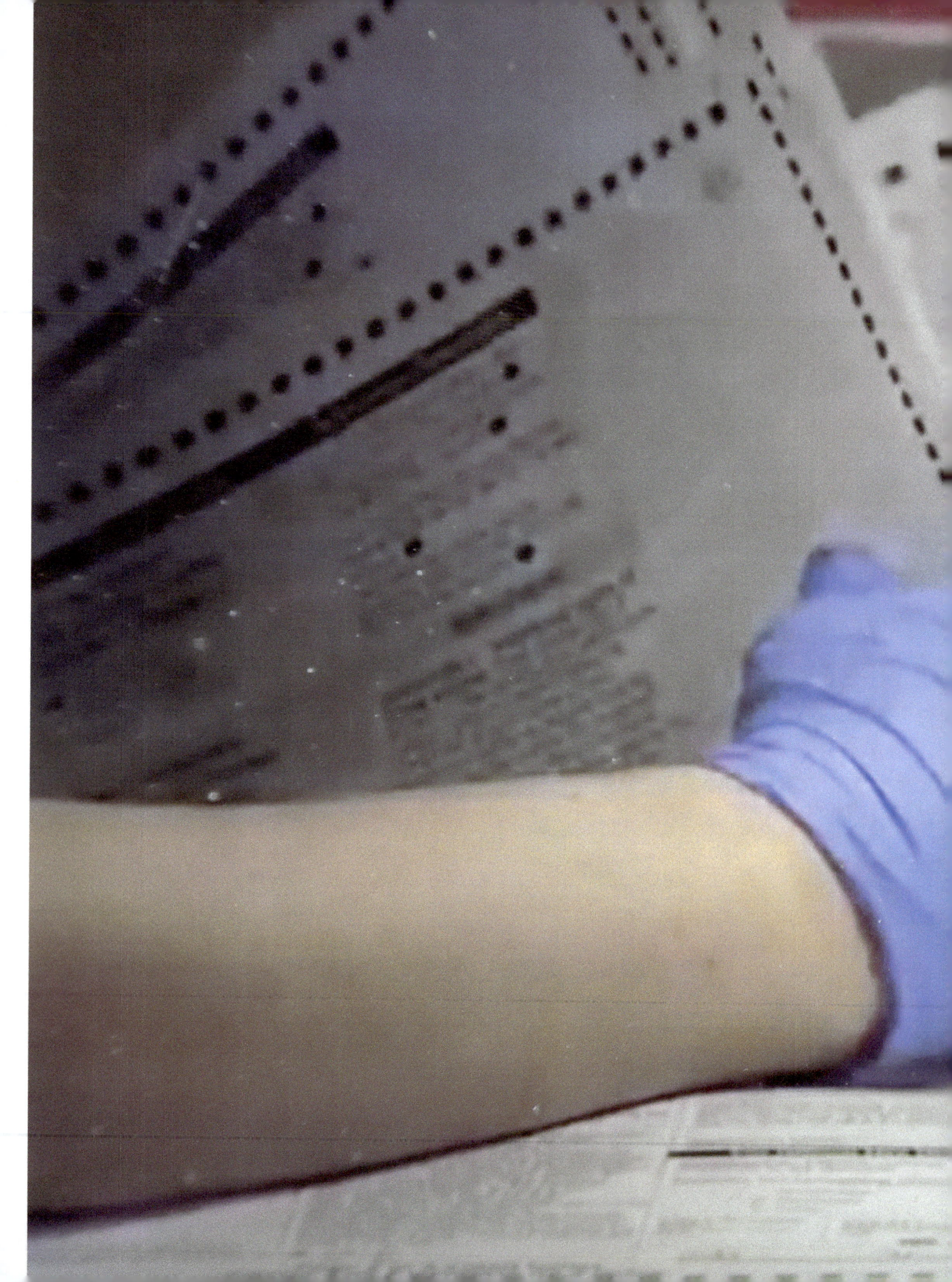

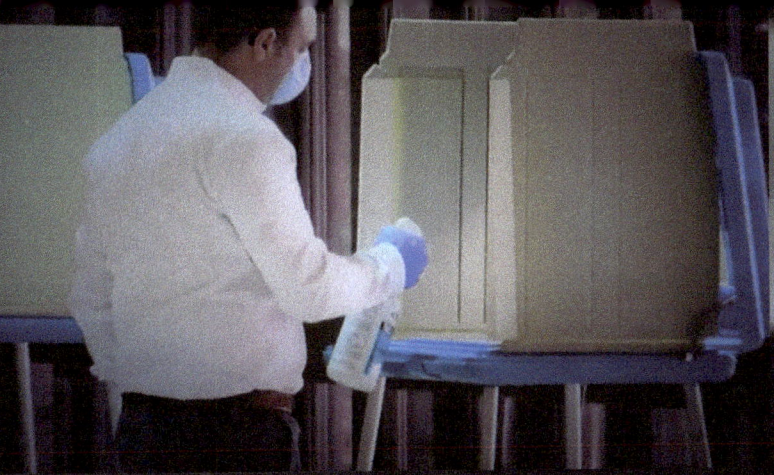

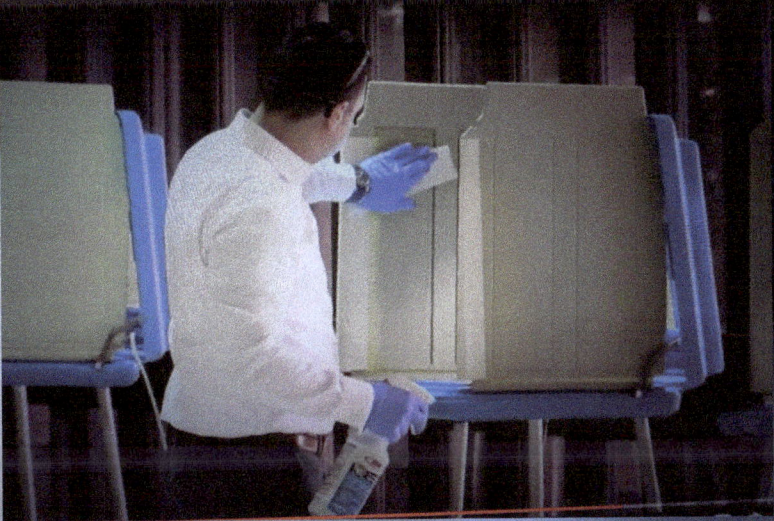

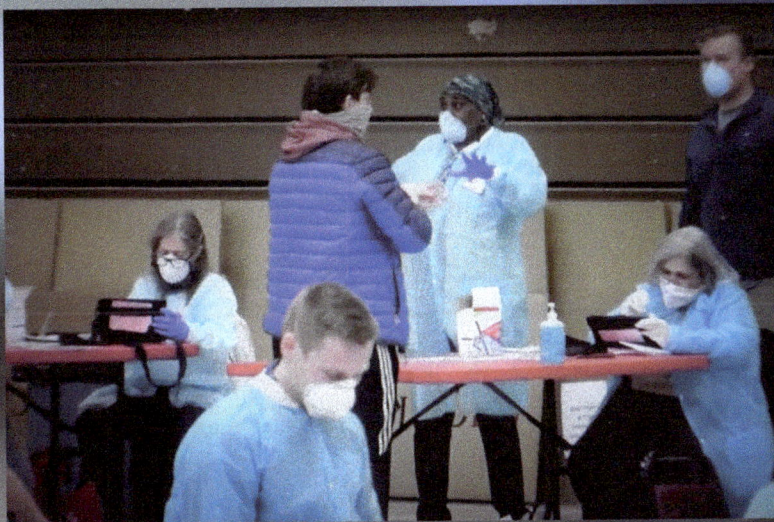

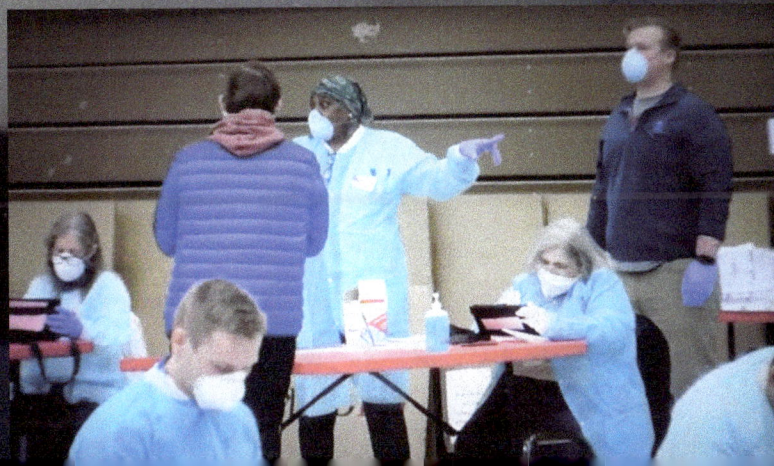

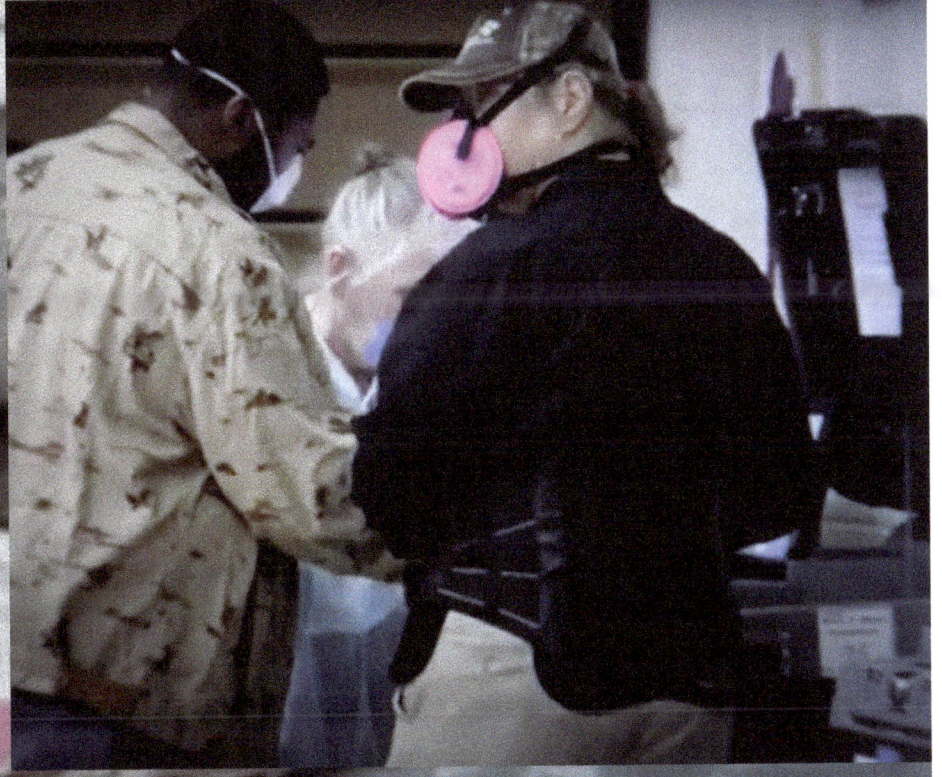

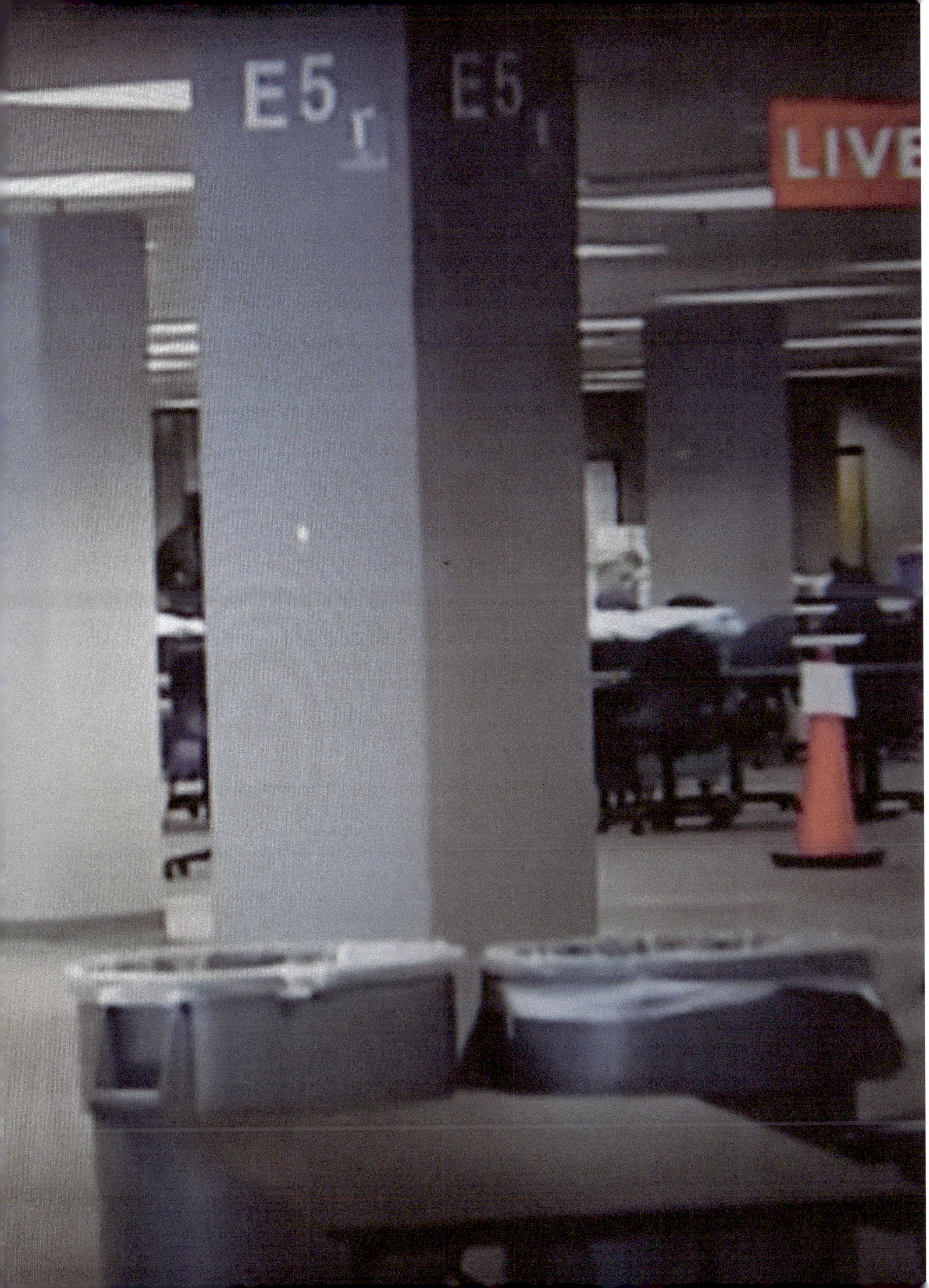
E5
E5
LIVE

Ellen Rothenberg, with Felicitas Hentschke

Insistence on Voting Despite the Pandemic is an Act of Resistance – An Interview

Ellen Rothenberg teaches at the School of the Art Institute (SAIC) in Chicago. But first and foremost, she is an artist and political activist who critically deals with socially relevant issues through installations, performances, visual essays, and other media. Her art is not limited to museums and galleries. She takes her work into the public space and seeks dialogue with passers-by.

In her work, she comments on issues and challenges faced by civil society. She draws attention to inequality and criticizes working conditions, especially in relation to women and others who are discriminated against on the basis of their gender, race, or class, from a historical and contemporary perspective. She encourages the communities around her to develop collaborative practices in response to these complex issues and challenges. In this sense, her art is very powerful and optimistic.

We invited Rothenberg to contribute a visual essay to this book. Like all of the other authors, we asked her how she experienced the coronavirus crisis and what touched her the most – without losing sight of the subject of work.

The result is a piece on the primary elections in the American states of Wisconsin and Georgia, which took place on April 7 and June 9, entitled "'This is Ridiculous,' Voting as Labor During COVID-19: A Report from the United States." She forces the viewer to look at the dilemma in which the citizens found themselves at the time, having to choose between a commitment to exercise their democratic rights and participate in the elections and a commitment to protect themselves and others during lockdown. An advantage of her way of working compared with the more linear texts penned by scholars is the simultaneity of the messages that she can express in their complex connectedness. This enables her to show the inequality, racism, and dysfunctionality of the social system at play more than ever during the elections under the condition of coronavirus – and that voting is a form of work.

In this interview we talk to her about all of these things and also ask her what impact coronavirus is having on her own work.

When we think about certain global moments in history – the first moon landing, or the 9/11 attacks on New York – most people who witnessed these defining events still vividly remember where they were and what they were doing when they heard the news. Coronavirus is a different kind of event, more a kind of phase, rather than a snapshot in history, that comes with drastic measures and consequences for each and every one of us and that will definitely remain in the collective consciousness for a long time. You were (and still are) in Chicago. How did it concern you personally – your daily life? Work? What are your observations on the pandemic experience in your city and on a larger scale in the United States?

Initially we became aware of coronavirus through the news, watching daily broadcasts concerning the situation in Wuhan and through discussions with colleagues, friends, and my international students. Understandably, students were anxious about the virus and its effects on their families and communities in their home countries. As COVID-19 spread to Europe there was a shift towards certainty, a new calculation of 'when' – not 'whether' – it would surface in the United States.

In counterpoint to the news, we were receiving official denials from our government and a complete lack of mobilization at the national, state, and local levels. There was an atmosphere of apprehension coupled with a sense of inevitability. It was only a matter of time before the virus would arrive in the United States. Then, with a shock, New York City was hit. The governmental and institutional responses occurred in slow motion after weeks of denial, hesitation, and waiting. The crisis flooded the country. Suddenly Chicago closed down. We experienced the extreme quiet, no traffic, no planes, no people on the streets. We were left in a vacuum without contingency plans, or clear information – silence.

Quickly and on a broad national scale the virus exposed the weaknesses and cracks in our economic and social systems. Without universal health care, and with an extensive history of health inequality, communities of color were disproportionally affected by the virus. Hospitals were overwhelmed and without the necessary equipment or facilities to care for the avalanche of sick patients or the supplies to keep their staff protected and safe. Gaps in the supply chain resulted in shortages of personal protective equipment (PPE), food, and daily supplies. The politicization of the virus by a president and his administration unable and unwilling to lead, to support scientific findings, and to unite the country has resulted in the current catastrophe. Vast economic divides in our society, in Chicago, and across the country directly impacted an individual's ability to survive the pandemic. The outrage and violence that followed became a call to action and people took to the streets to address them in publicly in "Black Lives Matter."

You created a photo essay for this volume "'This is Ridiculous,' Voting as Labor During COVID-19: A Report from the United States." What is its story? What do you want to narrate?

It is not a story per se, but a texture of relationships, a panorama both historical and contemporary, a landscape of conditions. The visual essay reflects the time we are living through. It is neither fictional nor personal. It is public and of the moment. It examines the media images of the primary elections from the distance of pandemic isolation through the screen. The primary elections in Wisconsin and Georgia occurred on April 7 and June 9, 2020, respectively. Despite very real risks, people were forced to vote in person during a pandemic lockdown, because of conflicting political efforts to skew or impact the vote. The images trace a national portrait of chaos and dysfunction. People standing six feet apart for hours, in the rain, to exercise their right to vote. They endured delays caused by a shortage of poll workers, closed or limited numbers of polling stations, malfunctioning equipment. It was a labor of citizenship inscribed across these events by ordinary people. Their frustration, their stoicism, their anger, and commitment appear within this essay.

What do you know about the protagonists of your story?

I don't know them, but I recognize them. They're clearly Americans, working people. They could be my neighbors, former students, friends, or people encountered on the street. One thing is clear, communities of color are being targeted with policies of voter suppression. Their insistence on voting despite the pandemic is an act of resistance. Voting rights suppression is a human rights violation and a strategy of repression familiar to generations of American communities of color.

In your work, the subject 'work and labor' is present in many projects. You are interested in feminist histories of labor and social action. How much 'work' is in your art work and specifically in "This is Ridiculous." For example, in your installation "For the Instruction of Young Ladies" (1989) and in "Beautiful Youth" (1992) you examine the history of education for women as a method of socialization rather than as a means of acquiring knowledge. Or, taking an example from another type of work, in "Industry Not Servitude" (1996) you are concerned with the history of the Lowell Female Labor Reform Association, the first labor organization for women mill workers in the United States. These women activists broke new ground in the area of women's rights and made significant contributions to anti-slavery movements and labor reform.

2020 is the centennial anniversary of women's suffrage in the United States and marks the passage of the nineteenth amendment giving women the right to vote. Currently I'm working on a public art work commissioned by the Weinberg Newton Gallery in Chicago, in partnership with the American Civil Liberties Union (ACLU) on voting rights. At this moment, when voter suppression is part of the current political landscape, there is a through line, a direct connection both to the suffrage movement and the struggle for civil rights and electoral access during the 1960s, which extends to the present. Today we are witnessing comparable contestations of human rights and social justice in the United States and on a global scale. The pandemic throws a sharp light on the institutional oppression and violence of our social, political, and economic systems.

You ask about coronavirus and how much this pandemic has influenced my thinking and current work. With the re:work invitation to participate in "Corona and Work Around the Globe" it's essential to speak about political activism and solidarity in times of isolation and social distancing, at a precarious moment of political instability and threat to our democratic system. As a 'high-risk' individual susceptible to the virus, how do I actively labor as a citizen from a state of seclusion? This is crucial.

Both the exhibition in Chicago and the essay in the re:work volume closely align with my commitments to artmaking, activism, and community. Publication and exhibition are discursive frameworks supporting possibilities of solidarity and resistance; opportunities to expose systemic inequalities uncovered by the pandemic, and disrupt official narratives. As a counter to isolation, they pose a critical public presence in conversation with others internationally.

In your precise working process, are you ever caught by surprise? Maybe by other stories you discover in the material you work with, stories also worth being told?

Artmaking, like research or writing, requires a series of returns to the material, to the place, to the archive, or to the image. It is only through repeated presence and attention that things come into focus and coalesce with meaning. The surprise is in uncovering connections. Often an oblique image or photograph, a tangential side note becomes key in understanding what's there.

As a very productive artist (and teacher) over the course of the last thirty years, you can look back on a long list of art installations and performances. In your self-description you say that you are very much influenced by the social and political actions of the sixties. You are used to working with historians, anthropologists, and archivists. What motivated you to work in an interdisciplinary context? And how do you collaborate with individuals in various disciplines in "This is Ridiculous"?

Working collaboratively and across disciplines always enriches and informs the work. We have the benefit of other perspectives whether the collaborators are academics or skilled professionals, tradespeople, or members of other countries or communities. They have an expertise, a knowledge based on a lived experience which would be impossible to duplicate or access in any other way. This generosity of exchange deepens my understanding; it takes me to places that would be off-limits otherwise. It's a privilege to learn this way and exciting to gain entrance to these multiple worlds.

What do you teach your students? New techniques to approach projects and their own art work? Do you give them tasks – to work on the theme of coronavirus? Or discuss critically the relation between social media and art? What is new or has changed in the classroom (beyond the fact that you meet online)?

Teaching during coronavirus shifts the emphasis toward developing an understanding of persistence, how to keep going, how to produce work under less than ideal conditions, in isolation, remote from the institution and institutional values. The crisis demands that we address questions of survival and ethics, to consider how our work functions in the world.

In photography you have to make a lot of decisions within split seconds. Maurice speaks of serendipity. You work with existing photographs and have time to look at them carefully and to absorb, to edit, and to modify them? What kind of previous knowledge do you need? Did you do a lot of research? How you approach the photographs?

Photography has been a kind of notation or record taking, a visual text that deals with physical circumstances and the materiality of the moment. It is a record of impressions.

Do you have a favorite picture in this essay? If you had to single it out and you had to give it a subtitle, what would it be?

The essay is a singular work with layered images, it's not possible to select one photograph for commentary or to subtitle. The layering produces a kind of visual noise, the dissonance of voting during coronavirus. The images contain artefacts of their construction, photographed off the screen, there are digital indicators of loading or broadcast. It's necessary to view them together as kind of a panoramic social snapshot. The collection of images reflects the simultaneity of activities and experience in the process of voting. Like a visual text it's temporal, a passage structured within the architecture of the publication.

If there is a narrative arc it articulates the voting process – people standing in line, being registered and sanitized, waiting outside, waiting inside. Poll workers in PPE, directing people, answering questions, cleaning the voting booths, counting ballots. Images of people as they labor to be citizens under the condition of coronavirus. "This is Ridiculous" in its layered presence asks for a kind of continuous return to 'reading' what is there, to encounter small details that on first glance might appear insignificant but are often telling.

Fighting for Justice in the Pandemic

Leon Fink
Police Violence and the Crisis of Work Authority in the COVID-19 Era

As the whole world knows, the health crisis in the United States associated with the COVID-19 pandemic has coincided with a crisis of racism and police violence symbolized by the suffocation of George Floyd in Minneapolis on May 25, 2020.[1] In the public discourse, these two stories converge around the theme of race: a disproportionate number of victims of both the virus and unbridled police actions are people of color. As such, it has become evident that our health care and public safety systems (not to mention the larger economy) are deeply infected with racial inequality and discrimination.

Defining the COVID 19 Era Working Class

As a labor historian, however, I also see another narrative playing out as COVID-19-era headlines inevitably invoke many different workers and occupations. At the forefront of the nightly cable news roundup are the medical professionals – doctors and nurses and their virtual army of supporting actors: ambulance technicians, ambulance drivers, janitorial and dietary staff, and nursing home attendants. A host of other service occupations have also suddenly gained prominence, such as grocery staff, home care workers, restaurant staff, and delivery drivers. Less noticed but equally relied upon and designated by their state governments as "essential workers" – i.e. those working on critical infrastructure operations required to remain open – are the warehouse workers from Amazon, Walmart, and Target bridging otherwise-broken supply chains. Also deemed essential, by a direct order from President Donald Trump, are the meatpacking and food processing plants.[2] Two further professions have received heightened attention. The central role of teachers (including day care providers) to the national economy is apparent as parents turn apprehensively to the still-uncertain trajectory of the coming school year. Finally, of course, we have all been reminded of the impact on our civic health of the actions of the municipal police – not to mention special forces deployed on presidential orders – in either containing or exacerbating social conflict.

This parade of workers may as a whole be said to comprise a 'public' workforce – not in terms of their source of employment, which encompasses both public and private employers, but rather their common impact on public welfare – but they are otherwise highly differentiated. Quite apart from issues of pay, itself a subject of vast differentiation, a considerable disparity – one might even say a vast chasm – separates these groups in terms of workplace authority. Each of these

---

1 Forced by the limitations of time and circumstances to make do here with a daily deluge of newspaper clippings and blog entries, I was lucky to be able to consult a few friends along the way, of whom I would specifically like to credit historians Joshua Freeman, Stefan Berger, Sam Mitrani, John French, Patrick Dixon, and Susan Levine, as well as labor organizers Anton Hajjar and Sarah Julian for valuable references and lines of analysis. Ongoing weekly meetings with the staff of Georgetown University's Kalmanovitz Initiative for Labor and the Working Poor throughout this period have also proven a most helpful stimulus.
2 Michael Dykes, "Opinion: Compensate Our Essential Food Industry Workers," *Agri-Pulse*, April 09, 2020, https://www.agri-pulse.com/articles/13464-opinion-compensate-our-essential-food-industry-workers, accessed July 16, 2020.

groups faces not only a distinct micro-environment based on the product or service rendered, but is also governed by different sets of industrial relations, whether shaped by collective bargaining agreements, government laws and regulations, or one-sided employer determination. Given the tensions accentuated by pandemic conditions, the inequalities of workplace voices – quite apart from the material disparities of economic rewards – take on enhanced prominence and have wider public repercussions. How much voice and/or control, we are obliged to ask, should employees themselves have over their jobs, their health and safety on the job, and their employment security? In keeping with the season's headlines, I am going to seize on two groups whose very polarity at opposite ends of the spectrum of control and collective influence raises increasingly pressing challenges for community health, welfare, and democratic self-rule: poultry workers and the police.

Plight of the Poultry Worker

Poultry workers, whom I portrayed in *The Maya of Morganton: Work and Community in the Nuevo New South*,[3] offer a clear stand-in for those many thousands of workers who find themselves at the lower end of workplace autonomy and control. Employed by an industry determined to dismiss any and all forms of meaningful union organization or contractual countervailing power, poultry workers have long languished on a gradient of wages, working conditions, and basic occupational health conditions far below the standard of most other industrial employees. Reflecting a broader trend among both poultry and meatpacking firms expanding across the rural South and Midwest, the Case Farms poultry plant in Morganton, North Carolina, had increasingly turned to low-wage, immigrant workers – including many undocumented immigrants – to fill its demand for labor. Yet neither poverty nor immigration status guaranteed quiescence. In the mid-1990s, the mostly Guatemalan and Mexican workforce at Case Farms responded to speedups, arbitrary dismissals, and denial of bathroom breaks with a sustained union campaign, including a hunger strike by two union leaders. However, even after winning official certification in a National Labor Relations Board (NLRB) election and winning a court order to force their employer to bargain with them for a year "in good faith," the Case Farms workers could not, under United States law, compel the company to sign a contract with them; the union campaign soon ran out of steam.[4]

Not surprisingly, amid COVID-19, the existing strains on everyday work relations in the food-processing industry have produced a public health disaster, which is likely only tolerated by the general public because the affected workforce is so residentially and culturally distanced from middle-class American communities and is already so politically disempowered that it can do little to escape its own suffering. The two government agencies charged with protecting workers' health – the Department of Labor and the Occupational Safety and Health Administration (OSHA) – have proved almost totally feckless, even as the Department of Agriculture signed off on a higher line speed for poultry 'disassembly' lines. As a laborer at Virginia Tyson Foods in Glen Allen explained: "It's very fast paced. It's very, very intense. Line speeds are designed to run 140 birds a minute.

---

3 Leon Fink, *The Maya of Morganton: Work and Community in the Nuevo New South* (Chapel Hill: University of North Carolina Press, 2003).
4 Leon Fink, *The Maya of Morganton*.

Everyone is standing not even arm's length apart. There's absolutely no way we can social distance within these plants...We may be feeding America, but we're sacrificing our own selves."[5]

The statistics are stark. "By July 7," as Jane Mayer documents in a stunning *New Yorker* report, "OSHA had received more than six thousand coronavirus-related workplace complaints but had issued only one citation, to a nursing home in Georgia."[6] Within the concentrated poultry plants of the Delmarva Peninsula (the slice of alluvial land jutting across Delaware, Maryland, and Virginia state lines), some 2,200 poultry workers had contracted COVID-19 by the end of May 2020, and at least seventeen had died. In the same period, three Guatemalans at Morganton's Case Farms plant also succumbed to the virus.[7]

Such shameful conditions and outcomes need not persist. A change in political regime accompanied by reforms in national labor laws could radically transform both the health and welfare prospects of low-wage workers. Perhaps the best summary of the required policy changes is contained in the "Clean Slate for Worker Power" proposal of Harvard Law School's Labor and Worklife Program. With only ten percent of United States workers unionized, Clean Slate proposes both immediate and longer-term relief in relation to the fundamental power imbalance that plagues labor-management relations.

First, to counteract worker invisibility in the COVID-19 era, Clean Slate proposes an amendment to both OSHA regulations and the Federal Mine Safety and Health Act setting out the creation of elected workplace health and safety committees as well as an elected safety steward in every workplace. Complaints from worker representatives would be dealt with through a collective bargaining grievance system (where applicable) or filed directly to government agencies and the courts. Following European precedents, Clean Slate also proposes complementing workplace-level reforms with a 'sectoral approach' to negotiations concerning baseline standards for an entire industry. Equally important, to ensure that workers have a protected 'voice' and freedom from retaliation on health or other issues, Clean Slate proposes a major shift in individual workers' employment rights. In place of the employer-friendly 'at-will' presumptions traditionally governing dismissals in the United States (at least wherever employers are not further bound by collective bargaining agreements or public-sector grievance systems), labor laws would switch – again, more in accord with standard operating procedures in Europe and elsewhere – to a 'just cause' model that would specifically ban dismissal on grounds of an employee refusing to work due to health concerns. Limitation of the employer's power of dismissal would inevitably have a ripple effect on both worker and union power in many sectors. By April 2020, for example, a number of warehouse workers at Amazon, a notoriously anti-union company owned by the richest man in the world, had reportedly been stricken with COVID-19 yet were warned against participating in protests on pain of losing their jobs. Over the last four decades, the biggest single driver of inequality, according to Harvard economists Anna Stansbury and Lawrence H. Summers, has been the decline in worker power and union organization, a trend exacerbated by the employer's near-absolute managerial authority.[8]

---

5 Jerald Brooks and Lakesha Bailey, "We're Feeding America, but We're Sacrificing Ourselves," *The New York Times*, June 15, 2020, section Opinion, https://nyti.ms/37w8tTX, accessed August 08, 2020.
6 Jane Mayer, "Back to the Jungle. A Meat-Processing Company Puts Its Workers at Risk," *The New Yorker*, July 20, 2020: 30.
7 Jane Mayer, "Back to the Jungle": 33; telephone interview with Basilio Castro, Western North Carolina Workers' Center representative, June 20, 2020.
8 Tim Bray and Christy Hoffman, "Amazon Has Too Much Power. Take It Back," *The New York Times*, July 29, 2020; Jane Mayer, "Back to the Jungle": 38; The classic, still-relevant text on the evolving justification of managerial power

Among other incremental reforms, Clean Slate offers suggestions for protecting communication and organizing channels as well as ensuring freedom from employer surveillance on digital platforms. In a further departure from traditional United States labor relations norms, Clean Slate also calls for the inclusion of community organizations in sectoral health and safety commissions. Amid the current enfeeblement of worker bargaining power, effective campaigns conducted recently by unions such as the Chicago Teachers' Union have reached out to community partners before framing negotiating demands that seek to defend not only the workers' immediate interests but those of the families and neighborhoods of their students. Clean Slate proposes adapting the strategy of 'bargaining for the common good' to health and safety issues as well. All in all, such changes, none of which by itself is outside the bounds of conceivable action but of course is by no means guaranteed even in the case of a Democratic executive and Congressional majority, would inject a new measure of worker power into labor-management relations and ultimately transform the American workplace in a humane and democratic direction.[9]

Police and the Badge of Authority

Yet, if most workers need and deserve a boost in workplace autonomy, what about selected public-sector work groups such as the police, whose employment rights, typically enshrined in law and set out in collective bargaining agreements, not only protect them from unfair dismissal by municipal authorities but also often 'shield' them from public scrutiny? The problem here, of course, is exacerbated by the racial disparity often separating overwhelmingly white police forces from the communities of color they are dispatched to control. As the death count of black victims of police violence has mounted since the deaths of Michael Brown in Ferguson, Missouri, and Eric Garner in New York City in 2014, the grassroots Black Lives Matter (BLM) movement has steadily shone a light on police violence. The May 25, 2020, strangulation of forty-six-year-old George Floyd in Minneapolis, Minnesota, who was arrested for allegedly using a counterfeit twenty-dollar bill in a local shop, set off shock waves of demonstrations across the country and around the world, despite the COVID-19 pandemic.

In the course of the protests, BLM and their allies have discountenanced the promises of police and public officials to promote reform and 'weed out the bad apples' in favor of an attack on police authority itself. In addition to training or retraining police to avoid the use of lethal methods of apprehension or crowd control, reform proposals regularly take aim at the fraternal work culture of the 'men [and small numbers of women] in blue.' Such measures also inevitably collide with the accumulated power of police associations and unions, which through administrative custom, collective bargaining, and legislation protect the actions (and jobs) of uniformed officers from outside interference. So thick has become the cloak protecting the police from transformative regulation that many racial justice advocates no longer choose to join a reform-oriented discourse. "Defund"

is Reinhard Bendix, *Work and Authority in Industry: Ideologies of Management in the Course of Industrialization* (New York: John Wiley & Sons, 1956).
9 "Clean Slate for Worker Power: Building a Just Economy and Democracy," https://lwp.law.harvard.edu/clean-slate-project, accessed July 28, 2020.

or even "Abolish the Police!" have emerged as prominent, if controversial, demands from the activist Left.[10]

For progressives used to making the case for *more* worker power and autonomy on the job (as exemplified above in the Clean Slate proposals), the police present something of a conceptual conundrum. They are both like and unlike other workers. In their collective organization and strategies for self-protection, for example, they draw directly on the legacy of skilled craft unionism, a tradition with a long reach into organized labor's white-ethnic past.

From the late nineteenth century onwards, big-city police (often of Irish and German-American descent) made several halting attempts to assume a place alongside other trades in citywide labor federations. For the most part, the labor movement itself initially rejected such bids, given that it was the police who were regularly suppressing their picket lines, but there were exceptions. The most famous case was that of the Boston police, who received an American Federation of Labor charter in August 1919 and then went on strike over wages and working conditions that included sixty-hour workweeks without overtime pay. Foreshadowing the latter-day response of then-president, Ronald Reagan, to striking air traffic controllers, Massachusetts governor (and future president), Calvin Coolidge, summarily fired the entire police force, while summoning the National Guard to beat back the spreading labor protests of the era.[11] Police unionism would again languish until it could join a larger wave of public-sector organizing in the 1960s and 1970s. Fueled – paradoxically – at once by state-based labor reforms encompassing collective bargaining rights for minority workers (such as the Memphis sanitation workers) and by white, middle-class fears of urban unrest, police representation was extended in separate affiliations such as the Patrolmen's Benevolent Association (PBA) as well as units of national unions linked to the American Federation of Labor and Congress of Industrial Organizations such as the United Food and Commercial Workers, the Service Employees International Union, and the American Federation of State, County and Municipal Employees.[12]

Moreover, once police unions found a foothold, they proved remarkably effective at using all of the political tools at their disposal for job protection and group empowerment. Dozens of police department contracts, for example, include provisions to delay officer interrogations following cases of alleged misconduct, and at least four cities mandate the removal of disciplinary records from personnel files after a certain amount of time.[13] Amid a larger culture of impunity, the Chicago Police Department (CPD) positively bristled with self-confidence. In 1968, only months after Mayor Daley issued a shoot-to-kill order in response to the riots following the assassination of Martin Luther King, Jr., a 'police riot' suppressed demonstrators around the Democratic National

10 Paige Fernandez, "Defunding the Police Will Actually Make Us Safer," *American Civil Liberties Union*, June 11, 2020, https://www.aclu.org/news/criminal-law-reform/defunding-the-police-will-actually-make-us-safer, accessed July 30, 2020; Mariame Kaba, "Yes, We Mean Literally Abolish the Police," *The New York Times*, June 12, 2020.

11 Brian MacQuarrie, "When the City Was Lawless: Recalling the Boston Police Strike of 1919," *Boston Globe*, September 7, 2019, https://www.bostonglobe.com/metro/2019/09/07/when-city-was-lawless-recalling-boston-police-strike/0YgNYLshnyfcxYkQnGKhvM/story.html, accessed July 30, 2020.

12 James R. Barrett, *The Irish Way: Becoming American in the Multiethnic City* (New York: Penguin Press, 2012): 45–46; Ross Barkan, "How Did Police Unions Get So Powerful?" *The Nation*, July 2, 2020, https://www.thenation.com/article/society/police-unions-nypd-history/, accessed July 30, 2020; Harold Meyerson, "Why Mainstream Unions Shouldn't Represent the Cops: Bargaining for the Police and for African Americans is an Exercise in Self-Negation," *American Prospect*, July 15, 2020, https://prospect.org/justice/why-mainstream-unions-shouldnt-represent-the-cops/, accessed July 30, 2020.

13 Rebecca Rainey and Holly Otterbein, "Local Unions Defy AFL-CIO in Push to Oust Police Unions," *Politico*, June 30, 2020, https://www.politico.com/news/2020/06/30/police-union-ouster-346249, accessed July 30, 2020.

Convention, and a tactical unit dispatched by the Cook Country state attorney's office stormed the apartment of Illinois Black Panther Party chair, Fred Hampton, and killed him in his sleep. Ruled a 'justifiable homicide' at the time, the victim's family would not receive economic restitution until 1982. In 1969 and 1970, "CPD officers killed 79 people... three-quarters of those killed... were Black... a rate three times higher than those in other major cities."[14] Across the ensuing decade, moreover, the well-funded campaigns of the Fraternal Order of Police succeeded in passing a variety of 'police bill of rights' legislation.[15] Indeed, only after sustained pressure in June 2020 did the New York state legislature revoke the infamous Civil Service Law 50-A, which barred the public from accessing police disciplinary files.

Prospects for Police Reform

Not surprisingly, over time, the political pendulum in various cities has swung back and forth from protection to righteous indignation and organized community determination to rein in police power and unionism. Yet, the reform record of the past decades offers a cautionary tale at best. Even where structural constraints have been imposed on police autonomy, the police rank and file have sought actively to undermine them. In Baltimore in 2015, for example, after six officers were charged for the in-custody death of Freddie Gray and the police department itself endorsed the principles of 'community policing' including the use of body cameras, a powerful police culture managed to undermine most changes. An unannounced work slowdown was soon followed by a citywide uptick in crime and the local public clamor soon switched from support for reform to calls for more aggressive, 'proactive' policing. Likewise, in June 2020, when a police officer was charged in Atlanta with the murder of a suspect, Rayshard Brooks, in custody, "some squads reportedly walked off the job and others called in sick."[16] In the meantime, technological fixes such as body cameras have been selectively adapted by the departments themselves to defend their actions. All in all, 'workers' control,' when it comes to policing, has not proved itself to be a progressive historical force.

But what about the basic rights to self-representation that we labor historians cherish – and wish to expand (as in the case of Clean Slate) – for every other work group? Here is where it gets tricky. It is not surprising, perhaps, that the political Right has been quick to draw the connections from police to other service-sector unions, especially teachers. "Collective bargaining, in the public-safety and educational sectors," intones one recent commentary from the right-leaning *City Journal*, "strips government executives of the tools they need to supervise and manage their workforces effectively. Police chiefs and school principals struggle to weed out poor performers."[17] Yet, even avowedly progressive voices look to administrative means to nullify police collective bargaining rights. While rhetorically pushing back against those who would apply similar strictures to other workers, Harvard Law School professor and Clean Slate co-founder, Benjamin Sachs, pro-

---

14 Maya Dukmasova, "From Soldier to Worker," *Chicago Reader*, June 10, 2020, https://www.chicagoreader.com/chicago/cops-union-history-fraternal-order-of-police/Content?oid=80542709, accessed August 01, 2020.
15 Maya Dukmasova, "From Soldier to Worker."
16 Baynard Woods and Brandon Soderberg, "Police Reform Doesn't Work: Baltimore Proves It," *Washington Post*, June 21, 2020.
17 Daniel DiSalvo, "Not Public Spirited," *City Journal*, June 8, 2020, https://www.city-journal.org/government-employee-unions-public-interest, accessed July 30, 2020.

poses amending state laws "to strictly curtail the range of subjects over which police unions have the right to bargain." While unions might still influence wages and benefits, argues Sachs, "collective bargaining over any subject that implicates the use of force, including...over disciplinary matters, would be prohibited."[18] What may be clear to Sachs may prove a distinction without a difference to conservative lawmakers. "Those who are looking to kick police officers out of the union movement should be very careful," warns New York PBA president, Patrick Lynch. "The rhetoric they are using now is the same rhetoric that has been used to strip union protections from teachers, bus drivers, nurses, and other civil servants across the country."[19]

The lessons of labor history, moreover, suggest that statutory controls on worker self- activity are likely to be ineffectual as well as deeply resented. A 'wages-and-benefits-only' approach to collective bargaining, for example, has long been applied to teacher unions – most recently by the viciously anti-union Wisconsin governor, Scott Walker, but also in Illinois, where teachers are formally instructed that they cannot bargain over vital educational issues such as class size. In many cases, however, employer representatives who sit down with such 'limited' worker representatives find that their counterparts have wriggled out of these straitjackets by formally making implacable demands on the allowed wages and benefits front until their 'real' grievances – over, say, class size for teachers or disciplinary matters for cops – have been attended to. Whether for the work they do, or the political style or leanings of their union leadership, tight work groups have long survived public and even prosecutorial adversity. Like the coal miners under John L. Lewis during World War II, Harry Bridges' longshoremen in the early postwar years, Jimmy Hoffa's Teamsters in the 1950s, or Mike Quill's New York City subway workers in the 1960s, it is not likely that an organized police force will meekly surrender its workplace power in the face of a liberal public onslaught.

Fortunately, police culture and, with it, the orientation of police unions, is not set in stone. Current-day European experiences – for the sake of argument, in Germany – for the most part provide an encouraging counterexample. In Germany, the main police union (Gewerkschaft der Polizei, GdP) is a member of the main trade union federation, the Deutsche Gewerkschaftsbund (DGB), which politically has long supported the German Social Democratic Party (SPD) in national politics. As German labor historian Stefan Berger summarizes, the GdP "has been at the forefront of demanding intercultural training in relation to non-German ethnicities in Germany and in relation to what I guess in the United States would be called 'race relations.'"[20] Acknowledging frequent allegations in the past of racial discrimination by the police – charges further confirmed in a July 3 *New York Times* exposé of right-wing infiltration of Germany's special forces military unit (KSK) – Berger nevertheless insists that both the government and the unions themselves have "always taken those [reports] seriously and started internal investigations. The union has been an important driver in the police to raise awareness of the need for anti-racism education."[21] As an affiliate of the European Police Union (EPU), a European federation of over 800,000 police officers,

18 Benjamin Sachs, "Police Unions: It's Time to Change the Law and End the Abuse," *On Labor*, June 4, 2020, https://www.onlabor.org/police-unions-its-time-to-change-the-law, accessed August 2, 2020.
19 Rebecca Rainey and Holly Otterbein, "Local Unions Defy AFL-CIO in Push to Oust Police Unions."
20 Stefan Berger, email to author, June 28, 2020.
21 Stefan Berger, email to author, June 28, 2020.

GdP's public message, at least, emphasizes the professionalization of standards, including current Europe-wide demands for better uniforms, equipment, and training.[22]

For the good of wider society, to be sure, the standards within any occupational group need to be monitored and balanced in some way by a broader democratic constituency. This point is signaled, for example, by a closer look at communications within the 'professional' culture of the German police union. Thus, in the very month of the *New York Times* exposé of neo-nazi sympathies within the national police forces, the monthly magazine of the GdP, *Deutsche Polizei*, featured a report on a different social threat: "Leftwing Extremism," ran its headline, "Brutal, Cynical, Arrogant."[23]

The balance of power, or effective work authority, of a given group of workers over their work environment depends on numerous factors. Among the most important, however, are formal regulations (or state-based encouragement/discouragement) on collective bargaining, the strength of the occupational work culture, as well as the economic (or budgetary) leverage for potential collective action. In the case of marginalized groups such as the poultry workers, it is the state's role that will likely hold the key to restoring a measure of workplace justice to the employment relationship. Yet, in the long run it may prove easier to intervene and empower a neglected work group than to disempower a group, such as the police, that has become politically swollen in its authority.

Despite the obstacles, there are doubtless some tangible reforms that can make a difference when it comes to police violence. The Justice in Policing Act of 2020, for example, passed by the United States House of Representatives in June on a largely party-line vote (and thus not going anywhere so long as the Republicans control the Senate), contains some practical strictures on police practices as well as incentives towards greater police professionalism. In addition to granting the justice department's civil rights division and state attorney generals greater power to investigate misconduct (including the creation of a federal registry of misconduct complaints), it would eliminate the 'qualified immunity' doctrine that currently protects local and state officers from lawsuits, requires body-worn cameras, restricts the transfer of equipment from the military to the police, and also makes anti-discrimination training a requirement for all law enforcement agencies that receive federal funds.[24]

For those who truly want to build worker power while limiting police violence, the most effective strategy might well be the simple slogan being shouted from the streets. As Veena Dubal, a University of California, Hastings School of Law professor, advocated after resigning from a toothless police oversight commission in Berkeley, the goal should be to "take the emphasis way from the unions and refocus on the defunding and abolition of police departments." Transferring some police functions to other professionals such as social workers and non-violent mediators is surely a good place to start. Only if communities shift the focus away from punishment and toward other priorities, thus allocating their spending in new directions, will police officers be incentivized to

22 European Police Union, "The Minimum Standards for Maximal Security Project," November 02, 2017, http://www.europeanpoliceunion.eu/.cm4all/uproc.php/0/minimumstandards/Project%20Overview%20(Press%20Release).pdf?cdp=a&_=15f7ba50448, accessed August 04, 2020.
23 "DP-Deutsche Polizei, Das Mitgliedermagazin der Gewerkschaft der Polizei," July 2020, https://www.gdp.de/gdp/gdp.nsf/id/deupolall, accessed August 4, 2020.
24 "George Floyd Justice in Policing Act of 2020," https://en.wikipedia.org/wiki/George_Floyd_Justice_in_Policing_Act_of_2020, accessed August 03, 2020; In early August 2020, a federal judge in Mississippi called on the Supreme Court to overturn the immunity doctrine, "Judge: Doctrine Shielding Police from Lawsuits is Wrong," *Jackson Free Press*, August 6, 2020, https://www.jacksonfreepress.com/news/2020/aug/06/judge-doctrine-shielding-police-law-suits-wrong/, accessed August 05, 2020.

change their behavior. As veteran trade unionist and social justice activist Bill Fletcher, Jr. rightly emphasizes, "The law enforcement unions are not the problem: the history, culture, and practices of the US law enforcement system are the problem."[25] To reform the police, defund the police.

---

25 Bill Fletcher, Jr., "The Central Issue is Police Repression, Not Police Unions," *In These Times*, June 12, 2020, http://inthesetimes.com/working/entry/22598/the_central_issue_is_police_repression_not_police_unions, accessed August 07, 2020.

Cristiana Schettini
"We did All the Work for You": Sex Work in Argentina in Pandemic Times

How did the first months of the COVID-19 pandemic impact on sex workers? In different parts of the world, journalistic accounts have described how urban circulation restrictions and the risks of contagion left sex workers even more invisible than usual to government emergency aid programs and even more vulnerable than usual to police abuse and criminalization. This chapter presents a closer look at the initiatives of a trade union of sex workers in Buenos Aires during first six months of the lockdown. The intention is to focus on the reaction of organized sex workers to the sanitary emergency in light of their recent history. The shift in the meanings of work over the last decades of Argentina's history has influenced the organization of sex workers, their position within the feminist field, and how they participate in the broader social organization of workers. For unionized prostitutes, the pandemic opened up a window to establish networks with the national state and to strengthen their historical demand for recognition as workers.

The Incident

On June 4, 2020, the Argentine minister of social development announced the launch of a digital platform to register the workers in the popular economy, the Registro Nacional de Trabajadores y Trabajadoras de la Economía Popular (RENATEP; the national register of workers of the popular economy). Accompanied by representatives of social movements, the minister stated that the government's initiative came "from below," and expressed the expectation that it would be the first step in access to work programs, social security, training, credit, and other forms of inclusion. He described the measure as a "springboard to building new rights."[26]

The website of the national government explained that the requirements to sign up were being over eighteen and working based on "skills and trades" in individual or collective production units involved "in asymmetric relations in the financial, commercial, or fiscal spheres." This definition of popular economy includes street vendors, market vendors, artisans, *cartoneros* (cardboard collectors), recyclers, small farmers, and workers in infrastructure and environmental improvement activities. The platform displayed more than two hundred possible occupations and activities. RENATEP acknowledged these activities as labor in order to enable further economic and social integration for those sectors.

The registry initiative responded to the debates that were already taking place prior to the pandemic about the government program of the Alberto Fernandez administration, in office since December 2019: its social agenda, its permeability to social movements, and the possibility of a universal basic income policy. The registry project provided for a few immediate measures, such as a certificate to recognize those registered as workers of the popular economy, and future measures, such as the opening of free bank accounts and access to public credit lines.

---

[26] "Lanzamos el registro nacional," https://www.argentina.gob.ar/noticias/lanzamos-el-registro-nacional-de-trabajadores-y-trabajadoras-de-la-economia-popular-renatep, accessed August 07, 2020.

However, it was announced at a time when it was already clear that the pandemic would mean the drastic impoverishment of vast sectors of Argentine society. The early establishment of compulsory preventive social isolation in mid-March brought a sharp halt to all economic activity and social interaction, and was especially devastating for these sectors. But contrary to what could have been expected, the launch of the platform did not provoke a public debate on social inequality, on the redistribution of wealth, the timing for establishing a universal basic income, or the possibility of taxing great fortunes. Instead, the controversy concerned whether Argentine state should recognize prostitution as work. Sex work was one of the hundreds of options in the registry, listed under "self-employment." In the first five hours of activity on the website, eight hundred of those who were able to access the platform chose to identify themselves as sex workers. Then the website collapsed. One month later, at the beginning of July, the website was reactivated, but this time without this category.

NGOs dedicated to combatting sexual exploitation and human trafficking joined representatives of the self-proclaimed "abolitionist feminism" movement and some government officials to denounce what they considered an attempt by the government to recognize and regulate prostitution. In fact, the news that the government had actually decided to withdraw the category "sex work," rather than it being a technical failure, was made public via the personal Twitter account of a conservative, catholic representative of anti-trafficking organizations, who at present holds an official post in the national government. Leaders and allies of the Argentine union of prostitutes, who had celebrated the chance to be acknowledged in a public registry as workers rather than victims or criminals, showed bewilderment and indignation at the interruption of the website with no official explanation. In the following days, they demanded an audience with the national authorities, but they did not succeed in having the decision reversed. Much as the government was permeable to social movements 'from below,' it was also permeable to other pressures.

What happened in this incident? At first glance, it looked like nothing other than a repetition of a debate splitting Argentine feminism, which has otherwise grown stronger and more united in recent years. Since 2015, the motto *"ni una menos"* (Not one [woman] less) has fueled massive marches against various forms of gender violence, particularly femicide. In 2018, the demand for the right to legal and safe abortion reached the national congress and mobilized forces across the political spectrum. Nevertheless, unlike abortion and femicide, the issue of sex work generated not only divisions but also violent confrontation between the groups of prostitutes organized around the demand for labor rights and the groups resisting the recognition of prostitution as work.

This episode also concentrates other layers of meaning and histories. Identifying them contributes to a reflection on the recognition as workers for vulnerable social sectors who find themselves trapped in the midst of a general precaritization of work relations. While the pandemic has caused a mixture of uncertainty, suffering, and alarm, it has also exposed the margins of political action for groups that carry out very heterogeneous activities and that share common experiences of vulnerability, invisibility, and exposure to risk. An articulated approach to the histories that converge in this episode also shows how racialized and sexualized bodies become the terrain for political violence and the political struggle for rights in Argentine society. The pandemic has converted social movements, the streets, and the state itself into arenas for the struggle for rights for those who are fighting to assert their identity as workers.

The Unionization of Whores

AMMAR (Asociación de Mujeres Meretrices de Argentina; the association of prostitute women of Argentina) was established at the end of 1994 during meetings between prostitutes who were tired of facing police violence on the streets. Until then, the edicts that had been in force during most of the twentieth century had entitled the police to define their own laws to deal with prostitution in Buenos Aires and other Argentine cities, in a widespread practice which persisted both during democratic periods and under authoritarian rule. The struggle to repeal these edicts during the democratic transition years, in the 1980s, brought together sex workers, gay, feminist, and human rights groups.[27]

Since its beginning, AMMAR has been a member of the CTA (Central de Trabajadores de la Argentina; the Argentine workers' central union), one of the main federations of multi-tendency trade unions. What mainly distinguishes the CTA from the CGT (Confederación General del Trabajo de la República Argentina; the general confederation of labor of the Argentine Republic), the other major established federation, is that while the CGT is a congregation of formal and industrial workers, the CTA unifies a diversity of workers excluded from the formal labor market. In its first phase (1991-2010), the CTA contested the neoliberal policies and resulting precaritization in labor relations during the 1990s. State unions played an important role in the CTA. But one of its most telling innovations was its openness to organizations that brought together unemployed workers, such as the *piqueteros* (unemployed workers movement), as well as organizations representing the homeless and retirees, most of whom were former workers in the companies that had either been privatized or gone bankrupt in the late 1990s.[28]

In the capital city of Buenos Aires, the system of police edicts was finally repealed in 1998. Almost simultaneously, prostitutes organized to stand up to the police in other urban settings. In the nearby city of Rosario, the battle of the incipient local AMMAR for the repeal of the misdemeanor code and against police extortion was followed by the murder of Sandra Cabrera, the leader of the organization in the city, in January 2004. This raised social awareness of the working conditions of prostitutes.[29] However, practices to control the organization of commercial sex in the urban space continued in the hands of the misdemeanor justice and the municipal police force.

At the turn of the twenty-first century, the emergence of sex trafficking as a social problem was concomitant with the growing distance between prostitutes, feminists, and trans people. While prostitutes developed a discourse focused on sex work as a basis for demanding rights, the other groups intensified their fight against prostitution as an expression of patriarchal domination. The approval of anti-trafficking laws, the actions of NGOs against sexual exploitation, and the impact in the media of cases of disappearance and murder of women, which were increasingly understood in terms of sex trafficking, led to a revival of the persecution of prostitutes. Since then, an increasingly pathologizing and criminalizing vocabulary informed the feminist abolitionist framework for

---

27 Leticia Sabsay, *Fronteras sexuales: espacios, cuerpos y ciudadanía* (Buenos Aires: Paidós, 2011); Deborah Daich, *Tras las huellas de Ruth Mary Kelly: feminismo y prostitución en la Buenos Aires del siglo XX* (Buenos Aires: Biblos, 2019).

28 Andrea Andujar, *Rutas Argentinas hasta el fin. Mujeres, política y piquetes, 1996-2001* (Buenos Aires: Luxemburg, 2014); Kate Hardy, "Incorporating sex workers into the Argentine Labor Movement," *International Labor and Working Class History*, 77 (2010): 89–108.

29 Maria Luisa Mugica, "La prostitución en Rosario: un análisis histórico sobre un Nuevo/viejo problema," *Actas de las X Jornadas Interescuelas* (Rosario: UNL, 2005).

understanding prostitution, and led to unprecedented animosity and harassment toward prostitutes.

Since then, prostitution has been increasingly treated as synonymous with trafficking in women. This has brought new challenges for AMMAR, including accusations of procuring.[30] In response, AMMAR built on its affiliation with the CTA and the increased tension within feminist debates to set out an argument repertoire of its own. A new collective identification emerged, detached from the judicial and criminalizing terms of the procurer and the victim-awaiting-rescue: the notion of sex worker took on new connotations and gave way to that of "feminist whore."

Between Unionists and Feminists

Prostitutes collectively organized as sex workers in different parts of the world during the late twentieth century.[31] Such initiatives did not always take the form of a trade union, although the vindication of a labor identity served to support the demand for basic rights, including the guarantee of physical integrity, access to health rights, and a retirement pension. Enrollment in the world of labor became a means of challenging the deeply rooted moral stigma that was found even in broad sectors of feminism. In light of the historical importance of the organization of the labor movement as a prominent political force in twentieth-century Argentina, it is not surprising that Argentine prostitutes have organized as unionized workers to face such stigmatization.

Nevertheless, feminism was present in the ways AMMAR defined sex work over its twenty-five years. At its 2008 national assembly, for example, its members ratified the decision to continue organizing as a trade union and demanding rights. In the final document, they asserted that they fought "together with all the people" for the "dream of a more just and egalitarian society, without exploitation or male chauvinism" until "no woman will be forced to stand at a corner for lack of opportunities."[32] One decade later, following diverse collective experiences, including women's meetings, workers' marches, feminist activities, the CTA, and networks with trans organizations, the meaning of sex worker gradually shifted: prostitution ceased to be referred as a symptom of capitalist exploitation and the patriarchy; instead, the word came to acquire positive and even feminist connotations, associated with conditions of dignity, pride, respect, and self-determination over women's bodies. Capitalist exploitation and the patriarchy remained core concepts, but rather than serving to highlight the coercion and the 'lack of opportunities' that affected prostitutes particularly, they now placed the experience of sex work in a critical position, with the capacity to point out and denaturalize the exploitation expressed in everyday patriarchal violence, and especially that targeted at workers forced to sell their labor power.

The change in formulation is, on the one hand, a reaction to the feminist abolitionist movement, with its insistence on prostitutes' victimization and on equating prostitution with trafficking

---

30 Deborah Daich and Cecilia Varela, "Entre el combate a la trata y la criminalización del trabajo sexual: las formas de gobierno de la prostitución," *Delito y sociedad*, 28, (2014): 63–86.

31 Joe Doezema and Kamala Kempadoo, *Global sex workers: rights, resistance and redefinition* (New York City: Routledge, 1998).

32 *Boletín Informativo de la Redtrasex*, 15, (2007/2008); http://biblioteca.redtrasex.org/handle/123456789/44, accessed August, 07, 2020.

in women.[33] On the other hand, it reflects the experience of participating in the CTA. The expansion of the conceptualization of work and workers allowed AMMAR to join the organizational structure of the CTA and amplify its visibility and its roots in different provinces. At the same time, for the CTA, the participation of a union of sex workers has enabled and legitimized its public intervention in an innovative way, even though, predictably, these gender formulations have also come up against conflict.[34]

The new meanings associated with the adoption of the term "feminist whore" as a political expression brought greater visibility for AMMAR and its secretary general, Georgina Orellano, in the media and among young, middle-class feminists who have adopted the denomination. Meanwhile, increasing animosity toward sex workers, as well as toward researchers engaged in the subject, came from abolitionist feminists, catholic conservative, and anti-trafficking groups. Critics assumed a perspective of moral superiority, characteristic of their interpretation of prostitution as human trafficking, while AMMAR began to combine media campaigns with its political trade union activities.

In 2019, in addition to continuing to participate in the CTA, AMMAR also established contacts with the CTEP (Confederación de Trabajadores de la Economía Popular), a confederation of workers of the popular economy. Created in 2011, CTEP brought together a new generation of social movements organized around a wide range of demands. These movements began to replace their identity as "unemployed," characteristic of late-twentieth-century organizations, with a self-identification as active workers who "invent their own work."[35] Their demands included the social recognition of their work as productive and necessary for the economic life of the country. This redefinition of work implies a direct questioning of the daily criminalization of their activities and of their vulnerability in the urban space, a particularly urgent problem for workers like *cartoneros*, recyclers, and street vendors.

Thus, at the end of 2019, AMMAR became closer to social movements representing people who work on the streets and who are exposed to police violence on a daily basis. Then the pandemic hit. In the first months of 2020, the neighborhood of Constitución, home to many vulnerable and informal workers, as well as headquarters of AMMAR, became the setting of its political action.

The Red House

When the pandemic reached Argentina in March, the government was quick to decree mandatory preventive social isolation. As confusion and fear intensified, the debate surrounding these quarantine measures highlighted a variety of situations. Many people were not able to stay at home, whether because they needed to earn their living daily, or because their home was not a suitable place to spend the day, or even because, as feminists have consistently warned, for some, the home means abuse and violence instead of protection and refuge.

These discussions took place online. The streets were deserted. But in the neighborhood of Constitución, dozens of people began to line up at the door of the 'Red House,' AMMAR headquarters since 2019, to receive bags of food. The protective measures put in place by the national gov-

33 Estefanía Martynowskyj, "Prostituicao e feminismo(s). Disputas de reconocimiento nos Encontros Nacionais de Mulheres (Argentina, 1986–2017)," *Sexualidad, salud y sociedad*, 30, (2018).
34 Kate Hardy, "Incorporating sex workers": 89–108.
35 https://ctepargentina.org/104/, accessed August 10, 2020.

ernment to prohibit evictions and to freeze the value of rents was not fully respected, and AMMAR union leaders devoted the early days of quarantine to negotiating with the owners of precarious hotels to dissuade them from evicting their tenants, many of whom were transgender girls who had defaulted because they were incapable of activity. The next step was to organize collective and solidarity initiatives to sanitize these places. According to a preliminary survey conducted by AMMAR, there were four hundred trans women living in 'family hotel' rooms in the Buenos Aires neighborhood of Constitución, for which they were paying extortionate rents. The pandemic context and the intervention of AMMAR increased the visibility of structural housing vulnerability, particularly affecting a population who faced implicit bias from the government of the city and who had their housing subsidy requests rejected on a frequent basis.[36]

In addition to public offices being closed due to the sanitary emergency, the police and other agents of the city government showed animosity toward transvestites, transgender people, and immigrants. Also, apart from not having the tools to reach the most vulnerable people, the national government was uninformed on the size of the different vulnerable social sectors. This became evident when enrollment for the Emergency Family Income (*Ingreso Familiar de Emergencia*) saw initial government estimates rapidly double, and then triple, eventually reaching nine million people. In the face of the emergency, AMMAR union leaders came into direct contact with national government officers to act as mediators in mitigation and welfare procedures. In June, the Red House began to be referred to as the "Ministry of Whores" in some journalistic accounts: from AMMAR headquarters, prostitutes distributed food cards and parcels but also oriented neighbors to fill subsidy requests, to follow through immigration and other documentation procedures.[37] Soon, dozens of African immigrants were standing in line with immigrants from border countries and sex workers.

The failed attempt to include sex workers in the registry of informal economy workers in Argentina is the result of the convergence of the many histories that became visible in the unexpected social catastrophe of the pandemic. The trajectory of AMMAR in relation to other social movements, its affiliation with the CTA, and its incipient rapprochement with the CTEP are all testament to the opportunities for political organization brought about by the shift in the meaning of work over the last decades of Argentina's history.

For organized prostitutes, this failed attempt exposes the degree of animosity and reluctance surrounding the organization of prostitutes as workers, especially in the dramatic situation produced by the pandemic. Beyond a certificate identifying the holder as a worker, which is of no small importance for sex workers, especially in a context of restricted public circulation, registration was not linked to the receipt of resources or income of any kind. It is evident that the vindication of sex workers mobilizes conflicts and tensions that largely transcend the distribution of material resources.

Facing a closed door, AMMAR found a new loophole as the state's difficulty in reaching vulnerable populations enabled AMMAR to increase its rooting in a small vulnerable portion of the urban territory. The pandemic context intensified perceptions of a shared experience with other neighborhood groups, who would be otherwise reluctant to approach the Red House. If the pandemic reinforces entrenched ways of organizing the social world, it also opens up narrow gaps for political action.

---

36 http://www.ammar.org.ar/No-tenemos-ningun-ingreso-como-nos.html, accessed August, 11, 2020.

37 Agustina Paz Fronteras, "Ministerio de Putas: cómo AMMAR articula con el Estado durante la pandemia," https://latfem.org/ministerio-de-putas-como-ammar-articula-con-el-estado-durante-la-pandemia/, accessed August, 12, 2020.

The impact of the pandemic is gendered. The heterogeneous world of Argentine feminism has witnessed diverse, collective reflections on the rights of those who do unpaid, feminized care work in these months of the health emergency.[38] This feminist perspective is also present in how sex workers think of themselves. In a recent interview, Georgina Orellano explained how the Ministry of Whores worked, explicitly stating AMMAR expectations:

> If the quarantine is lifted we have an open channel with the state to tell them: 'hey, look here, we are the ones that did all the work for you and now we want to talk about our working conditions.' Right now, we are providing pure social assistance, but so that it doesn't happen to us again, we want to go to the root, which is the recognition of sex work.[39]

Once again, the notion of dignified work is set in opposition to the work that others –in this case the state – will not or cannot do, a work described as "pure social assistance." Those who do it, in informal, precarious, and undervalued conditions, know how important and urgent such work is, an awareness that is expressed in the utterance "we did all the work for you." The recognition of rights, however, is still lacking. The failure of the state to register popular economy workers and the increased visibility of organized prostitutes at a time of generalized uncertainty raise both challenges and possibilities in the struggle for labor rights during and after pandemic times.

---

[38] For instance, the assemblies promoted by the School of Popular Feminism Nora Cortiñas and the Association of Women's Histories and Gender Studies under the motto "our rights are not on quarantine," http://www.hamartia.com.ar/2020/07/02/asamblea-de-trabajadoras/, accessed August, 13, 2020, and „Operación Bagayo", an Instagram community built to assist transgender people in vulnerable situation during the pandemic, https://www.instagram.com/operacionbagayo/, accessed August 13, 2020.
[39] Agustina Paz Fronteras, "Ministerio de Putas: cómo AMMAR articula con el Estado durante la pandemia."

On Barak

The Reserve Army of Labor in the Air: Military Support Systems for Furloughed El Al Pilots[40]

Introduction

Civil aviation was the key vector of the initial COVID-19 transregional proliferation, and one of the earliest and worst hit economic sectors. Closing the skies, as it were, by grounding airlines and shutting airports was a first measure taken by many governments as part of their attempts to contain the pandemic: according to a closed-borders, nationalistic view of public health, before a country could flatten its contagion curve, it had to shut down incoming transportation. Months after these measures were first taken, the resumption of activity to pre-2020 levels now seems protracted and uncertain.[41] As El Al CEO, Gonen Usishkin, wrote to the company's employees in early May 2020 to announce an extension of their furlough, "Civil aviation was the first sector to enter the [COVID-19] crisis and will be the last one to emerge from it."[42] It seems very likely that El Al, like other airline companies, will emerge from the crisis looking very different from when it entered. Expected mergers, consolidations, bankruptcies, government bailouts, and restructurings in the sector will surely affect workers. Yet examining the effects of the crisis on aviation workers reveals more than a sector grappling with severe uncertainty or workers in dire straits. Given the industry's significant role in spreading pathogens and worsening climate change and global warming, these workers' modes of adaptation and their different abilities to weather the storm will dictate the possibility or ease of introducing reforms to the sector. They are part of the conditions for an unsustainable business-as-usual model – that of the carbon economy writ large. Like industrial meat farms, or the notorious wet markets in Wuhan, China, civil aviation provides a case in which labor conditions are not only transformed by environmental change, but they also prepare the ground for further environmental damage or, potentially, mitigation of it. Given the acute demand for pilots in most airlines worldwide, these highly skilled professionals are a key industry bottleneck influencing the sector's ability to grow, change, or decarbonize.[43] Their ability to persevere in a polluting industry, to diversify into and out of it at short notice, their political clout, and also their ability to transition to other sectors permanently will therefore determine the chances of greening aviation and otherwise limiting its harm.[44]

This essay focuses on those labor arrangements in Israel in which the importance of civil aviation is arguably greater than almost anywhere else. Due to the country's geographical location and the Arab-Israeli conflict, which essentially nullifies cross-border ground transportation, the

40 I thank Avishai Ehrlich and Lesley Marks for reading early drafts of this essay, which was supported by the Israel Science Foundation.
41 "IATA: Passenger Demand May Not Recover Until 2024," *Flight Global*, May 13, 2020, https://www.flightglobal.com/airlines/iata-passenger-demand-may-not-recover-until-2024/138357.article, accessed August 8, 2020.
42 Hamal Editorial Board, https://www.hamal.co.il/post/-M6j_R2FkA-cy8Dgw9rt, accessed August 7, 2020.
43 Geraint Harvey, Karen Williams, and Jane Probert, "Greening the Airline Pilot: HRM and the Green Performance of Airlines in the UK," *The International Journal of Human Resource Management*, 24:1 (2013): 152–166.
44 Jonathan Watts, "Is the Covid-19 Crisis the Catalyst for Greening the World's Airlines?" *The Guardian*, May 17, 2020, https://www.theguardian.com/world/2020/may/17/is-covid-19-crisis-the-catalyst-for-the-greening-of-worlds-airlines, accessed August 8, 2020.

vast majority of entries into the country are by air. The other side of this coin is the fact that cheap airfares and growing demand for vacations abroad afford an outlet that has been cited as a reason for the deferral of a political solution to the conflict. As one analyst put it, the old dream of travelling by car to get humus in Damascus as the main benefit of a regional peace treaty was replaced in the 1990s by an affordable, all-inclusive vacation package in Turkey or Bulgaria.[45] As we will see, the conflict also shapes the contours of the Israeli aviation labor market and especially the leverage of a single group of workers – El Al pilots. In what follows, I will sketch out how these workers entered the current crisis and how they managed to keep their heads above water. There is much to learn from this creative, resourceful, and unified group and, in the tradition of the sociology and anthropology of elites, about power and inequality. Examining the particular support networks the pilots activated also raises broader questions about the role of labor in wider ecologies and that of non-human ecologies in labor, about civil aviation's connections to the army in Israel, about familiar conceptualizations of the stratification of the working class, and about work and its affinity to military service.

Indeed, the title of this essay seeks to throw into sharper relief how the military hierarchical structure of the capitalist workplace, commented on in the *Communist Manifesto* (and in many senses more relevant to the nineteenth century than the twenty-first), might offer an opportunity for a serious analysis that goes beyond the metaphors used by Marx and Engels. Here, not only the 'army,' but more specifically the 'reserve' element of the Marxist idiom are subjected to an analysis that takes particular military legacies in a specific workplace seriously. In a strange turn of events resulting from the COVID-19 crisis, the unemployed members of the reserve army of labor examined here are also members of a 'labor aristocracy' – another canonical Marxist term in need of revitalizing – whose aristocratic privilege stems from the same military-industrial context.

Shutdown

The pilots' unique position was revealed after the epidemiological crisis combined with a labor dispute to demobilize Israel's national carrier. In the month of April, after the initial termination of passenger shuttling in March, El Al started resuming operations, shifting to cargo instead (cargo transport was bolstered by medical equipment for fighting the pandemic and El Al signed contracts with global logistics companies that were supposed to engage the airline at least until October).[46] This shift created a rift among the pilots and within their union, pitting those operating the Boeing 787 fleet against the Boeing 737 fleet pilots now out of commission. The main organizing principle for a pilot's work status in El Al (as in other airline companies) is seniority, which is anchored in

45 Eli Oshrov, "Flights Free State," *Haaretz*, July 20, 2020, https://www.haaretz.co.il/blogs/radical/BLOG1.9005045?utm_source=App_Share&utm_medium=Android_Native&utm_campaign=Share, accessed August 7, 2020 (אלי אושרוב, "מדינה חופשית מטיסות,"הארץ).
46 Mikhal Raz Haimovitch, "El Al will Operate 150 Cargo Flights Worth Tens of Millions of Shekels," *Globes*, April 21, 2020, https://www.globes.co.il/news/article.aspx?did=1001326034, accessed August 8, 2020(מיכל רז חיימוביץ', "אל על תבצע 150 טיסות בהיקף של עשרות מליוני שקלים", גלובס); Mikhal Raz Haimovitch, "El AL Got Permission to Operate Cargo Flights in Tel Aviv- Istanbul Line," *Globes*, May 23, 2020, https://www.globes.co.il/news/article.aspx?did=1001329742, accessed August 8, 2020 (מיכל רז חיימוביץ', "אל על קיבלה אישור להפעיל טיסות משא בקו תל אביב-איסטנבול" גלובס); Sapir Perets Zilberman, "El Al Will operate 60 Cargo Flights from Wuhan, China through Israel to London, Paris, and Frankfurt," *PassportNews*, May 4, 2020, https://passportnews.co.il/אל-על-תפעיל-60טיסות-מטען-מוואהן-שבסין-דר/, accessed August 8, 2020 (ספיר פרץ זילברמן, "אל על תפעיל 60 טיסות מטען מוואהן שבסין, דרך ישראל ללונדון, פריז ופרנקפורט", פספורט ניוז).

the pilot's union agreements with management and is a key factor in their standing and prestige. However, the pandemic created a situation in which junior pilots flying a Boeing 787 (as first officers) were working and getting paid while their seniors from the other fleet (for example, captains) were not. Failed attempts to square this circle eventually caused the company to announce another shutdown in May. While this was not a labor strike, and the termination of activity largely resulted from a force majeure combined with management's calculations about profitability, the pilots' ability to insist on sticking to the old contract and to the principle of seniority against pressures to accept reforms is analogous to more conventional labor disputes in which trade unions support their members with a strike fund. Indeed, when other sections of the company's workforce succumbed to the pressures to sign a new labor contract in order to resume operations, the pilots stuck to their guns and to the existing contract.

Given that this was not a strike, furloughed workers could resort to unemployment insurance. Yet at the time of writing in August 2020, there is still no end in sight to the crisis. By now El Al has been shut down for six months, bringing workers to the maximum unemployment eligibility limit in Israel of 175 days' pay. Moreover, unemployment insurance covers up to only sixty percent of one's original salary (and, depending on age and other variables, sometime less); in cases of salaries higher than 10,000 NIS per month (around 3,000 US dollars, which is about one-third of what pilots normally make),[47] it is even less. All of this means that while pilots have benefited from some state support, it hardly covers their living expenses. How have they persevered through this ongoing and extended ordeal?

Pilots as Workers and Soldiers

More than most, pilots demonstrated versatility and creativity and were able to don many different hats in coping with the disruption. First, the El Al pilots' union created a special support fund to which those who were able to work during the crisis contributed. Second, pilots hail from a high socioeconomic background (this, as we will see, is mostly a result of the screening they undergo before enlisting in the air force, years before they join El Al). Earning about three times or more the average income in Israel, many are relatively wealthy, with substantial savings, real estate, and stock exchange portfolios. Moreover, pilots acted as individuals among informal networks of friends offering support to one another. Being technologically savvy, they deployed social media to organize and pool resources. Furthermore, many pilots have other professions – either previous jobs they had left to join El Al, or new occupations developed in the cockpit during the long, inactive hours on autopilot. Some quickly diversified into these professions or retrained for new ones. Again, this was often done in a collective manner – for example, teaming up to learn a computer language or the basics of product management.[48] Pilots (all but a small minority of whom are men) also acted to trigger the labor and other connections of their female partners; in turn, their spouses came together in existing and newly created mutual-aid networks. Finally, pilots acted

---

47 A captain earns 45,000 NIS while a first officer earns 30,000 NIS. See Yoram Gabizon, "El AL Management: The Pilots' Salary Has Reached to 160,000 Shekel Monthly," *The Marker*, August 2, 2020, https://www.themarker.com/markets/1.9043671?fbclid=IwAR1nZYfTj972fx_P2BeThZhUoSZmHT6YfRqLgviMdeexN2v90T1r9ok0Fuc, accessed August 10, 2020 (יורם גביזון, "הנהלת אל על: שכר הטייסים הגיע עד 160 אלף שקל בחודש", דה מרקר) Ten thousand NIS is currently about 2,900 US dollars.

48 Interview with pilot, May 31, 2020.

as unionized workers, sometimes in concert with the company's other workers, but more often against them. Such tensions re-opened a longstanding debate in El Al about whether this group is on a par with the company's other workers and whether the designation 'worker' is at all befitting.

Within El Al, pilots are not subject to regulation or supervision like other workers. For example, they have the prerogative to declare themselves unfit to fly due to illness (which they are not required to substantiate with medical records), thereby forcing management to find substitutes. They use this privilege regularly as a collective action against management instead of a formally declared strike (for example, when tens of pilots reported ill as part of a salary dispute in 2016).[49] They resorted to this strategy again during the May 2020 dispute, which, as noted, appeared as the mirror image of a strike. Indeed, the financial press regularly and rightly frames such illness within the sphere of labor relations: "[T]he pilot's sudden illness most likely resulted from the stress building up among pilots due to management's refusal to reinstate tens of pilots from the 737 fleet..."[50] Alongside such labor prerogatives and collective strategies, which they seldom use for the benefit of other workers, pilots' high salaries and their distinctive and often elitist esprit de corps – a solidarity forged, as we will see, in a different uniform from that of El Al – similarly turns them into a group unto itself vis-à-vis their fellow workers. Due to these differences, and their relatively small numbers among the workforce – about ten percent – pilots feel (sometimes justifiably) that the general workers' union does not represent their special interests and concerns. The union's ranks are manned mainly by maintenance workers, who always elect their own to the organization's leadership. Trying to have their cake and eat it, in late May the pilots' union both worked within the general workers' union and negotiated independently with management. When this was discovered by the union leaders, they stormed a board room violently and broke up a meeting of the pilots' union heads and management representatives. Subsequently, the El Al branch was disbanded by the Histadrut, Israel's General Federation of Labor.[51] This act formalized the thus far implicit rift between 'pilot' and 'worker' in El Al.

The ambiguity around the figure of the pilot is clearly rooted in the special skills and extensive training that this profession requires. However, at least in Israel much of it also arguably dates back to their military service and to another ambiguous distinction between 'pilot' and 'soldier.' Unlike regular 'green' recruits to the IDF (Israel Defense Forces), who normally serve three years, 'blue' pilots serve seven years – up until 2014 they served nine – and undergo a long training period which includes a university bachelor's degree and from which they emerge as officers. Indeed, while many enlist in the air force for ideological reasons or for prestige, many others also do so with an eye to the job market: one of the key reasons to enlist in the air force – as cited in the corps' materials given to candidates[52] – is the possibility of joining the labor market from an advantageous position. Their military uniform and salary also mark them out as both included and excluded from the category of soldier.

49 Itay Blumental, "25 El Al Pilots Informed: We are Sick," *Ynet*, March 3, 2016, https://www.ynet.co.il/articles/0,7340,L-4773588,00.html, accessed August 7, 2020 (וינט, "25 טייסי אל על הודיעו: אנחנו חולים", איתי בלומנטל).

50 Yoram Gabizon, "A Sudden Sickness: El Al's pilots have Returned to Disrupting the Flights," *The Marker*, June 6, 2020, https://www.themarker.com/markets/1.8908138, accessed August 9, 2020 (יורם גביזון, "מחלה פתאומית: טייסי אל על חזרו לשבש את הטיסות", דה מרקר).

51 Navit Zomer and Itay Blumental, "Troubles in El Al: Struggles between the Pilots and the Workers, Tension amongst the Pilots," *Ynet*, May 5, 2020, https://www.ynet.co.il/economy/article/rkPpYQFoU, accessed August 9, 2020 (נוית זומר ואיתי בלומנטל, "הצרות באל על: קרבות בין הטייסים לעובדים, מתיחות בקרב הטייסים", וינט).

52 Meitav, "Jobs: Pilot," https://www.mitgaisim.idf.il/תפקידים/טייסת/, accessed August 9, 2020 (מיטב, "תפקידים: טייס/ת").

If pilots are never fully 'soldiers' when they are formally part of the army, they are never fully 'civilians' once they leave it. Even after their discharge, air force pilots retain their status as members of the armed forces, a fact demonstrated, for example, by membership in the Hever Consumers Club, an organization that helps translate the power of this community into market terms. More pertinent to the current discussion is the fact that until well into their forties, many air force pilots serve at least one day per week in the reserves. During the COVID-19 crisis this was one of the key avenues for younger and hence more vulnerable furloughed El Al pilots to get by. Once furloughed, they immediately increased the number of days in their reserve units. With reserve compensation calculated according to one's civilian salary, a furloughed pilot could earn almost as much in the reserves.

Labor Aristocracy

One way to begin conceptualizing the place of pilots in El Al's broader ecology is through the familiar notion of 'labor aristocracy.' Since it was coined by Engels and repurposed by Lenin, this notion has undergone several rearticulations, with importance given to the special skills of a certain group of workers and to the benefits they gained from the fruits of imperialism. In its classical sense, labor aristocracy referred to stratification within the working class and to class conflict among the proletariat. This may happen on a local level within a given sector, or between monopolistic and competitive sectors, mainly on a global level, between what we might today call the global north and south. Imperialism is commonly seen in most of these discussions as an economic condition, taking the form of super-profits that allow the ruling class to bribe the unionized upper strata of the working class.[53] The value of the framework and theory of labor aristocracy has been challenged.[54] The current case suggests that if it still has any analytical purchase, such value might stem from focusing on elitism, the origins of which are continuously embedded in privileged registers of Israel's military-industrial imperialist complex, and on the social – not only financial – capital emanating from it. Just as race and gender help stratify the working class, military pedigree can be seen as another intersecting component: ease of access to employment, a resourceful support network, and various buffers in times of turbulence are some of the key dividends resulting from this.

Indeed, what is quite unique about our pilots is the fact that much of their 'aristocracy' bleeds into the labor relations within the company from a sphere quite distinct not only from El Al but also from the labor market more generally. El Al pilots have regularly been importing other kinds of capital from their military service. These include a high social status (captured by a famous 1960 motto "the best for flying" later criticized for its elitism), and a far-reaching network in key economic sectors. This collective ability to import social status from a sphere external to the job market significantly informs their maneuverability within it.

The cross-over from military to civilian aviation begins at the moment pilots join El Al. Only Israeli citizens can fly an Israeli plane, according to Israeli law. Because of this and the security checks required, and following a longstanding tradition, the vast majority of El Al pilots hail from

---

53 On labor aristocracy and imperialism, see Zak Cope, *Divided World Divided Class: Global Political Economy and the Stratification of Labour Under Capitalism* (Montreal: Kersplebedeb, 2012); Timothy Kerswell, "A Conceptual History of the Labour Aristocracy: A Critical Review," *Socialism and Democracy* 33:1 (2019): 70–87.
54 Charles Post, "The Myth of the Labor Aristocracy: Part 1," https://www.marxists.org/history/etol/newspape/atc/128.html, accessed August 10, 2020.

the Israeli air force.[55] Moreover, a striking anomaly of Israeli civil aviation law vis-à-vis international legislation is the fact that it allows military flight hours to count towards civilian benchmarks, regardless of whether the pilot commands a helicopter during his military service and is now applying for an airplane license. Since the cost of one flight hour can amount to hundreds of dollars, and one thousand flight hours are required in order to apply to El Al, the financial value of this practice is significant. The ability to translate years of military service into flight hours gives ex-air force men a significant advantage over other candidates. Military rank does not count in El Al, however, and within the company one can captain one's former squadron commander or fly under the command of a former cadet. Yet such combinations ensure that, in the revolving door between the company and air force, all sides have an interest in supporting one another with the resources at their disposal.

Not a Military Welfare State

Resorting to the army for help seems to fit a more general pattern in Israel's mode of addressing the coronavirus crisis. The famous Mark Twain quote "To a man with a hammer, everything looks like a nail" neatly applies to how the Israeli state first addressed COVID-19. Framing the public health crisis as a security threat, Israel quickly resorted to emergency regulations: it suspended civil liberties, mobilized Home Front Command Headquarters to issue instructions to the public, and ordered Military Intelligence to follow contagion curves and steps taken by other countries; it sent Mossad operatives to acquire ventilators from abroad, tasked the Shin Bet with deploying cellphone triangulation tools to aid contact tracing, and even charged Sayeret Matkal, the IDF's elite commando unit, with opening technical bottlenecks in fighting the disease.[56] However, the IDF was far less effective in meeting the surging contagion among its own troops.[57] Nonetheless, the securitization of the health crisis might have been a fitting framework for El Al's pilots – a military welfare state as it were.[58] However, this was not the case – at least as far as the 'state' component goes.

While El Al pilots indeed found refuge in their old air force units, there was no official decision to increase reserve duty. The opposite was actually the case – part of the IDF's general response to the COVID-19 crisis was to reduce unnecessary and expensive reserve duty.[59] It turns out that the

55 Avi Ashkenazi, "The Pilots on your Next Flight Abroad: A Barn worker, a Scientist, and a Parachute Instructor," *Walla*, May 13, 2019, https://news.walla.co.il/item/3235647, accessed August 9, 2020 (אבי אשכנזי, "הטייסים בטיסה הבאה שלכם" לחו"ל: רפתן, מדען ומדריך צניחה", וואלה).

56 Amiḥai Choen and Aidit Shafran Gitelman, "Securitization Under the Cover of Corona," *The Israel Democracy Institute*, April 12, 2020, https://www.idi.org.il/blogs/security-clearance/coronavirus-andidf/31286, accessed August 10, 2020 (עמיחי כהן ועידית שפרן גיטלמן, "ביטחוניזציה בחסות הקורונה", המכון הישראלי לדמוקרטיה); Yoav Zaitun, "Tracing after Medical Ventilators and Obtaining the Missing Compound for Testing: Sayert Matkal has been Recruited Fighting Corona," *Ynet*, April 3, 2020, https://www.ynet.co.il/articles/0,7340,L-5706746,00.html, accessed August 8, 2020 (יואב זיתון, "איתור מכונות הנשמה והשגת החומר החסר לבדיקות: סיירת מטכ"ל גויסה נגד הקורונה", יינט).

57 Lilakh Shoval, "The Soldiers' Outcry: 'We Were Abandoned to the Coronavirus'," *Israel Hayom*, July 13, 2020, https://www.israelhayom.co.il/article/780613, accessed August 9, 2020 (לילך שובל, "זעקת החיילים: 'הופקרנו לקורונה'", ישראל היום).

58 Jennifer Mittelstadt, *The Rise of the Military Welfare State* (Cambridge: Harvard University Press, 2015).

59 Amir Buhbut, "As a Result of an increase in Morbidity Rates: IDF Cancels Major Drill with the Participation of Thousands Of Reservists," *Walla*, July 8, 2020, https://news.walla.co.il/item/3372528, accessed August 9, 2020 (אמיר בוחבוט, "בצל העלייה בתחלואה: צה"ל מבטל תרגיל ענק בהשתתפות של אלפי חיילי מילואים", וואלה).

ability of many pilots to shift to the reserves hinged on the local initiatives of squadron commanders to help their struggling peers. In routine times, reserve duty is a burden that needs to be distributed evenly among people who in their civilian lives work as El Al pilots, in hi-tech companies, the weapons industry, or in the liberal professions. But during the crisis, more reserve days were being allocated to civilian pilots at the expense (and sometimes to the benefit) of other professionals. In other words, what the crisis and its mitigation brought to light was the fact that the IDF – or at least some of its branches – are not mere extensions of the state; rather, there are informal networks that connect the IDF to the labor market. This casts new light on the army and its various forms of potential for social change.

Importantly, however, this is not what Fredric Jameson described in *An American Utopia* as the army becoming a tool for generalizing public goods such as healthcare.[60] Indeed, to better understand what triggers such networks for El Al's pilots, a closer look at the privatization of the Israeli air force is in order. The informalization and privatization of the state of exception echoes processes of privatization of the IDF and other military forces. Indeed, the coronavirus crisis reveals how securitization might not neatly translate into the expansion of statist power.

Several sociologists and historians have analyzed the formation of Israeli society vis-à-vis the Arab-Israeli conflict and the resulting porous boundaries between military and civilian domains.[61] This insightful work tended to stress the militarization and securitization of Israeli society, the fact that its members are always at the ready as reserves for a potential conflagration, and, to a lesser degree, the privatization and neoliberalization of the IDF in recent years.[62] While aforementioned attempts to securitize and weaponize the coronavirus crisis fall neatly within the first framing, the pandemic affords another angle that breaks or at least softens this dyad. Indeed, rather than prioritizing the state or the market in an analysis of labor, this case study reveals the reach of a network that does not exactly belong to either; nor does 'civil society' capture this domain.

The interpenetration of El Al and the air force is two directional. Whereas the company recruits mainly military pilots, the air force has undergone an intensified process of privatization and thus 'civilianization' over the last decade and a half, especially in manpower.[63] This is true for technical operations whereby outsourcing to civilian contractors saves the need to train military technicians who will leave the corps after their three-year military service. All the more so for pilots, whose training is much longer and more expensive, resulting in longer service periods and greater reliance on these men in the reserves. Indeed, the air force is predicated on these reservists who constitute roughly sixty percent of the pilots in the corps. Not all of these reservists work as pilots in their day job, of course. This spread of reserve pilots in various sectors of the Israeli economy, with significant concentrations in the hi-tech sector (which was largely unaffected by coronavirus and was able to shift to remote work relatively easily) has special relevance during the COVID-19 crisis. Reserve duty of one day per week as the minimum for maintaining aptitude and keeping up

60 Fredric Jameson, *An American Utopia: Dual Power and the Universal Army*, edited by Slavoj Žižek (New York: Verso, 2016).

61 Avishay Erlich, "Society at War: The National Conflict and the Social Form," in Uri Ram, ed., *Israeli Society: Different Prespectives* (Tel Aviv: Breirot, 1993): 253–274 "הסכסוך הלאומי והמבנה החברתי", "חברה במלחמה: אבישי ארליך); Baruch Kimmerling, *The Invention and Decline of Israeliness: State, Culture and Military in Israel* (Los Angeles and Berkeley: University of California Press, 2001).

62 Yagil Levy, *Trial and Error: Israel's Route from War to De-Escalation* (Albany: State University of New York Press, 1997).

63 Noa Fenigshtein, "Staring The Civil Life," *Bita'on Hel Ha'avir*, June 1, 2015, https://www.iaf.org.il/8491-45233-he/ IAF.aspx, accessed August 9, 2020 (נעה פיינגשטיין, "יוצאים לאזרחות", ביטאון חיל האויר).

to speed as a pilot can be quite disruptive for a civilian career. Nevertheless, many pilots are interested in maintaining this arrangement for various economic, social, and ideological reasons. The air force, in turn, benefits from these men not only as experienced pilots, but also as more mature members of the corps with exposure to other sectors and institutional cultures that constantly rejuvenate the military.[64]

Conclusion: A Momentary Mask Slip

Between the two familiar poles created for many sectors by the COVID-19 crisis – that of government bailouts on the one hand and abandonment to the invisible hand of the market on the other – a prevalent coping strategy deployed by El Al pilots analyzed above casts a third or middle-ground option into relief. Informal and thus non-statist military aid to furloughed personnel reveals how the gradual and incomplete privatization of the army smooths its interfaces with the market while simultaneously revealing motivations that go well beyond the profit motive – such as mutual aid and esprit de corps. Had it not been the army, and if it could be extrapolated beyond the elites that currently have access to such networks, this strategy for surviving the economic effects of the crisis would almost be a cause for celebration for the resourcefulness and camaraderie involved, and for revealing a hidden sphere of social support.

Beyond these mitigating factors, it is important to remember that civil aviation is a polluting industry in terms of the seating proximity and the spread of pathogens, and the heat, particulates, and gases emitted by airplane engines that contribute to climate change and global dimming. The COVID-19 crisis thus prompted calls to condition government bailouts to airlines on greening measures and led to even more radical voices that advocate letting airlines fall.[65] The revolving door between El Al and the air force, alongside sectors like the defense industry that absorbs many former air force pilots, suggests that rather than diversifying to the green economy this manpower might bolster other problematic sectors.

Labor arrangements in the industry only partly determine how it emerges from the crisis. However, given the high level of initial and recurrent training required to pursue a career as a pilot, available manpower will be an important bottleneck in this process. According to the European Cockpit Association, "unlike other professions, pilots need continuous flying experience to keep their license and remain employable. This is a legal and mandatory requirement."[66] If in other airlines layoffs and even just months of grounding will curtail their ability to resume operations, the civilian-military nexus in Israel affords an outlet for maintaining aptitude, and hence limiting the pressures for radical reform.

However, as we have seen, access to this outlet is unequal and unplanned, in ways that reveal larger sets of inequality. Conventional characterizations of the state usually define this polity according to its violent means, such as the monopoly of the legitimate use of physical force in the well-known Weberian designation. Yet the surreptitious allocation of portions of the security budget in the form of reserves days that wildly expands and manipulates the notion of security

---

64 Yehoshua Brayner, "About Reserve Duty in the Air Force," *Walla*, June 16, 2009, https://news.walla.co.il/item/1486077, accessed August 10, 2020 (יהושע ברײנר, "על שירות המילואים בחיל האוויר", וואלה).

65 Jonathan Watts, "Is the Covid-19 Crisis the Catalyst for Greening the World's Airlines?"

66 Andreas Spaeth, "Will the Coronavirus Pandemic Result in a Pilot Shortage?" *Deutsche Welle*, July 1, 2020, https://www.dw.com/en/will-the-coronavirus-pandemic-result-in-a-pilot-shortage/a-54009473, accessed August 11, 2020.

hardly meets this standard. Things are thorny also when deploying Marxian ends-related understandings of the state and its relationship with the economy, in which the ruling classes and their corporate capitalism depend on the state to reproduce themselves. Not only do they depend on an active government that fosters economic growth, political stability, and social harmony, but also on governmental bailouts in time of crisis – something in the cards also for El Al. Indeed, as we have seen, the Israeli state underwrites many of El Al's operating costs, including training pilots in its air force and legislating that military flight hours will count for civilian aviation. However, the COVID-19 crisis exposed some hidden mechanisms and networks that also complicate such Marxian formulations, revealing the far reach of social networks that extend between various branches of army and industry, and informal support systems that are activated in times of need. These mechanisms in turn help direct attention to other features of Israeli aviation that are usually justified in terms of security – such as the aforementioned stipulations that informs who can fly an Israeli plane – and which now seem no less the effect of a powerful pilots' lobby and a web of former air force personnel in the highest echelons of Israeli politics. Indeed, the coronavirus helped expose tensions, frictions, but also unexpected synergies between securitization and privatization.

Despite the 'security' rhetoric that characterized Israel's treatment of the COVID-19 crisis, and perhaps exactly because of this language and due to the related blurred boundaries between the combined health, economic, and security crises, physical and national security seamlessly morph into job security and vice versa. As a result, public resources can be redistributed in an unplanned manner. In both civil and military aviation, the outcome is a differential aptitude – different pilots have different degrees of readiness – and, more important, differential aid – different citizens and even former air force pilots enjoy dissimilar access to state resources.

When Private and Public Spaces Become Blurred

Jürgen Kocka
Telework between Market and Family:
The COVID-19 Crisis as an Accelerator of Social Change

A long-term view of the COVID-19 crisis of 2020 so far[1] shows that it has not merely interrupted, suspended, and reversed major trends of our time; it has also accelerated some of them. At least this is what we find when we study how the pandemic and our reactions to it are affecting the world of work. During the crisis, political and administrative interventions into social and economic life, including work and labor relations, have been more intensive; social inequalities, including those related to work, have been more pronounced; telework has boomed and contributed to the return of gainful employment or paid work (*Erwerbsarbeit*) within the sphere of the family and household. In each of these three cases, the impact of the crisis has seen existing trends continue and accelerate. The long-term effects in each case are not yet clear, but a full return to the pre-COVID-19 situation seems unlikely even once the pandemic is under control. Rather, a search for a new kind of 'normality' will have to take place, the outcome of which is hard to predict. This essay focuses on the changing relationship between gainful employment and the family and household. A long-term perspective shows that what we are experiencing now is part of a fundamental reshuffling with as-yet-unclear consequences both for the world of work and for the sphere of family and household. Evidence will mostly come from German sources. But the questions asked and conclusions drawn also relate to other countries with advanced industrial or post-industrial economies.

1.

The spatial and institutional separation of household/family and gainful work was a secular and constitutive trend during the nineteenth and most of the twentieth century in industrializing countries such as Germany. It was something new, since in previous centuries the close entanglement between family/household and work for survival and earning had been the rule, in agriculture and industry, in peasant and artisan households, in cottage industries, merchant houses, and even in the sites of power such as royal courts, feudal manors, or local administration.[2] It was due to the factory-based industrial revolution and concomitant processes such as urbanization, and to the growing importance of mining, workshops, factories, and commercial-financial institutions, of construction sites, railroads, and other mobility-related infrastructure, and of administrative agencies, schools, and specialized service institutions that an increasing and soon-overwhelming amount of gainful work or labor would come to be performed in specialized workplaces, that is, outside the sphere of the family and household, and would gradually cease to be a constitutive ingredient in the life of most families.

Of course, this was only a dominant tendency, to which there were limits and many exceptions, but it had powerful societal consequences and concomitants. On the one hand, work now

---

1 Written in August 2020.
2 Jan de Vries, *The Industrious Revolution: Consumer Behavior and the Household Economy, 1650 to the Present* (Cambridge: Cambridge University Press, 2008).

took place in a relatively separate sphere of its own, where it could be experienced and evaluated as a distinct activity in contrast to non-work, and where it not only produced goods and services but performed other social functions as well, namely as a medium of communication and mutual recognition, of conflict and cooperation with colleagues, superiors, and subordinates, as a place in which social bonding and distancing could take place, which, in turn, helped to create identities and structure social relations such as those between classes. The nineteenth and twentieth-century rise of a work society (*Arbeitsgesellschaft*) could not have happened without the emergence of work/labor as a separate sphere with rhythms, rules, and constraints of its own.[3]

Since this was the dominant context, traditional homework (*Heimarbeit*; domestic work in the sense of market-related manual work/labor and cottage industries), which was performed at home as part of decentralized employment relations or by formally self-employed and, in reality, mostly very dependent people – for example in textile production and the clothing industries but also in the production of toys and, later, electrotechnical objects – became thoroughly marginalized. It had once been a mass phenomenon. In the 1850s, *Heimarbeit* still accounted for thirty-nine percent of all industrially active people in Germany, while factories and mines employed only sixteen percent (and handicrafts, forty-five percent). However, in the course of the late nineteenth and twentieth centuries this segment of the labor force drastically shrank and became a relatively marginal activity, representing less than one percent of the total labor force in the Federal Republic of Germany by the early 1980s. It involved work at home, frequently to supplement earnings, mostly performed by women on an irregular and part-time basis, it was usually considered low-skilled and was poorly paid (especially in textiles and clothing). It was precarious in many ways, being increasingly in competition with labor in low-wage countries; it was a phenomenon that was on the way out in countries such as Germany, but expanding in other parts of the world, especially in the global south. Cottage workers of this kind usually had no access to unions, which, for their part, rejected this kind of labor on different grounds.[4]

2.

In the early 1980s, a new type of homework slowly started to emerge and spread. New concepts were coined: 'remote work,' 'travail à distance,' 'telework,' and, as an English import into the German language around 2010, '*Homeoffice*.' The new micro-electronic technologies of communication, soon concentrated around the spread of computers, were the major driving force. It involved primarily non-manual office and communication work (text production, programming, data management), usually of a highly qualified and specialized nature, performed on computers at home by men and women who were either employed remotely, contractually bound, or self-employed. In

---

3 Jürgen Kocka, "Mehr Last als Lust. Arbeit und Arbeitsgesellschaft in der europäischen Geschichte," *Jahrbuch für Wirtschaftsgeschichte* 2 (2005): 186–206; again in id., *Arbeiten an der Geschichte: Gesellschaftlicher Wandel im 19. Und 20. Jahrhundert* (Göttingen: Vandenhoeck & Ruprecht, 2011): 203–224, 375–381; a shorter version: id., "Work as a Problem in European History," in id., ed., *Work in a Modern Society: The German Historical Experience in Comparative Perspective* (New York: Berghahn, 2010): 1–15.

4 Cf. Wolfgang Brandes and Friedrich Butler, "Alte und neue Heimarbeit: Eine Arbeitsökonomische Interpretation," *Soziale Welt* 38 (1987): 74–91, esp. 74–76; Friedrich Hegner et al., *Dezentrale Arbeitsplätze: Eine empirische Untersuchung neuer Erwerbs- und Familienformen* (Frankfurt am Main/New York: Campus, 1989): 1–25; Jan Breman, *Outcast Labour in Asia: Circulation and Informalization of Workers at the Bottom of the Economy* (New Delhi: Oxford University Press, 2012).

the 1980s and 1990s, growth of this type of work was slow, but 2002 saw the first European framework agreement on telework signed by the European social partners: "The agreement lays down working standards for people doing telework, defined as 'a form of organizing and/or performing work, using information technology, in the context of an employment contract/relationship, where work, which could also be performed on the employer's premises, is carried out away from those premises on a regular basis'." The agreement also emphasized that teleworkers should benefit from the same legal protections as employees working on the employer's premises. It aimed to define "a general framework for using telework at the workplace, in a way which would correspond to employers' and workers' needs. It concentrated on aspects which it regarded to be specific to working away from the employer's premises. It highlighted key areas requiring adaptation or specific attention such as employment conditions, data protection, privacy, equipment, health and safety, work organization, training, and collective rights."[5]

Telework was slow to expand. As of 2019, only between five and six percent of the labor force in all twenty-seven European Union member states (EU 27) *continuously* worked from home, a figure that had been more or less constant since 2009. However, over the same period, the proportion of people working *sometimes* or *occasionally* from their homes increased from five to nine percent. While telework was almost completely unseen among manual workers and rare among ordinary technical and administrative workers, it was particularly common in knowledge- and ICT[6]- intensive services. Yet, even within this category, there were pronounced national differences, with Scandinavian and some Western European countries at the top, and Germany as well as some Eastern and Southern European countries below the European Union average.[7]

It is against this background that we can understand the abruptness of the change that the COVID-19 crisis has brought about. Given the widely perceived need for protection against the threat of infection, the temporary lockdown of many businesses and the managerial strategies of many firms requiring large parts of their staff to stay and work at home, there was a vast increase – a jump upward – in telework. A detailed survey of nearly five hundred German businesses (different sectors and sizes, eighty-seven percent privately owned, twenty-two percent public, twenty percent manufacturing, fifty-two percent services, twenty-eight percent a mix) between May 4 and May 24, 2020, found that office work was being performed as telework from home, either totally or to a large extent, in the large majority (seventy percent) of enterprises. In addition, twenty-one percent of respondents reported adopting a hybrid structure, where around fifty percent of work is performed at home and fifty percent on company premises. Further, the majority of businesses said that they either had not, or had hardly, adopted telework before the start of the coronavirus crisis.[8] Clearly the crisis was the catalyst for telework in the majority of businesses. European data support this finding: by April 2020, over a third (thirty-seven percent) of the active labor force in the EU 27 countries had begun to telework as a result of the pandemic – this figure being relatively

5 Antonia Margherita, Sile O'Dorchai, Jelle Bosch, and Eurostat (European Commission), *Reconciliation Between Work, Private and Family Life in the European Union, 2009 Edition* (Luxembourg: Office for Official Publications of the European Communities, 2010): 126.

6 Information and communications technology.

7 European Commission, Joint Research Centre, "Science for Policy Briefs: Telework in the EU Before and After the COVID-19: Where We Were, Where We Head To," https://ec.europa.eu/jrc/sites/jrcsh/files/jrc120945_policy_brief_-_ covid_and_telework_final.pdf, accessed August 19, 2020.

8 Josephine Hofmann et al., "Arbeiten in der Corona-Pandemie – Auf dem Weg zum New Normal: Studie des Fraunhofer IAO in Kooperation mit der deutschen Gesellschaft für Personalführung DGFP e.V.," 2020, http://publica.fraunhofer.de/eprints/urn_nbn_de_0011-n-5934454.pdf, accessed August 19, 2020: 5f.

uniform at over thirty percent in most member states. The largest proportions of workers who had switched to working from home were in the Nordic and Benelux countries (close to sixty percent in Finland, above fifty percent in Luxembourg, the Netherlands, Belgium, and Denmark, and forty percent or more in Ireland, Sweden, Austria, and Italy). Germany was directly in line with the European Union average, at thirty-seven percent.[9]

In mid-July 2020, another comprehensive survey reported that three out of four German businesses had parts of their labor force working from home. More than half of these businesses indicated that they would maintain this decentralized working structure after the crisis to some extent, with plans to have more telework practices in place compared with before the crisis, and on a permanent basis.[10]

No doubt, many workers who have moved into telework during the coronavirus crisis will return to their offices, workshops, and other non-domestic workplaces once the pandemic has either ended or its threat is more or less under control. The present situation, as it emerged between March and July 2020, is not a stable one. In fact, a return to company premises is already being observed in July and August. However, as the recent survey of German businesses indicates, a full return to pre-coronavirus levels is unlikely. Telework will be much more commonplace after the crisis than it was before. Why?

First, firms have recently made substantial investments in new digitalized infrastructure and pertinent technologies to ensure fast and secure communication with their workers in spite of spatial decentralization. These technologies will still be available even when the crisis has either waned or ended altogether.

Second, we have had a lively public debate about the advantages and disadvantages of telework in recent months. Opinions differ, and there are pros and cons being espoused with many different shades of argument. But on the whole, the voices, comments, and statements leave little doubt that a lot of managers, employers, and business owners have let go of some of their previously held reservations about telework. For many, the last months have shown that telework is highly compatible with demands for work efficiency in several occupations and areas of qualification – albeit not in all fields – and that it also meets the need for the control that management is not ready to give up. It has become clear that telework can also help to reduce costs and therefore bring direct economic benefits, as, for example, there is less need for expensive office space or for workers to commute or go on business trips.[11]

Finally, it is particularly remarkable that so many dependent workers, different kinds of employees, as well as labor – especially union – representatives have come to see telework in a more positive light. Certainly, the disadvantages – for example, the diminished or lack of contact with colleagues, threats to privacy associated with almost unlimited digital availability, and the burden that working at home under unfavorable conditions places on family life – are acknowledged and deplored. But it is mainly the advantages that are emphasized: fewer and less-strict employer controls; greater freedom; the time saved by not having to commute; and more oppor-

---

9 Eurofound, "Living, Working and COVID-19. First Findings – April 2020", https://www.eurofound.europa.eu/sites/default/files/ef_publication/field_ef_document/ef20058en.pdf, accessed August 19, 2020: 5.

10 "IFO Institut: Mehrheit der Unternehmen will Homeoffice dauerhaft ausweiten," *Pressebox*, July 13, 2020, https://www.pressebox.de/inaktiv/ifo-institut-fuer-wirtschaftsforschung-ev/ifo-Institut-Mehrheit-der-Unternehmen-will-Homeoffice-dauerhaft-ausweiten/boxid/1014369, accessed August 19, 2020.

11 See e.g. Leibniz-Zentrum für Europäische Wirtschaftsforschung (ZEW), "Unternehmen wollen auch nach der Krise an Homeoffice festhalten," press release, August 06, 2020, https://www.zew.de/presse/pressearchiv/unternehmen-wollen-auch-nach-der-krise-an-homeoffice-festhalten, accessed August 19, 2020.

tunities to find a better work-life balance. It is telling that Germany's Social Democratic Minister for Labor and Social Relations, with the support of the Federation of German Labor Unions (DGB; Germany's most important labor organization), fights for a law guaranteeing every employee "*das Recht auf Homeoffice*" – the right to practice telework. While this plan has met with some opposition and may not be fully realized, such an initiative in and of itself is indicative of an increasingly positive attitude to telework among large parts of the German labor force.[12]

3.

Clearly, there are stark contrasts between the old type of *Heimarbeit* (see above p. 220) and the new breed of 'telework' (*Homeoffice*; see above). While *Heimarbeit* involved mostly manual work that was low-skilled, poorly paid, precarious, and usually performed at home on a part-time basis by women looking to supplement the family income, present-day telework is usually non-manual, often highly qualified and well paid, performed by both women and men, and sought-after as an advantage or even a privilege by many. While *Heimarbeit* sometimes included a domestic division of labor and the direct cooperation of different family members, this is rarely a feature of telework. While unions used to look down on and frequently rejected *Heimarbeit*, at least by the time it had become a marginalized, precarious phenomenon that was obviously on its way out, today's union attitudes towards modern telework are considerably more differentiated, nuanced, and largely positive as they acknowledge that it is on the rise. Everybody knows that it is neither possible nor desirable to perform all, or even most, gainful, market-related work in a decentralized way, that is, in or near workers' homes. However, decentralized work supported by digitalized technologies is set to be a growing and increasingly important element of the future world of work – either in a pure form or, more often, in varying combinations of decentralized work from home and centralized work performed at company workplaces.

This is a major shift; it is still ongoing and to be continued in the future. The COVID-19 crisis has accelerated and qualified this process of change. The social consequences are not yet clear but we can put forward some tentative observations and hypotheses. The intrusion of gainful employment and market-related work – and, sooner or later, legal and administrative provisions to protect and regulate this form of decentralized work – into the home is having an effect on the family and household. We are seeing less separation between family life and the pressures of capitalism and government regulation. Family life is becoming less private, with the boundaries between private life and the world of work becoming more blurred.[13] As we saw during the COVID-19 crisis, this can overburden and place on strain the family, but at the same time the family also gains more importance in relation to the marketplace and civil society. This could also render the gender differences

---

12 Corinna Frodermann et al., "Wie Corona den Arbeitsalltag verändert hat," *Institut für Arbeitsmarkt- und Berufsforschung*, IAB-Kurzbericht 13/2020, http://doku.iab.de/kurzber/2020/kb1320.pdf, accessed August 19, 2020 (results of a survey of 1200 employees, April–May 2020); "Digitalisierung und Homeoffice entlasten Arbeitnehmer in der Corona-Krise," *DAK Gesundheit*, press release, July 22, 2020, https://www.dak.de/dak/bundesthemen/sonderanalyse-2295276.html#/, accessed August 19, 2020 (survey of 7000 resp. 6000 employees, comparing December 2019 and April 2020); Carsten Lexa, "Gesetz zum Recht auf Home Office: Das ist der aktuelle Stand," *BASIC thinking*, May 28, 2020, https://www.basicthinking.de/blog/2020/05/28/recht-auf-home-office, accessed August 19, 2020.
13 Cf. Ines Janke et al., "Verschwimmen die Grenzen? Auswirkungen von Vertrauensarbeitszeit auf die Schnittstelle von Arbeit und Privatleben," *Zeitschrift für Arbeitswissenschaft* 68 (2014/2): 97–105.

deeply anchored within family life more influential in structuring working conditions and careers. There are good reasons to fear that women may be the losers in the new interlocking of family and work.[14]

Removed from the spaces of offices and workshops, from company premises, administrative agencies, educational institutions, and the like, workers are becoming more isolated and work is becoming more individualized. A sort of 'de-institutionalization' is taking place. Work is losing some of its socializing (*vergesellschaftende)* power, which is something that cannot be developed or exercised without intensive contact – through cooperation and conflict, formally and, particularly, informally – with colleagues, superiors, and subordinates. The importance of work as a basis for building identities will be further reduced. It will be replaced by other, more particularistic dimensions of belonging, collective self-determination, and social orientation: culture, imagined origins, nationality, and, perhaps, gender and age. New forms of inequality are gaining ground: for example, between those who are sufficiently qualified and – from the management perspective – 'trustworthy' enough to enjoy the right to work from home, and those who are not, comprising most blue-collar, construction, and service workers. Classical cleavages – such as differences in the interests and power of employers and employees – play a remarkably minor role in the present discussions about telework. They seem to have faded into to the background.

These changes are still underway and their outcome is hard to predict. These are unanswered questions; they are not yet thoroughly researched. But the coronavirus crisis has prompted us to pose them.

---

14 Karsten Hank and Anja Steinbach, "The Virus Changed Everything, Didn't It? Couples' Division of Housework and Childcare Before and During the Corona Crisis," *Journal of Family Research* (July 27, 2020), https://ubp.uni-bamberg.de/jfr/index.php/jfr/article/view/488/438, accessed August 19, 2020: 1–16.

Sandrine Kott

Work in Times of COVID-19: What is New and What is Not.
A Western European Perspective

There is nothing new about pandemics and the threat that they represent. The black pest killed between thirty and fifty percent of the European population between 1347 and 1352. In the more recent past, the Spanish flu killed more people than the war itself in four waves between 1918 and 1920. The main difference between the 1918-1920 pandemic and the one that we are facing today lies in the nature and the extent of the collective and public response. What is most striking is not the pandemic itself, but how our modern and highly organized societies, as well as the European welfare states, have dealt and are still dealing with COVID-19. In Western Europe, the state, which, since the 1980s, has been dismissed by neoliberal ideology as costly and inefficient, is back. Governments had the power to order and enforce the lockdown of millions of citizens without encountering any major resistance. Large sectors of the private economy were shut down while others had to quickly reorganize. Huge welfare provisions have accompanied these measures. The enormous impact that this has had on the world of work has been documented in many statistical surveys, and it has re-opened and reoriented lively debates on the 'future of work.'[15]

This is all unprecedented and it would therefore be very risky and even presumptuous to draw parallels with the past or to use history to understand the present. And yet, in many respects, the current crisis reveals or accentuates trends, contradictions, and problems that have already been identified and discussed by European labor historians. That is not to say that everything looks the same, but in what follows, I wish to use elements of knowledge on the history of labor in Western European industrialized societies to examine two widely discussed and closely related topics: women's work and remote or telework. This essay is mainly inspired by the French situation, with references to other Western European countries.

Women on the Frontline

The peculiar contradictions and tensions that have characterized women's labor since industrialization have become more extreme in times of COVID-19.[16] In the same way as during World War I, female workers and employees have been mobilized. This time, it was not to replace soldiers fighting on the battlefront but because their jobs are essential to collective society: supermarket employees and care workers – not only nurses – were on the frontline. Seventy or eighty percent of these workers are women, often migrant women.[17]

---

15 This was the topic chosen by the International Labour Organization at the occasion of its centenary in 2019: https://www.ilo.org/global/topics/future-of-work/trends/WCMS_545675/lang--en/index.htm, accessed August 13, 2020.

16 Anne Lambert et al., "Le travail et ses aménagements: ce que la pandémie de covid-19 a changé pour les Français," Population Societes 579: 7 (June 17, 2020): 14.

17 It would be another topic to discuss the question of the role that migrant workers have played in the European economy during the COVID-19 and how they have been affected by the crisis. The European Trade Union Confederation (ETUC) has published a short document on that topic: "Overlooked: Migrant Workers in the COVID-19 Crisis," ETUC, https://www.etuc.org/en/document/overlooked-migrant-workers-covid-19-crisis, accessed August 13, 2020.

In these vital sectors, women had to work under strained conditions. A French governmental decree extended the maximum working time from forty-eight to sixty hours a week on March 25, 2020, while the daily rest could be reduced to nine hours. In general, according to official surveys, women have been more affected by the increase in workload (thirty-six percent compared with twenty-nine percent for men). Similarly, fifty-five percent of women saw a change in the content of their work during the crisis (compared with forty-three percent of men) and twenty-four percent saw their working time increase (compared with twenty percent of men). However, in the same way as during World War I, this does not mean that women's work has been better paid or better rewarded.

In France, nurses have received a bonus of up to 1,500 euros (approximately 1,750 US dollars), with a salary increase negotiated in May 2020. Nevertheless, the average income of nurses is sixty-four percent of the average French salary and it is even lower in the United Kingdom. Nowhere is it seriously envisioned that this situation will drastically improve anytime soon. A significant rise in the wages of care workers requires a fundamental change in the values of society combined with a sustainable valorization of care and reproductive work. Yet these tasks still are seen as women's duties rather than proper, skilled work. The use of emotional language to describe their task – often endorsed and mobilized by the care workers themselves – reinforces this stereotype.

For these very same reasons, the population expressed demonstrative and symbolic support for the care workers. In France the "soignants" (caregivers) were acclaimed and applauded each day at 8:00 pm. And yet, health care workers who are routinely exposed to high levels of harassment in the workplace only became even more vulnerable during these months. They were confronted with new forms of harassment away from the workplace, with reports of nurses being evicted from their apartments or threatened by neighbors who feared that they might infect them with the virus. The same types of cases have not been reported for male doctors. Moreover, women were much more likely to be out of work than men at the end of the lockdown. Among those who were employed on March 1, 2020, only two out of three women remained in work two months later, compared with three out of four men. This same ambivalent position toward female workers –praised for their courage and involvement but also subject to suspicion and finally dismissed – also characterized what women experienced during World War I.[18]

This repetition of events is not just random; it is grounded in a structural problem that has been highlighted rather than created by the crisis. Since the beginning of industrialization, employed women are caught up in the contradiction between productive and reproductive work, between working outside of the home and having to take care of children or dependents at home. At the end of the nineteenth century, social laws implemented 'for' women – reduction of working days, protections for pregnant women, interdiction of nighttime work – did not aim to alleviate the burden of work. They were meant above all to reduce – if not solve – the contradiction between the economic necessity of female labor and what was seen, by most of the social reformers, as the natural function of women: being a wife and a mother. Because they saw these measures as discriminatory, some feminist organizations such as Open Door International began to fight against these specific dispositions in the interwar years. One century later, they have been finally abolished.

During the COVID-19 crisis, the closure of schools and other care facilities heightened the tension between the necessity to work and the role of most women as caregivers, in particular,

---

18 Two examples are Françoise Thébaud, *La femme au temps de la guerre de 14* (Paris: Stock, 1986) and Ute Daniel, *Arbeiterfrauen in der Kriegsgesellschaft: Beruf, Familie und Politik im Ersten Weltkrieg* (Göttingen: Vandenhoeck & Ruprecht, 2011).

but not exclusively, for single mothers and for homeworkers. Among parents of children under sixteen who continued to work, forty-three percent of women and twenty-six percent of men spent more than four overtime hours a day caring for their children. This situation affected more women working remotely: forty-seven percent, compared with twenty-six percent for men. Women who worked from home in more highly qualified jobs have seen their careers slow down. One survey shows that during COVID-19 women were less likely to submit papers to academic journals than men. Male experts were overrepresented in the media. In newspaper reports on teleworking experiences, women often complained that they were not even invited to Zoom meetings on the pretext that they had to take care of their children.

Remote Working, Working from Home. A Present without a Past?

This leads us to the heavily debated question of teleworking or remote working from home, which has been seen as the most important change brought about by the crisis. In what follows, only the situation of those working under an employment contract with a company will be discussed. The self-employed will not be considered.[19]

Remote working is not a new phenomenon but it has expanded significantly in times of COVID-19. In Europe, twenty-four percent of employees who had never previously worked from home before started teleworking, compared with fifty-six percent of employees who had previously worked from home occasionally. What used to be a choice and an occasional option became a solution imposed on a permanent basis. To be sure, working at or from home was the most common working mode before industrialization in Europe. Peasants or artisans worked at home, but unlike today they were more or less independent. Things have changed, with the generalization of the factory system during the nineteenth century, the generalization of wage-earning, and the distinction between workplace and home. Homework did not disappear, and in some rural areas – in the middle-range mountain areas in particular – it was still widely practiced, but homeworkers who used to be independent gradually became largely dependent on the merchants who provided them with raw materials and bought their goods. They were the poorest of all workers and the least protected. In cities, homeworking was common among women, particularly in the garment industry. In Germany, almost fifteen percent of garment workers worked from home in 1925. Being isolated, they were less organized, and up until the 1920s they were excluded from the social protections that factory workers could enjoy. Underpaid, they had to work very long hours in order to earn a living income.

Teleworking in Western European countries today differs drastically in many ways from this sad picture. First, teleworking is not a relic from the past, but rather was made possible by the progress of new technologies. Second, teleworking is generally practiced by the most qualified workers. In France, twenty-five percent of the active population has teleworked during COVID-19, with a very strong overrepresentation in the upper categories: almost seventy percent of the cadres could work remotely and only eight percent of unskilled workers. Last but not least, according to

---

19 For a definition of these terms see the ILO technical note "Defining and Measuring Remote Work, Telework, Work at Home and Home Bases Work," International Labour Organization, June 5, 2020, https://www.ilo.org/global/statistics-and-databases/publications/WCMS_747075/lang--en/index.htm, accessed August 13, 2020.

a survey conducted in April 2020 on a sample of 1,860 employees, the majority expressed positive views about their experience of teleworking.[20] This expression of satisfaction confirms a development that has been noted since the beginning of the twenty-first century. In France, where teleworking was less developed than in the northern European countries, the managers (cadres) were the ones who advocated more strongly in favor of a law to make it easier to telework for those who wished to do so. The reformist CFDT (Confédération française démocratique du travail), the most important union in France, strongly supported and supervised this demand at a time when business leaders were more reluctant. In 2012, teleworking entered into law. The Warsman law obliged employers "to cover all costs directly resulting from the exercise of telework, in particular the cost of hardware, software, subscriptions, communications, and tools, as well as their maintenance." In 2017, this commitment disappeared from the labor code but it became easier for employees to opt for teleworking. From now on, teleworking was an employee right, to be regulated and defined within the framework of a collective agreement negotiated with the trade unions or in a specific charter between employer and employees. This agreement or charter had to provide for the conditions for switching to teleworking, the methods for monitoring working time, and determining the time slots during which the employer should be able to contact the employee.

The strongest arguments in favor of teleworking expressed by the CFDT, as well as human resources representatives and employees themselves, are that it promotes and develops the autonomy and flexibility of the individual. These skills are indeed highly valued by the new management (or management 2.0) practices in hi-tech companies such as Google.[21] In place of a top-down management style inherited from the Fordist model, these companies encourage the autonomy and flexibility of their employees linked to an elasticity of space and time. For employers, these are the conditions for greater creativity and productivity, while for the employee this new desirable 'freedom' is not without danger. Accepting individual responsibility for an allocated mission means personally managing the contradictions of demands. As 'entrepreneurs of themselves,' employees face a greater psychological load and stress.[22] These same concerns have been expressed with respect to teleworking.

Nevertheless, employers, but also some trade unions, emphasize some advantages of teleworking: teleworkers spend less time on informal conversations, and, above all, they are required to deliver a job and not to count their time. Rather than a working day whose length has been carefully negotiated by the labor movement since the nineteenth century, telework is first and foremost task-based. Relabeled with new, fancy names like 'project,' this task-based work is not really new; it was already widely practiced in the nineteenth-century factory to increase productivity and was at the time heavily criticized by the trade unions as a way to foster and increase competition between workers and to undermine class solidarity. Has this issue entirely gone away today?

---

20 Thierry Pech and Martin Richer, "Coronavirus: regards sur une crise. La révolution du travail à distance. Enquête," Terra Nova, April 30, 2020, https://tnova.fr/system/contents/files/000/002/005/original/Terra-Nova__La-r_volution-du-travail-a-distance__300420.pdf, accessed August 13, 2020; and in general the initiatives of the CFDT.
21 See their website re:Work: https://rework.withgoogle.com/subjects/managers/.
22 Michel Lallement, *Le travail sous tensions* (Paris: Le Seuil, 2010): 43–58.

Teleworking: More Autonomy or More Isolation? The Past in the Present

At first sight, there is thus nothing comparable between the situation of a teleworker at the beginning of the twenty-first century and that of a poor, female nineteenth-century homeworker. And yet, the past has not entirely disappeared.

First, in the same way as for homeworking in the nineteenth century, one of the central arguments in favor of teleworking is the ability to combine work and family life. This argument is particularly prominent in countries like Germany or Switzerland, where the woman/mother is still largely viewed as the one in charge of 'her' children; it is less present in France, where the collective infrastructure for small children has a longer history, but even in France the argument is not absent. Nevertheless, this idyllic representation of homework as the optimal way to combine work and family life has been heavily challenged in times of COVID-19. Family members and in particular women were trapped between their employer's demands and the constraints of family life. Even if the reopening of schools has eased the situation somewhat, there are still dependents to be taken care of. For women, who are disproportionally the caretakers in the family, working from home is more often a trap than a real freedom. Especially since they are less likely than men to have a dedicated space or adequate equipment to allow them to work properly. On average during the lockdown, a quarter of women teleworked in a dedicated room compared with forty-one percent of men; most of the time, they had to share their workspace with their children or other household members. The gender gap was at its peak within the management group: twenty-nine percent of female managers had a dedicated room at home compared with forty-seven percent of male managers. In May 2020, the left-wing CGT (Confédération générale du travail) trade union conducted a survey on working conditions and the exercise of professional responsibility during the lockdown, and obtained 34,000 responses.[23] One quarter of the employees who responded said that no measures had been put in place by their employer to support remote working. They had not been given computer equipment, a telephone, or software. This lack of support was especially emphasized by teachers of all levels, a profession which is mostly (seventy percent in 2017) carried out by women.[24] The same survey indicated that more men than women benefited from financial support for internet connection, telephone, and software costs (seventeen percent of men versus thirteen percent of women) and they were less likely to be confronted with a lack of regular management support (thirty-four percent of men compared with thirty-seven percent of women). In the end, forty-two percent of those teleworking said that they perceived a sense of autonomy and freedom, but this was less the case for women (thirty-eight percent for women and forty-seven percent for men, especially in large private companies).

And yet, today just as yesterday, women are still caught up in the same contradictions, and express stronger preferences than men for a continuation of teleworking. What will their teleworking look like? If remote working began as a privilege for highly skilled male workers, more companies that have had positive experiences with teleworking during the lockdown are now tempted to

---

23 Dominique Martinez, "L'Ugict-CGT publie une étude inédite sur les conditions de travail en confinement," nvo, May 6, 2020, https://nvo.fr/lugict-cgt-publie-une-etude-inedite-sur-les-conditions-de-travail-en-confinement, accessed August 13, 2020.

24 Bernard Javet, ed., "Bilan social du ministère de l'Éducation nationale et de la Jeunesse 2017–2018 – Enseignement scolaire," 2019, https://www.education.gouv.fr/bilan-social-du-ministere-de-l-education-nationale-et-de-la-jeunesse-2017-2018-enseignement-scolaire-12098, accessed August 13, 2020.

expand it. In the short term, this is motivated by the necessity to comply with government social distancing regulations, notably the rule in France of four square meters per employee. In the long run, it could save costs that would otherwise be spent on office space. Moreover, managers have discovered that remote working has actually increased productivity. Not to mention that employees who save time on commuting often demonstrate more readiness to work longer.

In sectors like insurance and banking, there is now a clear trend towards increased teleworking in lower-level administrative positions, in which women are overrepresented. We can expect that companies will have time to better prepare for the new conditions than they had during the lockdown and that they will be better able to support their employees. Nevertheless, a growing number of remote workers in low-level administrative positions are already becoming entirely dependent on one piece of software, which leaves them with no opportunity to use their initiative. Their activities are already broken into small, simple tasks that can be easily measured, handled, and monitored from anywhere. In place of trust and autonomy, this kind of remote work is characterized by a careful reduction of initiative and constant surveillance. Again, women are more likely to be in these positions than men.

As we have already mentioned for France, the law provides a framework for teleworking but the quality of the relevant agreement or charter is dependent on the outcome of negotiations between the trade unions and employers. Right now, with the rise of unemployment and the decline of trade unions membership, the balance of power is generally weighted in favor of the employer. Moreover, in this peculiar situation, employees working remotely are isolated and find themselves at a disadvantage. This is especially true for employees working for European companies, a lot of them women on the other side of the Mediterranean.

One risk is that these employees are forced into self-employment, and, like those working for platforms such as Uber, deprived of any social protections. Less skilled teleworkers could also become modern-day 'pieceworkers,' as was the case in the garment industry of the nineteenth century. This all depends on the capacity of the trade unions to negotiate good agreements and the ability of the state to set out a legal framework for teleworking that counterbalances the weaker negotiating position of the employees.

Daniel Eisenberg
Through a Screen, Darkly: The Micro and Macro of Daily Life in the Early Pandemic Era

The truth is that nothing is less sensational than pestilence, and by reason of their very duration great misfortunes are monotonous. In the memories of those who lived through them, the grim days of plague do not stand out like vivid flames, ravenous and inextinguishable, beaconing a troubled sky, but rather like the slow, deliberate progress of some monstrous thing crushing out all upon its path.

Albert Camus, *La Peste*

A Pandemic produces new conditions and perspectives, reorients one's perception of time, space, and scale. In that spirit this essay attempts to capture the dramatic shifts that occur with breathtaking speed, leaving one to integrate a new register of experience...

———————————————

Even a pandemic begins imperceptibly, just as most illness begins with a single symptom – a tickle at the back of the throat, a dry cough, a headache that comes from fatigue or dehydration. But without any understanding of what a pandemic actually means, each one of us produces an image of reality outside of direct experience, and as if for the first time, framing each act of everyday life through the filter of safety; forging a path between fear and knowledge.

We watched the reports coming out of Wuhan with a kind of esthetic curiosity and detachment: the carless streets save a single bicyclist, the drone shots of skyscrapers and downtowns devoid of human presence; uncanny and strangely attractive.

Soon enough these would be our own streets and downtowns, far away and as unreachable as Wuhan. As the lockdown closes off all commerce and contact,' sheltering-in-place' becomes the term of the day.

And then we hear of the first cases penetrating the borders: first Thailand and Japan, then the cruise ships, then single cases in Chicago, Seattle, and San Francisco. Like a slow-motion tidal wave about to engulf us, we watched with curious detachment.

"You need to feel it on your own skin," those words spoken by my father come racing back to consciousness, this time with the understanding that an entire nation, in its resistance to the prescient advice of epidemiologists, infectious disease specialists, and health professionals, walked onto the beach to better view the approaching tsunami.

March 12

All of it becomes surreal and hyper-real at once. I am sitting at my editing desk on a rainy March afternoon trying to work on my film. On one of my breaks, I hear on the radio the World Health Organization's Director-General, Tedros Ghebreyesus, calmly declare:

... WHO has been assessing this outbreak around the clock and we are deeply concerned both by the alarming levels of spread and severity, and by the alarming levels of inaction.

We have therefore made the assessment that COVID-19 can be characterized as a pandemic. Pandemic is not a word to use lightly or carelessly. It is a word that, if misused, can cause unreasonable fear, or unjustified acceptance that the fight is over, leading to unnecessary suffering and death.

Describing the situation as a pandemic does not change WHO's assessment of the threat posed by this virus. It doesn't change what WHO is doing, and it doesn't change what countries should do.

We have never before seen a pandemic sparked by a coronavirus. This is the first pandemic caused by a coronavirus.

And we have never before seen a pandemic that can be controlled, at the same time...

... We have rung the alarm bell loud and clear.

Perhaps I should stock up on some supplies... who knows when it will get *here*, and how long this will last.

I drive to our nearby Target, looking for toilet paper – it's a virus, after all – disinfectant, perhaps some hand sanitizer. As I enter the place everything seems different; an air of quiet panic suffuses all human movement. The place is packed. I make a beeline for the paper goods. Entire aisles, usually stacked beyond all reasonable logic with hundreds of packs of toilet paper, paper towels, tissues, and napkins are now empty. How is this possible? I am able to buy some bleach and a few other peripheral items. I understand now. I am already one of the late ones. I spy a fellow shopper crouching in an aisle. We make eye contact. He is wearing a mask. A mask? It's already here; I'm already too late. I approach the checkout with a few items, but leave mostly empty-handed. I ask the checkout clerk what's going on. She says, "It's been like this all day."

After weeks of public reassurances and dismissals, that same evening, the president, Donald Trump, addresses the nation, and without any warning or time to prepare, terminates European air travel for thirty days.

In reality, European air travellers have already infected thousands of people in the New York City and other East Coast metropolitan areas. In a few short weeks New York will become the epicenter of the pandemic, and Elmhurst Hospital in Queens would become the scene of unprecedented urban devastation.

Many universities and colleges are sending their students home. We hear from our own administration on March 12 that we will conduct all our remaining classes remotely after an extended spring break.

We've stumbled into the abyss. We begin to understand the contours of what this feels like. 'Not knowing' defines our experience. When will it peak? Who is most susceptible? What can we do to protect ourselves?

The quiet, empty streets of Wuhan are now our streets. Rarely do we hear a car pass. Fear of the unknown, last felt on September 11, 2001, grips us.

The eyes and ears recalibrate. On our daily walks we see and hear the wind in the trees, now perceptible without the sound of traffic or airplanes to drown it out. It is early spring. Birds are beginning to migrate north again. The city is now theirs. We see birds we have never seen before, and the skies remain free of planes for many days. In these first few days we stay indoors, glued to our computers and televisions, somewhat relieved to be in our comfortable and familiar homes, with enough food to last a few weeks or so. Surely, that will be enough.

In Asia everyone is wearing a mask. We are told *not* to wear one, to keep the 'personal protective equipment' free for first responders. We do a quick calculation. If masks have been used for so long in Asia, with their experience of SARS and H1N1, then we should certainly follow their lead. We begin to cut up old table linens and hand-sew our own masks. Perhaps we are just giving ourselves some false comfort. Can't hurt?

Even before the series of fast-moving events that took over our lives in early March, we were already for quite a long time focused on our screens: smart phones, computers, tablets, and televisions; now even more of our day and our sensual universe will become defined by the screen.

'Screen' is a useful term, since so much of what comes through the image is hidden, edited, or predetermined... screened. Accustomed to it as packaged phenomena, one is inured to its deficiencies.

The physical space of *all* our interactions has become the interior space of the house. Evacuated of all presences other than our own, we find a way to make space for the virtual other, whether a professional encounter, a casual acquaintance, or someone already party to our private lives. In a few short weeks, we become savvy Zoom users, as every social, economic, personal, and professional transaction occurs in the uniform space of the screen.

> *In the first days of these Zoom meetings and Facetime 'quarantinis,' the bookcase, the living room couch, the kitchen counter or dining table, even the bed, become sites of signification... virtual and actual sets for our daily and professional lives. We become aware of stylized backgrounds and green-screened wallpaper, or the curated bookshelves where we quickly assess the political or intellectual disposition of our interlocutors. And for those unwilling to share their spaces or reveal their last vestige of privacy, their names are displayed in boldfaced type against a black background.*

> *We begin to perceive the sound of sirens on our phone calls and Zoom meetings with New York. In a few short days these would become an incessant background to all our communications. Soon, these sounds would become more vivid and present on our own streets, and soon after, an all-day, all-night chorus, as we imagine overrun hospital wards.*

In the first weeks of the pandemic, as labor migrated from office spaces to screen spaces and in those screen spaces to Zoom cubicles, we were bombarded with advertising and messaging about the heroism and valor of 'essential workers,' the medical professionals and the underpaid invisible service sector labor force delivering our packages and mail, those working in grocery stores, along with the transport, utility, and public service employees, and of course, the Patient Assistants (PA's) who clean the hospital bathrooms, tend and bathe the sick and dying. "We're all in this together" was the repeated mantra.

As if to compensate for their lack of power or agency, this public relations effort seemed to anticipate the economic leverage these workers were capable of employing at this moment of crisis, and attempted to preclude or short-circuit any demands for higher pay. These messages seemed aimed at neutralizing the thought of actually leveraging this newfound power towards safer working conditions or more than the meager pay raises that were offered to serve equally as brand promotion.

As low-paid, precarious laborers, many of these essential workers are unable to work remotely, unable to refuse unsafe working conditions, and as predominantly BIPOC (Black, Indigenous, People of Color), have reduced access to an underfunded health care system. In Republican states, many do not even have health insurance, as public health insurance options are still being resisted in these states, and health care access can be solely obtained privately at high cost or through an employment benefit. Now, with such widespread unemployment, millions have lost these health care benefits. Many, facing the virus directly, would get sick and die.

The pandemic is now some kind of new normal. We begin to lose track of the days; we relinquish future plans. When will we again be able to see our children, now isolated from us a thousand miles away? Trying to be disciplined in so many things becomes exhausting, takes more energy than everyday life, even though we are less physically active. We remain thankful for our health, our safety, and keenly aware of the privilege of our isolation.

During the last week in February, 2020, the United States unemployment rate stood at 3.5 percent.[25] Within just over a month, that figure would jump to 19.7 percent,[26] representing almost a fifth of the national workforce. Unemployment claims by the end of May reached over forty million.[27] This tsunami, felt worldwide, was of a particularly brutal nature in the United States, where there was no structural safety net in place for these millions of workers. The economic crisis, atop the existential biological crisis of COVID-19, produced a series of ruptures and dislocations unlike any seen before in recent history.

Although Congress rushed to *produce* a safety net for those in economic free-fall with the three-trillion-dollar Cares Act, two generations of political leadership had systematically defunded social welfare, leaving no adequate government infrastructure in place to administer or direct the economic response. As with the health care system – a haphazard patchwork that differed from state to state – the lack of coordination of unemployment benefits, loans made through local banks, and checks delivered by the Internal Revenue Service, produced at best wildly uneven results.

The confused and incoherent response from Washington was to invoke tired and inappropriate theories of federalism, passing off responsibility to the states for everything from personal protective equipment and ventilators, to unemployment benefits and hospital coordination. It was a massive and profound abdication of centralized government leadership precisely when a centralized, coordinated response was required.

Now in our own isolation there was a more personal need... the need to understand just how such a wealthy, advanced country could visibly fail to meet the demands of the coronavirus with such profound incoherence.

We've learned that the coronavirus is extraordinarily efficient in revealing the flaws and weaknesses in *all* national systems and forms of social organization. It demands very specific communal responses, requiring great discipline, competence, efficiency, and order. But in 2020, after forty years of the neoliberal mantra of privatization, personal liberty, and the wisdom of the market, a coordinated national response became impossible in a country whose leadership met the crisis with dogmatic political and philosophical resistance. It was simply against the prevailing Republican ideology to have a strong, centralized government response.

Magical thinking, conspiracy theories, and a radical call to resistance were more likely to be articulated than a respect for expertise or scientific knowledge. Much like their approach to economics, race, and class, which continually invoked personal and individual responsibility, the federal government approach seemed like just another form of Social Darwinism. Science and epidemiology are no match for that particular brand of libertarian American individualism.

---

25 United States Bureau of Labor Statistics, "Labor Force Statistics from the Current Population Survey," https://data.bls.gov/timeseries/LNS14000000, accessed August 10, 2020.

26 United States Bureau of Labor Statistics, "Labor Force Statistics from the Current Population Survey," accessed August 10, 2020.

27 Ben Casselman et al., "US Jobless Claims Pass 40 Million: Live Business Updates," *The New York Times*, May 28, 2020, https://www.nytimes.com/2020/05/28/business/unemployment-stock-market-coronavirus.html, accessed August 10, 2020.

Here we sit, in the most scientifically advanced society the world has ever known, with incomparable wealth and capacity – all squandered, made irrelevant, by the narcissistic impulses of a president and his sycophantic enablers. With public presentations devoid of reason or belief in scientific expertise, we quickly learned to listen past the wild claims and outright lies and instead listen to trusted sources.

The president is stoking revolts to lockdowns and quarantines, as his fear of a stalled economy and what it portends for his electoral prospects morphs into another polarization and amplification of division. With his belief in quack remedies, magical thinking, and the triumph of will over science, it is only a matter of time before these unmoored positions and kindled divisions explode into catastrophe.

Trump tweeted, "LIBERATE MINNESOTA!" followed immediately by "LIBERATE MICHIGAN!" and then "LIBERATE VIRGINIA, and save your great 2nd Amendment. It is under siege!" Gasoline on a fire.

This call to resist lockdowns and shelter-in-place orders, apparently motivated by the desire to jump-start stalled state economies, would prove to be more than rhetorical, as a few weeks later the numbers of cases would exponentially increase, after confrontations between mask-wearers and those resisting masks would flare up regionally.

As the death toll spiraled out of control, we were simultaneously tethered to our screens for information, news, and work, when we were confronted by the *next* crisis – watching in horror the eight-minute-and-forty-six-second murder of George Floyd by a squad of Minneapolis police, recorded by a bystander on a cellphone.

The pleas of the crowd to get off his neck, the theatrical display of dominance and deadly power, enacted with cold and brutal indifference... Immediately I am transported to my own childhood, hearing the stories of my mother's experience in the Radom Ghetto, and my father's witnessing of his own father's public humiliation on the streets of the Warsaw Ghetto... this endless continuity of cruelty.

The outrage of racial violence, atop the existential pressures of the pandemic, was too much to bear. Chicago ignited in flames, the governor called in the National Guard, and the city's downtown was sealed off. Overnight, many businesses had boarded up their glass windows, and now the sirens we heard invoked images not only of COVID-19 emergencies, but those of fires, police actions, and whatever other calamities we could imagine.

Locked in our houses we are also shocked by the alienating distance of these tragedies. Just miles away from our own homes people were suffering untold harm. We remained comfortable and secure... how deeply immoral.

These manifold crises: health crisis, economic crisis, racial crisis, one after the other, could be seen as separate, an unlucky sequence of misfortunes. But the tightly entwined factors of historical neoliberal labor policies, the privatization of health care, and the associated lack of profit in public health, the Republican Party commitment to dismantling government, its prevailing economic philosophy that markets should determine priorities, and decades of income inequality, all produced conditions for a perfect storm of related and inseparable crises... a domino theory of sequential catastrophes.

Over the past four decades, Republican and Democratic regimes alike have systematically cut taxes, defunded social programs, sold off the administration of government services as disparate as health care and incarceration to the highest bidder. These formerly government-managed activities of health, education, and social welfare, became profit-motivated generators of entirely new sectors of the economy.

In an economy that gives priority to profit, such areas as public health and public welfare – areas of the economy that have no potential for large profit margins – would inevitably suffer.

Conversely, the advent of a profit-oriented security infrastructure that includes prisons, paramilitary policing, and advanced surveillance technology proliferated precisely because of the profits these sectors produced. In no small measure, corporate political donations fed into a public policy fueled by fear, with an emphasis on the protection of property. Donald Trump instinctively leveraged these fears and longstanding racial grievances through his deft manipulation of the news cycle and social media.

In these decades of systematic disinvestment and a parallel offshoring of manufacturing, critical health care infrastructure became dependent on a 'just-in-time' supply chain. In a pandemic, a 'just-in-time' supply chain will never be adequate, and 'just-in-case' inventory management can't be quickly achieved.

The United States would spend four months scrambling to supply personal protective equipment and ventilators, testing equipment, swabs, reagents, and even cleaning supplies. And with the federal government off-loading responsibility onto state governments, individual states were competing against each other for critical supplies, bidding up prices while going further into deficit, as the prices for these supplies would rise exponentially. The absence of federal coordination also ensured uneven responses, including state governments that proactively resisted epidemiologists' mitigation strategies, giving great advantage to viral spread. One state would prioritize economic recovery and the opening of businesses, another would prioritize public health and sheltering in place, two strategies fundamentally opposed to each other.

The weeks following the murder of George Floyd and Breonna Taylor would pry many thousands from the safety of their interior spaces in small towns and large cities alike. Taking measure of the risks of public protest, determining that things were no longer a matter of silent endurance, protestors filled the streets for weeks. Veterans of the civil rights struggles of the sixties and seventies made note of the diversity in the crowds. This time was different. Amid such despair, there were some visible signs of change.

Income inequality, a major issue articulated in the campaign of Democratic candidate Bernie Sanders, has become the critical systemic weakness of the moment. Today's real average wage (that is, the wage after accounting for inflation) has about the same purchasing power it did forty years ago.[28] CEO pay at the top 350 firms in 2018 was 17.2 million dollars on average, according to new analysis by the Economic Policy Institute, and from 1978 to 2018 CEO compensation grew by 1,008 percent while the compensation of a typical worker rose just twelve percent. The ratio of CEO-to-worker compensation was 278-to-1 in 2018 – far greater than the 20-to-1 ratio in 1965 and 4.8 times greater than the 58-to-1 ratio in 1989.[29]

Even before COVID-19, thirty-seven percent of Americans did not have the ability to cover a four-hundred-dollar emergency expense.[30] Yet many with large capital formations have profited handsomely from this crisis, as the stock market approaches new records. Those on the other end of the income scale are now, after six hard months, frozen out of work or public benefits, with little or no capital to fall back on.

---

28 Drew DeSilver, "For Most Americans, Real Wages Have Barely Budged for Decades," Fact Tank | Pew Research Center, August 07, 2018, https://pewrsr.ch/2nkN3Tm, accessed August 10, 2020.

29 "CEO Compensation Kept Surging in 2018," Economic Policy Institute, August 14, 2019, https://www.epi.org/press/ceo-compensation-kept-surging-in-2018-the-ratio-of-ceo-to-worker-compensation-was-278-to-1/, accessed August 10, 2020.

30 Board of Governors of the Federal Reserve System, "Report on the Economic Well-Being of US Households in 2019–May 2020: Dealing with Unexpected Expenses," https://www.federalreserve.gov/publications/2020-economic-well-being-of-us-households-in-2019-dealing-with-unexpected-expenses.htm, accessed August 10, 2020.

As much of the economy has moved to working from home, the shift has mainly benefited college-educated employees who work primarily with personal computers. A Federal Reserve survey found that sixty-three percent of workers with college degrees could perform their jobs entirely from home, while only twenty percent of workers with high school diplomas or less could work from home.[31]

As of the end of the second quarter of 2020, jobs are back for the highest wage earners, but according to an analysis of Labor Department data by Opportunity Insights, employment is still twenty percent below pre-pandemic levels for workers earning under fourteen dollars an hour, and sixteen percent down for those making fourteen to twenty dollars an hour.[32]

The trend of income inequality and precarious labor continues at an accelerated pace during the pandemic, becoming an object lesson in the mechanisms of what civil rights activist James Lawson refers to as "Plantation Capitalism,"[33] the systemic dependency of low-paid workers on servile relations of debt, the technical surveillance of workplace efficiency, and the 'paycheck-to-paycheck' stresses of insufficient income.

Our sense of time has adjusted to new experiences of both long and short duration. As we become aware of the daily gradations of light and seasonal change, we see new continuities where before there were none; we see ruptures in the social fabric that were before less visible.

Our distrust of national leadership increases rapidly, as we witness the denigration of science, epidemiology, and expertise of all kinds coming from Washington, leaving governors and mayors to speak individually – we see their news conferences and reports, and along with all the information we ourselves have gleaned, fine tune our own understanding of truth and falsehood. We are left to control our daily input of news and information.

As he encourages his followers to get out and spend, the president knowingly or unknowingly extends the pandemic, exponentially fuels its dispersion. He is a master of chaos and distraction, never lets a crisis go to waste, ever dividing us for his own personal benefit. Or is he just witless? Incompetent?

Now, as we reach 170,000 deaths and over five million COVID-19 cases, we've seen a collapse of institutional credibility and any disciplined, organized response. The system has so little resilience precisely because it has been the project of this administration to actively hollow it out. The ideologically motivated dismantling of government has in some ways succeeded, with professionally qualified staff replaced by those of sufficient loyalty or allegiance.

August 12

It is now exactly five months since lockdown. With our daily walks, our Zoom meetings and Facetime conversations, our hourly check ins for news and our own projects, life has achieved some kind of rhythm, some sense of predictability. At some point on this hot, humid summer afternoon the skies begin to darken, the winds begin to pick up. As the skies enter some new and dangerous

31 Board of Governors of the Federal Reserve System, "Report on the Economic Well-Being of US Households in 2019–May 2020: Financial Repercussions from COVID-19," https://www.federalreserve.gov/publications/2020-economic-well-being-of-us-households-in-2019-financial-repercussions-from-covid-19.htm, accessed August 13, 2020.
32 Heather Long, "The Recession Is Over for the Rich, but the Working Class Is Far from Recovered," *Washington Post*, August 13, 2020, https://www.washingtonpost.com/business/2020/08/13/recession-is-over-rich-working-class-is-far-recovered, accessed August 13, 2020.
33 Jim Conn, "Plantation Capitalism," *Capital and Main*, June 5, 2013, https://capitalandmain.com/plantation-capitalism, accessed August 13, 2020.

phase, turning a dark yellowish green, our cellphones light up with automatic emergency warnings issued by the National Weather Service instructing us to seek immediate shelter in the lowest levels of our houses or in interior spaces away from windows. We've received a tornado warning, and moments later, sirens blare. We gather our things; some water and cellphones, a charger and computers, and head to the basement, not knowing what else to do. It's there that we wait it out, with our screens tuned to a live feed reporting the weather outside. They're calling it a 'derecho…'

We are left to imagine what's happening… and wait. Wait for a vaccine, wait for the election, wait for the ability to again move freely, and shape our own future. The virus, dependent on human weakness and impatience, is waiting as well… waiting for us to slip up, to lose discipline. It is ripping through, leaving a swath of ruin in its path.

When the storm is over, when we can come up from the basement and survey the thousands of trees uprooted in the storm's path, we'll replant and rebuild again, perhaps this time with a deeper sense of community that will make us each, individually, stronger still.

Contributors

Supurna Banerjee is an assistant professor at the Institute of Development Studies, Kolkata. Her areas of interest range from gender, labor, and migration to social space and activism. In her current projects she deals with inequality: the tea industry in West Bengal and the migration of women in India. She was a research fellow at re:work/Humboldt-Universität zu Berlin from 2018 to 2019.

On Barak is a social and cultural historian of science and technology in non-Western settings and an associate professor in the Department of Middle Eastern and African History, Tel Aviv University. He is a co-founder/co-editor of the *Social History Workshop*, a blog on the Haaretz website analyzing current Middle Eastern affairs through the lens of contemporary historical research. He was a research fellow at re:work/Humboldt-Universität zu Berlin from 2017 to 2018.

Larissa Rosa Corrêa is an assistant professor in the History Department at Pontifical Catholic University of Rio de Janeiro. She is a member of the working group Mundos do Trabalho and the Latin American Labour History Network. In 2017, she played a major role in integrating re:work in the Latin American and Caribbean conference "Trabajo y Trabajadores" ("Work and Workers") in La Paz, Bolivia.

Alina-Sandra Cucu is a historical anthropologist of labor. Currently, she is a Marie Curie postdoctoral fellow in the Anthropology Department at Goldsmiths, University of London. Her research focuses on the 'advance' of flexible capitalism in Eastern and Central Europe. She was a research fellow at re:work/Humboldt-Universität zu Berlin from 2017 to 2018.

Andreas Eckert is a professor of African history at Humboldt-Universität zu Berlin. Since 2009, he has also served as the director of the international research center Work and Human Life Cycle in Global History. He has widely published on nineteenth and twentieth-century African history, colonialism, labor, and global history.

Daniel Eisenberg is an internationally renowned filmmaker and professor in the departments of Film/Video/New Media/Animation and Visual and Critical Studies at the School of the Art Institute of Chicago. In 2018 and 2019, he jointly organized an international symposium and curated an art exhibition titled *Re:Working Labor* in partnership with the Sullivan Galleries at SAIC and re:work. He was a research fellow at re:work/Humboldt-Universität zu Berlin in 2018.

Babacar Fall teaches at the FASTEF, the School of Education of the University Cheikh Anta Diop of Dakar. Since 2018, he has also served as the director of the Institut d'études avancées de Saint-Louis du Sénégal. He is the author of many publications on education and social history as well as the coordinator of the Groupe pour l'Etude et l'Enseignement de la Population (GEEP) and chair of Schoolnet Africa. He was a research fellow at re:work/Humboldt-Universität zu Berlin from 2009 to 2010.

Leon Fink is a distinguished emeritus professor of history at the University of Illinois at Chicago and the editor of the journal *Labor: Studies in Working-Class History*. He has authored and edited numerous books and specializes in American labor and immigration history. He was a research fellow at re:work/Humboldt-Universität zu Berlin in 2015.

Paulo Fontes is a historian of Brazilian labor and working-class culture at the History Institute of the Federal University of Rio de Janeiro. He works on labor migration, the role of communities in working-class formation, and the cultural aspects of popular organization and politics. He was a research fellow at re:work/Humboldt-Universität zu Berlin in 2014.

Felicitas Hentschke is a historian and has been the academic coordinator at re:work/Humboldt-Universität zu Berlin since 2009. In terms of scholarly work, she has pursued projects such as on hostels, hostel dwellers, and labor in global history, on the role of photography and art in the field of history, and produced exhibitions on re:work topics.

The **Covid and Care Research Group** mainly comprises faculty members and current or former PhD students in the Department of Anthropology at the London School of Economics and Political Science (LSE), while a few have done or are doing their doctorates at Cambridge. One of the co-authors, **Deborah James**, was a research fellow at re:work/Humboldt-Universität zu Berlin from 2017 to 2018.

Chitra Joshi has taught for many years in the Department of History of the Indraprastha College for Women, University of Delhi, and has held visiting positions at the Center for Modern Indian Studies (CEMIS), the University of Göttingen, and the University of Innsbruck. She is among the founding members of the Association of Indian Labour Historians. She was a research fellow at re:work/Humboldt-Universität zu Berlin from 2016 to 2017.

Preben Kaarsholm is an emeritus professor in the Department of Social Sciences and Business at Roskilde University. He has enjoyed a long research career through grants and assignments at various research institutions. His current focus is on slave trade diasporas and the history of unfree labor in southern Africa and the Indian Ocean. He was a research fellow at re:work/Humboldt-Universität zu Berlin from 2017 to 2018.

Bridget Kenny is an associate professor in the Sociology Department at the University of the Witwatersrand. She works on gender, race, and labor in service work and precarious employment in South Africa. She is on the editorial board of various journals. She was a research fellow at re:work/Humboldt-Universität zu Berlin in 2018.

Jürgen Kocka taught modern history at the Free University of Berlin (1989–2009). He has broadly published on the history of labor, the middle classes and societal change in 19th/ 20th century Europe, and on the comparative history of capitalism. He was the director of the Berlin School for Comparative European History and president of the Berlin Social Science Center. In 2011, he received the Holberg Prize. Since 2009 he has been a permanent fellow at re:work/Humboldt-Universität zu Berlin.

Sandrine Kott is a professor of European contemporary history at the University of Geneva and at New York University. She has published widely on the history of social welfare in Europe since the end of the nineteenth century, on labor relations in European Communist countries, and on the International Labor Organization. She was a research fellow at re:work/Humboldt-Universität zu Berlin in 2011.

Marcel van der Linden is a senior research fellow at the International Institute of Social History in Amsterdam, the institute where he served for fourteen years as research director. He is also an emeritus professor of social movement history at the University of Amsterdam, and president of the International Social History Association. In 2010, he joined the re:work advisory board.

Nicole Mayer-Ahuja is a professor of sociology at the University of Göttingen as well as director of the Sociological Research Institute (SOFI). She is associated with the labor module of the M.S Merian International Centre of Advanced Studies "Metamorphoses of the Political" (ICAS:MP). She was a research fellow at re:work/Humboldt-Universität zu Berlin from 2010 to 2011. In 2015, she joined the re:work advisory board.

Mary Jo Maynes teaches European social history at the University of Minnesota. She specializes in the history of life course trajectories, autobiographies, as well as female labor in the European textile industries, especially in France, Germany, and Ireland. She was a research fellow at re:work/ Humboldt-Universität zu Berlin in 2013.

Ellen Rothenberg is an internationally renowned artist and professor in the Department of Fiber and Material Studies at the School of the Art Institute of Chicago. In 2018 and 2019, she jointly organized an international symposium and curated an art exhibition titled *Re:Working Labor* with re:work in partnership with the Sullivan Galleries at SAIC. She was a research fellow at re:work/ Humboldt-Universität zu Berlin in 2018.

Mahua Sarkar is Professor of Sociology at Binghamton University, New York. She was a research fellow at re:work/Humboldt-Universität zu Berlin from 2011 to 2012. She is one of the editors of this book series *Work in Global and Historical Perspective*.

Cristiana Schettini is a researcher at the National Scientific and Technical Research Council (CONICET) of Argentina. She teaches history at the Institute of Higher Social Studies in the Universidad Nacional de San Martín in Buenos Aires. She specializes in gender studies, social history, and sex work in South America, particularly Argentina and Brazil. In 2017 she jointly organized a summer school on labor, rights, and mobility with re:work at UNSAM in Buenos Aires.

Yoko Tanaka is a professor of economic history and of international and advanced Japanese studies at the University of Tsukuba in Japan. Her main research interests are business and labor history, labor relations, and labor policies, particularly in Germany. She was a research fellow at re:work/Humboldt-Universität zu Berlin from 2015 to 2016.

Ann Waltner teaches Chinese social history at the University of Minnesota. She specializes in the history of ritual, religion, gender and feminism, law, and religion, as well as the analysis of historical documentation. She was a research fellow at re:work/Humboldt-Universität zu Berlin in 2013.

Maurice Weiss lives and works as a photographer in Berlin. He is a member of the photographer-run agency *Ostkreuz*. Throughout the re:work years, he has been responsible for the portraits of all re:work fellows.

James Williams is an anthropologist interested in youth, migration, and work in African and Middle Eastern contexts of urban volatility, deprivation, and post-conflict. He was a research fellow at re:work/Humboldt-Universität zu Berlin from 2014 to 2015.

Bahru Zewde is an emeritus professor of history at Addis Ababa University, fellow of the African Academy of Sciences, and formerly vice president of the Association of African Historians. He has served as director of the Institute of Ethiopian Studies, executive director of the Forum for Social Studies, and board member of TrustAfrica. He was a research fellow at re:work/Humboldt-Universität zu Berlin from 2018 to 2019.

Picture Credits

"'This is Ridiculous.' Voting as Labor During COVID-19." 2020, Cover.

Eisenberg, Daniel, 'Authors on Zoom I.,' Front-end Sheet

Corrêa Fontes, Miguel, 'Coronavirus,' p. V

Tankha, Ishan, 'The Long Trek Home,' 2020, p. 30

Tankha, Ishan, 'On the Track,' 2020, p. 33

Mooketsi, Rehilwe, 'Man Rushing to Work,' p. 48

Bahru Zewde, Tsion, (Miss.T.Cal), 'Djibouti National Emblem,' p. 57

Bahru Zewde, Tsion, (Miss.T.Cal), 'Royal Furniture Masks,' p. 57

Bahru Zewde, Tsion, (Miss.T.Cal), 'Spiderman Mask,' p. 57

Bahru Zewde, Tsion, (Miss.T.Cal), 'Champion Liverpool FC,' p. 57

Bahru Zewde, Tsion (Miss.T.Cal), 'Bandana I.,' p. 57

Bahru Zewde, Tsion, (Miss.T.Cal), 'Bandana II.,' p. 57

Bahru Zewde, Tsion, (Miss.T.Cal), 'Bandana and Hijab,' p. 57

Bahru Zewde, Tsion, (Miss.T.Cal), 'The Lion of Judah,' p. 57

Weiss, Maurice, 'Black Ward' 1, p. 60, 91

Weiss, Maurice, 'Black Ward' 2, p. 61

Weiss, Maurice, 'Black Ward' 3, p. 62–63

Weiss, Maurice, 'Black Ward' 4, p. 64–65

Weiss, Maurice, 'Black Ward' 5, p. 66

Weiss, Maurice, 'Black Ward' 6, p. 67

Weiss, Maurice, 'Black Ward' 7, p. 68

Weiss, Maurice, 'Black Ward' 8, p. 69

Weiss, Maurice, 'Black Ward' 9, p. 70

Weiss, Maurice, 'Black Ward' 10, p. 71

Weiss, Maurice, 'Black Ward' 11, p. 72

Weiss, Maurice, 'Black Ward' 12, p. 73

Weiss, Maurice, 'Black Ward' 13, p. 74

Weiss, Maurice, 'Black Ward' 14, p. 75

Weiss, Maurice, 'Black Ward' 15, p. 76–77

Weiss, Maurice, 'Black Ward' 16, p. 78–79

Weiss, Maurice, 'Black Ward' 17, p. 80

Weiss, Maurice, 'Black Ward' 18, p. 81

Weiss, Maurice, 'Black Ward' 19, p. 82–83, 91

Weiss, Maurice, 'Black Ward' 20, p. 84–85

'A Right to Care.' Original illustration by Maggie Li, 2020, p. 110

Handler-Spitz, Rivi 'The Class of 2020 Has Had to Put Their Plans on Ice,' p. 150

Maturen, Stephen, "I Can't Breathe' Protest Held After Man Dies In Police Custody In Minneapolis', Getty Images News, Bild 1215368206, p. 152

Rothenberg, Ellen, "'This is Ridiculous.' Voting as Labor During COVID-19." 2020, p. 164–183

Eisenberg, Daniel, 'Authors on Zoom II.,' Back-end Sheet

Index